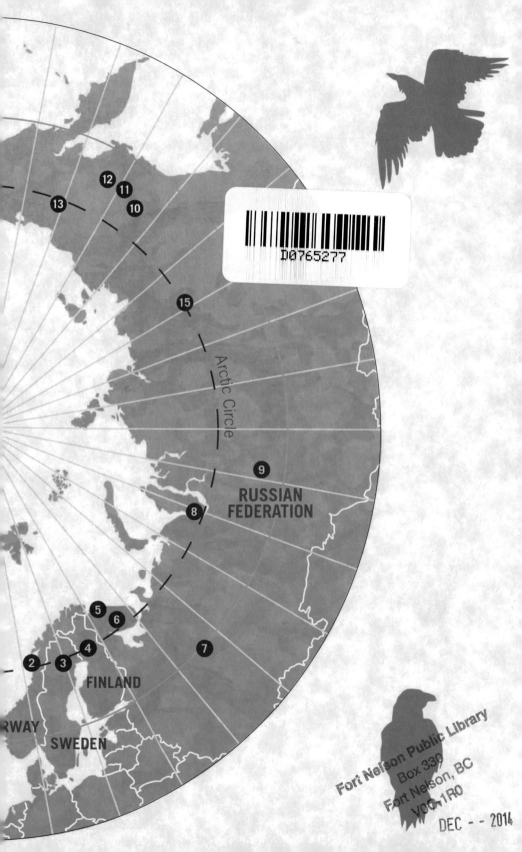

12
11
13
10

15

Arctic Circle

9
RUSSIAN
FEDERATION
8

5
6
2 3 4
7
FINLAND

RWAY
SWEDEN

Advance praise for CIRCLING *the* MIDNIGHT SUN

"*Circling the Midnight Sun* is travel writing at its best. Epic in scope and geography, it certainly does circle the most brutal and yet fragile landscape on earth. Raffan's a fantastic writer. He has that rare and great ability to see the big picture while refusing to judge. *Circling the Midnight Sun* is a must read for anyone concerned about the future of our planet. And boy, I hope that's everyone." —Joseph Boyden, author of *The Orenda*

"To me it's the most exciting region on the planet, and while we all talk about how the Arctic is being affected by climate change, how many of us have actually been there? My friend James Raffan has, and he takes being there very seriously— just look at where he went. Sir John Franklin would envy this voyage! . . . *Circling the Midnight Sun* is a fascinating read." —Peter Mansbridge, chief correspondent for CBC Television News and anchor of *The National*

"Start with a terrific idea: circle the globe along the Arctic Circle. Add an adventurous writer who has the energy, grit, empathy, vision, and savvy to get the job done. Presto! After four years . . . you have *Circling the Midnight Sun*: informed, entertaining, and important—a one-of-a-kind work with a ringing message for anyone interested in the north, indigenous peoples, climate change, or all three. This is the book James Raffan was born to write." —Ken McGoogan, author of *Fatal Passage* and *Lady Franklin's Revenge*

"Exploring the vast differences in culture, climate, and landscape, contrasting places like Repulse Bay in the barren Canadian Arctic to the smokestacks and mining pits of Luleå in northern Sweden, he shows how peoples throughout the circumpolar world are fighting to protect their identities. In this remarkable book, a man who has spent a lifetime studying and travelling the Arctic now gives you a chance to go there—and you should." —Whit Fraser, national reporter for CBC Television News and chair of the Arctic Children and Youth Foundation

"Hidden truths. Hard truths. James Raffan's sympathetic and insightful circumpolar voyage of discovery exposes the many challenges—and also the opportunities—that climate change is providing for the peoples and the biosphere of the north. . . . There are no easy answers . . . but Raffan, throughout his voyage, is certainly asking the right questions." —John Sloan, former Canadian ambassador to the Russian Federation

"By tracing one warm line through a land so wide and savage, James Raffan puts a human face on the circumpolar North." —Michael Byers, author of *International Law and the Arctic* and winner of the 2013 Donner Prize

"James Raffan has taken an unusual and difficult journey—around the world in Arctic latitudes. He has visited a diverse sampling of what Canadian Inuit would call *ukiuqtaqturmiut*—the people of the Arctic—an agglomeration of races, languages, and cultures united only by their residence in the globe's northern-most countries and territories. This wonderful and informative volume has given voice to their stories—human stories—often lost or ignored in a world newly enamoured of the Arctic but increasingly focused on the physical or economic aspects of climate change." —Kenn Harper, author of *Give Me My Father's Body: The Life of Minik, the New York Eskimo*

CIRCLING *the* MIDNIGHT SUN

CIRCLING *the* MIDNIGHT SUN

Culture *and* Change *in the* Invisible Arctic

JAMES RAFFAN

HarperCollins*PublishersLtd*

Published by HarperCollins Publishers Ltd

First edition

HarperCollins books may be purchased for educational, business, or sales
promotional use through our Special Markets Department.

HarperCollins Publishers Ltd
2 Bloor Street East, 20th Floor
Toronto, Ontario, Canada
M4W 1A8

www.harpercollins.ca

Library and Archives Canada Cataloguing in Publication
information is available upon request.

ISBN 978-1-44340-584-3

Bird silhouettes by James Raffan
Maps by Dawn Huck
Map data on endpapers and pages xi, 7, 27, 45, 57, 70, 86, 104, 119, 139, 158, 182,
196, 217, 239, 261, 271, 292, 303, 327, 345, 363, 377, 404, and 423 © 2014 Google.

Printed and bound in the United States of America
RRD 9 8 7 6 5 4 3 2 1

To Phyllis

CONTENTS

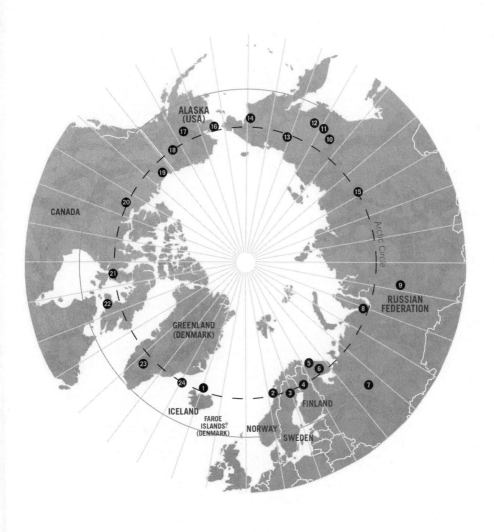

PROLOGUE

The idea of travelling around the world at the Arctic Circle had its genesis for me in two very different moments. The first was the decision that saw my newly married parents board the transatlantic ocean liner *Empress of Scotland* at the docks in Liverpool to travel to Montreal, to start their new life in southern Ontario. Since my first adventures by canoe, five decades ago, my parents have always been hungry to hear about the North and to revel vicariously in the life their choice created for their only son. My parents emigrated to Canada instead of South Africa or Australia, choosing north instead of south. And I have been increasingly conscious of this decision as my life as a first-generation Canadian has progressed.

The second moment was much more raw and recent. A group of British and Canadian politicians, bureaucrats, scientists, and academics—scholars all—who meet biannually to discuss an emerging world issue chose "The Arctic and Northern Dimensions of World Issues" as their theme in 2010. I was fortunate to be one of those invited to join them at a two-day meeting in Iqaluit, the capital of the Canadian territory of Nunavut, on Baffin Island. As often happens at gatherings such as this, there were a couple of Inuit presenting, but the delegate list was heavily skewed toward non-indigenous men and women, like me, with addresses in the middle latitudes.

A young British geologist listened carefully to a presentation by an Inuit woman who talked about two goals: preserving the natural world that is and has been since time immemorial the coastal precinct of her people; and supporting industry, particularly emerging oil and gas interests, in creating jobs for northerners. The geologist then asked how the Inuit could expect any sympathy at all if they said they wanted to preserve nature and fight climate change and then go on to hunt polar bears and support the very industry that was producing the fuel that was causing buildup of carbon in the atmosphere. Was this not a bit of a contradiction?

If looks could kill, that young geologist would have been vaporized on the spot. The Inuit woman paused and then quietly hissed, "We don't need your sympathy. We live here. This is our home. It is more complicated than that."

When the film *An Inconvenient Truth* plays in theatres worldwide, when its subject, Al Gore, wins a Nobel Peace Prize and the film wins an Oscar, it is clear that much of the world is looking north because of climate change. And in some ways, like so much of the exploration literature that came before, the reportage on global warming—*An Inconvenient Truth* as Exhibit A—is much more about physical and so-called natural science than it is about people or cultural science. For this reason, again in significant measure thanks to Gore's game-changing film, the poster child for global warming has not a human face but that of a polar bear. And, ironically, when it comes to raising money to build public awareness, this is not a bad thing.

But there are people who live in the Arctic, four million of them, in eight countries, speaking dozens of languages and representing almost as many indigenous ethnicities. These are the people who know the North best and, sadly, the people whose voices are least heard and little understood either by those who make decisions or by the rest of us, who are benefitting increasingly from the resources the Arctic has offered and continues to offer at an accelerated pace as the northern ice cap melts.

Life for these northerners, like life for everyone else on the planet, is changing. But global warming is the least of their worries. On whatever social index one might choose—measuring housing, health, education, violence, suicide, infant mortality, water quality, language erosion, or cultural decay—northerners are at the top, or bottom, of the heap. Occupants of the middle latitudes are worrying about climate change and looking north. Northerners are worrying about their very survival and looking south. They don't need sympathy. They need to be heard.

And that's how this book came about. Having crossed the Arctic Circle for the first time in 1977, when I stuffed a newly minted bachelor of science honours degree in my sock drawer and headed north to the Mackenzie Delta to build metal buildings for Esso—speaking of contradictions—I have spent part of almost every year since living, travelling, researching, visiting, drinking tea, and wandering somewhere north of sixty.

With the north as a constant reference point since then, I have come to see that while Western civilization appears to be on a crash course with itself, the North has wisdom that could come to bear on solutions to emerging environmental and geopolitical problems. So, having spent a goodly amount of time in the North American Arctic, I thought it might be timely and worthwhile to expand these travels and follow the Arctic Circle around the world, to see what I might see, to continue learning from northerners.

The first thing I learned was that it is much easier to *say* you're travelling around the world at the Arctic Circle than it is to actually get to that lofty latitude and move along the line. But that was the goal, and this is its story. It is not a textbook or a scientific tome—nothing of the kind. It is one person's account of getting a notion and enacting it, with all of the joys, fumbles, and surprises along the way, amply illuminated by the faces of northerners in Iceland, Norway, Sweden, Finland, Russia, Alaska, Canada, and Greenland who welcomed a "neighbour from across the pole" with open arms.

This story takes readers through twenty-four time zones and 360 degrees of longitude. The nominal latitude of the journey was 66°33' north, plus or minus, depending on who was around and what kind of transportation and infrastructure was available. However, a journey following the Circle exactly, were such a thing possible, would be 17,662 kilometres long. With one detour and another, my peregrinations totalled five or six times that length, door to door.

The story begins and ends at Greenwich Mean Time (where time zones begin) and as close to the prime meridian (0° longitude) as possible—in Iceland. Because it is located on an upwelling of the volcanically active Mid-Atlantic Ridge, Iceland happens to be the only place on the Arctic Circle where new land is being created. More significantly, however, Iceland is the only country among the polar eight that does not have an indigenous population. It is also the home of the oldest written texts anywhere in the circumpolar world. The story begins and ends in Iceland for all these reasons, and because this country provides a political counterpoint to the variety of projects in the other seven countries to devolve power to the indigenous peoples of the North. So from Iceland we travel east, toward the rising sun, across the Norwegian Sea to Scandinavia, Russia, Alaska, Canada, Greenland, and back to the tiny Arctic isle.

If the truth be told, however, although I've written the story sequentially by time zone and longitude, the various parts of the journey didn't always happen in the order they fall in this story. I had to take advantage of opportunities, seat sales, visa windows, and invitations as they emerged, so the tale as told here was crafted later to fit into a round-the-world arc of twenty-four chapters.

Because this book is about northern people and northern voices, I have presented their language authentically, in sense and in spirit, in ways that might offend some. For example, in Canada, the term "Eskimo"—originally from a North American Indian word, with a somewhat derogatory tone, meaning "eater of raw meat"—has generally been replaced by "Inuit," meaning "the people" in the Inuktitut language. But in Alaska and Russia particularly, "Eskimo" is still a term in common parlance, and it is used here alongside references to specific ethnicities, such as Inupiaq or Chukchi.

If you are offended, enraged, energized, or inspired by what this book tells you, then you will share some of what I experienced when circling the midnight sun between June 2010 and October 2013. To be sure, there are wrongs to be righted and much work yet to be done.

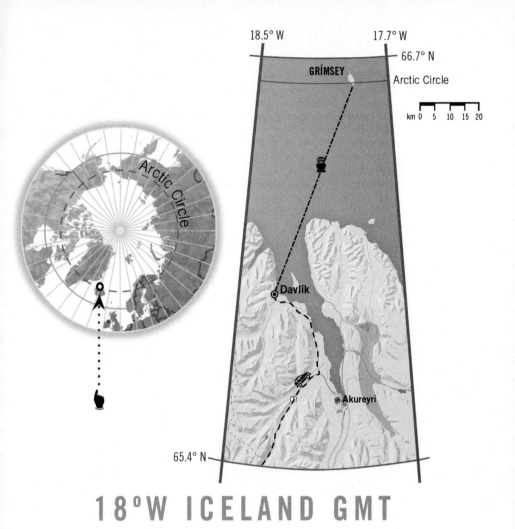

18°W ICELAND GMT

1: LIVING THE SAGAS

It was not the Arctic you might expect. It was lush and warm and greener than Greenland. There were blue poppies here the size of dinner plates. And the last polar bear to arrive here was shot dead as an undesirable. It was sad, really. There was a time when sea ice would last through the summer months in the Denmark Strait. Bears would use these rafts for loafing between spring and fall. But with global warming, that option was gone. Icelandic scientists reckoned this bear probably swam the last of the 430 kilometres from its winter range on the ice of eastern Greenland. The unsuspecting animal made landfall in the West Fjords region of Hornstrandir, in northwestern Iceland. It shook itself off and wandered up the beach, only to be dispatched as a threat to public safety by the local police chief, who feared that it might make its way to one of the towns on the other side of the broad Húnaflói fjord.

Icelanders have always done things a bit differently. The bear's role in municipal politics is one example. In the wake of the country's financial collapse in 2008, the comedian Jon Gnarr decided to run—successfully—for mayor of Iceland's capital, Reykjavik, a city of some two hundred thousand people. Gnarr and his Best Party promised free towels at public swimming pools and a "drug-free parliament by 2020"; moved by the bear incident, he semi-seriously proposed that instead of shooting hapless polar bears that turn up on Iceland's shores, authorities should instead put them in the municipal kids' zoo.

When I arrived in Reykjavik a couple of summers later, no bears had tested the proposed policy, but Gnarr was still mayor. Towels, sadly, in the many amazing geothermally heated public swimming pools in town, cost 350 Icelandic krónur (C$3). Neck deep in one of these human soup pots, cheek by jowl with beefy Icelandic men, I gazed beyond the fence to snow-capped mountain peaks in the distance through a haze of semi-fetid hot steam and lingering volcanic ash. During this geothermal interlude, I reflected on a populace that would elect a polar-bear-loving mayor and, more broadly, on this Arctic nation's commitment to letting the voice of the people prevail, even if the voice was as offbeat as Jon Gnarr's.

The tumult that immediately preceded Gnarr's electoral triumph was all about bad banking, megalomaniacal financing, and Iceland's struggle to recover after the economic crisis in 2008. The hero, or the pariah, of this financial drama was another Icelandic iconoclast: the president, Ólafur Ragnar Grímsson (elected for a fifth term in 2012).

When asked by the United Kingdom and European countries to cover the debts of three private Icelandic banks that had stiffed thousands of customers out of billions of krónur in savings, in the so-called "Icesave crisis," the Icelandic parliament— the Althingi—voted to pay for the bailout. However, before that decision could become law, President Grímsson, true to his Icelandic roots as a dyed-in-the-wool democrat, called upon the little-used powers of his largely ceremonial office to hold a referendum. Was this what the people wanted to do with public funds? A solid majority of voters responded with a resounding no. The president relayed this message to British prime minister Gordon Brown and many others in the international financial community. Brown had already put Iceland on the British list of terrorist states and agencies, alongside al Qaeda and the Taliban. Today, however, it is clear that the debts of these particular banks will be almost fully covered by the recovered assets.

Through Icesave, the loss of retirement funds, the collapse of banks, the bankruptcy of hundreds of firms, and 11 percent unemployment, the Icelandic króna dropped to half its value, but the Icelandic people did their best to stick to their principles and weather the financial storm. Some of the finance wizards involved in the economic crisis were later accused, tried, and convicted of all relevant charges, but that process is still not over. Homes of individual Icelanders in greatest need were saved through national mortgage protection, and other measures were instituted to help them pull through. In addition, political and judicial reforms were brought in. Now, the unemployment rate is 4 percent, but 9 percent of the population has fallen below the poverty line.

Although he did not play a direct role in the political rivalry throughout the crisis, President Grímsson was determined to change how business was done. The prime minister fell. There were riots in the streets until the change of government. The international community glowered at the Central Bank of Iceland, to whom no one in the financial sector was talking. Still, Iceland negotiated an agreement for a substantial currency swap with the Central Bank of China. Elsewhere, banks and corporations, notably in the United States, fell into crisis as well, despite the fact that they were propped up with public funds. But a US$2.1-billion loan from the International Monetary Fund and important support from the Nordic countries, Poland, and the Faeroe Islands allowed Iceland to stay its economic course. By 2011 it seemed to have turned toward safe harbour, but with continuing state debts, bank debts, and foreign exchange restrictions, the crisis has lingered for years.

As I read about all this in Canadian papers, Grímsson fascinated and inspired me, not only for his courage and his convictions during the financial crisis but also for his vision in other areas, particularly climate change and its implications for the rest of the world. When an opportunity presented itself for me to join a fellow writer and traveller, Ari Trausti Guðmundsson, in a delegation to visit President Grímsson at Bessastaðir, his official residence in the school-cum-farmhouse near an ancient Icelandic church on the verdant Alftanes Peninsula, I jumped at the chance to meet this modern-day political explorer before heading further north.

Over tea in china cups in the spacious living room looking out across manicured lawns to the mountains beyond, the president was charming and funny. He showed us photos of the Reagan-Gorbachev summit in Reykjavik in 1986, when Vigdís Finnbogadottir was president, and the elaborate clock the Russian had given her as a thank-you gift. ("As far as I know, it never worked," Grímsson said.) He explained that for most of the time that the American air base was operating at Keflavík using fuel brought in from the U.S., Iceland itself was running on oil imported from Russia. So much for Cold War solitudes behind the scenes in Iceland.

Climate change had been on Iceland's political agenda since at least 1996, when the country became a founding member of the Arctic Council along with Finland, Norway, Sweden, Russia, the United States, Canada, and Denmark (on behalf of Greenland). Grímsson was straightforward and direct in his pragmatic assessment of what was happening in the world.

"We should be concerned about the Arctic for many reasons. People have lived all over the Arctic for thousands of years.

When the Western world started waking up to Arctic issues, the Cold War covered them up. It is only in the last twenty years that we have been looking at things as they are. And now climate change has speeded that up to the point that the Arctic has become the most important part of the planet. First, the U.S. Geological Survey estimates from 2008 suggest that 13 percent of the world's untapped and undiscovered oil and 30 percent of undiscovered natural gas are in the Arctic. Secondly, climate change is happening three times faster in the Arctic. And thirdly, with the melting of the ice, you might even say unfortunately, there will be new shipping opportunities, which will reduce shipping distances by almost a half and have an impact on world trade, not unlike the effect of the building of the Suez Canal one hundred years ago."

He painted a picture of Iceland as a hub in this new international trading network, strategically situated at the terminus of both the Northwest Passage and the Northern Sea Route. As the summers have lengthened and the ice has thinned and become less extensive, tens of ships and thousands of tonnes of freight moving through Arctic waters are becoming scores of ships and millions of tonnes. Countries with no Arctic connection are building icebreakers and ice-hardened freighters. China's icebreaker MV *Xuĕ Lóng* (Snow Dragon) was well known to Grímsson; with his blessing, it would steam right across the top of the world from Shanghai to Reykjavik in the summer of 2012, confirming Iceland as the Arctic's central station: a port, a fuelling stop, a transfer point, or a handy stopping place on the way to or from almost every significant port in the world via the North Pole.

"If you talk to the leadership of China," Grímsson said, waving his finely manicured hand for emphasis, ice-blue eyes burning with sincerity, "when you ask them why they are so interested in Iceland, they would tell you soon in the conversation that when China has become the primary trading partner in the world, they will of course have to look at the northern sea routes between Europe and America and Asia to maximize efficiencies. And that is why I can tell you now that throughout my presidency I have received more delegations in Iceland from China than from the U.S., Britain, Germany, France, Italy, and Spain combined. When the European Union countries were pressuring us to take responsibility for the failed banks, and the United States authorities had simply lost interest in Iceland, the president of China and his prime minister, Wen Jiabao, were the people we were able to have a dialogue with. That's one of the indications that China is here now, not ten or twenty years from now."

Eager to touch the Arctic Circle in Iceland, I headed north toward the island of Grímsey, the only part of Iceland that reaches my target latitude of 66°33'N. As I travelled clockwise around the main island, the road was good, mostly an all-weather two-lane with traffic that became increasingly sparse as the day went on. Horses were everywhere. They were not wild, but they seemed to have the run of the place. In shadowed valleys I saw groups of recreational riders, some surrounded by dozens of riderless horses, sharing the common pasture; they seemed to have joined these posses just for fun. Having left Reykjavik in mid-morning, by early evening I was in a guest house in Dalvík, with a cold Viking beer in hand, watching the sun swoop past the northern horizon.

Early the following morning, I walked to the harbour to board the Samskip *Saefari*, a deep-hulled little stump of a ferry that looked ready for big seas, sitting quietly at the wharf. On that August day, the sky was clear and the weather report was good, but a couple of rough-looking deckhands still took the precaution of chaining down a tandem truck of asphalt that more or less filled the available automobile space on the vessel. There were a couple of cars tucked in under the passenger cabin on the deck above. And besides an assortment of mail and parcels that had come aboard in sacks for stowage in the purser's area, the only other cargo appeared to be a couple of tourists and a shrink-wrapped pallet of beer and liquor.

After a couple of hours at sea with the white-tipped peaks of the main island falling behind, Grímsey appeared, hardly bigger than the image on my map, a tiny island with a runway running up the middle like a zipper. Walking up the hill from the harbour and along Runway 36 (so called because it runs exactly north, 360° like the arrow of a compass) toward the Básar Guesthouse, located right on 66°33'N—the Heimskautsbaugur (Arctic Circle in Icelandic)—I ran the gauntlet of thousands of cranky and very territorial Arctic terns that seemed personally aggrieved that I had happened along. By the time the Arctic Circle monument came into view, I'd had my toque tweaked off twice, I was spattered with tern shit, and I'd had to resort to putting a stick into the collar of my windbreaker to deter these persistent, if beautiful, dive-bombing representatives of the Grímsey welcome committee.

The monument was a plain metal three-step stile over what looked like a piece of thirty-centimetre stainless steel oil pipe, the kind you would find in a refinery in Deadhorse, Alaska, Khanty-Mansiysk in northern Russia, or Norman Wells in the valley of Canada's fabled Mackenzie River, except that it was in the middle of a tundra golf course (one of two right on the Arctic Circle; the other is in Fort Yukon, Alaska). It was as if the designer of this unusual marker were asking the visitor to imagine the Arctic Circle as a circumpolar oil pipeline. Only 6 percent of the earth's surface is north of this line, but the industry estimated that this small zone of land, ice, and sea contained as much as a quarter of the world's undiscovered but recoverable oil and gas. The Grímsey monument's pipeline motif might have been closer to the heart of the matter than it first appeared.

I jumped up on one end of the pipe and, with my arms held out for balance, walked its length, imagining that if I continued tiptoeing along the line for 17,662 kilometres, I'd be back to where I started. Dismounting, I dug out my GPS unit and decided to "walk the line" from the beaches on the west side of the island to the ninety-metre cliffs on the east side of the island, a distance of maybe a kilometre and a half.

Convinced that no one was looking, I imagined myself balancing on the actual line, walking for the first few hundred metres with my arms out. The view brought horizons of infinite possibility. The sameness of undifferentiated smoky blue sky over smoky blue sea was contrasted by the richness of every tundra green imaginable and the chorus, near and far, of birds. The cry of the terns. The deliberately slow, slurred *chu-weet* whistles of the plovers. The bickering of razorbills and kittiwakes that ebbed and flowed over the beeline whirs of puffins, busily defying gravity on their travels between the water and their burrows along the cliff edge.

Then there came a familiar hoarse croak. It took a minute or two to locate the source, but eventually I spied two ravens sitting in the sunshine at the top of the cliffs that dropped down into the sea on Grímsey's eastern shore. If I were a raven, I'd hang out there as well, given the view, not to mention the bounty of eggs, chicks, and birds of every size and description on the menu.

Later, in one of the clutch of small houses clustered around the harbour, Ingólfur Bjarni, a gangly teen with a workingman's hands, invited me in to have a look at his family's collection of stuffed birds, which included some exotic migrants blown onto the island on the shifting North Atlantic winds. I mentioned having seen the two ravens on the island's eastern headland. "Yes," he said, "there are always just two ravens on the island," as if that were something everyone should know. "That is how it has been for nine hundred years. If one dies, the other goes to the mainland to find another. Or if a third tries to settle on the island, the other two chase it away. But always just two."

I had come to Grímsey to touch the Arctic Circle in Iceland but also to fish with Ingólfur's dad, Svafar Gylfasson, and Svafar's equally slim and handsome twin brother, Bjarni, in their fourteen-metre fishing vessel called the *Nunni*. This is what Icelanders have been doing since Ingólfr Arnarson, founder of the first permanent settlement here, arrived in the year 874. We set sail at four in the morning and pulled nets until mid-afternoon, filling the hold with stout wide-mouthed North Atlantic cod, bright orange *karfi*, silver saith, and a mixture of bycatch: *skata* (grey skate) and *skarkoli* (plaice). And I imagine that they had always done the job with the same devilish humour that caused Svafar's hired hands, Adam and Arni, to toss a vicious toothed catfish in my direction to see how far I might jump to avoid being bitten.

Like their Norse forebears, they fished with eleven *trossa* barriers, each consisting of ten thirty-metre gillnets tied together, with anchors and marker buoys on either end. Each time a *trossa* was pulled and reset, its placement was marked on the map so that when the boats went out—year-round—in darkness or in fog, they knew exactly where to look. Each net was pulled at least once every twenty-four hours to ensure that the catch didn't spoil in the water.

Between nets, the lads chatted, ate homemade cake, drank coffee, and smoked as the *Nunni* chugged its way to the next location, all within view of Grímsey. There was an onboard Internet connection and a laptop computer on the bridge that they used to report an estimate of their catch to the Icelandic Department of Fisheries daily, so that the taxman might keep track of how things were going. Like young people all over the world, Adam checked his Facebook page when the captain was below. There were no factory trawlers here, or near here. Svafar and his crew animated the sagas of the present day. Had global warming changed much in their lives? Not really. The fish might be a bit bigger, said Svafar, and they seemed to grow better in warmer water. What wasn't to like about that?

Back in the harbour each day by mid-afternoon, they weighed the catch as it was unloaded and hauled away on tractor-drawn wagons to be processed. The cod would be split and salted by another arm of the family business operating just off the Grímsey wharf, and the rest of the catch, sold fresh on the Internet before we even reached port, would be iced and packed in plastic shipping tubs that left town three times a week, stacked four high on the *Saefari* and trumping cars and other cargo for deck space. After a two-part brine-and-rock-salt curing process, the salted fish left the island, as less time-sensitive cargo, for shipment by air to grocery wholesalers in Spain and Portugal, who bought every delicious white flake that Grímsey could send.

One afternoon, after the *Nunni*'s hold had been emptied, the decks rinsed clean with sea water, and the hired help sent home, Safar asked if I'd like to join the family in checking herring nets set at various locations around the island. The herring, he told me, ran in schools along the base of the island's cliffs, close in to shore. The islanders did eat them, pickled, fried, or boiled, but herring was more of a staple food for their sheep. Icelandic sheep, the ones that produce the famous Icelandic wool, eat fish for protein in addition to forage from the Arctic heath.

The wheelhouse was crowded with more bodies than it saw most days. There was Svafar's father, who was still working another boat in the family fleet; Svafar's wife, Unnur, who ran Krían, the only restaurant on the island; and his twenty-one-year-old daughter, Gyda, who served at Krían when she was not at school on the mainland. Rounding out the group were Bjarni and his wife. It was a family outing, except for Ingólfur, who was working in the family's fish plant to ice and process the day's catch.

The herring catch was very poor; in fact, the only things in the nets beside seaweed were diving seabirds that had tried to swim through. But as the *Nunni* circled past the iconic yellow lighthouse on the bluffs of southern Grímsey, a cry from the deck drew everyone's attention to a pod of dolphins surfacing off the starboard bow. Svafar tugged my arm as he spun the wheel around. For a minute, it looked as if this fishing trip would shift into marine mammal sightseeing.

Hanging over the bow railings, the women pointed and called back to Svafar at the helm, to let him know where the dolphins were. Bjarni retrieved a pump shotgun out of a locker on the back wall of the wheelhouse, and he too headed out on the deck. Everything was happening so quickly. Momentarily, the pod disappeared. But then, after a few tense moments, it reappeared portside, farther away. The ladies cajoled the captain. Gyda was on her cellphone, calling friends with a high-speed inflatable to join the hunt.

In time, the *Nunni* circled and circled again and eventually synchronized with the sleek grey mammals. The pod glided alongside, as if to ride the bow wave of the boat. Suddenly there was a percussive thud.

At first, everyone thought Bjarni had missed, although that seemed difficult to believe, given that the animal was no more than a few metres away. But in time, it was clear that one of the pod was losing the ability to dive for any length of time. Blood streamed into the water from its back.

Aware that there was a chance the animal might die and sink, the women anxiously yelled directions from the foredeck back through the open wheelhouse windows, imploring Svafar to manoeuvre the boat close to the dying dolphin so that someone might get a gaff to grab it and pull it into the boat.

As the animal slowed in the water and tried to draw breath, its tail began to sink, and the intensity of the moment caught me totally by surprise. With the shrill voices fading momentarily into the background of engine noise and the movement of people within the vessel, I stood dumbfounded, looking at that beguiling "smile" of the dying dolphin's turned-up mouth as it looked up at the boat. The only other place I'd seen that face was on television as a kid, watching Flipper, the family-friendly and apparently so intelligent star of that long-running 1960s series. But suddenly Flipper was meat, the catch of the day.

"Come on, come on," the ladies cried, as Svafar manoeuvred the boat. "Quickly, quickly."

But to no avail. With everyone looking on from just out of reach because the big fishing boat could not get close enough, quickly enough, the dolphin broke the surface with its beak one last time, and slowly disappeared from view.

The women's shoulders dropped and their arms fell to their sides. Unnur, turning to look at the Canadian visitor, must have seen something on my face that hinted at the emotional intensity of what was going on inside. "Dolphin is one of the absolute favourite meats for the table," she said. "It's so disappointing to know that we came this close to filling the freezer with dolphin meat for the next few months. I hope you understand."

That evening, at Krían, Svafar exchanged his captain's gear for an apron and bussed tables. The place was full of British tourists who had come for the birds and to touch the Arctic Circle. As well, tables by the window were occupied by a boisterous shoal of fishermen from the Icelandic mainland who had moved north for the summer to work from Grímsey harbour.

Svafar drifted over and asked if I would like to try some dolphin. "There's a bit left in the freezer," he told me. The plate arrived with another ice-cold Thule beer. I closed my eyes to try to blot out the image of pan-seared Flipper, even if in my head I knew that what I was really struggling with was the clinical separation of life and death and the sanitization of my own carnivorous nature. The meat was dark, and rich and tender. The experience was more than a little surreal.

The following day, sitting at a concrete chess table in a little park overlooking the harbour where Grímsey youth were swimming and pulling each other around in a Zodiac, I saw the sail of a sleek sloop-rigged boat appear around the south coast of the island. It was a vessel of some size. As it approached, I could see an impressive graphic of a familiar big white form and, along the waterline, "Polar Bear" in large blue letters.

Later, during a quick tour of the Web from the comfort of another table in Krían, I learned that this was one of two vessels operated by a high-end Arctic tour company, en route from Britain to Greenland. As the crew lowered the sail to prepare to motor into Grímsey harbour, patrons lined up on deck in their parkas. In truth, it can be brutally cold at sea, even at more southerly latitudes. But the image of the bear and the parkas juxtaposed with that of Grímsey kids in bathing suits made me laugh at the *terra nullius* (meaning "land belonging to no one") expectations we southerners insisted on bringing north, before the people who live there gently showed us what was really going on.

Back on the Icelandic mainland, driving south from Dalvík to Reykjavik felt anticlimactic after Grímsey. But in the afternoon light, the iridescent glow of a valley of new-mown hay suspended between braided meltwater brooks fed by high alpine drifts pushed dolphins, ravens, and anything but the immediate presence of the place completely out of mind.

As I settled in for the five-hour drive to Reykjavik, the rhythm of the road polished the sights and sensations of Grímsey. A golf course! A polar bear on a twelve-tonne keel. A family that fished every day of the year on open ocean. No ice. Climate change, at least in the short term, was helping rather than hindering the day-to-day doings of a contented lot of seafaring folk. Ten thousand birds for every human on the island. "Air fishing" with big nets for puffins that ended up served with *ribsgel* (redcurrant) sauce on the Krían table. Terns that migrated seventy to eighty thousand kilometres each year, Arctic to Antarctic and back, and still had energy to fuss with strangers who dared to enter their personal space. And Flipper.

Interestingly, although Iceland was the last Arctic land to be settled or occupied, it holds the oldest written texts in the circumpolar world. As I approached Reykjavik to see them, I wound down past Mount Esja and around the bay to a guest house near the university. The following morning I parked by the big brand new glass honeycomb of the harpa concert hall. With map in hand, I found my way to the National Centre for Cultural Heritage, known as the Culture House, on a hill overlooking the Reykjavik harbour. It is here that some of these medieval texts, the Eddas and the Sagas, are kept and interpreted. Written in runic letters on animal parchments with vegetable inks, these documents were a literary phenomenon in the thirteenth and fourteenth centuries, but they reported on activities and explorations reaching back to the tenth and eleventh centuries, essentially the first written texts of human experience in the circumpolar world, another reason to begin my journey in Iceland.

After the brightness of the summer sun on the white plaster walls of the Culture House, it took some time for my eyes to adjust to the subdued indoor lighting. The Sagas area was even more dimly lit than the vestibule. But slowly, through text and imagery in backlit panels that gave a stained-glass-cathedral effect to the space, the place came alive. I wandered among busts, sculptures, and other artifacts placed on plinths and pedestals in the room full of ancient stories about the birth of Iceland, its Viking exploration roots, and its fierce allegiance to democracy. But after a while, having appreciated that what was on offer here were very cleverly and effectively wrought reproductions of the actual documents and the original texts, my initial enthusiasm was replaced by disappointment and thoughts of moving on.

Looking for the way out, I stepped through a darkened portal with the red glow of an exit sign above the door. It turned out that this was more of an entrance than an exit. *This* was the inner sanctum. Here, in even lower light, smooth surfaces of sealed glass cases reflected the faces of fellow visitors bowing to behold the real thing. The real Sagas were smaller than I'd imagined, especially after I'd soaked in the glorious (and colour-enhanced) enlargements next door. A story called Margaret's Saga was the smallest of the lot, with pages perhaps five by six centimetres. Beside this exquisite relic was an interpretive card that said midwives and new mothers often prayed to St. Margaret. Copies of this saga were sometimes placed against the thighs of women in labour to ease the birthing process.

Nearby were sample pages from the thirteenth-century Poetic Edda, a collection of Old Norse poems primarily preserved in a medieval manuscript called the Codex Regius, along with stories from the Prose Edda, written by Snorri Sturluson. Captivated by the notion of such antiquity right there in front of me, I have no idea how long I was there, barely registering the other visitors bumping into me as they moved past in the darkness.

The story that stood out was about the Norse god Odin, the ruler of Asgard, who always had two ravens in his company. These were Huginn and Muninn, his winged eyes and ears, who helped to keep track of goings on in the universe of the gods. Each morning, the saga said, these two ravens would be dispatched by their master to travel the world, then report back each evening with what they had seen and heard.

Odin, in his wisdom, gave these two special ravens the ability to speak human languages, so that they might understand the meanings of overhead conversations. Further, the saga relates, the names of these two birds are significant as well: Huginn is Old Norse for "thought" and Muninn means "memory." Huginn and Muninn are often associated in Norse mythology with *fylg-jur*, related supernatural beings directly connected to human fate and fortune.

Two ravens on Grímsey, never more than two, I could hear Ingólfur telling me. I could see in my mind's eye those two ravens sitting on the top of the cliff, talking like two old guys on the bench outside the post office. The story of the raven god suggested that thought and memory could control human fate and fortune. Perhaps the ravens were trying to tell us something.

I left the Culture House and headed through town to have a coffee and cogitate a bit on the Sagas, I settled in on a bench beside Hallgrímskirkja, the imposing church on the hill. In front of it was a well-weathered bronze statue of Leifur Heppni, the man himself, Leif the Lucky, Leif Ericsson—another star in the Sagas—looking very much like a Viking hero, overlooking the harbour. His jaw was set, his eyes firmly fixed on the horizon, and as I looked up at the gulls landing on his head, I saw the purpose of this circumpolar journey as clearly as ever.

The Sagas established that Ericsson and his crew had reached North America five centuries before Columbus. And yet Columbus got the credit for his "discovery" of the New World. Why were these northern voices, these northern stories written in vegetable inks on durable animal hides, not more included in received Western history? Was it because they did not ask or call out for recognition? Was it because they didn't fit into the Mediterranean exploration myth and mystique? Whatever the case, it seems the people of the middle latitudes have a long-standing habit of ignoring northerners and northern voices.

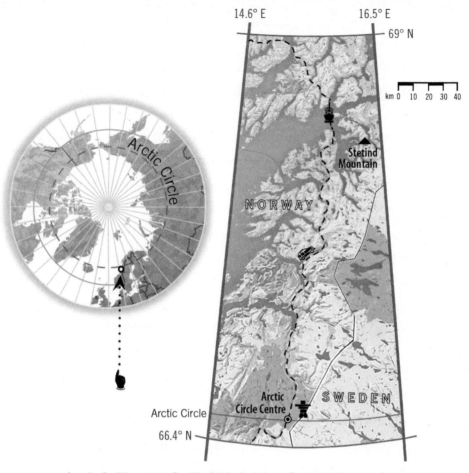

14°E NORWAY GMT+1

2: VOICES OF THE SACRED MOUNTAIN

As I moved east toward the rising sun in Norway, a bonus: my spouse, collaborator in life's adventures, and in-house editor, Gail Simmons, would be with me for a month in Scandinavia. The plan was to celebrate our thirtieth anniversary in Murmansk. We took a daytime flight from Ottawa to Frankfurt, en route to Oslo, where we'd rent a car to head north. It was a surprise to learn that air traffic controllers had routed our flight on an arc that intersected the Arctic Circle eleven thousand metres over the Norwegian Sea.

A lifelong reluctant flyer, Gail nevertheless wanted to travel partway around the Arctic Circle with me. For the flight, she was rendered more or less unconscious by relaxation tapes and a selection of little white pills from our most understanding family physician. I leaned over to point out on her seat-back map screen that we were actually flying over the intersection of 66°33' north latitude and the prime meridian—no answer.

Lost in my own little reverie, anticipating the tour we had planned that would take us up to the Arctic Circle by road in Norway, then east along the line through Sweden and Finland, followed by a great arc over the top of Scandinavia to Nordkapp and over the border into western Russia, I was caught off guard when the beverage service arrived. I was joined by three impossibly cute polar bears on the side of Coke's newest soft drink container. I was at the Arctic Circle, crossing into the space the Greeks called Arktikos, meaning "near the bear" (the Great Bear constellation), and there they were, the three proverbial bears.

Sipping my Coke, I reached for the in-flight magazine and flipped to the map at the back. It's basically the same world image that most Westerners have grown up with, a transverse Mercator projection that represents the middle latitudes most faithfully. The Arctic and the Antarctic are just grossly distorted white blobs on the edges of the page.

If we are to get closer to understanding the role that the North is playing and will play in our future, if we are to embrace the notion of a peopled Arctic, a different map needs to be etched in public consciousness. This is a map that President Grímsson knows well, the so-called polar projection. It is a view of the earth looking down from the North Star, a map with the North Pole in the centre and the equator at the margin, with the parallels (latitudes) as circles and the meridians (longitudes) as spokes on a wheel. There is a similar map for the South Pole; what sets the two apart is that the austral map shows land surrounded by water, while the boreal map is the opposite. Culturally, the poles are opposites as well: the North is peopled.

Although more often seen as a satellite photo than as a map, this is the image that has entered our lives with the incredible time-lapse photography of the summer minimum of Arctic sea ice. The polar projection also presents the adjacencies of the eight circumpolar nations and how connected they are by Arctic waters, instead of being strung out horizontally in a way that shows Russia and Canada, for example, as worlds apart when in fact they are neighbours across the pole. Although we tend to think of flights from, say, Ottawa to Frankfurt as following a straight line from west to east on the old school map, in fact the shortest distance between two points on the earth is always what's known as the great circle route, which, in this instance, goes well up into Arctic airspace.

Arctic as unknown wilderness. Polar regions as amorphous white blobs for text and legends at the top and bottom of our maps. Arctic as place of discovery. Arctic as exotic passage. Arctic as wilderness. Arctic as home of the bear. Arctic as laboratory. Arctic as thermostat, the melting ice an accessible metric of global climate change. And, increasingly, as changes in sea and land conditions have enabled more resource exploration and extraction, the Arctic is registering as a larder, a bank, even a battery.

Such are the shifting ways that this melting ice cap figures in the public consciousness. The Arctic as a homeland for people— more than four million globally at or above the Arctic Circle, including nearly four hundred thousand indigenous people of more than forty ethnicities spanning eight different linguistic groups—seems to be an elusive concept for residents of the non-Arctic to comprehend. And now Coke was connecting the consumption of sugar and caffeine to the preservation of bears that stand for all that is sweet and right and fuzzy and four-legged about the future of the Arctic and the planet. Jeez!

"Can you believe that?" I asked out loud, as I held up the empty can. And still my partner slept.

As we headed north from Oslo's Gardermoen Airport on Norwegian Highway E6, Gail was coming around. The rumble of the road and a good blast of fresh air washed away the worry of flying. We were like a couple of kids, giddy with the prospect of another Arctic adventure. Rolling north, we might as well have been in Thomas Hardy's Wessex or at home in eastern Ontario, watching farmers bale hay on neatly ordered green pastures between polite little towns. Thanks to warm equatorial waters surging north on the Gulf Stream and the North Atlantic Drift, the rolling green hills looked nothing like the Canadian Arctic.

It was June, and our goal was to be on the Arctic Circle on the solstice, to watch the sun complete its first full circle through all points of the compass in Norway. The joke on the Canadians, who generally think they know a thing or two about long journeys, was that getting to the intersection of Norwegian Highway E6 and the Arctic Circle in the compact coastal country turned out to be almost more than we could handle.

Our maps indicated that it was over a thousand kilometres from Oslo to the Polarsirkel-Senteret near Stødi. Gail and I routinely travelled from our home in Ontario to Nova Scotia, where most of her family lives, a distance of nearly 1,500 kilometres, which we usually did in one day, starting early and driving as fast as traffic and the law would allow, making our way down the St. Lawrence River valley, up and over the divide into New Brunswick, and then down the Saint John River valley to Nova Scotia.

Highway E6 was an excellent two-lane all-weather road, but with the undulating semi-mountainous terrain and insanely tight curves—clear mountain air on one side and grey granite on the other—we did well to reach top speeds of ninety kilometres an hour and averaged well below that. The landscape and the picturesque little Norwegian towns, as we made our way north through Ringebu, Folidal, Trondheim, and on, and *on*, were captivating in their contrast to anything we had experienced at this latitude at home. But on and on we went.

"Remind me what the big draw of being on the Arctic Circle on the summer solstice is?" Gail asked in a voice that was more "Maybe we should stop and continue in the morning" than it was "Gee, this fourteen-hour drive is just what I'd imagined our Arctic adventure would be."

"I don't know," I replied. "It's something to do with cosmic geometry and experiencing this important line I'm following around the world at the exact moment in the earth's orbit around the sun that actually defines the Arctic Circle. At every point along 66°33' north, for the first and only time this year, the sun will be visible all night long. That's cool, wouldn't you say?"

No answer.

"It's all about the obliquity."

"The what?"

"They call the earth's 23°27' tilt—the one that when subtracted from 90° gives us 66°33' or 66.6°, the latitude of the Arctic Circle, and the point on the earth's surface at which the sun is visible for twenty-four hours in the Arctic summer—the 'obliquity.' By that same geometry, that is the exact line where twenty-four-hour darkness begins in the winter. The obliquity is what defines the Arctic day and night, and it is also the angle that gives us the changing of the seasons. I thought it would be neat to be on the line on the day that the sun is visible for the full twenty-four hours, the longest day of the year."

"Right. I thought it would be neat not to spend the whole day in the car."

"Distances are deceiving here in Norway."

"Right."

By eight p.m., travelling in fog and light rain, we had made it to Mo I Rana, the administrative capital of Nordland County, which spans the Arctic Circle. But we still had ninety kilometres to go. By then, the road was even more challenging than farther south, with lots of hairpin bends and drivers who were clearly more familiar with the curves than we were. Norwegian roads, like most things Scandinavian, were much more economical in design than anything Canadian.

And, to make the driving even more interesting as we started up switchback grades into the Salffjellet Mountains, the Norwegian Roads Department had taken away the centre line, opting instead to mark a reference line on the edges of the road, so that when approaching a broad-snouted transport bearing down at high speed, you had to focus on the side of the road rather than the centre to stay out of harm's way. It took some getting used to.

The climb moved us away from bucolic farmland and into more wild country, scrub boreal forest, and eventually an alpine tundra plateau that looked, finally, like an Arctic to which we could relate. In fact, it started to snow as we passed a sign saying "Polarsirkel-Senteret 2 km." And finally we were there. At 9:37 p.m. on the summer solstice, Gail and I got out of the car and, to the extent that our road-weary bodies would allow, did a little dance right there in the parking lot.

The sign said that the centre would be closing at ten, so we rushed inside the domed-roof building, which looked inspired by a sea turtle, or perhaps a melting igloo. Signs in the foyer welcomed us in Norwegian, English, Dutch, Spanish, German, Italian, and French. A pretty summer student who was closing up the Arctic Circle photo booth apologized that she'd shut down the camera for the night but said that if we wanted to follow the red arrows on the floor and stand in the red box in front of the Polarsirkel-branded northern lights dropcloth, she would be happy to snap a picture with our camera.

Here, Polarsirkel ("Arctic Circle" in Norwegian) is actually a trademark that has been stitched, painted, transferred, tagged, or otherwise affixed to almost every type of merchandise imaginable, from pencils to pullovers. There were playing cards, key fobs, T-shirts, rock candy, stuffed animals, soothers, paperweights, neckties, towels, gloves, hats, underwear, lottery ticket scratchers, erasers, postcards, and more postcards. If you wanted cards postmarked with the Arctic Circle cancelling stamp, that cost a little more.

And you could mail these cards in the big red Arctic Circle postbox, which stood beside the rangiest-looking beanpole of a polar bear (apparently Europe's largest, although there certainly wouldn't have been a real bear at this location since the Pleistocene, if then), standing menacingly on its hind feet and stretching from floor to ceiling. I've never seen such a tall bear, in the wild or mounted. The specimen's only redeeming characteristic, besides its impressive height, was a very clean and fluffy coat that had been splendidly finished by the taxidermist with a creme rinse that smelled faintly of lavender.

The staff were now closing the till and locking up. A bit dazed by the inside of the centre, we headed back outside and into the gently falling snow. We took our coffee in Arctic Circle paper cups with us. Given the hour and the overcast sky, the view of the sun in the North for which I had hungered was obscured.

En route to the monument that marks the actual circle, we found ourselves surrounded by stone cairns—what Canadian Inuit call inukshuks, meaning "likenesses of men." As we walked up a rise, imagining that we were moving step by step along the Circle itself, things got even stranger. The scope of the phenomenon was staggering. All the way from this land surrounding the Polarsirkel-Senteret across reindeer pastures to the next ridge, which had to be at least a kilometre away, visitors had built these little monuments to mark the occasion of reaching the Arctic Circle. Where we expected to see evidence of the Sami, the Scandinavian indigenous people, we instead found a collection of lithic graffiti—"I was here" markers littering the tundra.

Returning to the car, we scared a couple of ravens chowing down inside a Dumpster outside the centre's cafeteria. They croaked and then lifted on wings that fluttered and squeaked in the still cold air. They circled once and then settled on top of the nearby monument, on the Arctic Circle marker. Thought and memory, in silhouette against the midnight sky.

The following day, we continued north above the Arctic Circle, still under an overcast sky, on the twelve-car E6 ferry from Bognes to Skarberget. "So where's this sacred mountain?" Gail asked as we chugged across open water. "What's it called again?"

"Stetind. And it's over there," I replied, checking my compass and pointing through the mist and rain in what I thought might be an easterly direction across Tysfjorden. "It was voted Norway's national mountain back in 2002. The Norwegian tourist brochure says it is visible for kilometres in every direction around here. Fishermen in boats on the open sea are supposed to use it as a marker, so surely we'd be able to see it from here, if the clouds weren't so low."

There were two compelling reasons to move north from the Polarsirkel-Senteret, instead of moving east or even west along the Arctic Circle. The first was an absence of roads in very rugged terrain. The other reason was to see if we might catch a glimpse of this sacred mountain and, after that, to get a view into the world of Norwegian enviropolitics as seen through the eyes of an inspiring young activist called Ingrid Skjoldvær, who lives near there.

Stetind is not the highest mountain in Norway, nor is it the most impressive—but, because of its smooth granite sides, it is perhaps Norway's most difficult challenge in technical rock climbing. Leading the team that first summited Stetind's 1,391-metre peak by its sheer west wall in 1966 was Arne Naess, the father of the deep ecology movement.

Naess, like Norwegian president Gro Harlem Brundtland, who was the first female prime minister of Norway and chair of the 1983 World Commission on Environment and Development, was a philosopher and environmentalist who called for a comprehensive examination of the causes of environmental degradation and decay rooted in the very DNA of developed Western societies. Naess died in 2009 but only after engineering a seismic shift in thinking about the relationship between people and place.

The year before he died, Naess gathered with a Sami shaman and healer, Eirik Myrhaug, and various other philosophers and teachers of *friluftsliv*, a distinctly Scandinavian philosophy of outdoor living, to redouble their search for new ways to move the principles of deep ecology into the mainstream. At this meeting they created the Council for Eco-philosophy, which they hoped would be a platform from which their messages might be more broadly communicated. The first communiqué of the council was the Stetind Declaration, which I held in my hand and pondered as the car ferry chugged on and we strained to see the mountain through the fog.

Like the Apostle's Creed or any other affirmation of faith, the declaration was meant to engage the convictions of individuals in working toward a new public consciousness. It reads, "We have gradually come to realize that our way of life has fatal consequences for nature and humankind, and therefore all life on Earth. The challenges that we face, as individuals and community, are not merely of an economic and technological nature. They concern our basic values and our fundamental conception of what it means to be human." And it goes on to acknowledge a set of related precepts and to assert a series of commitments related to renewing global understandings of the relationship between nature and humankind.

This declaration was duly signed by its creators and was then set adrift on the waters of the World Wide Web for others to embrace. Long before climate change would become a world issue, Naess and the other participants in the Stetind seminars were raising the contradictions of recycling in a carbon-dependent world of rampant consumerism. With this communication they did their best to lead by example and to spread the word. Above the Arctic Circle on Norway's rugged coast, looking back across Tysfjorden into swirling mists obscuring a view where the mountain should be, it's as if these voices were lost in the wind. But not completely.

Ingrid Skjoldvaer was sixteen years old and in grade eleven when she won a scholarship with Students on Ice to travel to Canadian Inuit communities by ship and join in the sharing of participants' stories from throughout the circumpolar world. I was a staff member on this expedition; when I returned, I prattled on to Gail about this fearless young woman who was leading a campaign to stop the Norwegian national oil company, Statoil, from doing seismic surveying in the ecologically sensitive seas near her home. In the months since we had met, Ingrid's group, Nature and Youth (Natur og Ungdom), in concert with other Norwegian environmental groups, had convinced politicians to refuse seismic surveying of the petroleum potential below the sea floor, a necessary precursor to eventual test drilling and production.

Safely off the ferry in the town of Skarberget, we continued to Narvik and then swung left around Ofotfjord toward the Vesterålen Archipelago, the northernmost part of Nordland County. Our drive up Norway had convinced us that there was no such thing as a house or a home on flat ground. Norway is all about split-level houses. We eventually found our way to Ingrid's family home overlooking Sigerfjord; it too was cut into a very steep hill leading down to the sea.

With her long blond hair pulled back in a matter-of-fact ponytail, Ingrid had a smile that lit up the tidy sea-themed living room. Although she was a little shy, it didn't take long—knowing Gail and I had been following news of her campaign on Facebook throughout the winter—before she produced a copy of the local paper with a photo of herself, beaming, in her mother's *bunad* (national dress) from southwestern Norway, holding a flag in front of a crowd of cheering onlookers under the headline "*Seir'n Er Var*," meaning "The victory is ours."

In the next few days, with Ingrid as our guide, we travelled by car, by canoe, by ferry, and by foot to coastal locations throughout her home region in the archipelago, where she introduced us to fishermen and to the reasons why, as an eleven-year-old, she had decided that the preservation of these home waters and the fish they nurtured was a cause to which she wanted to dedicate her life. Big thoughts for an eleven-year-old, but thoughts that had turned into impressive actions for a sixteen-year-old.

At the fishing port of Hovden, closest to the cod nursery coveted by Statoil, we walked among great wooden racks—called *hjell* in Norwegian—where split cod were dried by sun and sea air as cold-adapted bacteria slowly fermented and preserved the delicate white meat. Stockfish was the oldest export of Norway, Ingrid explained. It required energy to catch the fish, but after that, once the fish were cleaned and hung, drying was the most environment-friendly way imaginable to preserve it. "We still ship it all over the world," she said proudly. "For us stockfish is almost like bread. So preserving the cod fishery is important globally, but it is also very much a part of Norwegian culture and identity."

We met a fisherman on the Hovden wharf, cleaning a couple of fish for his supper. She introduced him and we talked about her campaign. "It's not a big victory," she said, "but without the permit to do the seismic testing, the oil companies will not be able to go any further, for now. It's more like a small battle in a bigger war."

At stake here were two of Norway's most significant resources: cod and oil. And because of the starkness of the conflict that had captivated this young woman, the more she explained to us, the more we read, the more it seemed that what was happening in Norway was emblematic of similar tensions throughout the circumpolar world. If it wasn't cod versus oil, it was reindeer versus mining, caribou versus dam construction, seals versus tourism, wilderness versus roads, natives versus non-natives, conservation versus development, citizens versus governments.

Here in Vesterålen, we found a nursery of the world's largest remaining population of cod, a biological fact that seemed at odds with the continued search for offshore hydrocarbons. Petroleum made up 25 percent of Norway's GDP—it was the largest per capita producer of oil and gas outside the Middle East—and while fishing was a significant source of food for export and for domestic consumption, Ingrid was quick to admit that economically it paled in comparison with oil. Nevertheless, "it is about more than money," she scoffed.

To see where she would go next, I couldn't resist baiting her a little by asking why anybody should care about cod. The western Atlantic fishery had collapsed and producers were turning to other species.

Without missing a beat, ever the professional in spite of her young age, she said, "It has everything to do with solidarity. We don't eat the cod that is caught here on a daily basis, but it does provide a livelihood for quite a number of Norwegians, and it does bring in quite a lot of money when we sell it to other countries. It's the biggest remaining cod stock in the world, and this coast is where these fish spawn. It makes no sense to risk it any further. We have to be able to say enough is enough."

Ingrid's passion, which infused her every word, was what compelled her to join Nature and Youth as a preteen. The organization was originally created as a forum for people under twenty-five who wanted to get out into nature, whether on the sea or on the rugged Norwegian landscape. But by the time the conflict over permission to conduct seismic surveying came along, the organization had evolved, and passion had pushed this remarkable teen well beyond Saturday fishing trips and walks in the woods.

Taking a leadership position in her local chapter of Nature and Youth, Ingrid helped her young colleagues develop their own brand of activism. "We were good sports," she said with a grin. "We made funny messages. We were rebellious. We made a cod cookbook and sent it to every member of parliament. We made a comic book. And, as the battle went on, we got to be a favourite item of the local media: not just because we were funny but because we always stuck to our case." All this resulted in a photo album she showed us that led to stories of a face-to-face meeting with Helge Lund, the CEO of Statoil.

"We made a song called 'Come On, Helge,' to the tune of Abba's 'Mamma Mia,' and then I ended up having to actually talk to him."

"Were you scared?" I asked.

"I felt kind of powerful with all of those people behind me. I met him and told him, 'There are lots of people who don't agree with you, and I hope your company will start focusing on renewable energy.' I did that old trick of imagining him in his underwear. At first, when he came to Vesterålen, they wouldn't let us into the meeting. But we leaked to the press that they wouldn't let us in. We said that it was outrageous. We asked, through the press, if Lund just wanted to talk to people who agree with him. Eventually, they let two people in. And that's when I got to talk directly to him."

Ingrid's conversation with Helge Lund led to further creative outgrowths of the Nature and Youth campaign that led to other confrontations and other meetings. The next thing Ingrid knew, she was in Oslo meeting with the prime minister. Norway was a huge producer of oil with a very small population, but its domestic emissions of carbon dioxide were minuscule compared with those of other countries. Still, she told Jens Stoltenberg, if he were to consider the climate effects of burning the gas and oil that Norway shipped around the world, its real carbon footprint would jump from less than 100 million tonnes of carbon dioxide to nearly 600 million tonnes per year. Norway should be working on ways to wean the world off oil, she said, and should be examining Statoil's request to find more reserves in that context. She implored Stoltenberg to start thinking long term about oil versus cod.

At that point in her report about the campaign and her visit with the prime minister, Ingrid flipped from storyteller to firebrand: "What are we going to do when the oil runs out? In forty years, we're going to have to do something else. Wouldn't it be terrible if we spoiled this amazing area, knowing we could have done something else? Because if there is one area that we should say is off limits to the oil industry then it must be here. This is one of the most vulnerable coastlines in the entire world! It's packed full of life. It's a beautiful landscape. It's my home. But it's also really rough, so if something happens, it would be catastrophic. At one point, you have to say stop."

Her blood was pumping, and she continued: "My organization made this *our* case. We got the debate to be about our future. And of course youth have more to say about the future because it is *our* future. Most of the people who are debating oil in the Arctic—or not, because they don't care—won't be alive when the oil starts flowing. We should be able to decide how we are going to live, what kind of world we are going to live in, and what industry should and should not be here."

In our conversation we touched on many subjects as we toured around the tunnels and byways of Vesterålen. We talked about inspirations—Gro Harlem Brundtland and *Our Common Future*, Arne Naess and the Stetind Declaration—and particularly how sustainable development, if there is such a thing, will not be possible while poverty and massive social injustices persist in the North and beyond. Ingrid told me how, through social media and the Internet, Nature and Youth in Norway had connected with a group of young environmentalists over the border in Murmansk, Russia, who were as concerned about the fate of the Sami reindeer herders and the aging Kola nuclear power plant as Ingrid and her colleagues were worried about Norwegian issues.

Nature and Youth in Norway secured funding for two young members to act as mentors for PIM, the Russian counterpart of Nature and Youth, in Murmansk. Communications from the Russians' hidden IP address, running under the official radar through Twitter and Facebook, have allowed the Norwegians to understand that the freedom they enjoyed to speak their piece to government was not shared by their Russian counterparts. The Russian government actively tried to quell their dissent, while the two Nature and Youth mentors were able to help them create an online petition and solicit the world for support.

Inspiring courage all around. If only all northern youth had the education, the means, and the confidence to create this sort of change.

20°E SWEDEN GMT+1

3: WE HAVE THE POWER

Back in the car and headed through the mountains to our next stop on the Circle itself—Jokkmokk, Sweden—Gail and I were still talking about Ingrid. "Sixteen!" Gail said, even more astonished after having had a couple of days and nights with her to get a full appreciation of her knowledge and commitment to the environment and to right living.

Before our journey to the part of the world surrounding Stetind, I had come to the conclusion that the deep ecology movement was a bit of a bust: it was right-headed but had essentially failed to make any headway into popular consciousness. But here was a teenager who had breathed the same Arctic air as Arne Naess and come to the same conclusions about how she would live her life.

The scenery along Highway E10 from Norway to Sweden was reminiscent of what one would see on the Canadian Pacific Railway running through the Rocky Mountains. Snow-capped peaks, cascading waterfalls, and deep valley vistas stretched off into infinity. Eagles and ravens soared near cliffs tall enough to impress Odin himself.

At the crest of a long hill just over the border in Sweden (where the quality of the road surface and the engineering of the curves and the roadbed improved *dramatically*), Highway E10 eased out into a link of crystalline lakes guarded on both sides by twin marches of snow-spattered hills. At the foot of 1,590-metre Vassitjåkka, the most commanding mountain in the range, was "the most northerly train station in Sweden," according to our guidebook. Set in the sweep of this majestic valley, the two-storey red-brick structure and its surrounding sheds and out-buildings along the twin-track railway looked like something out of a movie. We just had to stop and put on our hiking boots.

The crunch of lichen on grey granite, the rabbit's-foot feel of lush reindeer moss underfoot, the arresting pinks of mountain hea-ther bobbing in the sunshine all brought us back to a familiar place: the tundra. The air was clear and cool. The sky was blue. Pictures in a little museum inside the station indicated that the Sami used to drive reindeer by the thousand right through this place. Many times, as we walked quietly toward shadowed cliffs on higher ground, I imagined us following trails cut between the bearberries, crowberries, and fuzzy dwarf willow catkins by the feet of those animals, followed by the hide boots or skis of the herders themselves.

Higher up, we stopped, opened a flask of coffee, and watched a line of squat black ore cars pulled by two electric locomotives that appeared to the east, passed below us, and disappeared into a tunnel just west of the station.

As we looked down over the valley, Gail spotted a group of people sunbathing outside a building that looked like a dorm on this side of the track. On our way back down we learned that they were students from Luleå University of Technology, and what looked like a residence was actually their school's own "off-piste, self-catered ski resort," here in the mountains at 68.5° north. From this crew, here for a few days of hiking and mountain biking, we learned that many of their university's programs were directed toward jobs in the mining sector. Research happened at the Vassijaure facility, but, they added, "we might as well play as we learn. It is such a beautiful place."

In contrast to Vassijaure, Kiruna seemed like nothing more than a nasty little mining town. But the scope of the mine boggled the mind. Although it is billed as one of the most modern iron mines in the world, the first surface pit opened here in 1898. The ore body at that time was estimated to be four kilometres long, eighty to a hundred metres wide, and as deep into the earth as two kilometres, we learned—not that the numbers meant much as we sipped our Statoil coffee and pondered the tourist messaging. What did signal the sheer size of the operation was the fact that for nearly 113 years, trains had been hauling fifteen million tonnes of high-grade iron ore out of this mine each year and proven reserves were still over 600 million tonnes, meaning that the life of this mine, at current consumption rates, could go on for nearly half a century more.

Mining, of course, needs power. Another feature of our route back to the Arctic Circle at Jokkmokk was the massive power dams, holding water anywhere there was potential energy to be trapped in a natural pond created by the mountain landscape. On the Lule River alone, there were fifteen hydroelectric power plants. Not a great river for canoeing. But in terms of renewable resources in a time when the world was asking industry to scale back its dependence on fossil fuels, Sweden was ahead of the curve. And, of course, it was hydroelectric power that had run the iron trains for all these years.

We stopped at the visitors' centre operated by Vattenfall, the utility that ran Sweden's power generation and distribution grid. The original 480-megawatt dam on this site was built to power the mines and the original railway. Since then, many other dams, including the Harsprånget hydroelectric power station—at 977 megawatts, Sweden's largest—had been built on the Lule and elsewhere in northern Sweden, to energize the resource extraction industries. As we walked around the very creatively designed pathways, checking out viewpoints of the dam and reading the signage, I couldn't help wondering where all the reindeer were, right here in what was once the heart of Lapland.

Drawn to a grassy mezzanine with a park bench on it, in

among concrete terraces high up on the valley wall above the tailrace of the Porjus dam, we came across a massive piece of granite with what looked like a giant aluminum corkscrew heading skyward from its top. This was a four-hundred-tonne, fifteen-metre-high granite sculpture called *Kraft* ("power" or "force" in Swedish), created by a Swedish artist as a "memorial to the era of hydropower construction along the Lule River valley." The corkscrew was actually a stylized representation of falling water, which started to make sense in the context of aluminum renderings of shafts and turbines inside a top-to-bottom rift in the rock. Two massive handprints were carved into the side of the sculpture as if granite, in human hands, were as soft as pie dough. Without a word, the sculpture standing next to the massive hydro dam conveyed the incontrovertible message "We have the power. And look what we've done with it."

I awoke in a lakeside room at the Hotel Jokkmokk and realized that the racket right outside our window was an unkindness of ravens bickering over the spoils of some kind of large gathering that had taken place the previous day on the back lawn of the hotel. Gail had somehow slept through this whole avian argument, but I stood behind the drapes and peeked out into the sunshine to see what all the fuss was about.

The original reason to settle in Jokkmokk for a few nights, other than the fact that it is the biggest of four Swedish communities effectively located *on* the Arctic Circle, was that it was the centre of traditional Swedish Sápmi (Sami territory). Nine traditional Sami villages surrounding Jokkmokk had been incorporated with four Swedish national parks and two large nature reserves into one large protected area called Laponia, 9,400 square kilometres in total, that was designated in 1996 as a UNESCO World Heritage site.

By almost all official accounts of the Laponia project I could find, it had been a great success at protecting and perpetuating both the natural and the cultural values of the area. Within Laponia, the Sami could go about their reindeer-herding traditional activities. The reindeer had relative freedom to roam, almost as they had done before the advent of roads, mines, and power dams, or so the UNESCO literature let on. Tourists got a chance to participate in traditional activities, and Sami craftspeople were able to market their *duodji* (handcrafted goods), which brought outside cash to the traditional economy. The parks promoted their own conservation objectives.

Hungry to know what this unconventional form of co-management and collaborative self-rule was doing for the Sami, a bright young doctoral student called Carina Green, from the Department of Cultural Anthropology and Ethnology at Uppsala University in Sweden, took her questions into Laponia and conducted an elegant and thorough study of the situation from the indigenous point of view. What she found was a story that was quite different from that told by the other partners in the experiment. Laponia had not been a total failure for the Sami— some good had come from setting aside lands for their reindeer in perpetuity and from the increased awareness of others about who the Sami were and what their struggles looked like—but it had not been a great success either.

In particular, Green found that in the actual governance and management of Laponia, the Sami had been systematically marginalized in all manner of negotiations. To some of the non-Sami in the project, the indigenous inhabitants of the area were too *similar* to the dominant cultures in Laponia, so that it was often a non-Sami person who spoke for the people of the region, assuming that the Sami point of view was included in the remarks. But Green found also that the Sami were sidelined from constructive participation in Laponia affairs because they were too *different*, in that their worldview just didn't fit with that of the non-Sami people who were trying to make this experiment in collaborative natural and cultural conservation work. It was a classic Catch-22 situation.

But Green also found something else. Having been marginalized in the Swedish deliberations, local Sami people were now working within an international context as set by the UNESCO World Heritage site designation. Thanks to digital communications and channels that were opening as a result of publication of the Laponia story around the world, were starting to connect with indigenous people in other countries, such as New Zealand and Australia, where similar cultural/natural reserves have been created.

I was keen to settle into Jokkmokk and explore Laponia to find out what some of the insiders were saying about how things were going in the summer of 2011. Serendipity, however, had other plans that revealed themselves on our first morning in the Hotel Jokkmokk on the shores of beautiful Lake Talvatis.

From our window I could see what the ravens had discovered: wire bins full of old paper plates and napkins on the back lawn of the hotel. Beyond these, by the lake, was a constellation of large canvas teepees that were apparently being disassembled. I dressed quietly and headed out for a walk.

From the other side of the lake, I got a sense of just how dominant this canvas quasi-Native encampment was on the hotel property. It took up the whole back lawn. Some wedding! The set-up was reminiscent of photos of Sami encampments we had seen in pictures and museums, but without people to animate the scene, it was oddly out of place.

Curiosity brought me back around to get a closer look. Inside the teepees there was litter everywhere, including soggy papers, coffee cups, handouts, plastic name tags, and tattered programs for a conference called "Indigenous Terra Madre," which apparently had ended moments before our arrival. Scattered about were dozens of cheap single-use headsets, the kind used for simultaneous translation.

A crumpled list of participants indicated that there had been people at the conference from thirty-one countries. I sat down on the stack of flattened tables and had a closer look at the discarded program, which explained that the conference had been convened to explore "the relationship between man and nature from an indigenous perspective [and] how to explain that everyone needs to learn it in order to save the planet and the resources," all hosted by a local organization called Slow Food Sápmi. Bingo!

Feeling like something of a voyeur but intrigued by the energy radiating around the area and especially inside this unusual canvas-covered gathering place, I kept on sifting through the conference leavings. There were copies of speeches with what looked like presenter's notes, with last-minute edits. There were versions of at least two declarations made by conference delegates. There were handouts from some of the participating and sponsoring organizations.

With a muddy and disorganized sheaf of very tired and damp paper, I headed back to the room. Gail, who believes more than I do in the power of serendipity, awoke. Even before her customary kick-start morning coffee, she saw the notes, heard the sketch of the emerging story, and, still in her nightie, began helping me sift and sort the papers.

"Do you realize what you've stumbled onto?" she said with total incredulity. "This is a treasure trove!"

Now with a computer to aid in the re-creation of the conference, I was able to see just what it was that the Slow Food Sápmi had been up to at the Jokkmokk conference and what they had created. And it *was* a remarkable story.

Slow Food Sápmi, it turned out, was a branch of the international slow food movement, whose principal objective is the defence of biodiversity in the global food supply. In a speech delivered at the opening of the conference, Ol-Johán Sikku, the head of Slow Food Sápmi, declared, "The philosophy of the slow food movement is Clean, Good, and Fair. It strongly resembles the indigenous ways of thinking and living. The main thought is that clean food is attached to a clean environment. And a clean environment is attached to how we treat our planet. Indigenous Terra Madre is a fantastic start for lifting forward the power and knowledge that indigenous carry."

From the moment Sikku's remarks were placed into context, it was apparent that what was happening here was Sami looking after Sami interests, reaching out internationally, without benefit (or hindrance) from governments of any kind. Terra Madre was an established network of local producers, mostly indigenous, from around the world. They had been invited to Jokkmokk to share their concerns on the Arctic Circle. There were Native American producers from the Navajo-Churro Sheep Presidium. There were Tuareg milk, meat, and cereal producers from Niger, the Kamchatka Salmon Fishers, and traditional rice farmers from Malaysia who had brought their "agri-cultural" rituals, ceremonies, and celebrations. Also present, to my great surprise, were members of the Crofters Association from the highlands and islands of Scotland.

The problem was that not everyone who had been invited could come. The Swedish government had refused visas to delegates from poorer African countries, because of worries that without sufficient means and cash resources, they might disappear from Jokkmokk and become a future burden on the state. Bolstered by confreres from around the world, Chairman Sikku cobbled together a Resolution and Statement of Profound Concern, and called the Swedish government on its duplicity. In it, he pointed out that article 36 of the United Nations Declaration on the Rights of Indigenous People, which Sweden had signed along with 143 other countries, indicated that all indigenous people have a right to "maintain and develop contacts, relations and cooperation, including activities for spiritual, cultural, political, economic and social purposes, with their own members as well as other peoples across borders." And what incensed the gathering even more, so the document said, was that the UN Declaration stated further that in consultation with indigenous peoples, signatory states "shall take effective measures to facilitate the exercise and ensure the implementation of this right."

By now, Gail was with me on the back lawn, sitting among the detritus of this most remarkable gathering, still feeling the energy in the air. Bit by bit, we pieced together what had gone on. There had been sessions on traditional knowledge, land biodiversity, and indigenous food production; discussion groups on threats to pastoralism; and organized discussions about climate change, which, it was readily apparent, fell far down the list of threats behind agro-monocultures, dams, timber industries, oil and gas extraction, mining, and deforestation. The Sami hosts offered taste workshops, midnight sun walks, and cultural experiences serenaded by Sami artists singing joiks, traditional Sami songs.

Among the most interesting papers of all, once my litter pile was sorted and assessed, were those showing the development through consensus of a concluding statement. As this communiqué was coming together, early drafts were entitled "The Jokkmokk Manifesto," in the spirit of their first piece of business: to admonish the Swedish government on its responsibilities vis-à-vis the UN Declaration. In the final draft, "manifesto" had given way to "agreement," but the message was clear and the cause of much celebration. People were proud, none more than the Sami hosts, of what they had crafted.

Written in English, for maximum benefit in distribution, but simultaneously translated into as many languages as the delegates could muster, the final communiqué, a unique northern declaration, made clear that exactly the same appetites that were causing climate change were also threatening indigenous peoples and communities worldwide. Sustainable local food systems and food sovereignty were inextricably tied to maintaining cultural practices, spiritual values, and indeed the health and survival of the natural world, which, of course, is the source of all life on earth. Powerful ideas, scattered on a lawn right on the Arctic Circle.

The last piece of the puzzle was a dog-eared two-page speech, stapled in the corner, on which a delegate had written, "Jörgen Jonsson's Speech Closing Ceremony." Jonsson, president of the Swedish Sami Association, had begun with an old saying in his culture: "If the reindeer feel good, we feel good." He told the assembly that the conference discussions had helped him feel good, but that there was much work to be done. "We must stand up, speak our languages, share our knowledge, and feel confident that together we have the keys to create a sustainable society. We must at all costs raise our voices in a world where indigenous knowledge is neither valued nor heard."

We had the power. And look what we'd done with it.

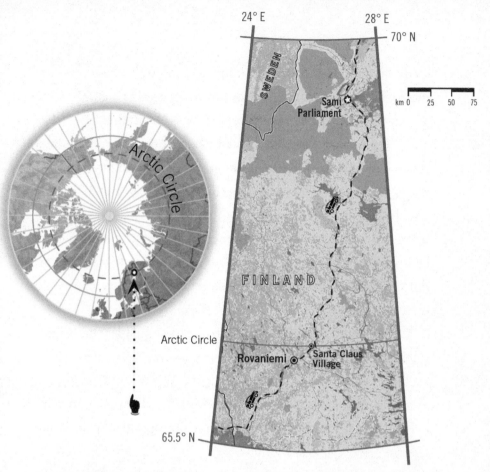

26°E FINLAND GMT+2

4: THINGS GO BETTER WITH SANTA

After the initial excitement of stumbling across the flotsam of the Terra Madre event, we met quite a number of Swedes and Sami in the shops and museums in and around Jokkmokk who were only too happy to confirm peaceful coexistence among the peoples of Laponia—but less so between traffic and the free-roaming reindeer. The main roads were fenced to some extent, but on the secondary and lesser roads, extreme caution was advised. Where there was one reindeer, there were always several or several dozen, and not one of them the slightest bit cowed by traffic.

As we moved east from Jokkmokk in our roller skate of a rental car (in order for me to change gears, Gail had to bring her knees together and close the map in the passenger seat), the first couple of encounters were funny. But after repeatedly coming upon gaggles of pot-bellied summer reindeer padding down the centre of the road, it occurred to me that relative to the substantial size and weight of the big male reindeer, our wee car would most certainly come second in any collision.

Cars coming the other way all had supplementary headlights stacked up like trophies along their front bumpers, which seemed totally incongruous at a time when the sun never sets. But we began to speculate about how difficult it would be to spot reindeer at night, especially with their white-dusted tawny bodies against a snowy background.

Down the road in the ghost village of Kuouka, we sat literally *on* the Arctic Circle in twenty-one-year-old Daniel Ohlsson's farm kitchen. Although Daniel's work was mostly in town, he still maintained a couple of tractors and worked the farm in his spare time. Here, the Jokkmokk reindeer story continued. He explained that many of the people in the traditional Sami villages throughout Laponia have moved to town. The Swedish government, like governments throughout the North, "encouraged" people to move to town, with financial incentives like preferential taxation.

"Does anyone still herd reindeer?" I asked.

"Yes, some. But everyone would still know someone or have a

relative who has something to do with reindeer herding. Reindeer are more like pasture animals now. They keep them around here in the winter and then move them by truck to the mountain pastures in the summer. In the old days they would have moved with them on the ground. They make money from selling reindeer but it's not enough. The herders need other jobs to earn enough money to live on. But everybody mostly lives in town now. I went to school with lots of Sami kids. They went to the Sami school for language lessons for a couple of hours a week, but other than that it was the same for everybody."

When he wants meat, or reindeer blood to make special black *palt*—a traditional Swedish meat-filled dumpling—he just checks with some of his Sami friends in town, who are usually happy to sell him meat under the table. "You can buy government-inspected reindeer meat at the supermarket," he explained. "But everybody knows somebody in town who can sell them a whole dressed reindeer for about three thousand kronor [C$475]. That's about sixty to seventy kilos. It's not really legal but the trade is not so great that the government gets upset enough to chase it. You can get dried and smoked reindeer too. They just smoke it and salt it and hang it up beside your house to dry. It's quite a bit more expensive, about four hundred kronor [C$63] a kilo. But it's more a snack for having with beer than an actual food item. We sell it at the gas station where I work. It's very popular all the time but especially with the people who come to the winter market in Jokkmokk."

The reindeer dodging continued as we made our way from Jokkmokk into Finland, where we approached the Arctic Circle from the south on Highway E75. From brochures we'd collected along the way, Gail and I had learned that Finns consider the Arctic Circle to be the "border of hastiness, where regular time changes into the magic time of elves and reindeer."

About reindeer time we had learned quite a bit; about elf time, we had learned less, except perhaps that travelling in twenty-four-hour daylight skews any notion of diurnal rhythm or anything as ordinary and predictable as three meals a day. But we also learned that elf wisdom can be elusive and that humans apparently can see elves only when the elves want to be seen, a bit like the essence of Iceland. That was definitely the case as we drove under a giant incongruous chevron road marker and turned left into Joulupukin Pajkylä, or Santa Claus Village, north of Rovaniemi. Here, the Arctic Circle was crawling with elves: diminutive Finns, some of them most certainly of Sami extraction, eager to get at the necessary task of cash-cropping tourists like us.

The first item of business was to find and walk the actual line, which had become something of a project ritual. Finding the Circle at Joulupukin Pajkylä, however, turned out to be a challenge, until we realized that we were standing on it: the location of the Arctic Circle was paved right into the village plaza, a wide white line that read, "*Napapiiri*, Arctic Circle," in deference to visitors who didn't speak Finnish. And, if we wanted, we could connect to Santa's wireless network for a small fee and call our friends and relatives anywhere in the world so they could see us crossing the magical line of latitude.

A particularly tinny broadcast of Mariah Carey's "O Holy Night," followed by a parade of other carols, put us in the mood to shop, despite the fact that it was a rainy July morning. Given the season, reindeer, dogsled, and snowmobile rides were out. We could go and pet the reindeer, but a couple of buses had already arrived and there was a lineup. Alternatively, we could follow the advice of a lovely young host in red vest and cap and make our way to Santa's Office for an audience with the man himself and a chance to have a picture taken. In multilingual posters around the place, it looked as if Santa had come straight from central casting in New York City or ho-ho-ho'd his way out of one of Haddon Sundblom's iconic ads for Coca-Cola, which appeared for the first time in the *Saturday Evening Post* back in 1931. Suddenly thirsty, we stopped for a cold drink and made our way to Santa's Main Post Office, where more happy elves were working the crowd.

Inside Santa's mailroom, the sound of music was replaced by the ring of several cash registers working transactions with visitors for mailables of every sort under the midnight sun—small postcards, medium-sized postcards, large postcards, Santa Claus Village stationery, bookmarks, and attractively branded envelopes and boxes to mail just about any item for sale on the premises, which, we gathered from looking around at Santa's tables, ranged from key fobs to fur coats. They'd cancel them today with Santa's special stamp (just like in Norway) or, for another modest premium, they'd set them aside and mail whatever it was in time for Christmas. But no, they wouldn't stamp your passport, even for a fee.

Bumping into fellow tourists at every turn, we made our way out, past a restaurant or two and into some of the other rustic-looking buildings on the site. Resisting an offer to descend into

Santa's underground grotto (some kind of cave complex with special lights . . . what he needed that for was a mystery verging on creepy), we opted to stay above ground and wander.

This place made the Polarsirkel-Senteret in Norway look like a roadside stand! Here, though, there were some very nice hand-crafted Sami and Finnish items as well as bowls and *kuksa* cups, made from classically made northern burled birch. There were canned meats and leather goods that made me hope none of the visiting children ever connected the dots between Rudolph and Santa's abattoir. However authentic all that was, the whole affair was gilded with the crass vulgarity of blinking lights, plastic holly, and canned polyester snow.

Stopping at a village map on an outdoor display board (Mariah's greatest holiday hits had come around again on the loudspeakers, making it seem even more intensely that we were in New York, Los Angeles, or Antler, North Dakota), we counted seven souvenir/gift shops, at least seven factory outlets for various Lapp products from polished gemstones to stylish reindeer purses, and about half a dozen bars and restaurants, all staffed by bored teenagers in red and green. As significant as the line of latitude on which it was situated may be, and as much as we had looked forward to experiencing the crossing in the heart of Sápmi—the wage-earning reindeer wranglers notwithstanding—this "village" on the Arctic Circle in Finland finally revealed itself for what it was: a strip mall dedicated in wallet, body, and soul to honour the Crown Prince of Kitsch, the omnipotent Deity of Consumption: Joulupukki, Père Noel, Ded Moroz, Baba Chaghaloo, Sinterklass . . . Santa Claus.

In an attempt to give the place its due, we wandered the mall talking to shopkeepers, all of whom spoke several languages with alacrity. A man minding a boutique full of diamonds and fine crystal told us that although things had fallen off considerably through the global downturn of the last couple of years, the village was still expecting to top four hundred thousand visitors for 2011. And that was in-person visits. Santa's Post Office would handle that number of letters and more during the Christmas season alone. People, he said, came singly or in couples and families by road. Meeting the "real" Santa was, of course, the big draw. Riding a real reindeer sled was a close second, although some visitors did carp about finding one plodding old reindeer, instead of a full team of Santa's handsome first-stringers, drawing them not through the snow-dusted forests of Lapland but around a dirty little track next to the parking lot.

"We're open 365 days a year, and sometimes that presents problems for staffing, especially when we're some distance out of town," the shopkeeper added, "but it is a business model that is working."

"Is the draw here Santa or to be on the Arctic Circle?" I had to ask.

"Both," he replied, surprised at the question. "But they likely would not come to the Arctic Circle if the village were not here to enhance the experience. Some of our biggest customers are people from the U.K. and central Europe who take advantage of one-day package tours offered by Thomas Cook and other travel wholesalers. They bring whole planeloads of people—parents, children, grandparents, aunts and uncles—just for the day. They leave a place like Manchester early in the morning. Guides warm them up with songs and stories on the three-hour flight to Rovaniemi. There they board Santa Express buses, and in three or four hours they get the full package: Arctic Circle crossing ceremony, reindeer and dogsled ride, lunch, meeting Santa, and, of course 'exploring the village,' which basically means shopping. Depending on the season and the carrier, I think the current price for that one-day package is about 350 euros [C$480]."

"Do Sami people have an interest in the village?"

"No, not really," he replied. "The village is a cooperative owned by the individual store and business owners, some of whom are Sami or of Sami extraction. We're all sort of in this together. And likewise there are all kinds of people who work here. Some are from the Rovaniemi area, which would certainly include Sami descendants, especially in the reindeer ride area. There are tourist operators in Finland, though, who have gotten into trouble with the Sami for dressing people in fake *gákti*— that's the Sami traditional garments—and performing rituals that are not really authentic. That is something we try to avoid here if we can."

"Would this have been Sami land originally?" I asked.

"Maybe," he replied. "I don't know."

Back outside, thinking it might be time to move on down the road, we stumbled into what turned out to be the most interesting and instructive aspect of the village. Napapiirin Maja, Arctic Circle Cabin, explained a lot.

Set apart from the other buildings and apparently right beside what was the bed of the original Arctic Ocean road running north through Finland from Rovaniemi, Napapiirin Maja was a tidy little cabin made of the slender conifers that grow at this latitude. Less than forty square metres, with a traditional Sami acorn-shaped clay hearth in the corner, the place had a homey and welcoming, almost cozy feel, more so than any other building in the village. This structure, we learned from a welter of trilingual interpretive panels, was where this entire installation at the Arctic Circle had begun in 1950. That was when Eleanor Roosevelt, the widow of American president Franklin D. Roosevelt, visited the site as part of her postwar work with the United Nations International Children's Emergency Fund, strange as that might seem.

During the waning years of the Second World War, after occupying Scandinavia for its iron ore and other strategic assets, the Nazis in retreat destroyed with brute force and fire just about every building and scrap of infrastucture within reach. The United Nations Relief and Rehabilitation Administration was set up to help rebuild the homes and lives of affected people. Although there had been a stake on the side of the road before that time to mark 66°33'N, it was only when Roosevelt planned a visit to northern Finland that a piece of land was purchased and the cabin built, in the hope that the project might boost tourism as a postwar industry.

Napapiirin Maja was built in a great rush. Legend has it that the logs, which were floated down the Kemijoki River, were taken from the water on a Saturday and the cabin was built by the following Saturday. The last timber framer involved in the last-minute construction flurry put the last nail in the trim around the front door just in time to open it for the distinguished American visitor on June 11, 1950. Crowds lined the road and came to the site by bus, as they did, as they do, as they will.

Eleanor Roosevelt kick-started tourism at the Arctic Circle in Finland. Who knew? I wondered if Mrs. FDR also inadvertently kick-started an American-style consumerism and way of doing business there. In hindsight, the coincidences and congruencies were portentous.

A month before Roosevelt's much heralded visit to Napapiirin Maja, the May 15, 1950, issue of *Time* magazine featured a story about how Coca-Cola was taking over the world. On the cover was a very striking illustration by Boris Artzybasheff showing an animated round red Coca-Cola sign feeding Coke to a globe cleverly portrayed as a person. The caption read, "World & Friend—Love that piaster, that lira, that tickey and that American way of life." The story, entitled "The Sun Never Sets on Cacoola" (Cacoola is Coke's name in Cairo), went on to detail the Coca-Cola Company's rapid expansion around the world, and the fizzy sweet brown beverage and the mega-marketing messages that went with it. As Roosevelt was cutting the ribbon at the Arctic Circle, Coca-Cola was flooding the world with the American way.

The first few decades of the company's growth were taken up with making Americans familiar with the soft drink cooked up by an Atlanta pharmacist in 1886, and the marketers had convinced consumers that it was a good thing to drink year-round. But one of the drawbacks of selling an "ice-cold" beverage was that winter sales, especially in colder locales, typically fell off quite dramatically. After the First World War, however, the company was eager to expand, and that was when it started a search for a way to convince consumers that drinking Coke in the winter would be a worthy and fun thing to do. That's when Coca-Cola turned to Santa as a pitchman.

Ads in the 1920s toyed with the idea of Santa as a character played by a regular guy. The ads worked, but not all that well. And that was when the company called upon Haddon Sundblom, an American-born artist with Swedish parents. Borrowing the likeness of a jolly friend of his, he created the first of many generations of Coca-Cola Santas who took the world by storm. Building on the poem by Clement Clarke Moore, first published anonymously in 1823 as "A Visit from St. Nicholas" but perhaps better known as "'Twas the Night before Christmas," Sundblom drew not a man playing Santa but instead the man himself, the "jolly old elf."

Unfortunately, of all the renditions of Santa that the Finns might have employed—including deep Sami traditions associated with late harvest, the winter solstice, and the sun's promise of return from the darkness of the twenty-four-hour Arctic night—the creative minds to whom it fell to develop programs for the increasing number of people who visited Napapiirin Maja chose a Santa mythology and image that looked strikingly similar to Sundblom's Santa, then "Coca-colonizing" the planet.

And that was the conundrum. All of Scandinavia having been decimated by the terrible years of war, people everywhere were in need of physical and economic "relief and rehabilitation"— among them the Sami, who were particularly hard hit by the war after a couple of centuries of conquest and assimilation. All of Scandinavia needed parts to build a new economic engine. Tourism was a likely place to turn. And in the strangest irony of all, the hope that arrived at Napapiirin Maja that day in June 1950 was attached to a way of thinking about development, a way of building an economy based on consumption, that would eventually be indicted for atmospheric changes that would melt the very snows to which people were drawn so they could experience authentic northern life at the Arctic Circle.

Worse still was the fact that the Santa character that the builders of the Finnish village chose to propagate included the image of cartoon little people, who looked in many of the drawings suspiciously like real little people who happened to live in that locale, with their reindeer, and who lived some kind of magical and happy life detached from the realities of pollution, oppression, and racial intolerance; people who seemed only too happy to stow their own cultural identity for one imported from the minds of poets and admen in the United States of America. In so doing, they bought into the consumer myth of a Santa cooked up to sell, sell, sell.

I went there to understand how people along the Arctic Circle were coming to terms with climate change. I'd come to learn and to appreciate what was going on culturally in these sparsely peopled northern lands. And what had I found? A most disturbing importation of a way of thinking about the world, with the chap in the red suit as its poster boy. Where I had hoped to find northerners, especially the Sami, tenaciously hanging on to their age-old traditions and connections to the land, I found a cartoon, a co-optation of a once-proud people and way of life feeding lines on a retail ledger. And it got worse.

The world changed. It got warmer. And like every advertising campaign, Santa got tired—or people got tired of Santa. Something happened, and Coke began looking for another image to boost those winter sales. Enter the polar bear and those impossibly cute ads that showed the animated bear family frolicking in the Arctic. Scrolling through YouTube, wondering when the connection was made, I tracked back to the transitional moment in 1994. It was a thirty-second TV spot that showed the bears on skates, whirling around and around on a rink shovelled out on an ice floe. One little fellow gets a bit tired and separates himself from the family. And . . . wait for it . . . into the frame comes Santa, who hands the cub a Coke. One thing leads to another, and the next thing you know the bears have walked right onto the can, and they're being served at ten thousand metres as flights cross and recross the Arctic Circle.

On the outskirts of Rovaniemi we passed a billboard with another very familiar brand. Come visit "the northernmost golden arches in the world," it said, in English.

"Do you think their Big Bacon Happy Meal is made with road-killed-reindeer patties?" Gail asked.

Somehow that would make the whole situation more palatable, I thought darkly.

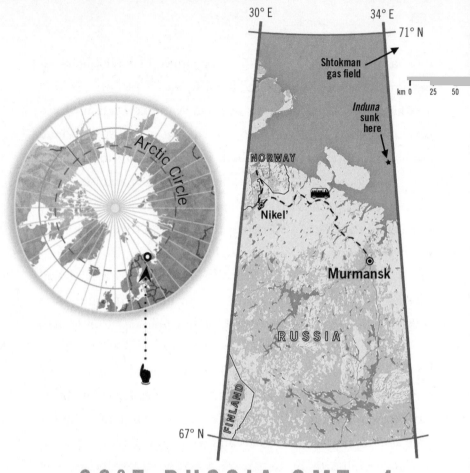

33°E RUSSIA GMT+4

5: HIDDEN TRUTHS

Finding our way east along the line from Rovaniemi into western Russia was complicated by the fact that our rented car was not licensed or insured to leave Scandinavia. Finland shares a long border with Russia, but we could not drive over it ourselves.

The alternative was to head up the Scandinavian peninsula and catch a bus to Murmansk from Ivalo, Finland, or Kirkenes, Norway. The Ivalo schedule didn't fit ours (we had been invited to a special Canada Day commemoration of the Russian-Canadian alliances on the Murmansk Run, the route used during the Second World War by Allied sailors to keep supplies flowing to Russia via the ice-free port of Murmansk), so we opted to drive straight north through Finnish Sápmi and into Finnmark, the most northeasterly county of Norway, to catch the Pasvikturist bus.

Driving up Finnish Highway E75 evoked boreal Canada, except for the heavy traffic at times, made up largely of reindeer, which seemed to be enjoying the relative absence of biting flies and mosquitoes on the road. We had learned about *sameby*, the groups in which the Sami herders are organized, economically and geographically, so we knew that every single one of these animals belonged to someone. More often than not, the reindeer with their big feet and ungainly gait would be gambolling down the middle of the road, and as we slowly drove by, often on the right shoulder, we would be close enough to see the nicks in the animals' ears that indicated where and to whom they belonged.

In the closeness of the car, there was ample opportunity as we rolled along to revisit what had happened in Laponia, either in conversation or in the privacy of our own thoughts, which brought us both to the conclusion that underlying the happy stories of cooperation and collaboration was a disturbing passive aggression toward the Sami. In Sweden, at least, the government had set in law that the Sami had perpetual rights to the land, but when any non-Sami came along with an alternative plan for the reindeer pastures, the Sami always seemed to have to move aside. The Sami didn't own the land; they had the right to use it, but what happened on the land seemed to be determined by everybody else. The Sami seemed to end up with what was left.

We arrived in the village of Inari, where the clear cold waters of the Juutua River empty into the expanses of Lake Inari, Finland's largest lake, and it didn't take long before we found ourselves in front of an impressive architectural work-in-progress to be called Sajos, the Sami parliament and cultural centre. Set against the clear blue of the northern sky and the sound of the rapids roaring in the distance, the strong vertical lines of the concrete walls and the gentle curved horizontal lines of the roof were strangely resonant with the place.

Finland was the first nation to establish a Sami parliament as an arm or agency of the federal government, back in 1973. And this brand new meeting place for the twenty-one elected representatives in the Sámediggi certainly added architectural gravitas to that original idea, which was to give the Finnish Sami, who live in Enontekiö, Utsjoki, Sodankylä, and here in Inari, a voice in Sami-specific economic, social, and cultural affairs, particularly education, language, and schools. Of the roughly ninety thousand Sami throughout Sápmi—formerly Lapland—ten thousand are in Finland, fifty thousand in Norway, twenty thousand in Sweden, and two thousand in Russia. Finland's move in 1973 was one of the first concrete steps, instituted in law, to devolve control of monies transferred from the state to the Sami people themselves. Although the Sami have a strong attachment to the lands and the waters, the Nordic states retain control of all Sami lands.

Norway created a Sami parliament in 1989, and Sweden

eventually followed suit in 1993. A winsome young Sami woman in her colourful *gákti* in one of several *duodji* outlets in town cut to the chase: "I was disappointed when I learned in school that the parliament doesn't have much say, really. It is, after all, a central government agency, and I think it is mostly there to make the government look good. The government still takes most of the decisions. We are very pleased to have a new building and maybe now things will change. Who knows."

Wandering through the town itself, we visited several *duodji* shops and turned over in our hands reindeer carvings and exquisite bone tools, many of which were patterned with the most intricate scrimshaw designs. Slowly, it dawned on us as we met and talked to the storekeepers that what we were appreciating was both a product and a process, both of which were part of modern-day indigenous life, particularly here above the Arctic Circle. The process of keeping these *duodji* going allowed master craftspeople to pass on the skills and traditions to the next generation. And the product was a source of outside money in a cash-driven economy.

Still, as we continued on our way, swinging west onto Highway 92 and over the border into Finnmark, it seemed a little sad to see aged Sami men and women huddling against freezing summer rain in roadside stalls offering genuine Sami goods for sale to anyone who happened by. As we entered Karasjok, home of the Norwegian Sami parliament, we realized that in all of our discoveries and conversations in Sápmi, not one person had said anything about climate change.

It was cultural change—perpetual efforts to claw back the control that their ancestors, for better or worse, once exercised over their nomadic lives—that was front of mind for all of these people. One woman selling dried reindeer meat on the side of the highway said it this way: "We are the professionals who know how to manage changes in nature with our reindeer, but can we manage the challenges created by man? No."

We finally made Kirkenes, a Norwegian harbour town full of aged Russian trawlers. The town of 1,672 was clean, orderly, full of fresh flowers in well-tended borders and brightly coloured houses in neat streets of cobbled stone. Once we learned that we could park for free at a harbour hotel while we were in Murmansk, we took a room and splurged on a late dinner of rare reindeer fillets with lingonberry reduction and red wine, having no inkling of how much things would change in the morning when we boarded the Pasvikturist bus for the five-hour, 230-kilometre ride into a very different world.

The "bus," an aging white van with sealed windows and broken seats, turned up two hours late, because of an accident involving another of the company's buses on the road we were about to take. The delay was lengthened by some administrative hassle the driver got into at the border, which left all eight passengers in limbo between Norway and Russia in a duty-free store that sold cigarettes, a few types of vodka, and an undrinkable whisky called King Robert Scotch. Once we'd tried it, we saved it for window-washing fluid for the rental car.

Once the border was behind us, any concerns we'd gathered earlier about errant mining practices, the aging atomic power plant we'd heard all about from Ingrid, and decommissioned nuclear-powered submarines quietly rusting away in an Arctic estuary were doubled and redoubled by the sight of the real thing. Pristine lakes and boreal rivers running through verdant forests in Norway were replaced almost immediately by nasty concrete-block houses, smokestacks, military checkpoints, and razor wire running atop fences that stretched out onto a tree-less post-apocalyptic landscape. And if the eighteen-year-old soldiers, with their Kalashnikovs at the ready, who poked their pimply faces into the van demanding to see our papers weren't scary enough, then the town of Nikel', with its faceless grey concrete flats and belching red and white stacks—where, they say, the sulphur dioxide effluent from the nickel smelter is so thick that the resulting acid rain will eat through an umbrella—was a crystal-clear indication that this Arctic was a world apart from anything we had seen or experienced in Scandinavia.

Occasionally, on the barren hills, we saw remnants of what looked like fences and corrals to direct reindeer at roundup time. But these were all greyed and often broken, leaving one to assume that they had not been used in a long time. We saw no reindeer or any recent evidence of reindeer either, on the road or off. And where reindeer footprints had prevailed for millennia before the march of Soviet progress, there remained only scars on the landscape where military vehicles on frozen ground had left a scatter of muddy ruts on tundra etched by acid rain and crisped by the unrelenting light of the midnight sun.

The invitation to visit Murmansk came through inquiries I had made to the Canadian Embassy in Moscow about my book project. Through correspondence it became clear that one of the Canadian government's priorities, given climate change, was the Arctic. Ambassador John Sloan and I had also figured out that both of our fathers had served in Allied ships on the Murmansk Run. This official junket to Murmansk was created to support Russian-Canadian business projects, but it was also an opportunity to mark the cooperation between our two countries, particularly the sacrifices of Canadian, British, and Russian sailors in Arctic waters during the Second World War. The two-day junket would culminate with a roundtable conference called "International Cooperation in the Arctic" aboard the legendary Russian icebreaker *Lenin*—the world's first nuclear-powered surface ship—now moored in Murmansk harbour and transformed into a floating museum and conference facility.

Having come by land to Murmansk, although conscious of the region's checkered history as a home for the now mostly decrepit nuclear submarine fleet, we did not appreciate until we got to the city the extent to which it was a maritime place and a bustling port. Whatever we heard, read, or saw, it became clear that to understand the history and significance of Murmansk, one must understand the geopolitics of war and revolution and the importance of an ice-free port in an Arctic nation, all set in the crumbling concrete boxes of Communism.

In the First World War, the Russians needed an alternative way to move supplies in and out of the western reaches of their nation, one that didn't involve waters directly connected to those of Germany, so they built a railway from St. Petersburg and Petrozavodsk to the north tidewater on Kola Bay. During the Russian Revolution, Murmansk was a port of strategic importance for White Army forces. Similarly in the Second World War, Murmansk was Russia's link to the Western world. And then, during the Cold War, Murmansk and sheltered harbours farther down its river estuary became home to the Soviet nuclear submarine fleet.

This history translated into a very curious set of stops on a Murmansk city tour with the Canadian delegation. Rolling up to the distinctively Russian Alyosha monument—a concrete model of a Second World War sentry in helmet and greatcoat, 35.5 metres tall, with a commanding view over the whole municipality and the harbour—provided a chance to think about Russians as allies in that war. But near the famous Russian Orthodox church, named for St. Nicholas, patron saint of sailors, was a smaller, much newer, and less imposing monument fashioned from the conning tower of the ill-fated Russian nuclear-powered submarine K-141 *Kursk*, the largest attack submarine ever built—a story about Russians as adversaries during the Cold War.

Moving on, the delegation's bus pulled up at a nondescript cemetery on a wooded hillside in the city. Here, with Canadian military attachés standing shoulder to shoulder with officers of the Russian navy, Ambassador Sloan made a touching graveside speech to the delegation about the Canadian whose name, George Auger, was carved into the plain grey marble monument. No doubt he thought of his father, as I did of mine, who survived naval service on the Murmansk Run.

The British merchant ship *Induna* had left New York in early March 1942 with a cargo of aviation gasoline, barbed wire, and other war materials. It sailed in convoy PQ-13 to Reykjavik, Iceland. Between rough seas, storms, and prowling U-boats on the way to the coast of Norway, the convoy separated and took some losses.

The *Induna* eventually formed up a new convoy with six straggler ships. They sailed through the Barents Sea well north and east of Murmansk, to try to avoid detection. One of these other merchant ships was bombed and incapacitated by German aircraft flying out of occupied northern Norway. Because of evasive manoeuvres, one of the *Induna*'s sister ships ran out of fuel. The *Induna* took her under tow and they both eventually got stuck in ice before another storm broke the tow cable and left both ships isolated and on their own in a hostile sea. Vulnerable and far from home in Arctic ice, the *Induna* was hunted and eventually sunk by German submarine U-376, the ambassador told the graveside assembly.

A Canadian merchant seaman, George Auger, was a fireman and trimmer aboard the *Induna*. He was badly burned trying to save the ship after it had been struck by one, then another German torpedo. Auger made it into a life raft and watched the *Induna* sink bow first into the ice-choked ocean. Then, in a cruel irony, as the men tried to shelter themselves from minus-twenty-degree winter conditions on the open sea, Auger got frostbite, adding insult to the fire damage to his skin. For four days they waited, and survived, in an ice-encrusted life raft. They were finally scooped up by a Russian armoured trawler and transported to hospital in Murmansk. But, having survived all that,

George Auger died on April 2, 1942. Many a moist eye watched as Ambassador Sloan laid a dozen red carnations at the foot of the plain merchant seaman's grave marker.

Later that day, at a reception for three Russian veterans of the Murmansk Run, Ambassador Sloan asked if I would join him in honouring these men with bouquets of flowers on behalf of the Government of Canada. Shaking hands with these three old sailors in their Russian Legion blazers festooned with medals and decorations of war, I looked into their rheumy eyes and thought of my dad, who would have been about their age had he still been alive, pondering how, even after all these years, Arctic allegiances were still shifting and how conflict is never very far away.

Images of George Auger and the *Induna* persisted as we drove the following day down the curving roads, past a sea of make-shift hovels, to the harbour. The *Lenin*, tied proud with a fresh coat of paint to the wharf bollards with thick new braided rope, was only about a dozen metres longer than the *Induna*, but even after travelling 560,400 nautical miles through frozen seas—its ice-hardened steel skin being declared too worn for further service—it fairly bristled by contrast. Its bridge stood five or six decks higher than the *Induna*'s, its weight was more than three times that of the little merchant ship, and its nuclear-powered steam generators and electric motors could generate a thousand times more horsepower.

We were met by naval officers and escorted smartly up a narrow companionway and into a room that made it clear the Arctic we now occupied was a different world again. The last retrofit of this pit bull of an icebreaker apparently had involved the removal of an upper deck and the creation of a cathedral ceiling and a modern all-purpose meeting space. Posters with the brightly coloured logos of Murmanshelf, a Russian association of suppliers for the oil and gas industry, the Murmansk Region Ministry of Economic Development, and the Embassy of Canada in Moscow stood on strategically placed easels before a theatrically lit giant screen and conference room that looked more like a meeting venue you might find at Disney World than a facility aboard a Russian ship.

The conference opened with pleasantries from the first deputy governor of the Murmansk Region, the chairman of the Murmansk Regional Duma (parliament), and Ambassador Sloan, who talked about Canada and Russia as northern nations cooperating within the framework of the United Nations, the G8 and G20, NATO, and, of course, the Arctic Council, of which both countries were permanent members. Sloan mentioned that both countries were working through the Arctic Council to protect the environment and to create conditions for sustainable development as the North became increasingly important to the world for shipping, resources, and energy production.

Several speakers detailed different aspects of plans to develop the massive Shtokman gas field in the Barents Sea and talked about ways for Russia and Canada to collaborate on that, if and when the economics of gas turned sufficiently to make this development feasible. Likewise, pointing to the *Lenin* itself as an exemplar of superior Russian icebreaking technology going back to the late 1950s, an official from the Murmansk Shipping Company talked about the Northern Sea Route and the implementation of the Arctic Bridge project linking Murmansk with the port of Churchill, Manitoba.

Nathan Hunt, president of the Moscow chapter of the Canada Eurasia Russia Business Association (CERBA), detailed a number of success stories between the two nations. It became quite clear that since the end of the Cold War, Canada and Russia had established strong bilateral trade in everything from oil extraction tools to firefighting equipment, language technology, banking, schooling, and computer technology, and consulting on just about every conceivable area from agri-tech to integrated efficiencies in the oil and gas service industry. But the biggest emerging Canadian interest, the conference delegates learned, was Fedorova Tundra, a major platinum deposit on the Kola Peninsula.

Exploration permits had allowed the Canadian resource giant Barrick Gold and its partners to demonstrate that the mine was a workable venture. Now they needed extraction permits and other permissions to get the mine operating to scale, and this was where the delicate give-and-take across the *Lenin*'s decks became key to the successful outcome of the gathering. Sergey Lobov, director of Fedorova Resources, had been part of the delegation as we toured around Murmansk the day before. When he took his turn at the podium, it was clear that he was speaking to those in the audience who might have political influence on producing the operating permits for the platinum mine.

The roundtable finished up with concluding remarks from Ambassador Sloan. Standing before a slide with the colourful logos of fifteen Canadian corporations, he highlighted more success stories of Canada-Russia collaboration, particularly in the North, and returned to Barrick's investment in Fedorova Tundra. "Governments point the way," he said, "and business does the work. But at some point, the government needs to get out of the way so that corporations can get down to the specifics of business. That is where we leave this gathering, knowing the goodwill that joins our two nations."

As the ambassador spoke, I did a quick scan of his audience. The only women in the room were in the translation booths at the back. That seemed a bit odd, but maybe not in Russia. Sami people were also absent in body and in spirit. Although there were plenty of maps shown of the Kola Peninsula, not one of them registered in any way that the area was once and, in parts, was still the grazing lands, pastures, and fishing grounds of the Russian Sami. It also seemed odd that as speakers talked about the future of business and development in the Arctic in northwestern Russia, there was not a whisper about climate change beyond the fact that the opportunities for shipping in the Northeast and Northwest Passages were improving.

A background paper by researchers from the Russian Academy of Sciences explained the situation this way:

> It should be noted that only a small section of the population of the region has thus far demonstrated an interest in the problem of potential climate change. To a large extent this is undoubtedly due to the fact that information on climate change in Russia remains both limited and contradictory. It is mainly provided by the mass media (which frequently adopts an ironic or apocalyptic approach to covering the theme) often focusing on large-scale cataclysms (typhoons, earthquakes, tsunamis etc). These phenomena have not of course affected the Russian North. As such it is

likely because of this that the majority of the area's population does not seem overly concerned about potential climate change. According to our estimations only about 5% of the population are interested in, or worried about, this problem.

The subtext of all the Russian contributions at the roundtable was that strategic interests had created Murmansk and now, since the fall of the Soviet Union, one of the biggest problems for growing the businesses of tomorrow in this corner of the Russian Arctic was people, or the relative lack thereof. At the height of the Cold War, supporting an active fishing fleet and an even more active base of operations for nuclear icebreakers and submarines, Murmansk had been a city of more than five hundred thousand people, the biggest in the circumpolar world. But now, since perestroika, that number had been nearly halved, with people, particularly the young, leaving for jobs elsewhere on a daily basis.

What was left on Kola Bay was the crumbling and often radioactive infrastructure of a fallen and nearly destitute superpower. Not a word at the roundtable about that. Nothing about the aging Kola nuclear power station, which had caused the remaining youth of Murmansk to reach out to Ingrid Skjoldvaer and Norwegian Nature and Youth to find a way to bring this potential disaster-in-waiting to public consciousness. Nothing about the municipality of Sør-Varanger, just over the border in Finnmark, where officials were worried enough about the nuclear power plant, the nuclear submarine bases, the nuclear fuel and waste storage sites, and other potential radiation sources—aware that it would take a nuclear cloud a scant four hours to envelop them after a disaster on the Kola Peninsula—that they had issued iodine pills to every household prophylactically, anticipating some kind of disaster sooner or later.

Nor was there any mention of the *Lenin* itself as a poster vessel for the deadly problems of nuclear power in a fragile Arctic environment. Twice, in 1965 and 1967, the ship's nuclear propulsion systems failed, resulting in the death of sailors aboard ship as well as permanent damage to reactor cores, which had to be removed from the ship, encased in furfural-based solidifying matter, and eventually dumped in the ocean on the eastern coast of the Novaya Zemlya Archipelago.

The last event in the Murmansk junket was a Canada Day social, to which were invited all the people the ambassador and his delegation had already met, in addition to an extra guest list that had been compiled to fill the room and add a festive feel to the celebration. Having been involved in a project with a couple of Kola Sami organizations about ten years before through the offices of the Arctic Institute of North America, I had been trying to contact a number of people who had come to Canada as part of that project. But I had more or less failed to make that reconnection, having names but no addresses from a time when email was less prevalent than it is now.

So when Gail and I were asked if there was anyone we'd like to invite to the Canada Day social, I passed on that short list of names to the ambassador's roundtable crew. To my great delight, through the embassy's business network, they had been able to connect with Nina Afanasyeva and a number of women from the Kola Sami community. So for us, the reception began with hugs and warm hellos from a bevy of handsome women in traditional Sami dress.

The ballroom of the Poliarnie Zori Hotel was festooned with Canadian flags and bunting, and the buffet menu was supposed to be of distinctly Canadian food (although I have no idea what sausages, cabbage salad, and warmed-over tomato pasta have to do with Canada . . . maybe the colour red?). Ambassador Sloan invited some of the dignitaries present to say a few words, and he himself spoke about the importance of the meetings of the last two days and about how the future for our two countries as northern nations was bright. With that, a group of Russian musicians sang a song, followed by an enthusiastic expatriate rendering of "O Canada" in honour of July 1.

Gail and I were standing with the Sami delegation during the national anthem and were surprised as it wound down to see Nathan Hunt of CERBA turn to the women and say, in Russian, how wonderful it was that the Russian song had been sung, but he wondered why the Sami ladies weren't singing a song of theirs as well.

"We haven't been asked," they said.

"Well, you're being asked now," said Nathan.

By this time, however, the ambassador had concluded the formal part of the evening program. Nathan did his best to pull people's attention back from the buffet and the bar to listen as the Sami ladies began their performance, but the focus was lost. The lingering image from the Canada Day reception was of a half dozen Sami women singing their hearts out in the function room of the Poliarnie Zori Hotel with hardly anyone listening.

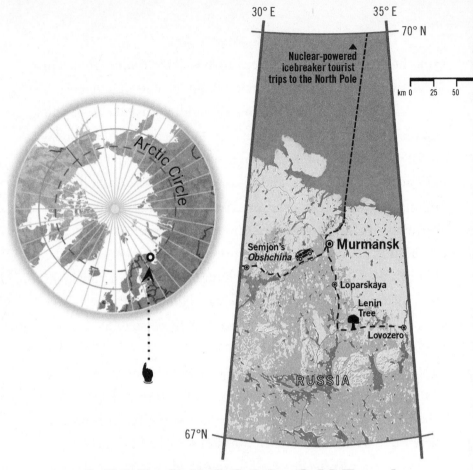

35°E RUSSIA GMT+4

6: SEMJON'S *OBSHCHINA*

The twenty-one-year-old Sami reindeer herder Semjon Bolshunov had a face that could sell almost anything. He was sitting on a backless kitchen chair in a ramshackle trailer in a sandy clearing in his ancestral grazing grounds on Russia's Kola Peninsula, just over the Finnish border. His eyes danced with radiance and conviction as he told me about his Sami aunts, who helped him to overcome a Russian father who "from the beginning tried to kill" the Sami identity he had inherited from his mother. His sun-burnished smile and animated delivery lit up the shack. But it was not a completely happy story he related.

In Soviet times, although the Sami were forbidden from wearing their national dress or marking their traditional ceremonies throughout the year, reindeer herding was done under state sponsorship and control and, all things considered, it worked. With the collapse of Communism in 1991 came the return of possibilities for Sami dress and language, but state support for herding vanished. The herders were left to fend for themselves economically. And this, with so many other pressures to be Russian, had a devastating effect on Sami throughout the Kola Peninsula. "Many of my cousins were ashamed to say they were Sami," he said. "But me? I wear Sami clothes everywhere, not just to festivals. I wear Sami shoes in the city, and when people ask why I am dressed so strange, I proudly answer that I am Sami."

My path to Semjon's *obshchina*—his forty-three-thousand-hectare ancestral homeland—began in the ballroom of the Poliarnie Zori Hotel in Murmansk on Canada Day. After they sang their songs, the newly elected chair of the Russian Sami parliament, Valentina Sovkina, and a host of other leaders in the Sami community (all women) hugged us both and said that it would be their pleasure to welcome us back at any time to see and do whatever our hearts desired in Russian Sápmi. I immediately made plans to return, but after a month away on this Scandinavian junket, Gail had a full slate of things to do at home and wouldn't be able to join me for a second adventure in the Russian northwest.

So six weeks later, I headed back alone to the Kola Peninsula. And just to make things interesting, the transport gods had arranged a little character-building exercise. The flight from Frankfurt to Moscow came in late, and the luggage queue gobbled up what few spare minutes there were to catch the night's last flight from Moscow to Murmansk. So I was left with my hello/goodbye/thanks/where's-the-bathroom/could-I-have-a-beer Russian to find out where one might go next. Several changes of airport levels, three ticket wickets, and a lot of hand-waving and watch-pointing later, it was nearly midnight and I had in my hand a voucher from my new friends at Aeroflot for a night's accommodation and a meal at an airport hotel.

Despite its surly desk clerk, burned-out light bulbs, and chipped ceramic tiles, the hotel was quite inviting, on the whole. The meal, however, was another matter. Ready for a cold beer and something spicy from what looked like some kind of Mexican-themed bistro off the lobby, I presented the smiling hostess with my voucher, expecting to be seated without delay, given that the place was nearly deserted. She took one look at the voucher, grabbed my arm, and perp-walked me to a nasty little room that smelled of animal grease and exhaust with bare walls and bad light. Repast, gulag style: a glass of warm tap water, a small bowl of tired greens, a piece of black bread, and a plate of soggy pasta dabbed with watery tomato soup made up my evening meal.

Suddenly my vibrating cellphone brought news of a warm welcome above the Arctic Circle. "Don't worry, James," said my Sami host, Anna Prakhova, on the phone from Murmansk, "we will adjust your schedule accordingly. What was going to be a busy few days will be a *very* busy few days. "

Another call brought even more good news. Again, thanks to connections and friendships made through the Canadian Embassy in Moscow, a one-time Russian visa had been transformed into a one-year multiple-entry visa, which would make things much simpler. If there is a good thing about Moscow as a central hub for all traffic in and out of what used to be the Soviet Union, it's that once you have cleared passport and immigration control on arrival at one of the three Moscow airports, all flights from there on, regardless of destination within Russia, are much less regulated and much less security focused.

It was a sovereign summery August day as the morning flight to Murmansk settled into its final approach. There was the *Lenin*, bristling at the wharf, the various military cemeteries and monuments around town, the Russian nuclear submarine pens on the horizon up the Kola River estuary, and, of course the winding road leading back to Norway.

Anna had told me on the phone that Valentina and the other Sami leaders would be joining us from time to time during the visit. She was very pleased to tell me that her employer, Frecom, a Moscow-based environmental consulting company, had given her leave to host the Canadian writer on behalf of the Sami of the Kola Peninsula on company time. "I hope you slept well as a guest of Aeroflot last night, James, because that will be the last time you'll be doing that for a while."

Time quickly blurred into a stream of faces and places, but with a very different constellation of actors than those who had animated the official visit with Ambassador Sloan and the Canadian delegation. The Kola is Sami country—this point was made crystal clear—even though the two thousand Russian Sami are almost all now off the land and living in communities. We met Sami in various walks of life in museums and public offices through the city. Anna connected them all back to their roots: Sea Sami, who traditionally fished the rivers and the coastal waters of the Barents Sea; or Reindeer Sami, who, before the Bolshevik Revolution and seventy years of Soviet collectivization, traditionally moved their herds toward the sea in summer and back up onto higher ground inland in the winter.

But Anna also took time in the schedule for a visit to the offices of the Murmansk Shipping Company, which had historically, until very recently, controlled the entire Russian nuclear icebreaker fleet. It also ran a diverse flotilla of ice-hardened cargo ships that for nearly a century had plied the Northern Sea Route from Murmansk on the Atlantic side across the top of Russia to Vladivostok and the Pacific.

Down the street from the Murmansk Shipping Company, in the Murmansk Museum of Regional Studies, we met a woman in a white tracksuit, a lawyer from Ukraine called Olga Sergeieva, who had just returned from the North Pole in a Murmansk Shipping Company Arktika-class behemoth, NS *50 Let Pobedy* (50 Years of Victory), the largest nuclear-powered icebreaker in the world, so far. Four days up, four days back, with a full two seconds right at the geographic North Pole. She showed me a photo on her camera of the ship's GPS readout indicating their position as exactly 90°N. The cost of this adventure? "Twenty-two thousand U.S. dollars, and you get to keep the fancy parka. It was the dream of a lifetime," she said with a sunburned smile.

The next morning, we picked up Valentina and some of the

other women from the Canada Day ceremony and drove about an hour south and east from Murmansk to Lovozero (known as "Love Lake"), where many of them had grown up. The town looked tired and rundown. Concrete buildings were crumbling. Not too many takers for the North Pole tourist trip here, I thought.

We went to the Sami National Cultural Centre, which appeared to be one of the newest and best kept buildings in town. Under a domed ceiling depicting the drum symbols of shamans long passed, Valentina convened a meeting of elders and others from town for a roundtable discussion with the visitor from Canada. With Anna energetically interpreting, Valentina and the others listened to my stories of people elsewhere on the Arctic Circle, of joys and struggles of the Inuit, of commercial fishing families in Iceland, and of the Sami I'd met in Scandinavia.

Slowly, the elders responded. They spoke of reindeer herding as it once was, of days when everyone spoke Sami, of change, cultural change, climate change, of how things were different now than they had been even a couple of years ago. They spoke of times when life was simpler and families were more connected to one another and to the land. But as the sun circled into the northwest and the shadows in the room lengthened, there was a sadness that started to overwhelm the meeting. Valentina spoke with quiet intensity, looking across the room into the eyes of her elders, of "pain in [her] heart" about the future of the Russian Sami. "We have talked about how things are warmer now, how winters aren't as harsh, of how summers are warmer, but that is not what is worrying me the most," she said.

"Climate change is happening. We notice it from year to year. But climate change is slow. Cultural change is something we see every single day. We are losing our language. We are burying our young people who take their own lives. Alcohol is a sickness too many of us struggle with. We are losing our way of life. First we were moved off the land, out of our *kova* [tents], out of our wooden houses on the ground, and into these concrete doghouses that rise high above the ground. Now we have quotas for fish and our reindeer are in pens.

"I feel pain in my heart," said the Sami leader, her blue eyes welling with tears. Turning to me, through Anna, she said, "Thank you. You have raised with us some difficult issues that we must discuss among ourselves. Our voices must be heard. We must use the resources we have, like our new parliament, to make our voices heard."

When the public event was over, we had tea with the elders. Then Anna and Valentina and I walked on litter-strewn streets to Valentina's office in the Sami college in Lovozero—her role as chair of the Sami parliament is unpaid—and we talked about just how difficult it had been for the Sami in Russia to have their voice heard by the powers that be. She told me of going to New York and speaking to the Tenth Session of the UN Permanent Forum on Indigenous Issues. She said she told them of governments saying one thing and doing another. Right from the reforms of Czar Alexander II in the nineteenth century, which established an early form of self-governance for Kola Peninsula Sami, to now, she explained, there had been official talk of rights, but these had always been trumped (or ignored) by just about every other type of political initiative.

Ironically, the collapse of the Soviet Union saw the overnight disappearance of many of the strictures on Sami life. Following the example of their kin in Scandinavia, Russian Sami started organizing and making requests of the government of the new Russian Federation that they be given leave to create their own parliament.

First the government just said no. The Russian constitution did not provide for establishing ethnic parliaments; after all, they were told, there were some forty different ethnic groups across Russia, and what a mess it would be if everyone set up their own system of governance. Then they were told, as described in a speech by the governor of the Murmansk Region at the time, Dmitry Dmitrienko, that "historically, there was practically no indigenous population present in the Murmansk Region" and that "all the people have in one way or another emerged from without."

Cut off from their kin in the part of Sápmi outside Russia throughout the Soviet period, and facing resistance from governments at every turn, even after the collapse of the Soviet Union, the Sami took things into their own hands, Valentina proudly explained. Supported by human rights organizations around the world, they persisted with the argument that establishing a Sami parliament would be a way not only to establish effective dialogue with the government but also to realize their rights as indigenous people to preserve and develop their language, national culture, traditions, and customs. This was still not possible, they were told.

And yet, through sheer persistence, the Sami were given permission to convene in 2008 the First Congress of the Sami People of the Murmansk Region, at which a decision was taken to move ahead with the creation of a Sami parliament anyway. Two years later, at the Second Sami Congress, convened in Murmansk on December 12, 2010, the Russian Sami parliament was created. One of the smallest indigenous groups in the Russian Federation had, however symbolically, taken matters into its own hands. Against all odds, the vote was pushed through by the Sami matriarch Nina Afanasjeva, and Valentina was elected chair.

After a full day in Lovozero, we had much to think about. On the way back to Murmansk, driving into the setting summer sun, we approached a tall pine tree on the side of the road that the driver asked me to have a good look at. At first, it looked like a very handsome, even iconic tree that might have been painted into celebrity by the Group of Seven. "The Lenin Tree," said Anna, pointing into the sunset.

It took a minute for me to understand what she was saying. It was like looking at a Rorschach blot or an Escher drawing, but when my brain finally saw in negative space what they were seeing, my chuckle of recognition brought howls of laughter from the others in the van: in silhouette, the tree against the evening sky perfectly etched Vladimir Lenin's familiar bald head, with his straight Russian nose and goatee.

"Welcome to the last monument to Communism," Anna said, "or so we hope."

Anna and Valentina had arranged for me to give a presentation about my work at the Murmansk Museum of Regional Studies the next day. It was a chance for the Sami to offer some programming for anyone who would like to hear from a guest they had brought to town; but, more importantly, it was also an opportunity for the guest—that would be me—to learn more about what the Sami were doing to change their decaying cultural and political fortunes, and about their growing public advocacy. There, in one of Murmansk's main museums, the advocacy took the form, in temporary space, of a new exhibit about the Sami. There were photos of elders and youth in non-traditional roles and jobs—working in schools and universities, in industry, on offshore oil rigs, and still as reindeer herders, remembering and reinforcing connections to the land and to the Sami culture reaching back into time.

The featured community member in the role of reindeer herder in the exhibit was the fresh-faced strapping twenty-one-year-old Semjon Bolshunov, who, said the interpretive panels, was from the village of Loparskaya. He was one of the leaders in the new Sami approach to herding. Thanks to Anna and the ladies, I would meet him at the end of an amazing road trip by the light of the midnight sun. Semjon was a cook by trade but took his turn, working with others on his ancestral community near the Finish border, at building a reindeer herd to keep the Sami traditions alive.

After the curator's tour of the exhibit was done and my talk had been delivered in the theatre of the museum, Anna explained to my delight that if I was amenable, we could head out when her husband finished work to visit Semjon on his *obshchina*. "It is a long drive, but we are going down there anyway. We have to pick up another herder who is in a community in the other direction and take him out to switch with Semjon. You would be welcome to come along. It will allow you to get an idea of what modern-day reindeer herding is like, James."

This indelible nighttime adventure began at about six o'clock in the fruit section of the grocery store near Anna's home. We bought a big sheaf of bruised bananas, "for the reindeer," Anna said, to my amazement. I took a couple of photos inside the store to mark the occasion. There was an insistent tap on my shoulder and something loud and officious being said, for my benefit. It took a second to realize what the fellow was saying. I quickly deleted my pictures. Why? Who knows. Habit? Bananas for reindeer? Who knew?

We headed back to the car. Anna had invited Olga, the lawyer from Ukraine, to come along, so we swung by her hotel for pickup. There were four of us in a late-model Lada: Anna and her husband, Yuri, a naval electrician, in the front and the North Pole lawyer and me in the back, the bag of bananas between us.

The original premise for making the trip was Sami looking after Sami. Alexi, one of the team charged with the responsibility of looking after this particular herd, had somehow gotten himself back to his village of Loparskaya, on the Kola River forty kilometres southeast of Murmansk, to see a doctor about his diabetes.

So before we could travel southwest from Murmansk to get to the *obshchina* where the reindeer were, we had to go southeast first, to Loparskaya. It was a nasty, rundown little community with hungry-looking stray dogs, grubby children playing in puddles on the side of the road, and tattered aboveground steam pipes from an earlier era. We pulled up outside a three-storey concrete box with cracked windows and mismatched curtains. Anna phoned up to let Alexi know we had arrived, and there was a long pause. At length, she spoke to her husband, who listened gravely, then nodded. And to me, she said, "Alexi is not ready yet. You and Olga will walk with Yuri."

As it turned out, the walk was a ploy to kill time, because Anna had learned on the phone from Alexi's wife that the herder, out on medical leave, had been self-medicating with vodka all day. She was trying to rouse him but not having much luck.

By the time our walk along the narrow, clean Kola River was done, Anna and Alexi's wife had him semi-conscious on the front steps of the building with a dark plastic bag of his personal effects collapsed on the concrete beside him. Yuri pulled the car up close to the building. Anna grasped him under one arm and his wife took the other; with his preschool children looking on, they poured him into the front seat of the Lada. All that stopped him from falling out of the car so that they might get the door shut properly was the seatbelt, which they reefed up tight as his drunken head lolled back against the seat.

With Alexi, the main reason for our journey, fast asleep in the passenger seat, the two women and me jammed ourselves into the back. We made our way back toward Murmansk and then swung west on Highway P11, the "Lotta Road" in local parlance, heading toward the Finnish border. It was only 140 kilometres to the road marker where we would pull off the main highway, but the road was curvy and bumpy and the going was slow. With the detour to Loparskaya, we didn't actually arrive at Semjon's reindeer camp until midnight.

By then, we were bathed in Arctic twilight, and frost was starting to crystallize on spruce fronds and on the rich beds of moss and lichen on the ground. Having driven down a narrow cart track for several hundred metres off the main road, we came to what looked at worst like a junkyard and at best like an abandoned gypsy camp. Tied dogs barked from indeterminate locations as we stepped out of the car and headed toward a rectangular cabin on a truck chassis, a house trailer of sorts, with a set of rickety steps leading up to a door on the back. After the rumble of the car for nearly six hours, a delicious quiet surrounded us.

In a wee-hours calm that felt almost conspiratorial, broken only by the dogs barking, Anna was first up the stairs. Before she could reach for the handle, the door opened and out came the young man from the pictures at the museum, fully clothed but looking like he'd just gotten out of bed.

"We've been expecting you," he said, with the magnanimity and welcome of a consummate host. "You will see that we set up a table and bench inside a picnic tent over there for you, because at this time of year the mosquitoes are bad." As we started walking toward this four-by-four-metre netting enclosure that looked like something out of *The African Queen*, Semjon paused, looked around, and asked, "Where's Alexi?"

"He's in the car," said Anna, darkly.

"Oh," Semjon replied, knowingly.

Over tea and crackers in the tent that progressed to beer inside the trailer after Alexi surfaced, with Anna interpreting and often (I think) correcting what he had to say, Semjon explained what was happening. Two things were evident from the outset: first, that although it was only through an aunt on his mother's side that he had learned anything at all about the actual mechanics of reindeer husbandry, this was something that Sami had done for generations—he seemed to know that more in his bones than in his brain; and second, anything he knew of Sami and reindeer had happened since the collapse of the Soviet Union.

He talked about two types of ancestral homelands that were recognized by the Russian government: one based on territory, and another based on family. Either way, he said, now that everything was happening in a free market economy based on private ownership, a person or a group of people actually had to apply to establish a case for being granted an *obshchina* by the Russian government.

Semjon and a group of friends and family members had been trying to establish this *obshchina* based on family ties, and they had been assigned this tract of land on the southwest Kola Peninsula to see if they could make a go of getting back into the reindeer herding business. "It hasn't been easy," he said. "We bought reindeer from a neighbouring *obshchina* and drove them here a couple of winters ago, but in the spring they all walked home. And we worried that they might drown in the river. But we got them back. And now I hear that there is a pipeline that is supposed to come through here and we might have to move."

At that point Anna interjected and said that was not the case at all. She added that the Russian energy giant Gazprom, the largest natural gas producer in the world, had widely promoted a series of public meetings to explain what was happening to the local people, including herders on all the affected *obshchiny*, but that attendance at these had been very poor. "Semjon might have done well to get to one of those meetings," she told me in English.

But he was building a reindeer herd, as his ancestors had done since time immemorial. And seeing as how we had come all this way, it would be Semjon's pleasure to take us out to meet the reindeer.

By now it was after one in the morning. The sky was luminescent and full of stars, and a moon was casting shadows on the ground, but it was difficult to see. Having come out of the generator-driven electric light of the trailer, where Alexi and another herder were fast asleep in skinny metal bunk beds at one end, we fumbled along without flashlights behind Semjon, through a fence that appeared to be made out of an old fishing net and on through ankle-deep reindeer moss. The bananas we had brought were distributed among everyone's pockets.

As a way to get the animals to be more compliant, and to keep them properly nourished, Semjon explained, as we walked, the herders had been feeding them a bit of grain. But there were no reindeer anywhere nearby. Semjon started to call, his young, strong voice echoing through the forest and fading into the silence of the Arctic summer night. He called again and again, each time waiting and listening to see if his animals had heard. And then, almost imperceptibly, through the still air came the hollow tinkle of cowbells. Different pitches from different directions, getting progressively louder.

Suddenly, we were surrounded by grey ghosts in the darkness, and one of them had just nudged me in the backside, aiming for the banana in my pants pocket. Fuzzy antlers were bumping against us. Bells were clunking as the animals jockeyed for the pocket spoils. Peels and all, they were devouring the bananas, sometimes wrangling them whole and other times biting through them and having pieces fall to the ground where, guided by furry noses, grazing teeth nibbled on shoes in search of the tasty treats from town. Anna was giggling. The normally stoic Yuri was telling them to stay out of his crotch. Olga was talking to the reindeer in her vicinity as if they were clients. And Semjon was lecturing his leaders not to be too bold, to let some of the females and smaller animals have their share of bananas as well.

The herd at this point was just several dozen animals. Semjon explained as we finished the visit and made our way back to the trailer that he and the others were hoping to build that number in the years to come. But it was going to be a stretch. They got a small stipend from the government to help, everyone hoping that the herd would provide meat for the Sami community and perhaps become something of a tourist draw in the area as well, but the actual work with the herd was mostly volunteer, he told us. The herders took their turns on the land with the animals, but they all needed other wage work in town, or wherever, if they could get it, to supplement their stipends.

Given the offer of a ride, which doesn't happen all that often, Semjon opted to return to Murmansk with us. As we headed back east on the Lotta Road toward town, Anna, Olga, and I again snug in the back seat, the young herder talked about everything from his view of Russian resource politics to how his reindeer all had different personalities. He explained that when he met new people, he remembered them by thinking of the animal in his herd that most matched their character and disposition.

By four in the morning, the sky was brightening and graded blue-grey mists shrouded the surrounding lands. There were no mines on this road, but the land as we got closer to town again took on a ravaged look. Semjon eventually fell asleep in mid-sentence. Anna told me quietly that she was ever so proud of Semjon and his irrepressible optimism, but that she feared for his vulnerability within a political system that could shatter his dream in ways he could never begin to imagine.

In truth, for all the novelty of this magical night among the reindeer at Kilometre 108 on the road from Murmansk to the Finnish border; for all of Semjon's optimism in thinking that this *obshchina* that his family organized in 1992 would somehow be the key to a happy future for Sami on the Kola; for all that hope in the face of what seemed like insurmountable odds, which was one of the most inspiring things I'd encountered to date on my travels around the world—for all of that, there was a sadness that covered the whole experience like a post-nuclear pall.

Even after a drink at four thirty in the hopping all-night disco in the Meridian Hotel with Anna and Yuri, I was wide awake and very much moved by the seemingly hopeless enormity of the challenges the Sami face. Back in my room, looking out on the grimy stacks of Murmansk, I took the cellophane off a CD that Anna had pressed into my hand as we left the hotel bar.

It was by the Sami singer Mari Boine. Mari's song

"Conversation with God," Anna intimated, could be an anthem for Semjon if he ever chose to ground his youthful optimism and see the world as it was. Sipping cheap Armenian Araat brandy from the minibar in my room, staring out the window with Semjon's sun-livened face very much in my mind, I listened to Mari's soulful voice through the tinny little speakers of my computer, releasing the day's many emotions.

Our Father,
They say you are in heaven,
Could You please tell me
Why things are the way they are?
Our Father,
Through Your name, they hallow and maintain
Injustice in the world.
Why do you allow this?
Our Father,
Why do You not deliver us from evil?
Are You not the Almighty?

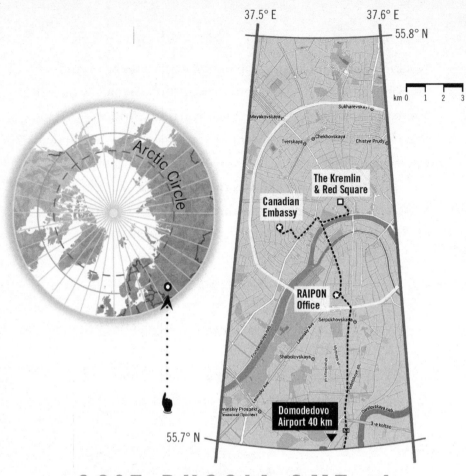

38°E RUSSIA GMT+4

7: A MASK FOR LUCK

On my own again and eager to build connections that would carry my research through Russia's 172 degrees of longitude and nine time zones, I parlayed contacts from my first visit into a multi-entry cultural research visa from the Russian Consulate in Ottawa. But there was more work to be done to secure the contacts and connections to get beyond the Kola Peninsula, and this all had to happen in Moscow. Through the Canadian Embassy, I was invited to deliver a series of lectures on Arctic Canada at various schools and universities in and around Moscow—part of Canada's ongoing efforts to support cross-cultural dialogue with its northern neighbours—and this circuit would prove instrumental in moving the research forward.

When I flew in this time, the impression I got of Russia while circling over Moscow in preparation to land at Domodedovo Airport was much more welcoming than the depressing scenes I'd glimpsed through the grimy windows of the bus from Norway. There were forested rolling hills on the city's outer rings, lined with orderly rows of commercial buildings and individual dwellings, all circling the bustle of the city's inner core. The scenery wrapped around a meandering oxbow of the Moscow River was more reminiscent of London, England, than of anything Cold War. But for me, a canoeist and geographer, the river—a secondary tributary of the mighty Volga flowing through the city and eventually south to the Caspian Sea—was not the kind of water I was hungry to experience. It was the north-wending rivers like the Lena and the Ob, which flow over and beyond the Arctic Circle for hundreds of kilometres—these were the rivers that would reveal the stories I'd come to hear.

Nevertheless, I was in Russia. I was closer than I had ever been to the secrets of Siberia, feeling more than a little apprehensive and giddy with jet lag and anticipation. In that state of mind, I perceived the chaos at customs and immigration control through a *Dr. Strangelove* lens, wondering whether the fellows in bad suits in the arriving throng were intelligence operatives spying on the texts I was hammering out on my phone. Eventually I emerged on the happy side of Russian officialdom and an embassy driver took me directly to meetings with embassy personnel about my speaking itinerary.

All of the presentations on this tour had simultaneous translation, which took some getting used to for the presenter and the audiences, especially when it came to parsing stories and information into bite-sized pieces that could be translated in a flow that built its own rhythm and cadence. (Note: jokes that work in Canadian English don't automatically translate into Russian.) The one exception was a professor in the Department of Regional Studies and Foreign Languages at Moscow State University who requested that I present without translation so that her students could practise their English.

Without question, the sleeper item on this remarkable itinerary was listed as "Luncheon at OR hosted by DHOM Gilles Breton, Duration: 2 hours." "OR," I learned from my embassy host, Elena Gaisina, was short for "official residence," and, by a process of jet-lagged deduction, I eventually figured out that Gilles Breton was the deputy head of mission (DHOM) in Moscow. "Guests," the itinerary went on, "will include Russian Arctic experts as well as representatives of Russian regional governments in Moscow (Komi, Yamalo-Nenets, Yakutia, Chukotka, Khaborovsk, Murmansk); International diplomatic community; CERBA, RACS (Russian Association of Canadian Studies)."

Having but the vaguest idea what happens in foreign missions generally or at OR luncheons in particular, I assumed that all these people had been invited but only one or two would turn up for a perfunctory hello and a very nice free lunch. Elena suggested that I might work up a brief illustrated presentation about my project. "Nothing fancy," she said. Nothing fancy. Right.

Having rushed in from a presentation to grade nine students at School N59, right across the street from a yellow and white art-nouveau-style chancery that houses the ambassador's official residence, I said hello to some of the embassy staffers and to Nathan Hunt from CERBA (who had encouraged the Sami ladies to sing in Murmansk) and was getting ready to relax a bit when in walked Anton Vasiliev, Russia's Arctic ambassador.

After my brief chat with Vasiliev, who, as it turned out, had spent quite a bit of time in Canada, Elena took my elbow and steered me toward other guests. It became clear that this would be far from "nothing fancy." As promised, there were people from various northern embassies, academic institutions, business, and government, all interested in the Arctic and all keen to have a conversation about the future of the North as it is being shaped by shifting climate, politics, and business opportunities.

Tatiana Vladsova, a leading researcher in the Russian Academy of Sciences Institute of Geography and head of the Russian Geographical Society, had me spellbound with the tale of her Integrated Arctic Socially-Oriented Observation System. I could have spent the rest of the lunch talking to any one of these kindred spirits, but out of the corner of my eye I saw a face that seemed very familiar. Full white beard. Oval, slightly tinted glasses. Balding, tanned, Semitic-looking features. Late sixties, maybe early seventies, but with the body and movements of an athlete half his age. Tailored blue suit. Maybe a Nova Scotia tartan tie. Two handlers. Serious twinkle in his eye. And then it dawned on me: that was the man who had dropped the flag on the ocean floor at the North Pole and single-handedly stirred up more controversy than a proverbial arctic fox in the northern henhouse. Arthur Nikolayevich Chilingarov. The very one!

But just as I was about to step forward to meet the Hero of the Soviet Union and Hero of the Russian Federation (so says his business card—honest!), Elena and the staff began gathering people in the living room of the official residence and directed me to move toward the podium for the DHOM's introduction and welcome and the start of my presentation.

To this august audience, I explained that my plan was to put a human face on climate change by travelling around the world at the Arctic Circle. After asking for advice or suggestions from anyone present, I mentioned that part of my draw to northern Russia was my previous book, a biography of the Hudson's Bay Company governor Sir George Simpson, who had circumnavigated the northern hemisphere, including a long overland portion from the Sea of Okhotsk to the Black Sea in 1841–42.

At the risk of the joke going horribly wrong, through a simultaneous translator who was standing beside me and speaking to the crowd, I slipped a portrait of Sir George onto the screen and mentioned that scholars reckoned he had sired seventy children across Canada, in and out of wedlock, during his tenure with the HBC. I added that although there had never been any mention of procreative activity during the Russian leg of his round-the-world journey, I was quite sure that Simpson's carnal appetites would have been just as enthusiastic on Russian soil as they were on his travels in North America. So I was hoping to meet some Simpsonian offspring on my journey across Arctic Russia from west to east.

With that, the Hero of the Soviet Union started speaking and pointing at the very dignified Ivan V. Rozhin, special advisor to the Russian vice-president for international affairs, representing Yakutia. I'd met Rozhin earlier and was hoping he would be instrumental in helping to set up a visit to Yakutsk. "He looks just like him," Chilingarov said in a loud voice. "Maybe that's the connection you're looking for right here in this room."

Happily, Rozhin smiled—or it might have been a diplomatic grimace—but with that utterance as an opener, I approached Chilingarov immediately following the presentation and in the spirit of his good humour said, "I am very pleased to meet the man who made so many politicians in my country mad."

He smiled broadly and said, "I don't know what the problem is. Your country and mine have been cooperating with science in the Arctic for many years. It is all about the science."

"Right," I replied. "It's all about the science. Say, when you were down there at four kilometres under the ice, did you happen to see the Canadian flag that was dropped through a hole in the ice at the North Pole by Fred Roots, one of our senior scientists, back in the 1970s?"

"No," said the Hero, with a slight rise in his eyebrows. "I have met Dr. Roots. He has done some very fine work."

"He has. It's all about the science."

"Absolutely," he said with a broad grin.

For all the contacts and connections that happened as a result of the embassy luncheon, an equally important reason to make a special trip to Moscow was to present my project to the leadership of the Russian Association of Indigenous Peoples of the North, Siberia and the Far East—RAIPON for short. I hoped they might endorse the project and link me to possible hosts across Siberia and the Russian Far East.

Unlike Canada, whose North is populated by just two indigenous groups, the Dene in the west and the Inuit throughout the central and eastern Arctic, or Scandinavia, whose North is the traditional land of just one main cultural group, the Sami, the vast Russian North is populated by dozens of indigenous groups in a number of language groups. Although all of them were subdued and assimilated into Russian culture—as were Christians and people of other faith, language, and ethnic groups—in the Stalinist era, the tatters of these peoples gathered and regrouped as best they could after the fall of the Soviet Union. In 1990, in the waning days of Mikhail Gorbachev's reforms, with support from indigenous groups around the world, leaders from these disparate oppressed ethnic groups from across Russia created an umbrella organization to represent indigenous interests in Russian affairs, particularly in the Russian parliament, or Duma.

Elena and I caught a cab at the embassy and accelerated down toward the Moscow ring road. The drive immediately felt more like a race or a demolition derby. At Zubovsky Square, just west of a big oxbow of the Moscow River, we had to cross at least sixteen lanes of seething traffic, maybe more. Had there been marked lanes, or if people in this honking, pulsating automotive mass had behaved as if there were lanes, getting over the river and across to the RAIPON office might have been less like doing a few laps at the Daytona 500 or the Monaco Grand Prix and slightly more relaxing.

But this was all in a day's work for the driver, who chattered incessantly, glancing at the road occasionally. It was never clear if he was talking to Elena, who was beside him in the front seat, or to other drivers out the window. Either way, he was right at home while I was quite sure we were near death. Somehow, by the grace of Providence, we made it through the chicane that funnelled the sixteen lanes into a measly six lanes on the Krymsky Bridge and up into the narrow streets of the old Moscow neighbourhood we were looking for. Eventually we pulled up at 44/2 Bol'shaya Polyanka.

This was a handsome old building made of what appeared to be hand-cut white stone. Architecturally, the place was Stalinist, with its arched windows and quoined corners, so distinct from the rough-poured concrete aesthetic of the drab Khrushchyovka boxes in the Moscow suburbs and beyond. But as well cared for as was the exterior, the interior showed the ravages of time and the want of maintenance rubles. The elevator was non-functional. The stairs were worn. And the corridor walls were long ago painted a smog-grimed pink, well chipped since then by passing people, furniture, and, by the look of the corners, perhaps the odd errant taxicab. The RAIPON office was of similarly tired Spartan decor, but it had its own kind of dignity, drawn from various photographs, paintings, and examples of hand-wrought aboriginal arts and crafts by members from sea to sea to sea.

We were met by Elena U, RAIPON's chief of staff, who intro-duced Fiera, a visiting teacher of Evenk language and literature from Yakutia. Next to her, at the end of the table, was Aleksei Vakhrushev, a documentary film director from Chukotka, also visiting Moscow. And along the way were Irina Kurilova, RAIPON's press secretary, and Dmitriy, a doctoral student in cultural studies from Lomonosov Moscow State University, who was in the office on other business and had asked if he might sit in. Sitting formally at one end of the small table, Elena passed along greetings and regrets from the RAIPON leadership, who were mostly away at an out-of-town conference. The atmos-phere in the stuffy little conference room with its grimy windows and antique phones was a bit pinched until someone's cellphone came to life with a rousing chorus of "I Like to Move It" from the animated classic *Madagascar*, as sung by Sacha Baron Cohen. Everyone laughed.

"So, you are on your way around the world at the Arctic Circle," said Elena, with a tinge of embarrassment through a blossoming smile. "This sounds like a very interesting project. We would be happy to hear what you need and to do whatever we can to help make it happen."

With that I unspooled a ten-minute synopsis of the project, finishing with the story of a meeting in Iqaluit, Nunavut, at which an Inuit woman threw up her hands and asked why for so many people in the South, the face of climate change and the North was the face of a polar bear, instead of a human being, a northerner. Throughout my story, which was accompanied by maps and photographs projected onto the cracks and patches on a cream-coloured wall, there were pauses while my words were translated into Russian, after which there would be a chorus of nods around the room.

"We are very interested in what is happening with aboriginal people around the circumpolar world," Fiera said. "You mentioned an Inuit who said climate change should have a human face instead of the face of a bear. Here, we don't think about bears and people as either/or. I think climate change should have the face of a bear *and* the face of a person, because if the bear dies we will also lose the people. The people will die without the animals."

She continued, "There is a saying among my people, 'If there is no bears, there is no Evenks.' In that sense, Evenks are half bear and the bear is half Evenk. Some people make fun of us because of this. We have this feeling that nature talks to us with its own language. There is an invisible thread connecting us. And still, when we explain this to other people, some of them believe we are not quite in our minds. But if the entire civilized world knew what we know, there would not have been the catastrophes, like climate change, we have seen."

By then, the formalities were gone, and with them any sense of barriers between correspondents around the table. For two and a half hours we talked, still through translation, but as if the give-and-take on topics of common concern were all that was required to make a connection and drive the conversation forward.

"How are the people in Canada's North adapting to climate change?" Fiera asked.

Not really knowing where to begin, I told them the story of walking along the shore of the Coronation Gulf with my friend Frank Ipakohak in Kugluktuk, Nunavut. "First," I told them, "he showed me a photograph of the island at the mouth of the Coppermine River where he had been born in a tent in the 1940s. Then he took me to a place where we could look out over the water. 'See,' he said, 'the island where I was born is gone, washed away. Climate change is something we have always lived with. We know how to adapt to changing conditions, and even though the change is happening faster now, we see evidence of change from season to season, from year to year. We see evidence of cultural change every day.'"

This story brought knowing glances around the table. Elena spoke first. "The same is true for the peoples of northern Russia as well. History has not been kind to us. We too notice the effects of climate change on reindeer pastures and on the plants and animals in what we call our 'feeding landscapes,' but there are other matters that are of greater concern."

Rising from her chair, Elena pointed to a map of Russia on the wall showing the territories of the various ethnicities and linguistic groups from west to east. As she spoke, I was struck by the idea of "feeding landscapes" and how similar this was to the ideas that were discussed at the Terra Madre conference in Jokkmokk. In addition to language preservation and the per-petuation of other cultural forms and motifs, security of land on which to nurture and nourish traditional foods is essential to survival for indigenous peoples.

"Not including the Sakha, who are the dominant culture

of Yakutia, we are thirty different peoples across Russia, totalling just over two hundred thousand among two million other Russians living across the Arctic. In Stalinist times, when it was forbidden to speak our Native languages or to practise our Native ways, other than to do the bidding of the state on collective reindeer farms and fishing operations, many of our people just disappeared. Now for many of our groups there are only hundreds, in some cases dozens, of people left who identify as part of these cultural groups. We are in crisis," Elena said.

"The situation for the Oroks, the Orochi, the Negidals, the Enets, and the Russian Aleuts is dire. Their low numbers and high rates of assimilation into neighbouring populations may well result in these traditions slowly dying out altogether over the next couple of decades, or ceasing to exist as independent ethnicities in our mix. Groups like the Dolgans, the Eskimo, the Sami, the Yukaghirs, and the Chuvans, of whom there are several thousand remaining, are stronger but their ethnic future does not inspire optimism. The strongest peoples in our membership, the Evenks—like Fiera—the Chukchi, the Nenets, and the Khanty and Mansi have worked hard to maintain language, cultural practices, and ethnocultural institutions, with the most stable ethnic self-consciousness. But even these peoples have yet to find an optimal model for the future. "

"But we are not without hope," said a male voice at the end of the table.

I turned to see that the documentary filmmaker, Aleksei, had moved forward to speak. "I have just spent the winter with a Chukchi man called Vukvukai—a name that means 'the little rock'—and his family on the northern slope of the Russian Far East on the Bering Strait. His life, still, is inseparable from the reindeer. Vukvukai and his community have been able to continue their way of life mostly by virtue of their isolation. Climate change will bring development closer to them every day, every season, but so far their nomadic Chukchi culture is virtually intact. It is an inspiring thing to see."

"This sounds more like the exception than the rule for Russian northerners," I replied.

"Yes, I suppose so. In time, life will be a struggle for them too."

Elena joined in once again and, after affirming the courage and insight of Aleksei and how pleased RAIPON was to be supporting his work in whatever way it could, she slid a package of materials across the table. "RAIPON is a permanent participant in the Arctic Council," she explained, "and this has been very good for us in telling our story to the international community. This has also allowed us to create materials that build understandings beyond the borders of Russia. We are determined to do what we must do to ensure that the new century is not the last in the history of the small indigenous peoples of Russia. Our priorities are set out in this review, which was published in English with the help of the Inuit Circumpolar Council and the Canadian International Development Agency within the Institution-Building for Northern Russian Indigenous Peoples Project."

"With help from Canada?"

"Yes," replied Elena, obviously having prepared this long ahead of time for the visiting Canadian.

A sampling of these priorities detailed the very steep hill that RAIPON members had to climb:

- Unconditional rejection of the policy of total state paternalism . . .
- Rejection of government care does not mean alienation of the state from decisions about indigenous problems . . .
- Preservation and maintenance of the still existing nomadic populations of the North . . .
- Allocation of territories for traditional land use . . .
- The traditional economy of the northern peoples shall be given a status of a special sector of the national economy . . .
- Urgent actions are required in social and demographic policy: to increase the birth rate in indigenous peoples, to sustain health care, and to decrease the consumption of alcohol, which is the main factor in the demographic crisis.
- The political aspect in development of the northern peoples becomes very important—establishment of local self-governance, indigenous representation in legislative and executive authorities at all levels. . . .

At my request, Elena made arrangements to provide a letter of introduction and support from the RAIPON leadership that could be used to make connections with a list of key people across the Russian North. "We are not huge in number, but now that I have learned a little more about your project, I think we can help," she offered. "Of all the people on this list, be sure to contact Vyacheslav Shadrin in Yakutsk. He is a senior chief of five districts in Yakutia, a scholar and teacher. He will understand your project and I'm sure be of great assistance."

Following Elena's lead, we all stood. Fiera motioned for me to come with her to the next room, which appeared to be the main reception area for RAIPON. She lifted a mask made of leather and wood from the wall and handed it to me, her dark eyes sparkling in her round smiling face. "For you," she said in English.

"I can't take that," I said, astonished that there was now a space on the wall where this artifact had been.

"You will need it," she said. "It is made by a craftsman in my community in Yakutia."

On a piece of tanned reindeer hide were three coins, drilled and tied like medals below the wooden chin of the mask. I slid my hand under each one and turned it over to see the obverse, appreciating the care and workmanship that had gone into making the piece.

"Those are for luck," she said, as she reached up and gave me a big hug.

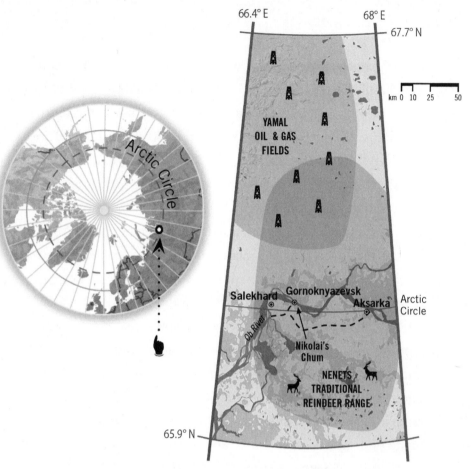

66.4° E   68° E

67.7° N

km 0 10   25   50

YAMAL
OIL & GAS
FIELDS

Salekhard Gornoknyazevsk

Aksarka Arctic
Circle

Ob River

Nikolai's
Chum

NENETS
TRADITIONAL
REINDEER RANGE

65.9° N

64°E RUSSIA GMT+6

8: YAMAL REINDEER

At first glance, the activity on the ice of the Ob River just north
of the Arctic Circle from Salekhard, the administrative centre
of the Yamalo-Nenets Autonomous Okrug, on April 1 looked
like a travelling fair and fun park. There was a garish red and
yellow pneumatic clamshell cover on a raised plywood stage
where singers and dancers in matching natty powder-blue par-

kas were entertaining an appreciative standing crowd. Food and merchandise vendors hawked their wares at tables lined up in the winter sun. Paralleling the shore but very much still on the ice were six or seven chums, Nenets travelling houses, made of teepee-style poles and covered with double-sewn reindeer hides.

Mixed in with the performers wearing modern outfits were Nenets women clad in full-length *yagushka* coats made of exquisitely embroidered and appliquéd white reindeer fur. Young Nenets men were wearing fur-hooded pin-striped *malitsa* tops, cinched at the waist, either with long woven sashes, if they happened to be in line for the ongoing wrestling match taking place on an uncovered stage, or with the classic wide black leather reindeer herder's belt with brass and chain ornamentation. And then there were the rosy-cheeked children, running and tumbling in their full-length hooded fur garments with mittens built right into the end of the sleeves. Nearby, a profusion of handmade sleds with leather traces were hitched to bridled reindeer eager to get on with the annual races.

There were both four- and five-animal hitches raring to go. Each animal was tacked with a broad, split-leather collar riding low on the neck, with a leather and horn bridle and a single trace heading back between the legs to a sled. Each team had a minder, young boys mostly, thwarting what could be a nightmare of tangling. A pair of inspectors put a stripe of orange spray paint on the neck of each lead animal, showing that the group was ready to race.

The course would take the teams upriver to a pole driven into the ice about a kilometre away, and then home. When the inspectors were done, the first two teams took off. In addition to the single leather rein to steer and encourage the lead animal, the drivers guided their teams with a slender stick called a *khorei* and called to their reindeer—"On Dasher, on Dancer . . . ," or something to that effect, in Nenets. Watching the tongues lolling and animals gasping for air as they crossed the finish line made me glad not to be a reindeer that day. But even they, the four-legged athletes, appeared to enjoy the enthusiastic cries of the very noisy and appreciative crowd at the Aksarka festival.

Herder Days, which are celebrated in various places through-out northern Russia, were in fact timed to coincide with the season when these families began the drive back to tundra pasturage hundreds of kilometres north. Started in Soviet times, and very likely building on a long-established tradition of getting together in the spring, these festivals were an opportunity for herders to gather, to share tales of the previous year's peregrinations, to have an annual meeting with representatives of the Departments of Agriculture and Education and other government officials, to sell meat, and to have a bit of family fun. I had to remind myself that this was not some kind of throwback to days of yore but a cultural happening in real time.

Through Venera Niyazova, my host and translator from the Yamal Department of Culture, I was welcomed into one of the chums at the race site for a meal by Viktor Laptender and his wife, Olga. Although the temperature outside was well below minus fifteen Celsius, the chum was hot and humid. Within its eight-metre diameter were at least eight little children with their mothers and older sisters and about a dozen other non-Nenets visitors from out of town, all feasting on the most amazing array of reindeer (frozen raw, smoked, boiled, or dried) and fish (frozen raw or boiled), dishes that came from the tidy little kitchen area around the tin stove in the middle.

When the festival was over, everything in this dwelling, from the hand-hewn floorboards to the tin stove and the thirty-five hand-trimmed spruce poles and the mix of canvas and reindeer hides that defined the living space, would be packed up on waiting freight sleds. The family would cross the river, reconnect with their reindeer, and continue on their yearly round. Somehow this was immensely reassuring, given Semjon's struggles in the fenced confines of his *obshchina* on the Kola Peninsula and the dying traditions of the Sami throughout western Russia and Scandinavia.

Our host was talking about the new railway that Gazprom had built up to the Bovanenkovskoye gas field, which was more or less in the centre of their summer grazing ground. Up to now, they had been able to work around the drill rigs and pipelines associated with this development, but the railway tracks across the landscape were new. Word was that the rumbling of the trains moving on the tracks was scaring fish away from places where normally there were plenty. Oil workers and construction personnel had been good customers for meat and handcrafts. The railway was a mixed blessing, as were the changes that were somehow timed with it.

The rivers on Viktor's yearly round were breaking up earlier and freezing later. For now, though, the pasture was as lush as he had seen it, which could have meant that the longer season was having an effect, or maybe it was just the way things were. Change was a fact of Nenets life, Viktor said. "It's a fact of all our lives," he added, with a sweep of his hand that included everyone at his table. In the end, he wasn't sure how things would work out, but he explained that they had adapted before and would likely be able to do so again.

What amazed me about this unlikely meal and its nomadic host was the fact that through more than seven decades of Communism, these herders in their family groups and brigades had prevailed. In postwar years, when the government decreed that all reindeer herding would be done through the administrative structure of collective farms, somehow the Nenets had managed to persevere.

When the Soviet Union collapsed, taking with it the notion of collective ownership, suddenly these herders were in a private market, with a very modest stipend from the government, charged with responsibility for production and marketing of meat, antler, hide, and other products of their labours that had be sold in a cash economy to make ends meet. And all the while, on the Yamal Peninsula, initial oil and gas discoveries in the 1970s were doubled and redoubled. As their reindeer were stepping over pipelines, the Nenets, opportunistically, found ways to market to the oilmen as they continued on their thousand-kilometre annual north-south migrations.

Each of Viktor's stories heightened my sense of wonder. Like children throughout the circumpolar world, Nenets children had been spirited off to residential schools since Stalinist times and forced to speak and learn in Russian. And yet, as soon as they returned for summer holidays, they returned to speaking one of eleven dialects of Forest Nenets or Tundra Nenets, depending on where their families ranged. Viktor added that without the Russian language, it would be impossible to market their meat. It was quite clear, as I sampled delicious chunks of frozen fish and pickled and smoked meats of every description, bundled up with slabs of homemade bread with lashings of butter or whole cream, that there was much more to be learned among these northerners than the finer points of reindeer racing.

With the exact same kindness and connections that had taken me into Viktor's inner circle at the Aksarka festival, Venera was able to connect me with Viktor's brother, Nikolai, and his family, who had been wintering downriver near a place called Gornoknyazevsk. The visit to Nikolai's chum began with another drive on iced roads. We stopped at an outdoor ethnographic museum, where a television crew materialized to interview the visiting Canadian. On arrival, I was encouraged to dress in full *malitsa* and *gus* (Nenets fur outfit). The B-roll they shot looked like I was trying to talk to the "living exhibit" reindeer. When in Siberia . . .

Set against the memory of the vibrancy of Aksarka, the absence of people in the outdoor museum made the installation flat. From a very helpful curator, however, I learned about the joinery on the sleds, the animist beliefs of the Nenets, and the rules and etiquette of the chum—how, for example, in a traditional family situation, an invisible line divides the space exactly in two, from the door back through the stove, with one side being the male domain and the other being the female side. "Men, for their part, should never touch the floorboards or the tent poles. These rules are what allow for efficient division of labour under what are often very cold and difficult working conditions," the curator explained.

We moved inside to the very pleasant ambient temperature of the museum's offices for a further chat. Katya, a beautiful young translator from the Department of Culture, motioned to a cloakroom off the foyer and said, "James, let us go in this room and take off our clothes." I blushed.

Here, with a map to aid the discussion, the curator explained the strong twenty-first-century presence of the Nenets on the Yamal. After the arrival of the Cossacks, the Nenets continued herding, managing to survive the sometimes oppressive tax regimes that various waves of newcomers imposed. But in a territory one and a half times the size of France, and with a habit of moving, coexistence was more possible than one might think. The Bolshevik Revolution more or less came and went without fanfare at this latitude, and it wasn't until the years of Stalin's terror regime that laws forbidding the private holding of land or animals and, among other things, the use of the Nenets language began the cultural decay for the Nenets above the Arctic Circle. Elsewhere in the Soviet Union, the policy of "sedentarization," moving women and children to houses in settlements in the name of better living conditions and improved education, broke up the family units that had followed age-old divisions of labour to make the pastoral life viable.

But even in 1961, when the Soviets collectivized the herds and created a number of state farms, or *sovkhozy*, the Nenets managed what others had not, by quietly insisting that women and children remain with the travelling herds rather than being forcibly resettled into settlement tenements. So when the Soviet Union collapsed in the early 1990s and many of the *sovkhozy* faded with the government, animals reverted to the families who looked after them and private reindeer herding took hold like nowhere else on earth. Today, the curator told me, there are more than 7,500 Nenets involved in traditional herding and something like three hundred thousand reindeer moving over one of the richest natural-gas fields in the world.

A handsome Nenets teen and his younger brother padded into the museum in their store-bought jackets, jeans, and new black Nike running shoes. The lad spoke quietly to the curator, who turned to us and said, "Your ride awaits."

Outside, a late-model Russkaya Mekhanika snowmobile sat with an old-fashioned handmade spruce stanchion sled attached, just like the ones in the ethnographic museum. The boys pulled blankets from under ropes tied to the sled, arranged a thick cushion of reindeer hides on the bed of the sled and then invited Katya and her boss, Venera, to sit on one side with their feet on the runner, and me on the other side. They then arranged what felt like thick horsehair blankets over the three of us, and we were off.

On the icy roads of town, I was worried that if my feet slipped off the runner, the rest of me would be sure to follow, leaving no option but to hand-wrestle with the snarling dogs that flew out to meet us at every turn, all spit and teeth. But in a few minutes, deceased cars, outhouses (there is no running water in most rural houses in Russia), and cobbled-together houses in the dilapidated "suburbs" of Gornoknyazevsk disappeared, and we were out on a hard-packed snow trail the boys had made on their way from their camp into town. Once on a less slippery surface they speeded up, leaving their passengers fighting to stay warm and hanging on for dear life.

The landscape was classic taiga with sparse copses of birch and spruce trees washed like thin colour across rolling snow-crusted tundra hills. Although the track we were following cut through new snow that had fallen overnight, washboard rumbles below the runners indicated that this was a well-used trail. We dropped down into a deep ravine and crossed an ice bridge over a stream and started to pick up tracks and broken snow where it looked as if many reindeer had been using their snowshoe-like feet to dig down for the rich green tundra lichens below.

Twenty minutes later, nearly frozen solid on the sled, we crossed another stream and roared up onto a rise. In the distance were two chums, like the ones we'd seen in Aksarka. In association was a semicircle of sleds, piles of firewood, and all the trappings of an active and ongoing nomadic winter camp. A boisterous black border collie ducked out under the door flap, closely followed by the man of the house, Nikolai Laptender, who waved heartily and welcomed us in.

Speaking Russian, Nikolai said how pleased he was to welcome a visitor from Canada into his home. He introduced us to his wife, Oustinia, who was busy tending the tin wood stove and preparing what looked like a feast on the low table near the fire, and to the other five of his seven children. He had six boys and one girl, Yalanya (the name means "sunny person"), who at about three years old was the youngest.

"But before we go any further," he said, looking directly at me, "I need to ask you to put your camera away. I would hate for you to publish a photograph of your visit here in a magazine that might be thrown in the garbage. It would show disrespect for the reindeer. The same goes for any other type of video or audio recording here. Please ask. You are welcome to use your note-book. The *tadibya* [shaman, the connector to animist traditions] insists that above all else we respect our reindeer and watch out for anything that might upset them. Without reindeer, I could not imagine living on this earth."

Pondering the simple profundity of that, acutely aware there were sounds and images happening inside this remarkable nomadic home that I would never hear or see again, I felt a surge of panic as I stowed the camera and looked for an instant at the digital recorder in the bottom of my daypack. This day in Siberia, whether I liked it or not, would be an immersion in the oral tradition—what I saw and what I heard, what I smelled, sensed, and felt was all there would be to build a mind map and memory of the encounter. Gulp.

As my eyes adjusted to twin beams of sunlight poking into the dim recesses of the chum through two portholes of heavy clear plastic sewn into the double-reindeer-hide walls of the structure, I could only marvel that in this very modest enclosure, there lived nine people with everything they owned: their clothes, bedding, food, firewood, sewing supplies, books, dry goods, kettles, toys, cooking supplies, pots and pans, and sacred things, all neatly stowed in less than fifty square metres. Of the many lessons I learned on my way around the circumpolar world, this was one of the most enduring. How gluttonous were we acquisitive dwellers of the middle latitudes with all our stuff, how spoiled and protective were we of space, personal and otherwise, and how much we could learn about the simple art of sharing and, apparently, interpersonal harmony from a nomadic family such as the Laptenders, who, for now, were ensconced so comfortably on the Arctic Circle.

Nikolai sat on a bundle of reindeer hides in the middle of one side of the chum and invited us to do the same. Without being asked, the five children settled in on the other side of the structure and set about either just watching the guests or quietly amusing themselves. In due course I was invited to wash my hands in a basin of warm water and rinse them in an ingenious reverse-plunger gravity-fed cold water reservoir that hung on three delicate chains from a horizontal bar tied to the main poles of the chum.

The low table Oustinia had been working on was moved in front of Nikolai, and on it was served boiled reindeer with bouillon and noodles, pieces of frozen raw reindeer meat, frozen *muksun*—sweet, delicate whitefish—butter and cloudberry jam, homemade bread, salt, sugar, store-bought meringues, salted fish, a dish of hard candies, cookies, and an opened can of sweetened condensed milk that everyone applied as liberally to almost every comestible on the table as North Americas would do with ketchup, as if it were a food group unto itself.

And we talked: about Gazprom, climate change, education, and how the Nenets world works. Since the collapse of the Soviet

Union, many of the family groupings—the brigades—from *sov-khoz* times have persisted as reindeer-working units on the same yearly round that Nenets have been tracing up and down the Yamal Peninsula as long as anyone can remember. Stipends from the government for tending this meat resource fell away substantially but were replaced, in some cases, with allowances and services from Gazprom that provided more ample compensation. Yes, they now owned their own reindeer. And yes, they still looked after some reindeer that were effectively owned by the state, but they did not have any rights to land or protections in law for their way of life.

Gazprom built schools and provided transportation and accommodation for some young people from nomadic families to attend them, which was a good thing for the most part, said Nikolai. The company gave assurances that grazing routes would not be impeded by roads, railways, or pipelines—although in practice, as I would learn later, these commitments weren't kept. Additionally, the corporation promised to ensure water quality throughout its exploration and extraction operations. Nikolai, reaching into an overstuffed leather folio for a glossy handout entitled "Yamal Megaproject," said Gazprom claims to take its social responsibility seriously. He read out: "One of the underlying principles of the commercial development in Yamal is maintaining a reasonable balance between industrial development and a solicitous attitude towards the traditional lifestyle of the indigenous minorities.

"That would be us," he said, waving his hand toward Oustinia and the children.

"We are worried about climate change, yes," he said, putting the handout away, "but we are worried about these oil and gas developments even more. So far, we have been able to carry on with our life as we have known it, moving north in the summer and back here in the winter, but with the new railway and more development to come, no one is sure what will happen to the reindeer . . . and what will happen to us."

That afternoon, dressed in a *gus* for each of us provided by the family, we travelled with Nikolai and the dog to find the herd and move it a bit closer to the camp. The dog rode on the back of the snowmobile until we started to encounter stragglers of the main herd, which were grazing happily in twos and threes throughout a wooded area along the banks of the river.

Nikolai stopped the machine and dispatched the dog, which circled and ran, traced a bigger circle, nipping at the hooves of the animals it would collect, and ran again, while Nikolai bellowed instructions to turn the growing group right or left or to bring them forward. His voice grew hoarse as he and the dog chased one cluster of deer after another. Working in Y patterns, the pair of them went up one fork of the Y, turned the animals around, and united them with the rest of the herd. As the three of us watched in total amazement, they marched the whole group back through a natural corridor in the trees to the place where the diversion had happened. It was only when we were all together and following along behind that I realized Nikolai was actually driving the herd along the snowy surface right-of-way of a buried gas pipeline.

By now, the man, the dog, and the reindeer were one, moving south, slowly but surely, in an undulating line. Clearly, the reindeer were used to this. The dog worked the sides and, in doing so, set the direction of travel, while Nikolai ran the snowmobile at the back of the pack, sometimes driving close enough that snow flung from the rear animal's splayed hooves would flip up over us. When Nikolai idled the machine to let the animals move ahead a bit, without the roar of the motor, we would hear the bells on some of the lead animals, animating a scene that has persisted, some would say, in spite of insurmountable odds.

With the herd settled like a hoarfrost ring around the camp, Nikolai gave a little lassoing demonstration before we moved back inside, surprising me with an invitation to take a couple of photos. After a couple of hours of running with a dog and a motorized man setting the pace, none of the reindeer seemed much interested in doing anything other than just standing there as Nikolai whirled his woven-leather line in the air and dropped it over their antlers. In the dying light of late afternoon, his two oldest boys chopped and split firewood from a pile of logs on a sled and stacked it neatly to one side of the chum. And inside, Oustinia was cuddling Yalanya and showing her how to wrap her doll in a kerchief, as she herself had been wrapped to ward off the cold not so long ago. The table was set again with sweets and tea, and we settled in for a second round of visiting before heading back to town.

What amazed me as Nikolai spoke, and Katya and Venera translated, was how remarkable it was that the Nenets people have persevered. As he talked, Nikolai reached behind the stove and pulled out a small case. He pointed to a wire leading up beside the tin chimney and out through the hole at the top of the chum.

"Cellphone antenna," he said. "But the battery is flat right now. We use it only when we have to. We have a solar charger that we use for the phone and for this," he explained, pulling out a laptop computer. "We are experimenting all the time with these things," he said, "figuring out what will work and what will not work. Living in town is not the answer. We are reindeer people."

But then came the *pièce de résistance*: he spoke to Oustinia, who handed him a one-litre plastic bottle full of what looked like green dishwashing soap. "This is concentrated cleaning solution," he told us. "Being concentrated, it is excellent because we cannot have too much weight when we are moving. It is environment-friendly, which is important to us. And the manufacturer says that it has twenty-nine different uses. It can clean people or pots and pans, hands, hair. . . . We have tried all twenty-nine applications and found it to be an excellent product. We have even found a thirtieth use that the manufacturer doesn't know about yet. We have found that it works well for curing reindeer skins."

"Who makes it?" I had to ask.

"A company called Amway," he said with no irony at all in his voice or his face. And with that, Nikolai launched into a story of how he went to a seminar in Yarsale, one of the towns they passed twice a year on the way from here to the summer grazing grounds in the north.

"It might have been sponsored by Gazprom," he added. "I can't remember."

But, clearly, he had taken in everything that the good folks from Amway—short for "American Way"—had to say, as evidenced by his description of sales pyramids. He explained that if he became a distributor of the products, with his own customers, he would be able to purchase this soap and other Amway products suitable for the nomadic lifestyle for much less.

"Please," he said, "take my card." His business card had the logo of the Yamalo-Nenets Autonomous Okrug, with its prominent reindeer and an oil derrick or gas flare poking out of a crown symbol and, of course, the characteristic tricoloured Amway logo as well.

A man with no fixed address had just handed me his business card.

"Yes," he said, "our telephone number is on there and we have a postbox in Salekhard where mail can be sent. Please note that the card also has my dealer number on it. If you and your family ever need an Amway product, even back in Canada, just put my number on the order and our family will benefit."

The Arctic trails have their secret tales.

With the kindness, patience, or perhaps curiosity of local people in Salekhard, time on the land with Viktor and Nikolai Laptender and their families led to an invitation to attend a meeting of a group called the Intelligence of the Indigenous Peoples of the North (elders representing Nenets, Khanty, Komi, and Mansi peoples of the Salekhard area). Because other meetings had run long, Katya and I were late and found a group of stone-faced people waiting in a government conference room, looking at their watches.

But after a round of apologies and some initial pleasantries, the elders took me one by one through what turned out to be a common story of steady migration of nomads to settlements, with their complaint that Russian law gives the ones who remain on the land no real protection against the march of progress in the oil and gas industry. Each in turn talked about the seductive lure, especially for their young people, of TVs, computers, cellphones, and wage work to earn the cash to buy and service these attachments to the world outside. I asked whether they had been following the Arab Spring, where social media had been the vector of inclusion that was changing the politics of these places in front of the world's eyes. "Not really," was the answer.

But the talk of revolution struck a chord. One of the leaders agreed that it would take something like that to get the Russian government's attention and make the process of law-making more responsive to the needs of indigenous peoples. However, Leonid Ivanovich Khudi, the Nenets representative, went into a long explanation of how that kind of fight, that kind of very public resistance to authority, was just not in his people's nature. It was a moment that was so revealing and, in some ways, so sad. But it illustrated how these people, who were only a generation or so away from being pastoral nomads, have rolled with the world they've found themselves in.

The elder stopped and thought and said, "You know, the oil in Yamal is going to run out in thirty or forty years. And when it does, the reindeer-herding people will be prepared, still living on the land, still working with uncomplicated resources."

"So you're looking forward to when the oil runs out?" I asked, somewhat incredulous.

He broke a toothy smile and said, "Da, da, da, da, da."

All of a sudden there was a strange and quite wonderful flush of optimism in the room. Everyone, it seemed, knew the situation for indigenous people in the face of ongoing development in Yamal was going to be a continuing struggle, but this man, Leonid Ivanovich Khudi, in his own quiet and lovely way, had broken through all that, if only for a moment.

The last stop in Salekhard and probably our most important meeting was with Sergey Nikolayevich Kharyuchi, the Nenets president of RAIPON, who had written and signed the all-important letter of support for my project. Thinking Kharyuchi would have another job to pay the bills—NGO work, worldwide, seems to be largely a labour of love with many rewards but sometimes some very modest remuneration—I had asked my hosts in Salekhard if they knew him and if we might catch up with him at some point to say hello and thank you.

"Oh yes, we know him," they said. "He is chairman of the Yamalo-Nenets Autonomous Okrug Legislative Assembly, just one step down from the governor, and one of the most powerful and respected people around."

So on the appointed day at the appointed time, we made our way to the very handsome new government building sitting on stilts in the permafrost by the river in Salekhard. We climbed the marble steps and presented our credentials to security. The only comparison to the tired building in which the Moscow RAIPON office was housed was the fact that the elevator in this new building didn't work either. At the end of a climb to the fifth or sixth floor of the legislative office building, we were met by a member of the chairman's staff, who took our coats and offered us sweets and seats.

Sitting there in the Yamalo-Nenets corridor of influence, I found myself awash, even a little embarrassed at my own erroneous assumptions about how the world works. That an indigenous person might become the speaker of the House of Commons in Canada, a position roughly equivalent to chairman of the Legislative Assembly, while not totally out of the question, would certainly be unusual—and not because there aren't Canadians of indigenous origin capable or worthy of assuming such a position, for there surely are. But before I could ruminate much more on that topic, the padded door to the inner sanctum opened and a big man in a bespoke suit stepped out, shook my hand, and said, "Welcome. I am Sergey."

If the quality of the tea service, the size and thickness of the burnished meeting table, and/or the acreage of leather-topped desk and credenza were indicators of the status and stature of the officeholder, clearly Kharyuchi had done exceedingly well for himself by any standard. Although very much the voice of RAIPON, Kharyuchi had parlayed his postgraduate studies into a PhD in law, which had led to senior government positions. When I asked about his role in changing the fortunes of the small indigenous peoples of the Russian North, he handed me a bound copy of his dissertation, a comparative analysis of the laws governing indigenous peoples throughout the circumpolar world.

As we drank hot tea from bone china cups, he asked about my project, having read the prospectus months before, when writing his letter of support. Although the conversation took place in Russian, his eyes clearly saw much more than mine as they looked through the cultural divide between us, at the table and in space and time. It was one of the few times in my whole journey, even with what I took to be Katya's very competent translation, that I wished for unmediated conversation. Kharyuchi was a wise and gracious human being who had thought deeply about the blessings and curses of the North and of northerners and, as I engaged his dark eyes across the table, I had a palpable sense that there was much in this interaction—meaning, nuance, metaphor—that I was missing.

As he talked and Katya translated, I found myself thinking of a member of my doctoral examining committee, who said as often as he could that "a unilingual doctorate in cultural geography is a contradiction in terms." As if in reply to my insecurities about fumbling my way to his office, Kharyuchi concluded by saying, "I am so glad you are doing this work, James. It is important. It is not that northern people are voiceless, but sometimes what we say must be amplified for the world to hear. As president of RAIPON, I am very pleased and proud to support what you are doing."

And then, like a besotted groupie, I asked if he would sign his book for me.

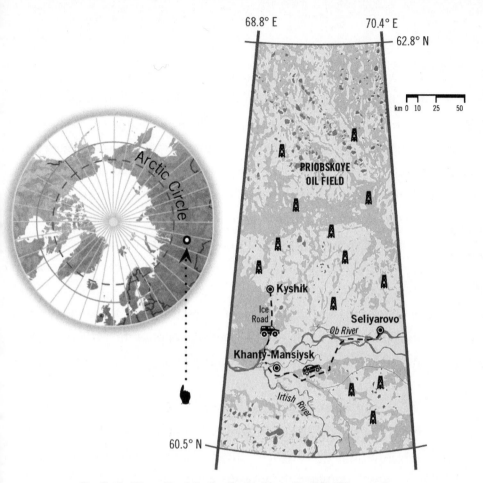

69°E RUSSIA GMT+6

9: UPRIVER

The ideal way to move east along the Arctic Circle from Salekhard would have been to follow the ghosts along the Railroad of Death to Igarka, 1,300 kilometres east from the estuary of the Ob River to the banks of the Yenisey River. The original routing of the railway actually headed southeast through the town of Nadym before curving northward again and eventually through the improbably boggy tundra/taiga terrain. Scholars estimate the venture cost three hundred lives per month for the four years it took Stalin to realize it was a bad idea.

Although the prospect of following seismic lines and newer ice-road infrastructure through what is now one of the richest oil fields in the world appealed to my sense of adventure, it was unlikely, given my budget of time and money. Instead, again using Sergey Kharyuchi's letter and the encouragement of the Canadian Embassy to share stories of the Canadian Arctic with our neighbours across the pole, I made my way upriver from Salekhard to the traditional territory of the Ob-Ugrian people, the Khanty and Mansi, which is now the Autonomous Okrug of Khanty-Mansiysk, and into the very heartland of the Russian oil patch.

First stop after arriving in the namesake boomtown of the region, the city of Khanty-Mansiysk, population eighty thousand, was at the offices of the Salvation of Yugra Peoples Association, the first non-governmental indigenous organization created after perestroika. The welcome by the association president and a group of elders and officials with frozen fish and vodka at ten in the morning on a brisk winter day was almost overwhelming.

Amply aided by Vladislav (Slava) Rishko, an interpreter from the Khanty-Mansiysk Department of Public and International Affairs, I started into my presentation. When I got to the part about the fiery Inuit woman in Iqaluit observing that climate change needs a human face instead of the face of a bear, an elder at the end of the table, Nikita, interjected with a long story about how Siberian peoples don't make such distinctions "because the bear is our brother," he said. When I had finished, around the table we went over the next hour or more, with each person in turn saying something about what they did for the organization and why they were pleased to be here to help welcome a Canadian.

"Most Mansi people are small, but I am big," said Oleg Gustavovich Shatin, from across the table. He had been introduced as the manager of a private commercial fishery. And now, after a few brimming bumpers of Beluga vodka, he was almost effusive. "I offer you a big welcome and a toast. We must take you out onto the ice on the river to show you how we fish. A toast to you and to the river and to our upcoming fishing expedition."

I shot a quick glance at Slava as we drank Oleg's toast, knowing that our schedule for presentations and travels for the next several days was already packed. The pair of them just smiled and sipped, as if to say, "Just go with it, James."

The following day we had a van booked to drive fifty kilometres north on the ice road to the Khanty village of Kyshik. But we came out of our hotel to find Oleg, large as life in reindeer boots and an improbable fur hat, exhaling plumes of white breath into the exhaust cloud of an even more imposing six-wheeled Trekol semi-armoured amphibious all-terrain vehicle. "We promised fishing. So fishing you will get," he said, as Slava asked the driver of the waiting van to follow us.

Over the next hour or so, we stopped by two independent

crews who were getting around on recycled military single-ski snowmobiles and pulling nets set through the ice of the Irtysh River. For the first while, we drove around with apparently no idea where the crews were actually working. Oleg was on his phone, petulantly yelling at whoever was on the other end. At one point, he turned to me and said, "I think I should fire every-body involved in this operation. Oh . . . whoops . . . I guess I can't fire myself, as I'm the boss."

He explained, "In Soviet times, Irtysh River *muksun* used to be a delicacy that was salted and sold in southern markets. Now, we sell what we catch locally. The market is much bigger now that oil has been discovered and the population has increased. But the water quality is not as good either, which has diminished the catch. Farther up the river, around Kyshik, where we are going, there is a very special fish called *chebuk* that is still a delicacy. The water there is still very clear, much less polluted by habitation and industry than it is here."

Although it might have made sense to travel to Kyshik in the Trekol, we had to decline. After an hour of bumping and swerv-ing through metre-deep drifts on the river ice, it was a relief to say goodbye to Oleg and board the rented, warm, and shock-absorbed Toyota van that was the original chariot of the day. To our surprise, Oleg lumped his largeness into the Toyota as well, apparently having made the decision to accompany us for the next leg of the journey. With a government driver, arranged by Slava's boss, we headed back to town and eventually over the river ice again, heading north, but this time on a track that had been plowed and packed by previous traffic.

Cattails and sedges in the frozen marshes through which we travelled were dusted with ice crystals. White birch trees stood sentry among snow-covered conifers. And all was bathed in the light of a strengthening Arctic sun that threw shadows across the blue surfaces of the Siberian snows. We bumped across frozen flats, sometimes taking precipitous drops onto stream beds only to lift up the other side, like off-road rally drivers flying through the air with wheels spinning.

What surprised me most about the journey, however, was that Oleg and our driver were on the phone most of the time. Cell service, at least in this part of western Siberia, and in spite of what appeared to be vast expanses of land without power, power poles, or cell towers, is far better here than it is at this latitude in Canada. My only conclusion about that was that the oilmen must need to talk to one another.

When the faded green houses of the village came into view, we slowed down and picked up a vanguard of stray dogs that loped along, yapping at our tires, as if they'd been expecting us. We went directly to the village office, where we were welcomed by the village head, Natalya Paulovna Bachman. "We are honoured to have a visitor from Canada," she said, as she introduced us to the member of the regional Duma who happened to be in town. "Where *is* Canada?" he asked, in all seriousness.

"We are neighbours across the pole. I have come to say hello on my way around the world at the Arctic Circle," I replied through Slava.

"I always thought Canada was way over there," he gestured, waving to his left. "Far away over there." But then, pointing upwards, "I suppose we are closer over the North Pole."

Bachman explained that as a Russian woman, she had come to Kyshik, a majority-Khanty town, to work. And this is how she came to be involved with local politics. "The population here is 778 right now," she said, "62 percent of them Khanty. We have a couple of Forest Nenets living here. The rest are a mix of Russians and others who wish to live a more traditional lifestyle, hunting and fishing on the surrounding clan lands. We had twenty-nine newborns this year, and 211 of our population are under twenty. The traditional activities of hunting and fishing are supplemented with income from state donations. We have a good school that teaches Khanty language and culture," Bachman told us.

"Since the collapse of the Soviet Union things have been more difficult here. Fewer people are connected to the land. We are trying to encourage tourism and to make souvenirs, but it has been a difficult mental transition for local people. The Khanty have never been traders. Trading was not a part of their way of life. So we are trying. The thing we need most is a road, because through the summer months—and the summer is getting longer, it seems—we are accessible only by boat.

"What we are most excited about," the village head continued, "is our school. This is a test site for a Khanty component in the curriculum. We are seeing children who identify as Khanty getting more involved in who they are. Twenty-five years ago, no one said very much about who they were or what their cultural background might be. But now, I think there is a return of pride in being Khanty.

"Come. The children have prepared a concert especially for you."

What followed was a series of skits and dances to recorded music on the tiny school stage, performed by children in the flowing colours of traditional Khanty dress with woven headbands, empire-waisted knee-length dresses with square yokes and shawls over ornately patterned knitted socks and moccasins. The final dance involved four teenage girls twirling on the stage with their heads, shoulders, and faces covered with intricately patterned and fringed shawls.

"This is part of the bear dance," the head teacher explained. As I had learned at the Salvation of Yugra Peoples meeting, the bear was prominent in this culture. "During the bear festival, it is important that the bear be respected at all times, but because the Khanty are relatives of the bear and worried about reprisals from the spirit world for participating in the killing of a bear, we celebrate the hunt with our faces covered."

Thinking this performance at the school might mark the end of the visit, I expressed my thanks for the program that had been presented, especially the dancing and music in the school, fully expecting that the next event would be getting back into the van for another wild ride through the frozen tundra marshes back to town. The community had other plans.

Yefim Mikolaevich, the diminutive leader of the cultural program at the school, beckoned us to follow him to a small sod-roofed log house set into a copse of trees at the centre of the village. The gentle yellow glow of candles flowed out through small frosted windows into the fading afternoon. With the flair of a maître d', Yefim gestured with a sweep of both arms.

"Welcome. Please come in. This is a traditional Khanty winter house that is here as a kind of open-air museum. Please come in and we will share a meal."

And share we did. First, before a table laden with fresh apples and oranges, newly baked bread and butter, fish sandwiches, chunks of rare Kyshik *chebuk* both boiled and frozen, dried reindeer sausage, cheese, bannock, pickles, instant coffee, and lashings of quality Beluga vodka, Yefim asked us each to pick up a coin off the table, close it tightly in our hands, and make a wish. He collected these in a large red cloth that he tied up and invited me to toss into the fire, crackling in a clay fireplace in the corner of the building. "These will bring us all good luck," he said as the cloth caught fire and sent flames licking up the packed earthen flue. "Being here in this place reminds us that we must cling to our land, we must cling to our melodies. We know from what you have said that this is part of what you are trying to do by coming here and writing your book. Welcome to Kyshik. A toast to you, our Canadian visitor."

I sat on a low bench, looking at candlelit faces around the table as the meal progressed, with Yefim's toast echoing in my mind: "We must cling to our land. We must cling to our melodies." In the midst of territorial, cultural, political, and economic complexities that had long since started my head spinning, a human encounter over food had forged a meaningful connection that transcended differences and difficulties. At one point, as if to meld all these sensations and all this learning into one musical whole, a woman at the table took out a piece of split reindeer shin bone, the Khanty precursor to the modern-day jaw harp, and played a few traditional songs to aid digestion.

By the time the meal was well over and everyone had had their fill and was getting tired, it appeared that Oleg had developed quite an affection for Natalya, the village head, who sat beside him in her flowing full-length sheared mink coat, lecturing him on the proprieties of where and where not to fish in her jurisdiction. Oleg, for his part, undaunted and unbowed, and on the back side of a half-litre of vodka, said, "My wife left me. I still don't know why. I long for the days when I might go home with the smell of a woman on my clothes instead of the smell of fish, tobacco, and beer."

"Maybe it is time we started getting back," said Slava.

A couple of days later, we set out in the opposite direction from our base in town, this time on a paved road that led to smaller tracks of frozen gravel surface, where we had to swing in tight to the windrows of snow to allow the massive drill rigs and other oil patch service equipment to pass. On either side of the road were criss-crossing networks of pipelines, all bathed in the eerie light of gas flares illuminating the dim light of morning. A couple of hours brought us to a settlement called Seliyarovo, a hundred kilometres from Khanty-Mansiysk.

Unlike Kyshik, or any northern community in Canada, this village of 560, located on a high bank of the Ob River, included no indigenous people on its census. And where once travellers might have used the river or the stars to navigate, there were gas flares marking every cardinal point on the compass. As we approached, the village constable pulled ahead of us from a lay-by where he'd been waiting and escorted us to the school, where we were welcomed by village officials and the school principal. The students sang a song, accompanied by Eduard, a three-fingered accordion player, who became our guide for a walking tour of the rest of the small village. The highlight was a simple frame Russian Orthodox church with a new coat of paint.

"It was built in 1837, mainly with donations of the people," Eduard said, obviously proud. "People learned about the Revolution and Soviet power also inside these walls. In 1932–33 the crosses were taken down and the church became a collective farm office. Then it was a library, a club, a village meeting hall, and, for a while after that, a store. And now you can see it is again a place of worship. The revival of the temple is the revival of our soul, our heart, and our motherland. What a day it was, after the fall of Communism, when we were again able to raise the cross onto the steeple."

We clumped inside in our boots and parkas and carefully wiped our feet on mats inside the door. The place was heated, presumably with local gas or oil, and comfortably warm. Light from dozens of slim votive candles in ornate brass holders bathed intricately painted images of the saints on the walls, highlighted with gold leaf, and accented the fine woodwork in the polished floor where people would stand during worship ceremonies.

Back outside, the cold dry air seemed more oxygen-rich than

ntented Icelandic horses bask in the light of the midnight sun not far from Dalvík,
ere the ferry departs for the Isle of Grímsey.

e author at the wheel of a 1969 Saab 95 station wagon that has seen better days—a
ssic vehicle in the classic taiga landscape of northern Sweden, where roads criss-cross
  Arctic Circle. (Photo: Gail C. Simmons)

Who knew? Reindeer on the Kola Peninsula in northwestern Russia like to eat bananas. Cuts on the animal's ears and more modern tagging systems help to identify the individual reindeer and its owner.

Impromptu revelry in a herders' cabin on the Kola Peninsula. The author in blue with host Semjon Bolshunov (*left*) and Sami guide/interpreter/lawyer Anna Prakhova. Beh (*l–r*) North Pole lawyer Olga Sergeieva, Alexi, and a third herder. (Photo: Yuri Prakho

Polar bears are found throughout the circumpolar world. WWF International estimates that of twenty to twenty-five thousand bears worldwide living in nineteen distinct subpopulations, 60 to 80 percent reside in Canada.

the reindeer races on the frozen Ob River at the Arctic Circle, near Aksarka, Siberia. sides a special halter and single trace on the lead animal (*right*), the driver uses a long k called a *khorei* to steer the five-deer hitch.

Hardy Nenets children play with a balloon at the Aksarka Herder Days. Hand coveri are partially sewn to sleeve ends so that mittens are never lost.

Nomadic Nenets reindeer herders (and Amway representatives) Nikolai and Ous ia Laptender with five of their children outside their chum, on the Arctic Circle n Gornoknyazevsk, east of Salekhard. (Photo: Venera Niyazova)

a rural school in the village
Kyshik, in the Khanty-
nsiysk Autonomous Okrug
northern Russia, a student
forms a traditional Bear Fes-
dance. A scarf masks the
of the dancer so that the
cannot identify her.

traditional Khanty winter house made of Siberian logs, host Yefim Mikolaevich (in
by the clay fireplace) toasts a visitor from across the pole.

After the toasts, songs, and speeches marking Epiphany in the Russian Orthodox calendar, the celebration moves outside for wild dancing as the afternoon sun sets over frozen ground. (Photo: Vyacheslav Rishko)

Outside the palisade of the museum and community hall in Seliyarovo, Eduard, the three-fingered accordion player, leads an old Russian goodbye song as a visitor from across the pole departs.

A desk made of ice in Ded Moroz's (Russian Santa's) underground village, created in a repurposed Cold War food storage tunnel carved into a permafrost hill near Yakutsk, Sakha Republic. (Photo: Ruslan Skrybykin)

Oktyomtsy, north of Mongolia in the Sakha Republic, midwife/farmer Marta xandra Uvarov (*right*) poses with her engineer daughter, Olga.

matter where a traveller goes in the circumpolar Arctic world, the Bear constellation, 3ig Dipper, always points to Polaris (the North Star), which itself is often bathed in the ting greens, pinks, and blues of the aurora borealis.

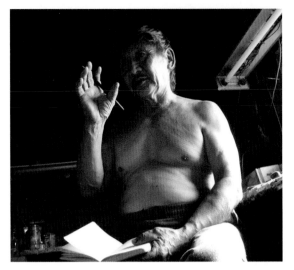

Boris Fedorovich Neustroev, a.k.a. Mandar Uus—incomparable artist, blacksmith, blessing maker, and Son of Raven—in his forge on the Road of Bones.

Mandar Uus etches intricate carvings into a sacred cup called a *choron*. This cup is used to serve *kumys*, a drink made of fermented horse milk.

Molten slag is separated from doré—an amalgam of pure silver and gold—in the refinery of Kupol mine, north of the Arctic Circle in Chukotka.

that inside the church. Not really knowing what was happening next, Slava and I followed Eduard and the rest of the fur-clad delegation through the narrow streets of town until we came to the house of the original nineteenth-century merchant, Yevgeny Iohimovich Ryazantsev, who had put this town on the map.

After a walk through the main house, we headed out into an enclosed compound. With a showman's flair, Eduard threw open the double door of the wooden outbuilding and ushered us inside. Before my eyes could adjust to the light, and before I could really absorb the visual feast of colour and frill and form against the backdrop of log walls, an ample woman with a beaming smile, in a brightly coloured kerchief, pearls, and an intricately embroidered Russian *sarafan* dress, swept forward from the group holding out a round golden-brown ceremonial loaf of bread. Set into a round hole cut into the egg-varnished and braided top of the loaf—called a *karavay*, as Slava later explained—was a ramekin of sea salt.

"Please," she said, pushing the baked masterpiece toward me. With the eyes of several dozen villagers focusing on this tableau, I had a momentary flash of panic, not having a clue what to do. But one of the people just behind the woman stepped forward and pantomimed two movements. She put her hands together, rolled her thumbs apart, then held one hand flat and tapped it with closed fingers of the other. And that's when it twigged: staff of life, salt of the earth. Welcome.

Still not really wanting to damage the perfection of the loaf, but with the urging of the crowd, I reached out and tore off a piece of the bread. My instructor was nodding vigorously and repeating the tap-tap-tap hand gesture. Following somewhat blindly but now getting swept into the energy of the place and the people, I tap-tap-tapped the torn morsel of bread into the salt and popped it in my mouth. People clapped and cheered. Others followed suit. A blessing was given.

"What the hell is going on here?" I whispered to Slava. "Have we just stumbled in on a day when something like this was happening?"

"Yes and no," he replied conspiratorially. "Normally on the last day of Svyatki, of the Russian Orthodox Christmas season, which happens between January 7 and 19, there is a feast. This is to celebrate Epiphany, the day we celebrate the baptism of Jesus. On this day, all waters are holy. They are saying that waters connect all life. These people knew you were coming, so they just held off with their celebration for a few weeks. You have been welcomed with *khleb da sol*: bread, from wheat, the staff of life, and salt, a symbol of loyalty and friendship. The round loaf symbolizes the sun. Sharing these sacraments at the feast of Epiphany means that you, as a guest, have joined with the master of the house in friendly relations, to share your joys, troubles, and worries with everyone who shares in the meal."

"Jesus!"

"Yes, James. Enjoy."

And so we sat down and the toasts began.

"To the Russian frost," called Eduard, who had changed into a ceremonial shirt.

"To the Russian frost," was the communal response. Slava did his best to explain some relationship between vodka, which was

40 percent pure alcohol, and ambient temperatures in this area, which often approach forty below. Toasting the frost with vodka was somehow a way to revel in the hardships of Siberian life. Or something like that. But before I could delve any deeper into that mystery, the meal was served.

We began with *czarskaya ukha* (three-fish soup), which, Slava explained, must be served with vodka and the words of an elder. And from there, our culinary migration moved to boiled reindeer tongue, pressed rolled meat with pickle, and more beautiful breads. Then chunks of *muksun*, that succulent whitefish, some salted and some served fresh frozen in chunks, landed on the table. That was followed by pickled herring from downriver with cranberries from up on the ridge. Pickled cabbage from the garden, salted down and loaded with vitamin C. More toasts. More food. More laughter and stories. Then songs.

Just as the dancing began, there was a percussive rap on the door. And another. Without further warning or ceremony, in blew a host of young people in peasant dress, wearing masks and loud makeup. They yelled, cheered, sang, and twirled wooden clackers like ones you might see at an English soccer game. Like mummers in a Newfoundland home invasion—soulers, galoshins, guysers, gypsies—whatever they might be called, the needy had crashed the feast, and with them was a smallish person dressed as a bear. With aprons and skirts cupped up into baskets the mummers swished and swirled around the room collecting food and sweets, all the while insulting the hosts and berating the guest, all in good fun, of course.

It was a scene straight out of Tolstoy's *War and Peace*, Book

Seven, where "Hussars, ladies, witches, clowns, and bears, after clearing their throats and wiping the hoarfrost from their faces in the vestibule, came into the ballroom where candles were hurriedly lighted. The clown Dimmler and the lady Nicholas started a dance. Surrounded by the screaming children the mummers, covering their faces and disguising their voices, bowed to their hostess and arranged themselves about the room."

A century and a half later, that is exactly what played out in Seliyarovo that Arctic winter evening. The visitors with corked eyebrows and mustaches (most of the Seliyarovo mummers seemed to be young women) stuffed their pretty little faces with handfuls of food on the fly as they harangued their way around the tables.

The room was infused with rhythm and energy, but instead of dancing inside, the instigators grabbed the Canadian guest by the arm, scooping up my coat, and whisked me out the door and into a frozen courtyard where music and singing blared from a pair of speakers that had been set up. Suddenly the courtyard was alive with bumping, turning, promenading, boogying revellers. At minus twenty-five, breath from fifty "perspiring, flushed, and merry faces" hung like smoke against distant gas flares and emerging stars in a deep blue Arctic sky.

At one point the chief mummer, a winsome woman in her twenties, in an outrageous curly blond wig and with lipstick smeared all over her face, hip-checked me into a snowbank, before reaching to yank me back into the action with a deft elbow swing and cackle of delight. Seeing that this was now an acceptable dance move, others did the same, and it wasn't long before there were dancers wallowing in the snow and a friendly snow-ball fight was in full swing, all in time to the music, of course.

All too soon, it was time to say our goodbyes and reload the van. While we had been collecting our things to depart, Eduard had once again shouldered his accordion and, with a group of revellers who had spilled out through the fence surrounding the playground, was singing some kind of goodbye waltz, which everyone knew. Above them in the dim light fluttered a flag with Seliyarovo's stylized crest showing reindeer antlers, a bird, a fish, a tree, and a spurting oil pipeline all in equal proportions. But it was the open faces and the energy of this still robust group that brought tears to my eyes.

Still psychically sated by all that had happened, I contemplated the realities of the continuing journey as I made plans to pack and move on. On the way to the airport for an early morning flight a few days later, I was concerned about the excess-baggage charges of travelling with winter clothing and lots of books, CDs, and bottles of maple syrup for gifts. Slava told me not to worry. "We'll find someone who is leaving without luggage and they will take your extra bag."

"Come on, Slava," I replied. "What is the chance that some-body is going to be leaving Siberia in the middle of the winter with no luggage? And what about security regulations? I don't think you are allowed to check anyone else's bag, are you?"

"No, not technically," he said. "Everyone does it. You will be fine."

When we arrived in the ultra-modern airport in Khanty-Mansiysk, I got into line behind a group of tall handsome men in fancy red and blue embroidered parkas and natty warmup suits. "These guys are part of the Russian biathlon team," Slava whispered. "There are five of them and their coach has a baggage allowance for eight. I told him you were Canadian. He agreed to take your bag. I hope you don't mind—I just gave him the maple syrup you just gave me as a gift. Please give me your passport."

There I stood, a passportless Canadian who had just foisted one of his bags onto the coach of the Russian biathlon team. I looked at the broad shoulders and slim hips of the willowy blond, clean-shaven biathlete who stood directly ahead of me in line. This thick-waisted, middle-aged Canadian Viking would surely never be mistaken for an Olympian, even if the luggage tags matched. In the nick of time, Slava returned without the bag and gave me my passport. I was checked in without incident, through security and in the departure lounge.

The flight boarded on time, and by the luck of the draw I landed in an aisle seat next to two of my fellow team members, neither of whom had any idea that I was now one of them. Two others and the coach sat across the aisle. The flight was full and everyone was seated. But nothing was happening. Things started to get interesting when a police officer, with his braid and brass and distinctively upswept military brimmed cap, came aboard and conferred with the in-charge flight attendant. She consulted a list and together they started making their way toward the rear of the cabin. My heart missed a beat when they stopped at row 16.

I was just about to offer a full confession, certain that our luggage ruse had been discovered, when the flight attendant turned the other way and asked one of the young athletes to come with her and the security officer. A few minutes later, the chap returned and spoke to his coach, whose gaze fell to me while he was speaking. Then he began speaking to me in Russian. Mercifully, Elena Gaisina from the Canadian Embassy was booked on the same flight and seated nearby, and it was she who intervened and clarified what the coach was saying.

"One of the bags belonging to the team has failed security screening," she explained. "At first they thought it was the bag belonging to the first team member. But the bag was not his. They have come to the conclusion that the offending bag is yours. You will have to go with the officer. I will go with you."

I stood up and began to wonder whether the rest of my natural life could be spent in the gulag. Without a word, Elena and I walked up the plane, feeling the stare of every eye on our backs. With one officer ahead and one behind, we were escorted up the jetway, back through the departure lounge, back through security, into the main concourse of the airport, downstairs to the departure area, where we had checked in, and through a locked door into the luggage sorting area.

Because this was the only flight leaving at the time, the luggage sorting area was completely bereft of luggage, except one piece, my camera case, which stood on a conveyor belt with a beautiful drug- and-bomb-sniffing German shepherd sitting beside it.

Blanch.

The senior of two more uniformed security officers spoke to

me in Russian. "They want to know if this bag belongs to you," said Elena.

I nodded.

And then, in English, the officer said, "Open bag."

Referring to an X-ray image on a nearby console, the officer started rifling through the camera and recording equipment, pulling various things out, one by one, and asking what they were. Each piece, in turn, had to be powered up, powered down, and then taken apart until the officers were satisfied with its purpose and function. Eventually, near the bottom of the bag, they pulled out a small hand-sewn leather pouch containing my father's chiming gold pocket watch.

"You are wearing a watch. Why do you need a pocket watch?"

"It belonged to my father, I carry it in his memory. " In truth, I carry it in my dad's memory wherever I go. The daily meditation of winding it ties me back not only to him but also to the early days of exploration and navigation at sea. It was only after the invention of the chronometer that sailors could determine longitude with any accuracy. This chiming gold watch connects my travels to that tradition, but it also is a tangible connection to a very fine moment in the evolution of ideas and design. But as I stood on the cusp of certain arrest for a baggage misdemeanour, even with Elena translating, there was no way all that was going to be communicated without further misunderstanding.

No response. The officer kept digging. I thought of patting the dog to curry favour with that member of the security detail but thought better of it.

Directly under the watch was a plastic container that held twelve AA batteries.

"What is this?"

I motioned for him to pass it over and showed him a dozen spent batteries lined up like little sticks of dynamite, all lined up six-on-six. At that point I began to wonder if, in the X-ray image, the watch and this item had looked like a miniature bomb.

Cords, flashes, laptop computer, other batteries, lenses, camera bodies, digital recorder, notebooks, lens cleaning brush and solution, miniature tripods, gloves, lint-free lens cloth, extra glasses, traveller's cheques and spare credit card under the lining were finally all removed and scattered around on the conveyor belt as if they had exploded from the waterproof black plastic Pelican case. The head man motioned for Elena and me to stand back as he turned and conferred with his colleagues. Then, with a wave of his hand, he indicated that I should return all of the gear to the case and move along.

Elena and I were escorted back upstairs to security, through the departure lounge, down the jetway, and back into the plane. By now, having had twenty minutes or so to talk among themselves, word would have spread about the Canadian terrorist aboard the flight. Eyes on both sides of the plane all the way back to row 16 said as much, or maybe it was just the beginnings of an adrenalin hangover. I know for sure that the coach of the Russian biathlon team won't be doing anybody any favours with luggage any time soon. Nevertheless, it was a gesture of kindness I won't soon forget—but a rough exit from Khanty-Mansiysk.

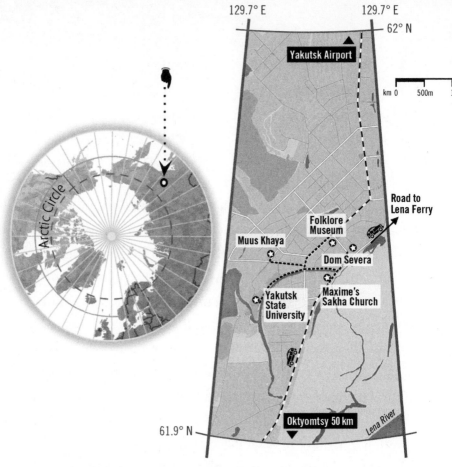

130°E RUSSIA GMT+10

10: SHAMAN'S DREAM

As I had explained back in Moscow at the ambassador's luncheon, one of the original discoveries compelling me to undertake this circumnavigation of the northern hemisphere was the around-the-world journey taken by Sir George Simpson in 1841–42. While I was writing a biography of Simpson, my curiosity was piqued by the many similarities—the Native people, the climate, the company infrastructure—between the North American fur trade and the Russian fur trade. The Russian-American Company, chartered as Russia's first joint stock company by Czar Paul I in 1799, was not as old as the Hudson's Bay Company, chartered in 1673, but it was every bit as robust, and Simpson was able to use its supply lines to travel from the port of Okhotsk, on Pacific waters, to St. Petersburg, just below the Arctic Circle on waters leading to the Baltic Sea.

Simpson had been particularly fascinated not only by what he had heard of the trade in furs in the Russian Far East but also by the trade in the precious ivory of woolly mammoths, being unearthed regularly by indigenous people who fished, hunted, and husbanded reindeer throughout what is now the largest Russian subnational jurisdiction, the Sakha Republic (also called Yakutia). "Sir George was impressed with the price of ivory on the Yakutsk market," I wrote in 2007 in *Emperor of the North*, "as well as with the fact that Providence seemed to have provided an inexhaustible supply of this organic raw material. Yakutsk, after all, is almost at the Arctic Circle."

Now, sitting in a private dining room in the Muus Khaya (Iceberg) restaurant in Yakutsk, I was thinking of Simpson being royally wined and dined by the governor of the city when my elfish translator, Ruslan Skrybykin, leaned over to me and said, "James . . .James, do you . . . do you know what you are eating?" (Ruslan, whose main income stemmed from teaching English as a second language, always said things twice, or three times, with pedantically careful enunciation.)

"Delicious rare tenderloin," I said quietly. "You asked if I would prefer fish or meat, I said meat, so . . . I'm guessing this is . . ."

Unable to contain his enthusiasm for life in general, and for today's main dish in particular, Ruslan interrupted. "It's foal. F-o-a-l. You are eating foal, foal. Do you? Do you know what that is?"

"Baby horse."

"Exactly. Exactly. Exactly. Have you had baby horse before?"

"Not knowingly," I told him, adding that there had been instances of horsemeat getting into fast food restaurants in Canada. By now, Ruslan had leaned well into my Western personal space and was staring intently at my mouth as I chewed.

"How do you? How do you like the taste? The taste?"

Our host, the restaurateur Igor Makarov, who spoke a little English, had overheard enough of this side conversation to draw his full attention.

"Do you like it?" he inquired.

In truth, it was the best meat I'd eaten since the melt-in-your-mouth dolphin steak that Svafar Gylfasson had served me at the Krían Restaurant on Grímsey. Fine-grained, tender, juicy, and grilled to perfection. But I was also glad that, in contrast to the day we shot Flipper, I did not have to witness the demise of the doe-eyed little fellow before his journey to the table began.

Through Ruslan, Igor asked if horsemeat was available for sale in commercial supermarkets in Canada. I said no, but that there were specialty butchers who prepared it for certain ethnic customers.

"We have horses at home," I went on. "My wife and daughters are competitive riders. They are horse lovers. Horses are a big part of our family's life as well. But I'm not sure how they will react when I tell them that I enjoyed a meal of foal here in Yakutsk."

"Here in Sakha, horses are sacred," Igor explained. "They are part of who we are. They have been part of Sakha culture as long as anyone can remember. And, for my part, I can't imagine loving a horse and *not* eating them."

My arrival in Yakutsk had come with high expectations. This was the administrative centre of the largest Arctic republic in Siberia. Having connected through the RAIPON office in Moscow to the much respected Professor Vyacheslav Shadrin, I had decided this thriving Siberian city of 270,000 inhabitants would be a perfect next stop for my research.

But it is a long way from Moscow, the centre of all things Russian. Struggling with the five-hour time change during the six-hour Transaero flight that had delivered me to Yakutsk at five in the morning local time, I finally met Professor Shadrin, barrel-chested and over six feet tall, a gentle giant of a man in his early forties, at the airport. We took a taxi into town and I learned that he had been far busier on my behalf than the paucity of email communication had led me to believe. As a teacher at Yakutsk State University and the Russian Academy of Sciences and a member of the local indigenous council, he was very interested in helping a writer from Canada understand and appreciate what was happening with culture and climate change in Yakutia. What I did not know beforehand was that in addition to being a young academic of considerable intellectual heft in Yakutsk, he was also the headman of the Yukaghir people in Siberia, now numbering just over one thousand and living in pockets spread out over three time zones throughout the Russian Far East.

As we travelled over frozen gravel and broken pavement, Shadrin—Slava—shyly explained in halting English that he had just been elected to his third five-year term as chief. Between calls on his mobile phone as we rumbled and bumped our way through potholes between snowbanks, he said, "They call me about everything. I wish I could solve all of their problems but I can't."

After a brief nap at my hotel, I staggered downstairs to begin exploring Yakutia. I found Slava in the lobby, on his phone, and beside him a diminutive Sakha man in khaki-coloured overcoat and grey woollen toque. This was the inimitable, indefatigable Ruslan.

"Hello. Hello, James. Slava has asked me to translate for you while you are here in the Sakha Republic. He and I have known each other for a long time. I am not cheap but I am very good. I give good value, very good value. I have been teaching English for a long time. In fact, Slava and I met in his home village, Nelemnoye, just north of here, near the Polar Circle. Actually . . . actually, it was very funny. I was a military translator first. But I went there to teach English in the school in Nelemnoye, and the kids asked me, 'Why are you teaching us English?' They did not seem to under-stand why I was there. They said, 'Do the reindeer need to speak to us in English?' Ask Slava, he will tell you. James. James, I am at your service."

At the table in Igor Makarov's restaurant, Ruslan turned and said, "Horsemeat is very good for absorbing radiation. Very good. We have sent horsemeat to Japan since the nuclear power stations were damaged by the tsunami." I didn't have the heart or the time at that point to ask how he came to know this, but given Russia's spotty history with nuclear power, including using thermonuclear bombs to assist with the creation of some of the big diamond mines in Yakutia, I had no reason to think that Ruslan was having me on.

As the meal continued, Igor explained that the Yakut collective spirit that had resisted conquest by the Cossacks was the same vigorous resistance that had kept the Bolsheviks at bay, culturally speaking. And it was this collective feistiness that saw the creation of the Yakut Autonomous Soviet Socialist Republic in 1922. "There are Yakut primary, secondary, and post-secondary schools," he said proudly. "There are Yakut writers, poets, artists, and academics. Yakut politicians. Yakut businessmen, like me. We like to think we govern ourselves, which has always been a bit of delusion."

"We live in a refrigerator," Ruslan quipped. "Things keep well at fifty below."

Slava in his quiet and determined way had planned a week-long agenda for my first visit to Yakutia that left my head spinning. With Slava as the tall and stolid straight man and quixotic Ruslan for editorial comment and one-liners, it was like going to the circus with Abbott and Costello.

As a courtesy Slava arranged a meeting right at the start of my visit with Afanasiy V. Migalkin, chief of the Department of

People's Affairs and Federative Relations of the Sakha Republic. Migalkin seemed neither interested in nor engaged with anything Slava or I had to say, choosing instead to stick close to received government truths that indigenous peoples had thrived during the Soviet period, all of which was dutifully translated by Ruslan.

Afterwards, we had barely stepped onto the street before Ruslan let loose. "Here in Russia, we say, 'There is no truth in legs,' meaning that you are more likely to be given the straight goods by a person who is sitting down. But in your country I believe what you just heard is called bullshit."

We moved from there to Dom Severa, the Northern House, where elders met to discuss important matters. "It used to be," said one elder, "that in this permafrost area, even in summer you had to build a fire to dig a grave deep enough to bury a loved one. Now that is not the case. In town, back in the 1960s, they used to have to build buildings on piles driven four metres into the permafrost to ensure that they would be stable. Now they have to put the piles twice that far, eight metres, into the ground to make sure a house won't topple."

Elsewhere in town, in a square near my hotel, I had seen a great bronze statue of Comrade Lenin on a massive marble base slowly sinking into the melting permafrost. Instead of standing straight-backed, pointing the way to the future, he was leaning dangerously to the right, his place on the square eroded by free-market currents or climate change—take your pick. "The whole city is about to collapse," quipped Ruslan. I told him about the "last monument to Communism" on the road from Murmansk to Lovozero, which left him speechless, if only momentarily.

Like conversations elsewhere, this parley in Dom Severa began with observations about climate change and moved before long into deeper and more troubling matters. "Changes to landscape bring changes to our souls," said one of the elders. "When lands are destroyed, our souls are destroyed too," added another. "And we don't have much say in any of what is going on the land."

"You are from Canada," said an elder who sat directly across the table and who, until this point, had said very little. "What is happening in your country? Is it the same as what is happening here?"

Prompted by Slava, I launched into a sketch of Canadian indigenous land claims in general, including the story of the creation of Nunavut, explaining how, much as in Russia, Aboriginal and treaty rights are enshrined in a constitution as well as in our Charter of Rights and Freedoms. I mentioned that both our governments had issues with the United Nations Declaration on the Rights of Indigenous People; Canada had voted against it initially but eventually endorsed it, and Russia abstained.

The main difference between our two countries was that treaties such as the Nunavut Land Claims Agreement are predicated on fee-simple land ownership, meaning that many indigenous peoples in the Canadian North get to participate fully in development decisions, with all the costs and revenues that those decisions may generate. "It's not perfect but it is very different from here," I explained.

"How did they do that?" the man asked.

"Through resistance, persistence, and negotiation . . . and patience," I replied. "But what is written in law and what happens on the ground are often very different and, in that sense, my country in many respects is no different than yours when it comes to many of the issues that are of greatest concern to you today."

"What troubles us most is the disappearance of language," said Slava, to a full table of nodding heads. He continued, "The Sakha language is strong but the number of speakers is dropping. In the four spheres where language is used—official language, work language, home and family, and communication outside the jurisdiction—the dominant language, Russian, gets stronger every day. For the Evenks, the Evens, the Dolgans, the Chukchi, and my people, the Yukaghirs, there are fewer and fewer speakers every day."

From across the table, another voice added, "A loss of one language is a loss to all mankind. Indigenous languages are far more precise. The soul of a people depends on language."

At that point Ruslan, as was his way, sat forward, dropped his elbows onto the table, and spoke. I was not really sure if he was translating or speaking on his own behalf, but he said, "James. James, if you lose your language you have only your body left. Without language you are no longer human."

Still pursuing the theme of the invisibility of ordinary people, we travelled by car to the agricultural village of Oktyomtsy, population 2,787, fifty kilometres upriver from town. Yakutsk Radio serenaded us with the Beatles singing "All My Loving" as we headed south. There we met Marta Alexandra Uvarov, a gracious seventy-one-year-old who lived in a modest seven-by-ten-metre log home, built by her deceased husband. Attached to this was a garden plot, a tenth of a hectare, that has faithfully produced a hundred forty-kilo sacks of potatoes annually that she has sold to supplement her pension or bartered for meat and milk with her neighbours.

"I was a midwife for thirty-five years," she explained, "working for a time in the north of Yakutia, not far from Nelemnoye, Slava's hometown. But we came back and settled here in 1985. Now my husband is gone. I must live on a pension of eleven thousand rubles [C$350], which would be okay except that my monthly bill for gas and water is seven thousand rubles [C$225], so I must grow potatoes to make ends meet. And, since the flood, I have lost all my seed potatoes. I am now in the process of trying to start again but it is difficult."

The mention of a flood took me by surprise. I had expected that the story would have some kind of connection to climate change or a tale of unexpected extreme weather events that might be tied to changing global weather patterns. Indeed, this was a phenomenon throughout the world, including the North, that seemed to be occurring with increasing frequency. But as we toured the village after our meal, admiring the wandering cows and the sturdy little Siberian horses that had survived the flood, and as we sat down for another pot of herbal tea, the story Marta had to tell about the flood was more a cautionary tale about government and speeded-up resource development in the Russian North, and who participates in decision making—or not.

In the spring of 2010, Marta's husband was in hospital and she had to spend a lot of time running back and forth to Yakutsk to be with him. Her son, Alexander (Sasha), looked after a couple of cows they had and made sure that the house stayed warm. But that year had been a year of very little snow. It had been cold but there was not much precipitation on the ground. The broad Lena River was as low as it had been in some years when it froze in October, and many came to the conclusion that the river likely froze right to the bottom that winter.

So when spring came and the sun started to melt the snows on southern slopes, and rivulets of water turned into streams that found their way to mighty Eh-Beh—the Mother River— there was no place for the water to go, because the main channel was blocked with ice. Sasha was at the farm and got a message through to his mother to say that he was taking what he could onto the roof but that no one knew if the water would rise. Gas and electricity supplies to the village were cut off. And that was the last they heard until a few days later.

The water peaked at four in the morning on May 20. Sasha did his best to protect their belongings, but the water rose over the root cellar, ruining the next year's seed crop for the best potatoes in the republic. Horses and cattle drowned. Before the water started to recede, a few days later, Oktyomtsy was devastated and Marta's husband had died in hospital. By the time she was able to get back to the farm, the seed stock was mouldy and covered with silt in the root cellar, and the house her husband had built, the place that had shaped her life and her children's character, was a total shambles.

"People said this was the first flood our village had experienced in a hundred years," Marta said, with tears in her eyes. "Other times when the river would freeze solid or an ice dam would form at the confluence of the Olyokma River and the Lena, the government would use bombs to blast the ice and let the water through. This time, though, there was no bombing because of the gas pipeline that runs in the bottom of the river between here and Yakutsk."

"So this flood had really nothing to do with an early spring, or a freak weather event that might have been related to a changing climate?" I asked.

"No. They would not blast the ice for fear of damaging the pipeline."

"So they damaged the lives of the people of Oktyomtsy instead?" I continued.

"Da. Da, da, da."

Proposed in 2001 to move Russian crude oil 4,857 kilometres from Tayshet in Irkutsk to Skovorodino and on to the terminal in Vladivostok, the Eastern Siberia–Pacific Ocean pipeline included a leg constructed between Oktyomtsy and Yakutsk in

March and April of 2009. The original plan called for a tunnel below the riverbed, but the modified plan, which was ultimately approved, set the 1.22-metre-wide pipe in a trench on the bottom of the river. It was particularly sturdy pipestock that was used in this section of the corridor and it was built to withstand anything the river might throw at it, but it was not designed to withstand conventional Russian techniques for blasting ice dams to keep villages like Oktyomtsy from being flooded.

"The government compensated people for their cows," Marta said. "But they have said that we should all move or we will not get one more ruble of help. I don't want to move. This house is a monument to my departed husband. He built it with his own hands. We raised our children here. When we came here, the soil could grow only grass. I have worked that soil with my hands, year by year, and have made this little farm very productive. I am proud of what has been accomplished here. I will not move."

"Can't you go to the government to say that that is not good enough? Can't you complain?" I asked.

Marta visibly deflated and her eyes lost their spark. "This topic is closed for public discussion. We don't speak to the government in this country like you do in your country. Now they are talking about a bridge near here. I am worried that this will create another whole series of problems for us," she sighed.

"So we do what we can. I do my yoga. And I am president of the Grannies' Club in this village. Our motto is 'Help yourself.' Please, have more tea."

It is only looking back on that first winter experience in Yakutia, which was followed by a second visit the following summer for another series of adventures in the Siberian Arctic, that I can see a very carefully constructed curriculum created by the kindness, generosity, and genius of Slava Shadrin, professor and Yukaghir chief.

As happened in Murmansk and Moscow, Salekhard and Khanty-Mansiysk, my itinerary included visits to a number of museums where aspects and artifacts of indigenous life would be arranged in some kind of linear narrative that invariably began with geology and dinosaurs, volcanoes and woolly mammoths, and worked its way through dioramas of noble savages living off the land and reindeer pulling sleds then and now, to the silvered extravagances of czars and kings, the triumphs of the revolutions, the sacrifices of the patriotic wars, and eventually the contradictory successes of Soviet supremacy. But Slava did his best to set all that in a real human context, in its many dimensions. A case in point was a pair of visits with two people who routinely left the realms of conventional time and space.

First, Ruslan and I were invited to visit with Aiza P. Reshetnikova, the director of the Yakutia People's Music and Folklore Museum. Aiza, Slava told us, had been a concert pianist in her younger days but now devoted her life to gathering, protecting, and preserving folklore of all the various peoples throughout the region. I wasn't really sure what the visit to Aiza's museum might add to other folklore learnings. Slava obviously knew otherwise.

Aiza welcomed us into a conventional museum setting, lined with outfits and artifacts, printed wall panels, and various TV screens that flickered in the subdued overhead lighting of the building. But rather than set us loose to pick a path through the various stops and exhibits, she pulled up three plain wooden chairs and told a story about the creation of the world.

In the beginning there was darkness, she told us. "This is the Yakutian folk tale that I have suggested should be told at the opening of the opening of Sochi Olympics in 2014." The Olympics were opened with a spectacular show that included a host of uniquely Russian stories but, alas, Aiza did not get her wish.

In the beginning there was a big ballgame in this area. People played and played in the darkness until their ball disintegrated. At that point, Raven—"I've met Raven at every stop on my Arctic journey so far," I just had to tell her—flew high into the upper world and brought back two balls, which he returned to the middle earth in his big beak. From one appeared the sun and from the other appeared the moon.

Joining all this together was a sacred tree, whose branches reached up into the heavens and whose roots plumbed the depths of the underworld. Raven then created two special characters in the middle earth to help humans to navigate this complex cosmological environment, Aiza explained. The *algyschyt*, or blessing maker, connected to the upper world, and the shaman or black shaman (an Evenk term) to the underworld.

Aiza led us to a huge diagram on the wall that showed the great tree and the concentric layers of both worlds, upper and lower, converging in mirror images as orange and yellow corn kernels or magnetic force fields joining in the middle of the image. The only animate figure on the entire image was a raven that appeared to be on its way from the second layer of the underworld toward middle earth.

"Shamans were very important connectors in all the cultures of Yakutia. But after the Revolution, they were given a choice by the Stalinists," she said "They could break and burn their drums or be shot. Many of them died by their own choosing, given that option."

Just as I was getting ready to accept that what the director was describing was something long gone, long past, she explained that with the founding of the Russian Federation and the collapse of Communism, shamanism has come back across northern Asia. Some consider it the official religion of the Sakha Republic. "There was a shamans' conference here in Yakutsk back in the early 1990s," she said, with a smile. "It is a spiritual tradition that lives on."

"What is the connection between the shaman and the raven?" I had to ask. "Are they one and the same?"

"Well, not exactly," replied Aiza, "but they are related. The raven god, Uluu Suorun Toyon, lives in the fifth layer of the upper world. His sons are the shaman and the smith, the armament maker, both of whom are connected with fire and with the sun god, Urun Ajyy Tojon. The smith or *algyschyt*, the blessing maker, connects people with the goodness of the upper world."

She beckoned us to follow her to an electric piano she had set up in the centre of the shamanic area of the museum. "The power of the shaman is legendary," she explained as she sat down and her practised fingers touched the keys. "Normally a shaman's dream journey to heal a person would last several hours, maybe all night long. I have written a composition for piano that is much shorter, but it is meant to take you into the shaman's journey. I would like to play it for you now."

As if she were entering some kind of trance, Aiza paused, and we watched as she gathered herself physically and mentally before starting on the lower registers of the piano. First she created rumbling sounds with her left hand that were answered with much lighter chatter in the upper register played with the right hand, as if her two hands were talking to each other. Notes in the lower register increased in volume and intensity and became more dissonant. As the energy of the piece built even further, her right hand began beating like a bird's wing on an oval drum sitting on the upper deck of the piano, where sheet music might have been.

With her eyes closed, her body swayed from side to side, sometimes rhythmically, sometimes spasmodically, as the walking beat of the music accelerated to a jog and then a run, broken by splashes of discordant notes played with fingers together on flat hands. High crashes followed by low crashes were joined with occasionally melodic chords and ascending or descending notes in the middle octaves of the piano. The tempo by now had accelerated to a sprint, and the sound was so loud that it was banging off the glass cases in the museum and making the skin-covered drum dance on the upper deck of the piano. As I rested my eyes for a brief moment on that drum, it occurred to me there was something more going on here than a strictly musical performance.

With the music at panic pace, her fingers ran up and down the keys, like some kind of a cross between the scary bits of

Mozart's *Magic Flute* and the scratchy underworld fiddle talk of the Charlie Daniels hit "The Devil Went Down to Georgia." The mix of chords, discords, and chaotic tonal jumps up and down was building, intensifying. Her whole body was now driving the performance. Finally, at the end of an intricate glissando that emerged from the continued deep rumbling from the bowels of the instrument, there was a percussive filigree of high notes that sounded like a shriek, and she finished by drawing both hands from high notes to low, black notes and white, in a cascade into silence that left even the usually talkative Ruslan speechless.

"In the end, the shaman loses consciousness," Aiza said after she opened her eyes and returned to the verbal storytelling. "Now that he has identified the evil spirit hiding in the great tree of life, he instructs his assistants to make sparks using stones. Lightning then seeks out and kills the evil spirit. And when he returns to consciousness, the shaman would usually describe to the sick person what he has seen, what he has done about it, and what he has seen of your future in the other world."

Aiza continued and Ruslan started to laugh, which seemed somehow incongruous with the intensity of the tone of the musical storytelling that had just happened. "Aiza says that while she was playing, she was thinking that your travels will be very fruitful for you and useful for us."

Having beheld this remarkable performance, I began to wonder if this pianist-cum-composer might be as much shaman as museum director.

There was no doubt, however, when Slava set up a meeting a couple of days later with a man he called "the last of the Evenk shamans." "He has agreed to meet you in his worshipping place down near the river. He has a wedding to attend in the middle of the afternoon and one in the evening, but he has some time between."

At the appointed time, Ruslan and I walked past a number of *sergey* (ceremonial Sakha horse hitching posts) and up the steps of a handsome wooden building, which, like Dom Severa, appeared to have been inspired by the multi-sided Sakha birchbark-covered summer houses we had seen in the countryside around Yakutsk.

When the wedding party moved to a more informal grouping for photos, Maxime Duran, a wisp of a man, much younger than I'd expected, approached us. He wore baggy grey flannels, a baby-blue cable-knit sweater, and wire-rimmed tinted glasses that he was forever pushing up the bridge of his nose. Around his neck on a lanyard was a wooden stick, like a little canoe paddle, with a hole burned through its distal end. We shook hands. He pointed to a table with paper plates, plastic cups, bread, cake, and jugs of what looked like rancid whey or curdled milk, and then suggested that we enjoy some refreshment while we waited.

Just as Sir George had done, though not from plastic cups, we drank *kumys*, fermented mare's milk. The taste was as I'd imagined it to be, acidic like yogourt or sour cream, though thin and nearly clear as vinegar as it rolled over my tongue. It was the lumps and other particulates in the mix that brought on an almost instant gag reflex.

Twenty minutes later, Maxime reappeared and beckoned us into the sanctuary of his animist church. Inside was a large real tree with branches reaching up to a skylight in the top of a rotunda at least three stories above our heads. On many of the branches were beautifully carved white cranes. Spring sun streamed in through the skylight, highlighting wisps of smoke lingering from the wedding ceremony. He invited us to sit down on carved stools beside a small round table.

Taking a seat himself, he snapped a lighter and lit a mixture of herbs in a small bowl. Bending forward, he laid his head sideways on the table and for several minutes breathed quietly on the embers, nurturing them to continue burning with smoke but no flame.

The purification ritual complete, we began our conversation. Although I was full of questions, with the air thick with sweet smoke, it seemed an unlikely time to begin any kind of inquisition. Not knowing what Slava might have told Maxime about the Canadian visitor, Ruslan started in with a bit of an explanation about my journey around the world and my interest in peoples of the circumpolar world. There was a long pause after Ruslan had finished. Maxime put his head down again and encouraged the smudge with his breath.

After another awkward pause, he took the burnt stick on the lanyard around his neck in his right hand. He put it up to his eye like a jeweller's loupe. Looking through the hole, he leaned down again and examined the tendrils of smoke. Then he sat up and looked above and beside me on either side but not directly at me.

As he was doing that, Ruslan said, "A shaman is called a person with an open body. They are open to what is in the air and they are able to see things that we can't." But as quickly as he had taken up his shaman's loupe, Maxime let his tool fall back down onto his sweater and picked up the smallest of four or five ceremonial wooden drinking vessels.

"The *choron* tells us many things about our culture," Maxime began. "It is made of birch, our sacred tree. It is used most often for drinking *kumys*, our sacred beverage. It has three legs, which reminds us that a man has three parts to his life, three worlds, three souls, three parts to his beliefs."

Running his fingers along and around the ornate vertical and zigzag patterning around the cup, he added, "These circles remind us that all nations are eternal. The *choron* is open on the top, reminding us that all blessings come from above." He launched into a version of the story Aiza had told us about the sacred tree and the middle world joining the nine layers of the upper world and the nine layers of the lower world. But then things got personal.

"People have had this wisdom for a long time," he continued. "First the Christian church came, and at that point much of traditional spirituality was pushed out of the mainstream. After the Revolution, these teachings were forbidden. My great-grandfather was killed by the Bolsheviks. He had a choice of either breaking his drum or forfeiting his life. He would not break his drum. My grandmother and my mother were healers too, although in their day shamanism was still forbidden. No one talked about it in the open."

"So how did you learn to do what you are doing here?" I asked.

"First, I studied to be a doctor in the Russian system. Then I did studies in Evenk and Sakha culture. I learned Chinese medicine and other alternative healing techniques like herbal remedies and leech therapy. I also learned the skills of a cashier, so that I could get enough money to keep my studies going. I am thirty-seven now. Since the collapse of the Soviet Union, it has been possible to practise more traditional spirituality right here in Yakutsk.

"Since the days of the Cossacks and the first Orthodox priests coming into our area, people have kept almost a double belief system. These young people getting married this afternoon were doing what they are now free to do. They got married officially in the Orthodox cathedral in Yakutsk, but they came here for a traditional Sakha ceremony." At that point, Maxime had to take a call on his cellphone.

While he was on the phone, Ruslan whispered, "Shamans are healers. They have always been responsible for people's health. Shamans also perform rituals and ceremonies, like what happened here today with the wedding and what is going on now. Sometimes the healers who do that are called white shamans. The shamans who get involved with the evil spirits and work themselves into a trance and a situation like the one Aiza described in her music are called black shamans, brought by Raven. Many Sakha believe all diseases and human problems are caused by invasions of evil spirits or the escape of one of their souls. For that, they come to Maxime. In a contest in Khabarovsk a while ago he was recognized as one of the best seers, one of the people with the best extrasensory perception in Russia."

Maxime finished his phone call, but before he could start in again with his teaching, Ruslan decided that what should happen next was a little demonstration. After a somewhat lengthy conversation with Maxime, during which the shaman looked to be protesting and looking at his watch, Ruslan turned to me on his little carved stool and said, "Maxime has agreed to look into your future to see what's in store for circling the midnight sun."

Maxime gestured for me to stand and then crossed the wooden floorboards to the centre of the room. He flicked the lighter, fired up the smudge another time, and wafted sweet smoke all around me. Then, with his loupe, he started examining the air around me, circling, moving closer and then farther away.

This went on for perhaps ten minutes. Different positions. Different places in the room. Eyes open. Eyes closed. And then we all returned to the little round table.

Maxime sat silent on his stool with his eyes closed.

"What did you see?" asked Ruslan impatiently.

"I didn't see anything, really," replied Maxime. "You are closed."

"Perhaps it is a cultural difference," I suggested.

"No," said Maxime, "I didn't see much at all. All I saw was a line."

He drew an imaginary line on the table with his finger. "There are dots along the line like this," he added. "And then there is another line here, and another straight line here, touching the first line here. There are more dots here. And then here, there is a wavy line," he said, again making an imaginary mark on the table with his finger. "This may be the shore of a lake." Retracing with his finger the lines and dots he had drawn, he stopped his finger on a particular place and said, "Do you live here?"

Ten thousand kilometres from home on the dark side of the circumpolar moon, as it were, the man in the blue cable-knit sweater had drawn an almost perfect map of the roads, lane-ways, and scattered houses in the village where I live in eastern Ontario, right down to the odd angles of intersection of various streets, the relative distance between houses, and the proximity to a lake—Cranberry Lake in the Rideau Waterway between Kingston and Ottawa.

Totally unfazed by my surprise and incredulity, Maxime persisted with his contention that he had not seen much of anything in my aura. I, however, was absolutely intent to hear what might come next from his mouth.

"I see a big blue mountain. You might be climbing a mountain backwards. What you are doing is challenging. And somehow," he added after yet another pause, "I see the number thirty-five as significant in your life."

"Does any of that make any sense to you, James?" Ruslan asked.

"The map for sure. The blue mountain, the backward mountain climbing, and the number, not so much. Perhaps time will tell." In truth, however, the words didn't come easily, as I was still more or less speechless from having watched a total stranger halfway around the world draw a detailed map of my hometown with nothing more than information gathered "in the air."

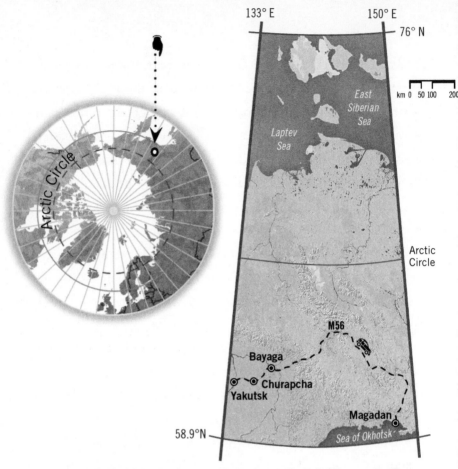

132°E RUSSIA GMT+10

11: ROAD OF BONES

All too soon, the winter visit to the Sakha Republic came to an end, forcing me to scuttle home to tend to other things. But the following summer, with Slava's continuing help, I returned. I found myself squeezed in with two strangers in the back seat of a battered and dusty four-wheel-drive mud buggy barrelling down a dirt road in central Siberia—a road that is smooth only when it's frozen.

It was August and the road surface was definitely not frozen. A couple of decades ago, summer permafrost could be found eighty centimetres below the surface at that time of year. Thanks to a warming climate, the lower limit of this "active layer" had crept farther below the surface year by year to nearly twice that distance. That night, the only thing the adjective "active" modified with any accuracy was the surface of the road, alive with mud where rainwater had pooled and seething desert dust everywhere else.

Driving as fast as fate would allow on either surface caused the knobbly tires to swoon and the vehicle to twitch unpredictably. Had there not been three of us shoehorned into this minuscule back seat, providing onboard padding for one another, this would have been an impossible ride.

At the wheel, with his thinning dark hair sticking up on top and cropped right to the skin about his ears, was Kassiean, driving as if he were in an armoured personnel carrier or possibly a tank. Hands at ten and two on a custom steering wheel the size of a dinner plate, he saw no rut too deep to enter at speed. If you can drive into it, then you can drive out of it, either on the ground or in the air, with most of your rattling bits still attached.

Apparently, Kassiean had once driven roads like this, and some rough tracks too, for his job as a military driver. That was before the Soviet Union collapsed and left thousands of military jarheads to their own devices with little but the uniforms on their backs and a few rubles for bus fare home. For Kassiean, the device of choice was a tired old right-hand-drive Nissan Safari Granroad, which, with a little tinkering and some new tires, reconfigured the unemployed soldier into an occasional cross-country taxi driver.

In the other front seat was my loyal confidant and research convenor Slava Shadrin, who had orchestrated my winter visit a few months previous. This second Sakha sojourn had started a week ago with a discussion in a classroom in Yakutsk with Sakha leaders from all walks of life, to see where my research might go from there. There were a couple of college professors, a publisher, an artist, and others who listened intently as Slava spoke of my quest to understand how northern peoples are responding to shifting climate and the other forces of change that are affecting their lives.

At one point, as the group mined their own contact lists to see who could help answer the kind of questions I was asking for my book, two or three of the group got on their cellphones and called people across the region. It was an almost comical scene, these well-dressed, confident people, stuffed into 1950s-era student desks that we'd pulled into a circle for this meeting, talking on the latest digital devices.

It was through this collective investigation that they realized the revered Sakha cultural leader Boris Fedorovich Neustroev—affectionately nicknamed Mandar Uus, Mandar the Artist—was in town for a teachers' conference, and he was looking for a ride home. A few more calls and everything was settled. Mandar was keen to return to his village, Bayaga, in the Tattinsky district of central Yakutia, right on the Kolyma Road. So if the visiting traveller would like to find a vehicle and pay for its hire, Mandar would be happy to go with him and host the traveller at his home.

This was a win-win situation, with one small catch, which everyone thought would be just fun. Mandar had been asked in his capacity as an *algyschyt*, Sakha blessing maker, and something of a cultural celebrity, to say a few words at a wedding in Churapcha, an agricultural community of seven thousand people about halfway along our journey. The Canadian traveller would be welcome there too, he told the group over the phone.

I overheard a couple of people in the group talking and nodding enthusiastically as this call was going on. "They are saying that they might like to spend such time with Mandar as well. They are saying you are fortunate to have this opportunity," said Slava.

So in the back of the Nissan, behind Kassiean, was this character Mandar, a diminutive man who seemed bothered not at all by the limited space for legs and feet behind the driver's seat. Between the two of us was Sergei, Slava's young cousin who had just graduated with a degree in English literature from Yakutia University. A skinny kid in pointy black leather shoes, skintight stovepipe pants, and a T-shirt that said "Abercrombie NY" in bold red letters, he seemed a bit ambushed by Slava's offer of temporary employment as a translator. Ruslan, alas, was translating at a conference at a resort on the Black Sea and was unavailable. It soon became clear that Sergei had not done much in the way of oral practice to get his English degree. He seemed to know how words and concepts flipped from one language to the other, but he couldn't quite get them out of his mouth. What was clear, and quite charming, was his excitement about being with Mandar.

I caught Mandar's dancing eye from time to time as he chatted with Sergei and Slava in the car, his sun-livened face and expressive hands speaking volumes about his role as a revered member of the Sakha community. Mandar's trade, handed down to him by his father, who had received it from his father before that, was smithing: making armaments on a forge. Fitting, I thought, as the story of this polyvalent vocation unfolded, that the one who makes breastplates, swords, and helmets is also one of the principal keepers of culture in the Sakha tradition. In truth, the *algyschyt* is only one rung down the Sakha spiritual hierarchy from the shaman. Mandar was a man of very considerable influence.

Given centuries of czarist and Communist oppression, which saw shamans and Christian clerics crushed with equal zeal, it was no easy job being the keeper of anything non-Russian. Travelling along the Kolyma Road exemplified the massive dimensions of Mandar's challenge.

Snaking east just below the Arctic Circle for about two thousand kilometres from the village of Nizhny Bestyakh, on the east bank of the Lena River opposite Yakutsk, to the city of Magadan, on the Sea of Okhotsk, the Kolyma Road is one of the most storied trails in Russia, possibly the world, and it's not a happy story. The Arctic here, as elsewhere around the circumpolar world, is rich in lumber, gold, silver, platinum, tin, tungsten, mercury, copper, antimony, peat, coal, and oil and gas. To access the gold of the Kolyma region, Joseph Stalin used forced labour to build a road to those resources through what Aleksandr Solzhenitsyn came to call the Gulag Archipelago.

Here in Kolyma, so Slava said, there were twelve months of winter, and the rest of the year was summer. There had been a little less winter since the advent of global warming, compared with conditions back in the 1920s and '30s when the road was built, but the area was legendary for its harsh conditions. Ask anyone who had built such roads in Greenland, Scandinavia, or North America. It was an ideal place neither for construction nor for the construction workers. If the winter cold didn't kill, the summer bugs would. Prisoners built the Kolyma Road through cold, insects, starvation, disease, exhaustion—every hardship imaginable, and some that went well beyond that.

No one knows for sure how many died because, unlike the Nazis who carefully documented their terminal detainees, no one really kept track of individual fates of the artists, scientists, writers, philosophers, intellectuals of all stripes, men and women, young and old, who were summarily convicted as "counter-revolutionaries" under article 58 of the Russian penal code and shipped to their deaths.

Conservative historians estimate at least a million people died on this line through the coldest inhabited land on earth. This midsection of the road became known as the Pole of Cold and Cruelty. Every two metres, on average, a *dokhodyaga* (goner) died and was bulldozed into the roadbed where he fell. For this reason, the track we were on was called the Road of Bones.

Slava and Mandar's indigenous forebears went about their business on the land while all this was going on, farming, fishing, herding reindeer, moving from place to place with the game and the season, trying to stay clear of the government forces. But they too were subject to cruelty by local Communist authorities and, eventually, to state collectivization. In time, like the dissidents and the Christians, the Native people were herded and pressed into service on the Road of Bones. I imagined all of us—the soldier, the student, the smith, the writer, the academic—side by side with picks and shovels, hungry for thin soup and a possible future.

Inside the Nissan as the hours limped by, Kassiean wielded his power as driver and owner of the vehicle like a Kalashnikov, smoking cigarette after cigarette and saturating the cab with the incessant bump and screech of Russian techno-punk dance music. The front speakers were broken or disconnected, so the speakers in the back, which were just above our heads, were pressed into extra-loud service so that the music might make its way to Kassiean at sufficiently numbing volume.

Mandar, Sergei, and I were effectively sitting in one another's laps with our knees around one another's ears. Our voices cracked from yelling over the music. Our throats were clogged with a delicate mix of unfiltered Belomorkanal cigarette smoke and Kolyma dust. While the sun was up and we could see one another, conversation was vaguely possible. But afternoon gave way to evening and, in spite of our northern latitude, the August light waned. By ten o'clock we were being bombarded with techno-punk in darkness. We had long since given up trying to talk in competition with the semi-rhythmic caterwauling of Kassiean's musical divas.

The window on my side wouldn't stay up. And so the talcum powder dust—road material pulverized by logging and supply trucks that ran this road year round—billowed in uninvited. The throbbing music, the cigarette smoke, the dim light, the dust, the oily vapours of five bodies after twelve hours in a hot box, the rodeo lurching of the vehicle, the thinness of the seats—all contributed to creeping claustrophobia bordering on panic.

Fourteen hours in, we had done the wedding and were back in the car. I was fighting the urge to scream as rippling cramps seized my hamstrings. The Kolyma Road. The Road of Bones. It was all I could do to focus away from the discomfort and into the instructive simplicity of happenstance. Skating on the thinnest thin edge of comfort I had known in some time, it dawned on me that this dust we were breathing was not like the dust that used to dance in sunbeams that speared through the old house I grew up in in Guelph, Ontario.

The Kolyma dust contained the DNA of dead dissidents. That night, circulating in the air were the hopes and dreams, the triumphs and disappointments, the first cries and final breaths of the *dokhodyagi*, the doomed. We were breathing the genetic coding of long-ago efforts to tame this land and its people. For what? Gold? Oil? Natural riches? Compliance with the ruling powers?

And then the Nissan started faltering as if it too were thirsting for fresh air. As if in answer to my prayer, Kassiean wheeled to the grassy side of the road as our transport stalled with a final lurch and cough. I have to say that for the first and perhaps the only time in my life, I was happy to be stranded in the middle of nowhere, in the dark, in a bit of a language bind, with four strangers, because stopping meant that breathing fresh air was again, however fleetingly, possible.

Slava and the other two milled around Kassiean, who rummaged through the back to find what he needed from the hodgepodge of a repair kit that he pulled out of a greasy cardboard box. I had taken Latin when I should have taken auto mechanics. There was no chance of technical assistance from the Canadian, even if he could have spoken Sakha or Russian.

To get the blood flowing again, and to stay out of the way, I walked back the way we'd come, into the twilight. With each step, I was engulfed by fresh night air and sweet silence, broken only by the fizz of my ears recalibrating to natural sounds and by the startled croaks of a pair of ravens that apparently hadn't been expecting company at two in the morning.

In the darkness, on the side of the road, my feet crunched sun-dried caribou lichen atop rich carpets of sphagnum moss, which brought to mind the musty smell of cardamom and black olives. And with the dustless cool air came the balm of possibility and black spruce that I had experienced so many times in northern wilderness journeys back home. I'd never been so glad to get out of a vehicle in my life. I walked on.

There was such unspeakable violence in the forced making of this road under my feet. But only steps from the scene of such tragedy was taiga land that showed no human mark. Some called it wilderness. Some called it homeland. The politics of resource development brought joy to some, riches to others; for prisoners of the gulag, it had brought the end.

But in the open spaces, where development seemed distant or detached, something precious loomed in the viridescent silhouettes of stunted conifers against the star-spangled indigo of a fleeting Arctic night sky. Suddenly, far from home, seriously out of my cultural element, entirely dependent on strangers, I was in a very familiar place. I was in the North, in the oneness of the boreal world, with my Canadian Arctic just over the pole. The realization warmed my innards like old malt.

Against the chill in the night air, that insight brought to mind a constellation of experiences I've had across Arctic North America over the past thirty years. The first secrets and the first silences I knew in the Arctic were those found by canoe and showshoe, by dogsled, by ski, and later by snow machine and motor canoe. River campsites. Barren Lands hunts. Winter fishing holes where the wash of the wind and the light filtered through cloud, ice fog, and sky would tinker with perception, causing the horizon to flutter.

These places were etched in memories of sounds underfoot and smells that whisked me to spots on rain-spattered maps in my imagination. Awed by place or by the presence of an all-encompassing whole filled with bears or birds, whales or wishes. We ask, in our dreams, am I the first person ever to sit in this very spot? This is the explorer's conceit, as present and alive today as it was in the glory days of Columbus and Martin Frobisher, or maybe even Leif Ericsson.

In those books and imaginings of my youth, I learned about the naval captain John Ross, who sought the Northwest Passage in 1818. Sailing north up the Davis Strait between Greenland and Baffin Island, he broached pack ice and stopped at what we now know is the mouth of Lancaster Sound. In the ship's log he reported that on the horizon to the west, instead of the continuing waters of Lancaster Sound, there was a range of snow-covered peaks, which he named the Croker Mountains after John Wilson Croker, first secretary of the British Admiralty. There was, as time would tell and as the local Inuit already knew, nothing of the kind at that location. Ross was humiliated when the folly of his observation was revealed.

But the story of the Croker Mountains points to the ease with which misinformation about the ends of the earth got into public consciousness. What the North was and what it was not to the people who lived in the middle latitudes of the earth differed substantially from the views and perceptions of northerners. What we saw in the visual renderings of travellers and explorers and what we read in their accounts could not really be tested for veracity until, as with the Croker Mountains, others followed and found that in a different year, in a different season, with a different set of eyes, the ice at the reported location of Ross's mountains was actually the eastern opening to the fabled passage to the Orient. The stars in whose light I bathed that night would have been there for Ross. To pinpoint latitude, he would have shot Polaris, the North Star, with his sextant. But sometimes even the stars can be deceiving.

How views of the North differ between residents and visitors, however, can be much more subtle. Here in the Arctic, as the Greeks believed, we were "near the bear"—the celestial figure. Ursa Major, the Big Bear, points to Polaris, the Pole Star, which lights the tail of Ursa Minor, the Little Bear.

These bears (which are known even in Polynesia, where bears are never found and the constellations are absent in the night sky) are synonymous with north for any navigator on sea or sky in the middle latitudes of the northern hemisphere. Because Polaris is directly above the geographic North Pole, it is the only star that appears stationary from a rotating earth. As such, Polaris is a guiding star that indicates direction; but also, for those like John

Ross with the ability to determine the angle between the ground and the star, this bearing is equivalent to latitude. At the equator, the Pole Star is right on the horizon (0 degrees, if it can be seen at all), and at the North Pole the Pole Star is directly overhead (90 degrees).

Even in the fading blue of the night sky over the Kolyma Road, I could see Polaris, just barely, nearly 66 degrees over the horizon, for I was sitting just south of the Arctic Circle. With the tink-tink-tink of Kassiean's tools sounding in the background, other perspectives on Polaris drifted into my mind. The Inuit call Polaris Nuutuittuq, and no doubt the Yukaghirs and the Sakha, Slava's and Mandar's peoples, have names for this iconic star as well. But for many indigenous northern travellers throughout the circumpolar world, the star is actually too high in the sky, too far overhead to give them an accurate fix for direction finding. The star that guides us southerners north will not serve us when we get there.

At most stops along the way during my two-year circumnavigation of the world at the Arctic Circle, I explained to people, like Svafar Gylfasson in Iceland, the Sami ladies on the Kola Peninsula, and the Intelligence of the Indigenous Peoples of the North group in Salekhard, that because of climate change many, many people in the middle latitudes were looking to the North. And for many of us, as a result of popular science programs, films like *An Inconvenient Truth*, and campaigns by corporate giants like Coca-Cola, the face of climate change—the crystalline image of all that is right and all that is wrong with the North—is the polar bear, *arktos*, in a warming sea. That night I saw clearly that such interpretations are as illusory as Captain Ross's detailed relief map of the Croker Mountains.

During my memorable meal in the Khanty winter house in Kyshik in the valley of the Ob River, a woman dressed head to toe in fur had assured me that for her people there really is no distinction between bears and people. "We were all bears once and some of us will be again," she said. Maxime Duran had explained to me that he regularly travels in time and space and through the North Star, the portal to his other world. "Just as some people were bears once, and bears were once people, that star is the place where the cosmic traveller can pass through the bottom of the sky into the upper world to have a look around. Let me tell you a little bit about what he sees," Maxime said, as he drew a map on the table of a place he had never been. How little we dwellers of the middle latitudes knew about true exploration.

In time, the banging stopped and I could see by his relaxed silhouette against the brightening sky that Kassiean was having a smoke for the road. The problem turned out to have been an air filter so clogged with dissident dust that, when he pressed the accelerator, the motor would flood with fuel that it could not burn for lack of oxygen. Life's like that sometimes. By then dawn had awakened the green glow of the taiga trees and tundra, and the Nissan threw an elongated shadow over my footprints in the stained yellow roadbed. The stars had faded.

As I turned from where I'd been sitting with my journal—I'd written "You are here" in the middle of an empty page—I saw a tree without bark standing head and shoulders above the rest. A flash on its wind-polished trunk caught my eye. Here in the middle of nowhere, in Siberia, were a few coins and even a couple of Russian bills carefully placed in cracks in the bark. I dug through a mixture of Russian and Canadian coinage in my pocket, looking for a quarter with a caribou to place beside these other offerings. All I had was a toonie, a two-dollar coin with the queen on one side and a polar bear on the other. *Arktos* as an offering. In the moment, it seemed fitting.

The only motivation to get back into the vehicle was the promise of getting to the end of this journey. With its filter clean again, the motor roared strong and off we went. Kassiean lit a cigarette and flipped the tape another time. The music started thumping and soon was mixed with dissident dust. By then the sun had come up, and light on the scene made the whole situation slightly more tolerable. But, truth be told, having been awake for nearly twenty-four hours, I was asleep when the rumbling finally stopped. It was six o'clock, and as memorable as the scene was—of warm morning light bathing small houses and compact log barns, contented cows and a few stray dogs sniffing along fence lines—it was the clean sweet cool air filling my lungs that marked that moment of arrival.

Everyone in Mandar's household was still asleep. So after a quick trip to the outhouse, we quietly entered his mud room and took off our shoes. At Mandar's direction, Slava and Kassiean flopped down on couches in his main room. He ushered Sergei and me up a small spiral staircase to the second floor, where Sergei pulled up a cover on a roll-out mattress in the hall. I was ushered into what appeared to be a child's room, where the woven woollen blankets were neatly folded back in expectation of a visitor. I was road sore from eighteen hours of cramp, and the comfort of being able to stretch out, finally, took me instantly to a place far, far away.

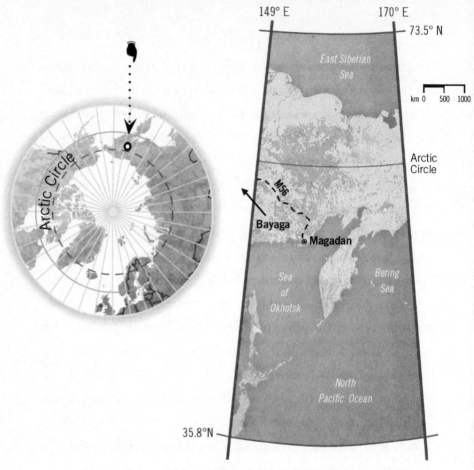

133°E RUSSIA GMT+10

12: MANDAR'S SMITHY

I awoke mid-morning on the second floor of the house that Mandar had built and that he shared with his wife of many years, Fedora Borisovna, and several grown children, their spouses, and his grandchildren. Registering the reassuring smell of fish frying, I closed my eyes again. By contrast to the din and claustrophobia of the road, the quiet of the house, the delicious comfort of the bed, the sunlight filtering through sheer drapes on the window, the occasional raven's croak outside, and the faint memories of home evoked by another family household gave the arrival of this first morning in Bayaga a gauzy, dreamlike quality.

Aside from the muffled kitchen clinks of Fedora cooking, there was no other movement or sound inside the house. I padded down the stairs, sliding my hand down the burnished tree branch that served as an ingeniously installed spiral banister. Fedora smiled and pointed to a wash station near the door. As in every Siberian household I'd been in—perhaps in deference to the dark months of searing cold and the year-round permafrost that lay less than a metre below the ground, where pipes would most certainly freeze and burst—running water consisted of a small metal jug suspended from the ceiling with a metal spigot that released water onto your hands, into a sink, and thence by pipe onto the ground under the house. The toilet was a privy out back.

As I stood by the sink brushing my teeth, Fedora busied herself in the kitchen, where a table was being prepared with butter and waffles, deep-fried bannock, fresh milk, cream, yogourt, condensed milk from a can, dried cranberries, and a glass pot of lingonberry jam. Slava was heaped up under blankets on one couch, still asleep. Kassiean, woken by the sound of my descent on the stairs, had dropped his feet from another couch and, with blankets still around his middle, had lit his first cigarette of the day. On rough-hewn shelves around the main room were books, birchbark baskets, an ornate hand-carved *choron*, papers, family pictures, and drawings. And in among all these effects, situated on tables and low stands, were a couple of radios, a CD player, a flat-screen TV, and a desktop computer.

Heading for the outhouse, I spied a large dish antenna and two other antennas that gave the impression that television, Internet, and probably phone service came to this remote Siberian village by satellite. Stepping past a curious black-and-white cow that had ambled down to investigate the stranger, I was on my way back from the privy when Mandar appeared from an outbuilding with a huge smile. He shook my hand and greeted me in Sakha, communicating with the firmness of his grip and through hazel eyes sparkling in an open face. His day, it appeared, had begun much earlier than mine, even though we had both travelled the same long hours to get here. Oblivious to the language barrier, in the warmth of an Arctic summer sun that had not really set through the night, he gave me a tour of his place. He pointed out the family's first house, a dung-covered vertical log byre or winter *balaghan*, where Sakha families traditionally lived, sharing warmth and living quarters with their stock, mostly cattle. I gathered that he and Fedora had lived here before they built their present place. And, most importantly for the purpose of my visit, he pointed to another log outbuilding, the 160-year-old blacksmith shop where he practised his ancient craft of forging armaments, mostly knives these days.

Standing maybe five foot one and already a grandfather, Mandar still had the shoulders and upper arms of a much younger man. "Welcome, traveller. You are welcome in my home," he said as we moved inside and sat down for breakfast, Slava translating through mouthfuls of hot tea and deep-fried bannock. "I am a traveller too. I have spent my life travelling and learning. It does not surprise me that you have come here, because we are both part of something bigger that is happening in the North along the countries of the polar belt," he said. "Today, we will work in the smithy. I will show you how to make a knife the Sakha way. And we will share stories about our travels."

He picked up the last piece of buttered waffle and led us out. In minutes a hemlock fire was crackling away in the forge and Mandar fed the food to the fire, mentioning that the spirits always had to be thanked before the work could begin. Then he led Kassiean, Slava, Sergei, and me to an anteroom off the smithy where he picked out a couple of rusted tines from what looked to be a fork on a mechanized hay mower. These would be the raw material from which our knives would be heated and hammered.

For the next several hours, we took turns heating the steel in the fire and hammering it into shape, guided by Mandar's instruction. During pauses in the process, when the metal was heating or cooling or when someone was resting from the hot work of hammering, Mandar would sit down on a stool beside his workbench and talk. It was as if the whole thing had been scripted as a trimodal tutorial involving head, hand, and heart; food, fuel, and fire; underworld, middle world, and upper world; stranger, shaman, and smith, to teach the visitor the answers to the questions he had brought to the master's door.

"I am a lucky man," he began with a twinkle in his eye. "I have a good life, a good wife, and a good knife. That is all a man needs." He then situated what we were doing in the biggest possible frame: nine layers in the upper world, nine layers in the lower world, just as Aiza's diagram had shown at the folklore museum. "The place where light and dark, good and evil, come together is the middle world," he explained. "This is where humans live with the spirits of nature. The shaman is the only person who can travel in all three worlds, the smith somewhat as well. Both know how to work with fire. The shaman and the smith are related that way: they are both sons of Uluu Suorun Toyon, the raven god, who inhabits the fifth level of the upper world."

"So both the shaman and the smith are related to the raven?" I asked, testing what I had learned from Aiza.

"Absolutely," he replied. "The raven is a very spiritual bird, a very important animal in Sakha teaching."

"A very important bird throughout the North," I said, explaining how the raven had been a seemingly constant companion in my Arctic travels.

"That doesn't surprise me one bit," Mandar replied. "It doesn't surprise me that you come here either, really, circling the midnight sun."

"Why is that?"

"A long time ago, I had a dream. Maybe fifty years ago. But I remember this dream. It is a dream about uniting peoples of the northern belt—maybe the Arctic Circle, or maybe the belt of stars in the galaxy that can be seen by peoples of the North. It is a dream about a day when northern peoples will have to come together to be heard. I think that day is near."

"Tell me about your dream."

"I was climbing the side of a big mountain."

"Was it a blue mountain?"

"No, it was just a mountain as we have to the east in Sakha country. I discovered an opening in the side of the mountain that led to a cave. Inside the cave, it was very dark, and wet and cold. As I made my way back into the recesses of the cave I could only go by feel. I had to see with my hands. Eventually, I saw a tiny light far away at the back of the cave. I went toward that light for a long time, and when I got close I saw that there were eight people sitting around a fire. They were all elders from different northern peoples: Chukchi, Eskimo, Evenks, Yukaghirs, Sami— all indigenous elders. There was one empty place at the circle. They invited me to take that place.

"I was a young and foolish man at the time. I thought they were just sitting there at the fire doing nothing. But they were talking, and I listened. They were saying that one day there would come a time when peoples of the Arctic belt would be struggling to be heard, and that the only way for their individual voices to be heard would be to unite and speak with one voice. And then I woke up. But I remember that dream always. In hard situations in my life, I remember that circle of elders, and the light circle, and that image helps me in harsh situations. But I think what you are doing is related to this somehow, travelling around the world at the Arctic Circle, bringing northern voices together."

Mandar took his seat by the bench once again. The light of a noon sun detailed the symmetrical movements of his compact hands. It was as if his fingers were tools. They were short and tapered toward trimmed, dirty nails. Muscles and sinew bulged between the joints. The flat surfaces were more or less clean, but the creases and lines in the palms were darkened from years of handling charcoal and black carbon steel. As he spoke, each point had a gesture and a rhythm that made his body and hand movements an integral part of the communication.

"We have three types of language. This you need to understand, if you are to understand what climate change is doing to peoples of the North. First is our inner language. This comes from the heavens and attaches us to a particular place. People from the Sahara Desert have a different inner language than the Sakha. In frost, we will do better. In the heat, the Bedouin will do better because of that inner language. You might think of the inner language as the language of the *salgyn-kut*, the air soul that grows from and into the natural world. The sounds we make are connected to our physical body, which in turn is connected to our breath, and our breath is connected to the heavens. This is why the sounds of language vary in different places on the earth. The earth is different, so the inner language is different."

The crackling of the fire had given way to the glow of coals. "The second language," Mandar continued, "is our mother tongue. The mother tongue is the voice of a nation, the voice of a particular people, like the Sakha, or the Yukaghirs, or the Eskimo, all of the elders around that northern circle of light.

"And the third language appears when nations have relations with other nations. They connect and influence each other. When the Russians came here for the first time, we took words from their language into our language, and they did too. This is called the language of time. In the days of our ancestors, time language was under control of the mother tongue. But now, since contact with the Cossacks, since the Revolution, this time language comes to our mother tongue like a master. And what happens when a guest comes to your home and directs you to live by his rules? Is it possible to be a family under those conditions? I ask you. It is very difficult," he told us.

"So to climate change: the world has been changing since the

Sakha have been on the earth. Our inner language has been changing with the changes in the earth that have happened during that time. But the changes are happening more quickly now. Where there was pasture, there are now shrubs. Where there were small trees are now big trees. The birches used to push against the frost and create the burls I use for my knife handles right at ground level. Now the frost is farther down in the ground and the burls are not as common. Global warming is affecting our inner tongue. And as our children live lives that are less connected to nature, that affects their inner tongue as well. Without a strong inner language, we are less able to defend our mother tongue against the forces of globalization and the mastery of the time tongue. I am concerned.

"In our nation, only the person who knows his own language in its three dimensions can be a great person. The most famous people in Sakha come from the countryside. Why is that? Very few famous Sakha come from cities. Why? It is the inner language that is connected to the land. This makes them strong and wise. Inner language allows a person to receive new information and create new ideas. This is why every person in town needs to visit the land from time to time. That connection to nature is critical to keeping and developing the inner voice."

By afternoon, we were finishing our knives, as much as they would ever be finished, and Fedora had come into the smithy with a pan of freshly cleaned *sabo*, little fish that looked like perch about the size of one of Mandar's expressive hands. She set them in the coals where the steel had been heating, and the fire baked them until their skins were crispy and black. We followed her in for the evening meal: fire-roasted fish, boiled fish soup, pickled fish, more whipped cream, condensed milk, yogourt and whole milk, smoked horsemeat, and fresh bread. After dinner Mandar performed on a *khomus* (also called a *vargan*, or jaw harp). He could hardly wait to finish so he could ask questions about what else and who else I had met on my travels.

We moved to the main room, where Mandar had set out examples of twenty-four styles of knives he made, based on the traditions of a Sakha smith. "They are not weapons," he explained. "Each has its own purpose, for cutting, for carving, for skinning. If they were weapons they would have finger grips cut into the handles. Each of these comes with a purpose and a teaching that was passed on to me by my ancestors." I sat listening, captivated, but then started to smile: all this earnest traditional teaching was courtesy of a set of authentic Sakha props laid out on a pink tray illustrated with Disney images of golden-haired Cinderella. Too funny.

Next, Mandar extracted a dog-eared folder filled with a sheaf of art paper. To my utter astonishment, he launched into a two-hour explanation of a series of visual interpretations of dreams he had experienced. At the bottom of each drawing was one of the classic Sakha patterns that you might find on a *choron* or on the wall of a winter *balaghan* or birchbark summer house. But on the main body of each sheet of heavy white paper were pen and black ink sketches of the most fantastical series of images I had ever seen. Planets, stars, galaxies, drums, faces, skins, horses, people, each one the vision of a particular dream he had had sometime in the past.

One of the recurring motifs in this remarkable set of drawings was hands, the most beguiling of which showed hands with facial features in the creases: eyes, ears, noses, and sometimes mouths. "In some fairy tales," he explained, "people use their hands to see and to hear. All of the earth's cosmic waves are invisible to our normal senses. It is only with the eyes and ears of the hands that they can be truly felt and understood. You can't smell a person's cosmic waves. You can't hear them. You can't see the devil. You can only feel them with your hands." And there they were, the smith's hands, gesticulating in perfect harmony, while Prince Charming and Cinderella looked on from under the knife collection.

He continued, "If we spoke a common language, if we found a time language we could share, describing and explaining what is going on in each of these images would take two or three days. Speaking to you now, through translation, the message is much shorter. But you, traveller, should understand that we are all connected through the cosmos, through the land, through who we are. When we lose connection to the land, to the cosmos, we stop being who we are. We must look after those connections. That is my job within Sakha culture."

By then, it was nine o'clock at night and all of us were dog-tired. Having started at noon the day before, we had crossed the river, driven along the Road of Bones, attended and officiated at a wedding, and carried on along the road until six in the morning; then we'd all had a nap, made knives, eaten handsomely, and travelled the cosmos. I, for one, was exhilarated but exhausted. But Mandar had one more thing to do. At his urging, we sat down, and he presented each of us with a finished knife in a handmade leather sheath. "These you must take, with the ones you made here, as a souvenir of your visit. We are so glad you came. Be careful, though: they are sharp." Taking one of them out of its sheath, he made the point by slicing a piece of paper he held in the air into thin strips that cascaded one by one onto the floor.

"I have written a note on yours, traveller," he said. Slava took the knife and read the inscription that was etched into the polished steel along the spine of the blade. "It is written in Sakha," he said. "It says, 'May the rich god of the forest give you the best animals and send them to your path of life,' and it is signed 'Mandar Uus.'"

"I don't know how to thank you for what you have taught me in the last twenty-four hours, Mandar," I said. "This knife, and the terrible one that I have made, speak to lessons I will be pondering for a long time."

"We should go," said Slava. And as quickly and unceremoniously as we had arrived in the morning, we left in the twilight, at ten. Back on the Kolyma Road, we headed west for the lengthy return trip to Yakutsk.

Without Mandar in the vehicle, leaving just two of us in the tiny back seat, I was just getting used to the idea of having a little space to stretch out when, out of the dust and darkness, appeared the taillights of a disabled vehicle. As we were in the proverbial "middle of Siberia," it made sense that Kassiean would stop to see what he might do to help out. The driver of the disabled vehicle knew exactly what was broken. There being no such thing as an auto club to call for service in this remote corner of the world, the best option for repair was for one of the occupants of the disabled vehicle to go with us to Yakutsk to get a replacement part. And so we were again three in the back seat, me against the window; Kassiean was chain-smoking at the wheel, and the thump, thump, thump of the same twelve songs from the techno-punk hit parade squawked from the speakers beside my head.

All things considered, however, I was in a very different state and frame of mind on my return from Mandar and Fedora's home. Exhaustion, dust, and the onset of some kind of gastrointestinal insult that had turned my bowels to water notwithstanding, we were now driving down a road with coordinates in three dimensions instead of just two. After Mandar's cosmic tutorial it felt as if, instead of being on a road heading west through Siberian taiga, we were now travelling through the cosmos, complete with a hitchhiker from some other galaxy. We bumped along, heads bobbing, the music blaring, the smoke and dust circulating, until we crested a hill and before us saw the Lena River bathed in the golden light of six in the morning. Eh-Beh the Mother River had never looked so good.

After a couple of weeks together spread out over several months, I had become very fond of Slava. On both my visits, on the strength of the initial RAIPON connection from Moscow, he had dropped everything and made my education his priority, arranging interpretation (although Slava had a strong command of English, not as good as Ruslan's but better than that of some of the stand-in translators like Sergei), smoothing logistics, setting up drivers and meetings, and generally making sure that this project of mine would be as well served as possible through his agency as host and fixer of all things.

With coffees in hand, being careful not to crush the flimsy cups, we walked through the loose dry clay down the bank, boarded the ferry, and sat on a bench on the port side of the wheelhouse looking out over the Lena. As we waited to cross, we talked about Mandar and language and revisited the many topics of discussion during our whirlwind knife-making tutorial and Sakha cultural immersion experience.

"What about Mandar's notion of genetic memory?" I asked. "Can language and tradition be maintained that way?"

"Maybe," he replied with a sigh. "Yukaghirs believe in reincarnation. We don't speak of genetic memory. We believe that humans come back as animals who perhaps come from spirits or who, in death, transcend to the spirit world. As such, the world we inhabit is, in a sense, what one ethnologist called a 'hall of mirrors' where spirits, animals, and people are all doubles of one another through the process of reincarnation. This is why I believe Mandar was right when, somewhere back in our conversation, he said that teachers don't really teach, they only help students remember what they may know from a previous life. They know it. The knowledge is inside them. And language is part of that knowledge. But in the case of my people, the Yukaghirs, it may be too late."

As deckhands loosed the lines and the ferry slipped into the sinewy reflections of the calm river waters, Slava relaxed into yet another story. In the latter years of the nineteenth century, he began, a Lithuanian Jew called Vladimir Jochelson had run afoul of the czar because of his activities with the revolutionary organization Narodnaya Volya, which was intent on overthrowing the monarchy. He left Russia to study anthropology in Switzerland but kept involved by editing the newspaper of the organization. As a result, when he returned to Russia in 1884 he was arrested and imprisoned, and after three years in Petropavlovsk Prison in St. Petersburg he was sentenced to ten years of exile in Siberia—near the Arctic Circle in Yakutia.

While in exile, Jochelson made two major expeditions to live among the people of Yakutia and learn their ways. Even at that time, Slava explained, the Yukaghir people and their languages, customs, and traditions were dwindling. Using the academic discipline he had acquired in Zurich, Jochelson made a special study not only of the language, manners, and folklore of the Tungus and Yakut peoples he met but also of the Yukaghirs, who, in nomadic and seminomadic fashion, fished and hunted bear, wild deer, and moose. He also met a separate group of tundra Yukaghirs who herded reindeer and moved more often than their taiga brethren. Jochelson was credited with discovering, on one of his expeditions, two Yukaghir dialects that, even then, were thought to be extinct, Slava said.

"Jochelson wrote a book," Slava went on, "a very thick book that was first published in English in the 1920s but just six years ago was published in Russian. It is called *The Yukaghir and*

Yukaghirized Tungus. As strange as it may sound, Jochelson's book is the keeper of our culture. He is helping us remember who we are, who we were, who we will become. We have folklore ensembles in Nelemnoye and Andriushkino and in Yakutsk, and we have our artists, writers, poets, and musicians, but we also have many challenges as a people. With all of the development that is coming, I am not sure what will happen. You don't see the future very clearly if your culture is not good. You talk of climate change. We speak of cultural survival."

The following day, Slava returned to his world. Ruslan and I visited a school and that evening dined again at Igor and Marina Makarov's home. They spoke of their desire to come to Canada, perhaps for an exhibition of some of Igor's photographs of backcountry Sakha, perhaps one day to emigrate. But the intensity of all these travels and experiences in Sakha had taken their toll and I had to fight to stay focused and alert, especially through the vodka and fine wine that was served in equal measure to the Makarovs' flowing hospitality. The Road of Bones had taken more out of me than I'd thought.

Ruslan and I said our thanks and goodbyes and headed back to the hotel in a cab. But Ruslan, instead of heading home in the cab, asked if we could spend a few moments talking in my room.

I was exhausted. My head was swimming. My bowels were still unsettled. My body had not really shaken off the hum of the Kolyma Road.

"Ten minutes, James. Ten minutes, that's all it will take. You are leaving tomorrow. There is something I want to show you and something I would ask you to do."

So up the stairs we went, Ruslan carrying a grey gym bag. Any desire I might have had at that time of night to muster energy for another conversation, after all that had happened in the last few days, was diminishing with each step. We sat down across from each other on twin beds and Ruslan unzipped the bag.

"First, James . . . First. A toast to our fathers with the drink of your ancestors."

He reached into the bag and pulled out two glasses and a half-empty bottle of Famous Grouse Scotch whisky. He might as well have pulled a rabbit out of a hat. I was speechless.

"Like yours, my father has passed. But James, having been with you in the spring and again on this visit, I know that your father, who I feel I know through what you have said to people as they have asked about your family—I know that your father would be proud of what you are doing."

The wash of exhaustion and resentment, and now guilt, that had followed me up the stairs dissolved into tears that quietly dripped on the bedspread between my legs as Ruslan poured two generous doses of blended malt. "To our fathers with the drink of your ancestors," he said as we clinked glasses. "*Cheh!*"

Completely blindsided, I began to babble about how fortunate I felt to have met Slava and Ruslan and how these experiences—east, west, south, and north from Yakutsk following a line just south of the Arctic Circle in the Sakha Republic—had taken my research to places I could never have imagined. Ruslan reached again into his bag and took out a well-thumbed paperback book.

"James. James. As you . . . as you know . . . I am a translator by trade. I have here a seminal work in the Sakha tradition by

Aleksei Yeliseevich Kulakovsky, one of our greatest writers. It is called *Ouian's Dream* [The Shaman's Dream] and it is a long-form poem, a prophecy really, written in 1910—illustrated, incidentally, by our friend Mandar Uus. The government contracted me to translate this book into English. I did that, to the best of my ability. But I have never heard my words, my translations, voiced in English."

Now feeling a flush of remorse on top of regret, feeling like a total cad for even *thinking* of rebuffing Ruslan's only request in the whole time I had known him, I began to read *Ouian's Dream*, page by page, astonished at the veracity of the predictions of how indigenous people would be beaten down but then would rise up again and find their feet and their identities in a new world. Ruslan, for once, just sat quietly and listened.

"Is it a good translation?" he asked. "Is it a good translation?"

"I don't know, " I said, laughing. "I haven't seen the original text."

"To Kulakovsky. *Cheh!*"

"To you, Ruslan, a fine translation. *Cheh!*"

"Now James, James . . . I want you to go back and read this part again because I think it relates to what we are doing here, what we have been doing during your visits here on your way around the world."

And so I picked up the book and read again, as Kulakovsky wrote of his own quest to find truth in the craft of his channelling the shaman's dream. He had foretold with astonishing detail the coming of electrical power, various wars, and the subjugation and eventual re-emergence of Russia's indigenous peoples as a

viable political force. With Ruslan hanging on my every word—
his every word—I continued:

May my aspirations for good
Raise me like the most powerful feather
May my yearning for noble deeds
Lift me like the strongest wing feather
Purity of my thought
Has turned into the swiftest wing
Loftiness of my thought
Has become the mightiest wing
In anticipation of happiness
I have spread my wings
In anticipation of carnage
I am shooting upwards

This time, Ruslan could not contain his enthusiasm. At that
point in the reading, he blurted, "James . . . James . . . this is . . .
this is *you*, man. This is about circling the midnight sun. This is
you who is going to ascend. This is you who is going to fly. Yes.
You are escorted by the midnight storm. May your aspiration
for good raise you like the most powerful wing feather. Purity of
your thought has turned into the swiftest wing. That's you, man,
circling the midnight sun."

At that point, the tears welled again, any lingering inhibitions
stripped away by the Famous Grouse. After this effusive affirmation that had set my project on something of a pedestal, I couldn't
think what to say to this remarkable human being, knowing that

my journey would have been impossible without the resolve and spirit of people like him who had helped along the way.

Up early the following morning, wondering if the whole *Ouian's Dream* encounter was in itself a dream, I met Slava in the lobby and together we taxied to the airport. I told him about Ruslan and he just nodded and laughed. "Kulakovsky is someone you should pay attention to," he said. "We do."

But then, knowing this would be our last time together, he said, "Before you go, James, I need to tell you a story that I began on the ferry but didn't get a chance to finish." And so in the cab, and then on a bench in the tiny crowded Yakutsk airport, Slava said his goodbyes with his own tale.

"Fifty years ago, or so, in a place on the tundra near the sacred blue mountain, an old shaman died. There are two ways to become a shaman: to learn as a young man with a shaman teacher; or to spend time away from people, on the tundra, in isolation with the gods.

"Many or most shamans live as ordinary people. Around this time, a young man, who had a wife and family, a herder, an ordinary man, felt a calling to spend time alone on the tundra. Even though he had a family, he did this," Slava related.

"One fall, he went away to the tundra and did not come back. Effectively, he disappeared. That spring, wolves started coming around the reindeer herd. One wolf in particular was very aggressive, and so the elders conferred and decided that they should kill this wolf. They set about trying to trap him. Their best hunters tried, but every time their traps were foiled as if the wolf was one step ahead, as if he knew all the tricks.

"One time, they came to a trap that was sprung and noticed a human footprint mixed with the wolf tracks. They knew then that the man who had disappeared was living with the wolves. But his wife and family were missing him. They wanted him back. And maybe this would stop the wolves from attacking the reindeer."

Slava continued, "So there was another shaman in the community who had stopped practising in the Soviet period. They said he should destroy his drum or he would be killed. He had destroyed his drum and returned to living as an ordinary man. The hunters went to this man and told him the problem of the wolf they couldn't catch. And they asked him what they should do.

"The old shaman said that they should go to the sacred mountain on the night of the full moon. 'The wolves will be there,' he said. 'You need to take the whole community and make a circle around the whole pack of wolves. When you get the wolves circled, make a break of one person in the circle. And then let the wolves out that gate. The last wolf will be the man who disappeared. When all the other wolves are gone, you can catch the last one, the man wolf. But don't just use one lasso. Seven people must get their ropes on the wolf because he will be very strong.'

"So they did what the retired shaman said. They went to the mountain on the full moon and circled the wolves, and seven of their best hunters lassoed the wolf. He was very strong, as the shaman had told them to expect. With these seven ropes, they captured him and tied him tightly to a reindeer sled and took him back to the village.

"As instructed, they left the man wolf on the sled for three days, and at the end of the third day, the wolf spoke like a man and asked for a drink of water. When he drank the water, his metamorphosis back into a man was complete. The man then went back to his family and lived again normally with his wife and children. He helped people with healing from time to time. But mostly he lived a normal life."

Slava watched me pass through security. Looking back through the front window of the airport I caught a glimpse of him heading to the cab. I looked again and the cab was there, but he was gone.

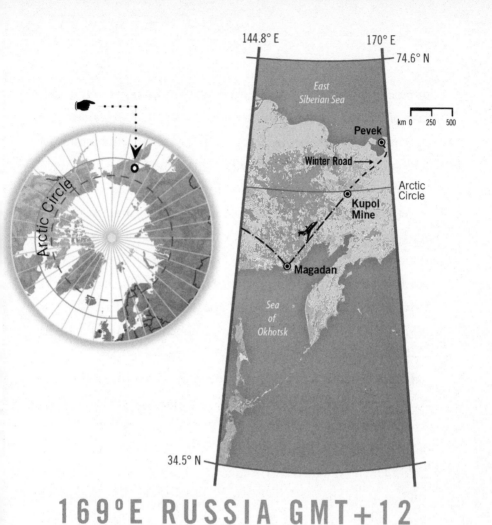

144.8° E   170° E

74.6° N

East
Siberian Sea

km 0   250   500

Pevek

Winter Road →

Arctic
Circle

Kupol
Mine

Magadan

Sea
of
Okhotsk

34.5° N

169°E RUSSIA GMT+12

13: ARCTIC GOLD

Next stop along the Arctic Circle from Yakutsk was a gold
mine in the Chukotka district of the Russian Far East. And, as
had happened so many times in Russia, it was anything but an
easy proposition to get there. Fortunately, Lou Naumovski, the
Canadian who is vice president of Kinross—the Canadian company that owns the mine—and head of its Moscow office, had

attended my presentation at the embassy in Moscow in the early days of my research. When he offered to help, I explained that help in getting to this gold mine, called Kupol, in the middle of nowhere in eastern Siberia, would be just the ticket.

Nearly a year after saying goodbye to Slava, I had managed to get a permit to enter Chukotka—a process, it seemed, even more complicated and fraught with delays and setbacks than getting my Russian visa. On the one day of the week when you can travel east by actually flying east, without backtracking to Moscow or another Russian hub, I passed through Yakutsk again en route to Magadan on the Sea of Okhotsk, not far from where Sir George made landfall in 1841.

I found myself sitting with a dozen or so people in the back of an ancient Antonov turboprop. Designed in the 1950s for service on short gravel airstrips in the Russian outback, like the Beavers, Otters, Twin Otters, Dash-7s, and Dash-8s made by the de Havilland Aircraft Company in Canada, the AN-24 had wings set over the fuselage to prevent gravel, ice, and snow from being sucked into the air intakes or damaging the propellers. This one had been kitted out for cargo in the front. Behind a movable bulkhead, there were a few rows of tatty canvas seats in the back, complete with a bored flight attendant. Ancient ex-air-force khaki emergency oxygen masks, or maybe they were life preservers—one couldn't be sure—were stuffed into the pockets for good measure.

Among the great trials—and joys—of travelling are moments when circumstances collide to propel the traveller into an exis-tential crisis of one sort or another. In this instance, just as I was thinking how good it would be to leave this twin-engined museum piece, the plane bumped down and rumbled along a cracked asphalt strip at Sokol Airport near Magadan. My phone, which had never really found a service to which it could relate anywhere in Yakutia, suddenly lit up with an incoming text message: "Hey Daddy, I don't know where you are or if you'll even get this but you should know that your friend Marty Bergmann was killed in an Arctic plane crash a couple of days ago. So sorry. xo Molly."

And there it was. The guy flying in a new (relatively speaking) Boeing 737-200 on First Air Flight 6560, making its final approach to the controlled airstrip at Resolute Bay, Nunavut—a place I had landed on occasion with Marty, who headed the Canadian government's Polar Continental Shelf northern research support program and had a deep passion for the North—had come to the end of the line when his skilled and certified Canadian pilots had flown into a hillside, temporarily blinded by low-lying fog over the airstrip. Meanwhile the guy flying in the back end of Siberia, in the hands of unemployed Russian fighter pilots on a plane held together with pop rivets and tin cans, survived. I felt slapped in the face with circumstance. Work in the North involved risk. I ached for his family.

Inside the terminal, a swarthy fellow in a leather cap held a piece of paper with my name on it. "*Dobriy vyechyer!* Good evening!" I said, unleashing 50 percent of my vast repertoire of Russian greetings, pleased that the connection had been made so surely and promptly. He just nodded and pointed to a hole in the wall where, apparently, the luggage would be appearing.

My case arrived, complete with Mandar's knife and my own, which of course had tripped the security alarms on the way out of Yakutsk. But, as Mandar had promised, they were allowed through as cultural artifacts on the strength of an official certificate he'd given me when we left Bayaga. Still without saying a word, the Kinross man hefted my cases up into the back of a new Toyota sport utility vehicle, opened the back door, and gestured for me to get in.

As we turned right onto a two-lane paved road, I saw a sign indicating that we were on Highway M56, the Kolyma Road. Instantly, I flashed back to those long hours with Slava and the others on the Yakutsk half of this notorious two thousand kilometres of pain and suffering. That reverie popped when the Kinross fellow reached back over the seat and handed me an envelope.

In it was a big brass key, like something from a medieval castle, and a typed note that said:

> **Dear** Mr. Raffan: **Welcome to Magadan. You are on your way to the Kupol site! TODAY IT IS** Tuesday, August 23 **IN MAGADAN**. Today you will overnight in Magadan. The driver will take you to an apartment on Karl Marx Street. On Wednesday, August 24 at 7:30 a.m. the driver will pick you up from the apartment and take you to the airport for Kupol charter. ***Welcome to Kupol!***

When we were stopped at a police checkpoint near what appeared to be an abandoned military airport, the whole arrival scenario started to take on a shadowy Mission Impossible cast. As I sat in the back seat of an anonymous late-model black vehicle with tinted windows, my imagination ran rampant. I began to wonder if I should eat the note.

We crested a hill and before us, on a narrow isthmus of land set north/south between verdant taiga hills and east/west between the brooding waters of two bays, was the beguiling jumble of buildings, power pylons, smokestacks, and antennas that was Magadan. To our right, high on a hill overlooking the isolated town, was a giant concrete head, reminiscent of Easter Island. This I took to be the *Mask of Sorrow*, a famous monument that commemorated the countless souls who came here by ship, and who lived and died as exiles building roads and mining gold for the Stalinist regime.

On the edge of town was a shabby corona of dilapidated wooden shanties with little fenced vegetable plots and hungry-looking dogs. Closer to the centre were buildings, some new and sound and colourful, others made of old concrete and steel in need of roofing tar and a lick of paint. We passed a monument of MiG fighters, old rockets, and a helicopter welded up in flying formation onto monkey bars made of old drill pipe. It appeared to be a place for young kids to climb and for older kids to practise their tagging skills.

The road name changed to Prospekt Lenina, and now the facades were clean, with pink stucco and paint and the classic lines and curves of nineteenth-century czarist architecture. Set back from wide sidewalks and new street lamps, they presented a much more sophisticated face to the street. Rising behind and above them all were five golden turrets on what appeared to be a brand new monolithic white cathedral.

We turned off the main drag and laddered our way along narrower streets and laneways bordered by much tawdrier buildings, some of which appeared to have been halted in mid-build. We crept past a stalled truck and pulled up in front of a wooden door hanging off its hinges on a crumbling concrete stoop. We'd arrived: 54 Karl Marx Street, such as it was, a five-storey walk-up.

At that point my friend at the wheel turned and held up four fingers on his left hand. "Turn key four times, four times," he said, waggling his digits so that I might understand. Holding the key in my hands, I looked at it and then again at his fingers. "Four times?" "Da. Turn key four times."

The apartment block ran the length of Karl Marx Street, a few hundred metres. Above the first-floor exterior—coated in unbelievable amounts of graffiti, some of it vaguely artistic—the upper stories, with their alternating stripes of cream and yellow paint, gave the impression that somebody actually cared for the place. Standing there with a brass key in my hand, all I could hear in my head was the theme music for the American spoof spy series *Get Smart*, which got louder as I entered the building, heard a door slam, and started to make my way up the urine-stained stairwell.

Six flights up, I arrived at a battered steel door. Number 26. I inserted the key and turned it four times, each turn producing a percussive click in the tumblers of the lock. Lo and behold, the door swung open, revealing another more conventional wooden door inside, which was open. And beyond, to my great relief, was not some Russian thug with a gun but a very nice, perfectly normal-looking three-bedroom apartment with a large kitchen, dining room, and sitting room. It had a washer, a dryer, full cooking appliances, and a large-screen TV.

I assumed I was all alone in the apartment until I heard the toilet flush. Instead of an armed intruder, a compact American contract geologist from Centennial, Colorado, called Brad Margeson, emerged in clean jeans and plaid shirt. "Make yourself at home," he said. "Take any room you like. I'm heading back to the States in the morning."

Margeson explained that since gold was first found in the Kolyma region back around 1912, geologists like him—although exclusively Russian rockhounds until the collapse of the Soviet Union—had been prospecting and sampling the rich and ancient rocks of the Russian Far East. As they worked their way north from the first gold finds close to Magadan, the gold- and silver-rich quartz vein system that became the Kupol mine was discovered in the mid-1990s just above the Arctic Circle in the remote region of Chukotka.

Since the mine opened in 2008, it had produced something like two million ounces of gold and twenty million ounces of silver, which, even in this remote location, was still a very profitable undertaking, he told me. "I've been working with a team on opening two other deposits, called Dvoinoye and Vodorazdelnaya, that are located about a hundred kilometres north of Kupol. The plan is to truck high-grade ore from these mines to Kupol for processing, which will both add to Kupol's results and extend the life of the whole project."

After a great tall glass of Russian rum, cola, and real ice, I crawled into the clean sheets and had a chuckle at the key on the bedside table before passing out with visions of another day in Russian airspace, another trip over the Arctic Circle starting first thing in the morning.

Woken by either barking dogs or ravens mimicking barking dogs, or both, I was up and showered and well ready by the time, as promised, another driver in a van turned up at Karl Marx Street. Chattier than the last guy, he talked about working for Kinross and all the jobs it had brought to what was otherwise a pretty desperate place. We drove around town picking up four or five other people heading to Kupol before turning north on M56 for Sokol Airport and the charter flight to the mine.

The plane was a vintage Russian AN-26-100, the so-called tactical version of the AN-24, which included a retractable ramp at the rear of the plane for loading cargo and small vehicles and, presumably, for offloading the same by parachute over hostile terrain when the spirit moved.

After three-plus hours in the air, we touched down onto the gravel airstrip at the mine. "Welcome to Kupol," said a sign, followed by a set of rules about things you could and couldn't do, things you could and couldn't bring in and out of the mine, where you could and couldn't go on the site, and why management reserved the right to examine, X-ray, and hand-search your goods and your person in microscopic detail to ensure each visitor's "safety and comfort" while at the mine site. Basically, surrender your passport while here; no booze or drugs in; no gold or silver out, anywhere in your system.

As my carry-on case included audio and video recording equipment, cameras, a GPS unit, and other electronic gizmos,

I braced myself for a full going over when it came my turn to pass through arrival security. Mercifully my host, Lyudmila Ukhtomskaya, was there on the other side with Alexander Petrovich Romanov, the deputy site manager, who stepped forward and waved me through. In no time at all we were en route to the mine facility itself, which stood fortress-like on top of a distant rocky tundra ridge.

Every aspect of this impeccably run mine—from food, accommodation, and recreation facilities for the workers to the mine itself, with both aboveground and underground ore extraction processes; from the mill and refinery that crushed, cooked, and concentrated high-grade ore into twenty-kilo doré (gold-silver amalgam) bricks to the oilers, mechanics, machinists, road workers, security, translators, and administrators who each did their part in the 24/7 operation of the mine—demonstrated that if you can build a mine here, you can build a mine anywhere.

Pool tables, megatonne off-road dump trucks, computers, metallurgical reagents, workboots, and bandages—everything here had been shipped by sea to Pevek on the Russian Arctic coast and then driven, dragged, or hauled over a 360-kilometre winter road. Though it was hard to imagine from the inside, this small town with beds and comfortable living facilities for over six hundred people was actually a creative assemblage of trailers from Alberta that were shipped to Pevek, rolled up the winter road, and put together like dominoes on a crushed-gravel pad to make the man camp. And, presumably, anything left would all be moved the other way when the life of the mine was done.

But in all the stories of early road building and gold mining in the Kolyma region, conspicuous by their absence in any of the historical books or reportage were the indigenous peoples who inhabited these lands long before 1912, when the first Russian prospectors turned up. As it did elsewhere across the Russian North, Russification involved rounding them up into collective farms, breaking the shamans' drums, and indoctrinating all and sundry, regardless of creed, culture, or language, into working for the good of the Russian whole. Mines, since their inception here and elsewhere throughout Scandinavia and Siberia, are something that the reindeer have just had to walk around.

Although there were no conditions on the licences governing the operation of the Kupol mine regarding relations with nearby indigenous communities or about hiring or training local indigenous people at the mine, I was intrigued to hear about Kinross's relatively bold statements of corporate responsibility, which, company documents profess, guide all activities at Kinross projects all over the world, including in the Russian Arctic.

Four of the ten guiding principles for corporate responsibility were directed toward fair and ethical treatment of people for whom the locations of Kinross mines were home:

3. We promote an ongoing dialogue and engagement with stakeholders in the communities where we operate, maintained in a spirit of transparency and good faith.

6. We conduct all of our activities in accordance with accepted standards in the protection and promotion of human rights. We respect the cultural

and historical perspectives and rights of those affected by our operations, in particular indigenous peoples.

8. We seek to maximize employment, business and economic opportunities for local communities from our existing operations and new projects.

9. We provide lasting benefits to the communities where we work by supporting sustainable initiatives to develop their social, economic and institutional fabric. We recognize that every community is unique, and we work with our community partners to ensure that our support matches their priorities.

With the help of the corporate responsibility manager, Evgeniya (Jenya) Saevich, I was able to explore the application of these principles with various office personnel at the mine. But the conversation I was most anticipating was a chance to sit with four Chukotkan employees at Kupol.

We met down in the Solstice Café—a place with fancy coffee machines and a fully equipped musical stage where the Kupol house band performed—in the orderly confines of the modular man camp. Pavel Ermakov was a blaster who had learned his trade in the open-pit part of the operation. Vladimir Korange, Vladislav Itegin, and Nikolay Rol'tykvy were labourers working their way into the system thanks to Kinross training and affirmative action programs. Pavel was from Ilirney, a rural settlement of about 150 people between Kupol and Bilibino, a nuclear-powered gold-mining town and administrative centre set up in the 1960s.

Vladimir was from Keperveem, another reindeer-herding community in the region. The other two didn't say where they were from and clearly were present for the conversation because they'd been told that this was something that would make the boss happy.

They had all grown up in a reindeer-herding culture in the context of Soviet collective farms. Those were good times, relatively speaking. Reindeer were far more plentiful then than they are now—Pavel said that when he was young in the late 1970s and 1980s, there were eight herds, each with its own brigade of families that moved with it over the tundra lands around Ilirney. "Now," he sighed, "there are two." The fall of the Soviet Union summarily withdrew government support and cooperation for reindeer herding and dumped the herders and their families onto the open market to fend for themselves. "Reindeer herding is part of your soul," Pavel said, "but not so good for finance. I had to look for work."

Part of Kinross's process in setting up Kupol, compelled primarily by its own Corporate Responsibility Code, involved travelling to Ilirney and Bilibino and Keperveem and other communities around the mine site to speak with the people and to tell them personally about what was happening at the proposed project. Company representatives spoke of the steps that would be taken to ensure minimal impact on lands and waters. They reassured community members about commitments made to themselves and to the Russian government about doing their level best to hire and train local people whenever possible.

For many, like Pavel and Vladimir, it was an opportunity they felt they should explore because the future of reindeer herding was so bleak. Chukotkan women as well, though fewer in number, applied for positions with Sodexo, a multinational food and facility management company that operates the man camp, or with the mine itself.

When the conversation was over, I asked Jenya if Kinross was close to reaching its targets for hiring indigenous people from the area. "We don't really have targets, as such," she replied. "It's more of an attitude and an ongoing commitment to communicating with the communities. In many cases, the people, like Pavel, who apply for jobs with the mine and who do well, working their way up the ladder to positions of increased responsibility and increased pay, bring money back to their families in the community but at the expense of their connection with the land and the herding way of life. I have heard more than once from indigenous community leaders, 'Don't take our best herders from the community because they never come back.'"

On a tour of the mill, proud employees explained how eight-tonne scoops of ore dumped around the clock into the hopper at one end were reduced to a "pour" of near-pure silver and gold at the other. Just as it was funny when a worker in a Canadian radar station on Baffin Island explained in the dying days of the Cold War that the only place left in the world to source tubes for Canada's antiquated tracking equipment was behind the Iron Curtain, I laughed when I saw these US$300,000 bricks of Russian doré being carefully stowed in individual weathertight U.S. Army 2.56-millimetre M2A1 ammunition cans for transport to southern markets.

I listened to songs in the music room by a Russian-born

Canadian from Calgary. I had conversations with people from all over the world in the cafeteria, many of whom had worked in mines on almost every continent. They spoke of airports, bars, and bistros in major cities and out-of-the-way locales as if they knew them like the backs of their hands, because they did.

Over surprisingly drinkable coffee, an Aussie called Jason Lever, the continuous improvement risk manager, told me of his "commute" to Kupol from Guatemala, where he owned a terrace bar and bistro called Lava, in La Antigua, Sacatepéquez. During subsequent cafeteria meals, I learned more about Jason's Ducati 250 motorcycle and his love life than was probably necessary, but it was just table chat in a dry camp with very little else to do besides work, sleep, and carry on—four weeks in, four weeks out. "I've come to the point now," he proclaimed, "that next time I feel like getting married, I'm going to do what Rod Stewart did. I'm just going to find a woman I hate and buy her a house."

Outside the man camp and beyond the mill, with the requisite training and safety briefings at each step, I went with willing guides and translators deep underground to meet the people working there. I visited the open-pit part of the operation, which they were in the process of closing down, and saw the polymer-lined cofferdam where the cyanide extraction fluids, now neutralized with chlorine, were being collected in a substantial tailings pond.

On a drive out to the airport, I saw skids of shrink-wrapped ammunition cases being quietly loaded on a backhaul flight to Magadan—a plane full of doré bricks. Hijack that and you've got riches to fund a revolution! Past the airport, I chatted with workers running off-road dump trucks and massive bulldozers to build the hundred-kilometre all-weather road to the sister Dvoinoye mine, which Kinross was in the process of opening. Ore from there would be trucked back to the Kupol mill, thereby increasing the efficiencies of this Kinross Arctic operation.

This road building, the guys told me, was coming to a halt until freeze-up because they'd run out of heavy-duty enviro-cloth to lay on the tundra under the road. Still, they were busy making perfect the grades on the road they had built, and there was my friend the raven supervising from a perch on the edge of the dozer blade.

Back in Magadan, with the *Get Smart* theme again running in the back of my head, I turned the big brass key four times and found a new set of roommates at 54 Karl Marx. With them for company in the evenings, I spent a couple more days in Magadan, continuing my conversations with company personnel at the Kinross office.

Jenya Saevich introduced me to Alexander Kazantsev, site services supervisor for Kinross at its ocean port on the Northern Sea Route at Pevek. He took me back to the very early days of the mine and showed me photos of himself taking a six-wheeled amphibious all-terrain vehicle, much like Oleg's Trekol on the Ob River near Khanty-Mansiysk, out over the tundra to find the remaining nomads and their reindeer still roaming on the lands between Kupol and the coast.

Their first encounter had been in April of 2004. Kazantsev showed me pictures of his team sharing meals with a herding family in the smoky confines of their yaranga made of bent saplings covered with dried reindeer skins. "We see these families occasionally now during the winter months when we are hauling freight to the mine," he said, "but now that the connection is established, the herding families tend to drive their animals toward the mine in late July or early August each year. At that time, they can join us for a meal or two and also get supplies of tools or other things they might need."

Jenya interjected to tell me about another way Kinross has made the benefits of the mine more tangible for the herders and the people they support in neighbouring communities. "We have established the Kupol Social Development Foundation, which is devoted to supporting worthwhile projects in maintaining traditional lifestyles as well as aboriginal health care, education, and entrepreneurship. This was started in October 2009, when the company put $1 million into a foundation fund to support a US$250,000 annual operating budget for grants to local people and local projects."

Jenya led me down the hall to meet Ludmila Danilova, a Chuvan woman who was the executive director of the foundation. She explained how the staff go about deciding which projects and whose communities win support from Kupol's charitable support arm. "There are eight members on the tender committee," she told me, "whose job it is to decide on which projects to support. One of the early successes was a film called *The Book of Tundra*—"

"Oh," I blurted out, "by Aleksei Vakhrushev."

"Have you seen the film?" Ludmila asked.

I hadn't, but I told her that I'd met Aleksei in Moscow and we'd spoken in the RAIPON office.

She continued, "To date we have supported more than two dozen projects, from getting bone carving going in one area, to helping to provide fur clothing and dental care for herders in the Bilibino district. We have helped to create a health centre in Anadyr to promote exercise and wellness and to reduce the incidence of diabetes and obesity. A grant went to a group who have created a mini-farm to provide fresh eggs to the community. And we are working with a group to see about getting our core boxes—wooden boxes for miles of drill core—made locally. In another location we are helping to promote cultural identity as an ecotourism development driver. We try to send funds to where they are most needed, and we do our best to ensure that projects are aligned and not in competition or conflict with social programs and initiatives by local or regional agencies. We give out about seven million rubles [C$225,000] a year."

That afternoon, I left the Kinross office in Magadan and walked back to 54 Karl Marx thinking of well-intentioned people doing the right thing, of a mining operation above the Arctic Circle where everything is being done properly. Still I couldn't get out of my head the image of Pavel, the Chukchi blaster who talked longingly about attachment to the land. He was getting on with wrangling a future for himself and his family in the wage economy of resource extraction. I wanted to believe that this was a good thing, that this was a possible future for people like Pavel. But I was haunted by his comment about reindeer herding being part of his soul. There was something sad about that, but maybe there are also things a traveller could not or did not see.

Kinross must have been one of the biggest employers in Magadan and in Chukotka, if not the biggest. It employed 1,600 people in all, infusing 1.3 billion rubles (C$41 million) in wages and benefits into the local economy. It purchased over 4 billion rubles' worth of goods and services each year, working with two hundred local enterprises and entrepreneurs as business partners. The mine trained people, students particularly, and supported local communities through its foundation. Still I couldn't shake the notion that the power balances here, as elsewhere in the circumpolar North, were askew. Kinross was taking its corporate responsibility very seriously, far more seriously than the Russian companies that had been popping up in the mining sector since the collapse of the Soviet Union. Access to resources was increasing thanks to climate change, but without effective laws and regulation, or self-regulation in Kinross's case, that included the people who lived where these extractions were taking place, there remained a potent sense that the decay and eventual collapse of these languages, these cultures, these land-based ways of life was a necessary consequence of progress.

That night, I went to a *banya*, which involved amazingly hospitable Kinross men flaying themselves with fresh birch branches in a subterranean spa—some aspects of what happened in

Siberia should probably *stay* in Siberia. I had a delightful meal and many toasts "to neighbours across the pole" with Jenya and some of her colleagues from her team at the Green Crocodile Restaurant on Pushkin Street in Magadan. Then I accepted an offer from Roman Karabets, the more talkative Kinross driver, to take me on a tour around town.

We went first to the *Mask of Sorrow*, which I'd seen on arrival. Inside the concrete head, the sculptor Ernst Neizvestny had created a life-size tiny cell to represent the place where many people perished. The tears falling down the face from the eye, which is actually a barred window, were faces, faces inside tears. In the back of the sculpture, the part you couldn't see from the road, were two human figures in bronze. There was a headless man on a cross high up. Lower down was a grieving woman on her knees. Someone had placed red carnations in the crook of her arm. The effect of the work silenced us until long after we were back in the car.

On the way back to Karl Marx Street at the end of the tour, we passed the five golden turrets, which Roman explained were part of a new cathedral, the Church of the Trinity. We passed an army of workers slaving at midnight to finish installing marble steps and terraces of precast paving stones. "Why are they building a new cathedral when it appears there is another smaller one at the other end of the main street?" I asked.

"We had a governor here called Valentin Tsvetkov who thought he was the czar. He collected graft from all of the local businesses, who had no choice but to pay. And he used public funds to pay for private ventures with all sorts of underworld connections. He got rich by taking advantage of his position and his greed. He started building this church back in 2002 and then got assassinated in Moscow later that year. People have been trying to get the thing built since then. Apparently the patriarch of the Russian Orthodox Church, who has never been to Magadan, is coming here tomorrow to open this place. I call it a monument to God and corruption," Roman scoffed.

The next morning, before boarding my flight to Anadyr, I went with Jenya to the plaza outside the new cathedral where the consecration service was in full swing. Security was very tight and the square was crowded, but we managed to get close to a screen where the proceedings inside were being broadcast. The ornate artworks on the walls and ceilings of the sanctuary were like nothing I'd witnessed in any other church, in Russia or elsewhere, with the possible exception of the Sistine Chapel.

After we'd stood for a time watching the screen, Jenya suggested I go inside. "When was the last time you got to attend the opening of a Russian Orthodox cathedral? When was the last time you got to see the great Kirill, patriarch of the church? Go—I'll be in my office across the road. Just come there when you are ready, and I'll take you back to your apartment to get your things."

Eventually I realized that there was a semi-organized line in what was more or less a sea of people milling in the plaza, and I waited my turn in that to go through security. An old woman in a big woollen greatcoat down to her ankles took exception to the young army officer who embarked on a pat-down. She cuffed him with her purse and spat something derogatory in his general direction before he backed off and held up his hands in submission, moving on to the next person in line.

There were men and women streaming across the newly finished pavers. The men looked up at the shiny gold turrets and the women drew kerchiefs out of their handbags and covered their heads as they made their way up the broad white marble staircase. I thought of Eduard, the three-fingered accordion player in Seliyarovo, and how excited he was when they were once again able to erect a cross on the top of the church in that town, the church that had become a store and a meeting hall during the seven dark decades.

Inside, as the blending of human voices chanting and singing echoed and reverberated off depictions of saints and the stations of the cross, I watched a parade of stone-faced mostly old men in glittering liturgical splendour, led by Patriarch Kirill himself, with their candles, incense, and incantations, move through a sea of men in plain clothes and women with their heads covered and eyes averted.

I thought about who plays, who watches, who wins, who loses. I wondered where was the healer, the shaman of this golden temple? Was it the patriarch? Was it the gold? I stood there thinking of Solzhenitsyn, who wrote, "Gradually it was disclosed to me that the line separating good and evil passes not through states, nor between classes, nor between political parties either— but right through every human heart—and through all human hearts. This line shifts. Inside us, it oscillates with the years. And even within hearts overwhelmed by evil, one small bridgehead of good is retained."

Outside, a raven dropped from a nearby tree into the crowd and snagged a chocolate bar wrapper with some chocolate still in it that someone had dropped on the ground. A boy, maybe six or seven years old, pulled away from his grandmother's hand and lunged toward the bird, missing by a mile, but stumbling and dirtying the knees of his Sunday-best pants.

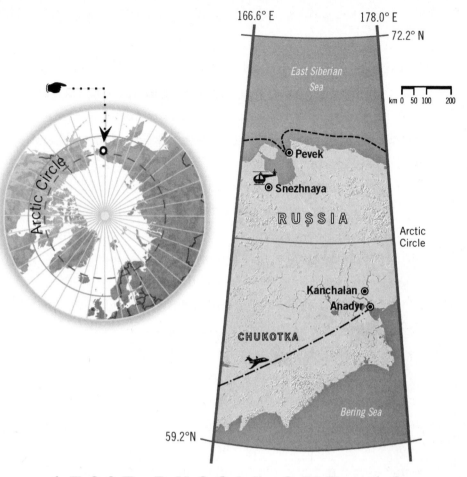

178°E RUSSIA GMT+12

14: SNOW WIND

My last stop in Russia was Anadyr, capital of Chukotka, located just across the Bering Strait from Alaska in the farthest east of Russia's nine time zones. Grigori Tynankergav, a Chukchi geologist, member of the Chukotka Duma, and chair of the Chukotka Council of Elders, seemed very comfortable as he traced his finger along a map and talked about his first job. Although he had no experience with the development of tin and tungsten mines in the 1930s, which was when mining began in the Russian Far East, he was very much a part of the early development of placer mining, which had led underground to the creation of Kupol, Russia's second-richest gold mine. Sifting through kilometres of river aggregate and alluvial sand for gold—the exact same process that had brought miners north to the Yukon and Alaska in the great gold rushes of the nineteenth and early twentieth centuries—had had its effect on the pastures of reindeer that had been herded since time immemorial by his people.

"My first assignment as a government geologist," he said, "was to travel along the coast of Chukotka to speak with the reindeer herders who migrated there in the summer. As a person familiar with herding as well as with geology and gold mining, my job was to explain to them what was being planned and when the gold mining would start. I can say that the population understood what gold mining was. They knew from the stories of the Kolyma gold mines to the south, in the days of the gulag, that when placer gold is being mined, entire valleys are removed from Native use. They knew that after the mining process is done, at this latitude vegetation does not reappear in those places for fifty years."

Grigori wore a natty grey sports jacket, blue V-necked vest, and tie. His strong hands still touched places on the map as if doing so brought back the sensations of actually being there at times during his forty-year career. Speaking Russian that was being translated into English by an Eskimo interpreter, he said, "Of course the population agreed with the need to develop the gold resources. From one side they were very critical. A lot of them knew about the Kolyma mines, but when I spoke with them about the country's need for resources, they understood. While on the one hand they knew that some of their ranges would be given over to placer gold mining, they also knew that there were other valleys they could move toward and that government money and collectivization projects could help raise the quality of their living conditions. Nobody asked their opinion about any development project."

We were talking in Grigori's spartan beige parliamentarian's office in the State Duma building. Although there were aspects of this story that seemed lost in translation or that didn't add up, there was truth in his eyes that was compelling. He had put his name forward in the recent election because he wanted to contribute to making his homeland a better place to live for all, including his people, in what remained of those collective farms and villages; a few remained on the land with the remnants of the 540,000 reindeer that had once flowed like blood through the Chukotkan landscape. What had driven him to that level of public service was a debacle that should never be repeated, in the Arctic or elsewhere.

After the Second World War, Chukotka's strategic import-ance resulted in large inflows of military personnel and resour-ces to support the international bristling of the Cold War, this being the closest part of the Soviet Union to North America. As well, the regime offered large-scale incentives for Russians to come and help develop the riches and resources in this back corner of the Arctic. At the height of the immigration explosion in Chukotka, in the late 1980s, the nearly static and well-distributed indigenous population of 20,000 to 25,000 was buried to the point of invisibility in a total population of 160,000 immigrants, mainly Russians.

Then came the collapse of the Soviet Union and with it a massive out-migration of military and mine workers, who were suddenly out of work. "At the same time," said Grigori Tynankergav, as he offered more tea in the Duma's chipped china cups, "the reindeer population dropped catastrophically, to less than eighty thousand animals. And with far fewer animals, a lot of Native people became unemployed. They moved to town to look for work. But there was no work. And there was no support. Whole villages were deserted. In many places the reindeer just disappeared. For nine or ten years following the collapse of the Soviet Union, times were very hard for the tundra populations of all kinds. They were hard for coastal people too, but for tundra people it was hard times, very hard times. Abramovich changed all that, at least partly for the better."

Grigori recounted in capsule form the almost unbelievable story of how vulnerable the Russian North was politically. The player who "changed all that" was thirty-four-year-old Roman Abramovich, a Russian oligarch and eventual owner of the Chelsea Football Club, a plum team in the English Premier League.

In 1992, Governor Aleksandr Nazarov was elected to fix the post-collapse economic, cultural, and social mess. He closed the region to outsiders and attempted to kick-start the resource industry. People who had been enticed to the ends of the earth with high wages and subsidized costs of living were leaving in droves. Thinking it might compel indigenous people back into the Soviet-style wage economy, Nazarov reduced any remaining agricultural subsidies. By the late 1990s, problems of daily power outages, staple shortages, and corruption were replaced in the aboriginal sector by widespread starvation and disease.

And that, said the parliamentarian, was when Abramovich appeared. Having risen like a rocket after the collapse of the Soviet Union, from selling plastic ducks on the black market to co-ownership of Sibneft, Russia's biggest oil company, for reasons that no one really wants to talk about—some say he was just a good, public-minded businessman and others said he was avoiding prison—Abramovich banished *himself* (some say with a nudge from the Kremlin) to Siberia by being elected to the Russian national parliament as the representative for the Chukotka Autonomous Okrug.

With proven massive resources, both in the ground and offshore, and lots of unproven potential to make money, Chukotka seemed a natural place for a business operative like Abramovich to migrate to continue building his empire. But in the fall of 2000, he surprised many people by running against Aleksandr Nazarov for governor. Amid allegations of corruption, Nazarov eventually withdrew from the race, and in December of that year, with 90 percent of the vote, Abramovich became governor of the most resource-rich, socially impoverished, dysfunctional state in the Russian Federation.

For better or worse, Abramovich and his team transformed Chukotka. He established a charity called the Pole of Hope, through which he directed personal funds to better the lives of Chukotkans living on the land, including the reindeer herders. He travelled to North America to talk up investment in the Chukotkan mining sector. In Alaska and in Canada's Northwest Territories, he sought out advice on everything from health care to housing to improve the life and lot of post-Soviet Chukotkans—as if American and Canadian northerners had something in these areas to be proud of.

A Polish reporter, Zygmunt Dzieciolowski, wrote about a typical visit of Abramovich's to an Eskimo village on the north coast: "Many of the Chukchi resembled tramps, dressed in worn-out clothes. Some were obviously drunk. The school stank of walrus meat. The meeting was over quickly." But in the next scene, apparently the young governor did what he had done all over Chukotka. "He walked to his helicopter, rapidly dictated instructions to his assistants. First, there was to be a new school, then a power station and a clinic, and new houses for everybody. When they reached the helicopter, [Abramovich] asked his bodyguard for a bottle of vodka. It was not for drinking. It was to disinfect his hands."

As his first five-year term as governor was coming to an end in 2005, Abramovich announced that he would not be seeking re-election. Some thought that perhaps he had decided his sentence was done, that his mysterious debt to society had been paid. Unfortunately for him, he had done such a stellar job by all accounts—particularly those circulating in the halls of the Kremlin—that, by the powers vested in his office, President Vladimir Putin scrapped the law under which gubernatorial elections were conducted and appointed Abramovich to a second term. By 2008, when President Dmitri Medvedev accepted his letter of resignation, it was estimated that Abramovich had somehow managed to flow something in the order of US$2.5 billion into the crumbling social and economic infrastructure of Chukotka, half of which was rumoured to have come from his personal bank accounts.

My fixer in Abramovich's world was Elena Bologova, a representative of the Chukotka Mining and Geological Company, who had helped to stickhandle my "CP"—my Chukotka Permit, which is required for anyone from the outside to enter this final Far Eastern segment of Siberia. Because my visa stated my business as "cultural research," CMGC could not sponsor my visit, so it was Elena who took my letter of introduction from RAIPON in Moscow to the leadership of the local branch of the Association of Native and Smaller Peoples of Chukotka. Without their enthusiastic support for a Canadian traveller, this last Russian stop would never have happened.

It was Elena who had introduced me to Grigori; then she took me to the offices of Deputy Governor Leonid Gorenshteyn, who had signed my CP. It was Elena, who spoke impeccable English, who had arranged for the services of Ivanna, a lovely Eskimo interpreter who she felt would better reflect the nuances of answers to questions I might have. It was Elena who arranged nearly a week of meetings, activities, and outings around Anadyr that took me inside the troubled history of the area but also inside the curious and brightly coloured hope that had been painted on everything by Abramovich and his people while they were in charge from 2000 to 2008.

After our conversation in the Duma and the executive offices, Elena and I climbed the stairs to the meeting room of the CMGC's offices, where we sat down with the leadership of the indigenous groups in the Anadyr area. At the table were Anna Otke, a professor of ecology and vice-president of RAIPON in Chukotka; Petr Klimov, manager of social affairs, deputy general director for the CMGC and a newly elected member of the Presidium of the Supreme Soviet in Moscow; Larissa Abryutina, a social worker and educator in Anadyr; André Alexandravich Klimko, a RAIPON board member and newly retired chief of police from Kanchalan village; and another RAIPON board member, Valentina Sobolkoya.

They talked about what it is like to shift from an indigenous population of 20,000 in a general population of 160,000—one eighth of the whole—to an indigenous population of 20,000 within 50,000—two-fifths of the whole, as a result of Russian emigration from the Far East. "The inequities and injustices become much more apparent," said Valentina.

She went on, "Because the overwhelming majority spoke Russian, we spoke Russian. We had to learn Russian in school. Native languages are being lost. And now, when we might work at bringing them back into everyday life, the young people are not interested or able to join in. Even in the villages, language decay is happening.

"And although we are now nearly half of the population, Grigori Tynankergav is the only elected member in the Duma from the Native community out of thirty seats. We have problems with unemployment. When people moved to town after the collapse of the Soviet Union, there were no jobs, even if we did have the right education. That was a sad experience, when the collective farms were closed, because we entered the market without any knowledge of the rules. We were not educated as owners. So while young people might be educated now to be owners and learn about business, after they come to school in town they don't want to return to village life."

Anna spoke up. "Another difficult aspect of reindeer herding is that there are very few women. If there are no women in the yaranga, there is no sense in keeping the herd. And without women on the land, there is no one to teach the girls how to sew and prepare skins. Reindeer herders are freezing on the tundra because there are no fur garments to keep them warm." As the others were nodding in agreement with that, I thought back to the Kupol foundation and its project to produce fur garments for the reindeer industry. Hearing this helped put that project in context.

Someone else added their voice: "There is no European clothing that will replace fur. Fur doesn't allow the frost to penetrate and doesn't let the heat escape. There is nothing better than fur. The same is true with all of the attempts to replace our skin-covered yarangas. All of them have failed. All of those structures have been lost on the tundra. All of those good ideas from the engineers and the government turned out not to be good at all."

Our time together was running out. Petr Klimov explained that for many years he denied his Chuvan ancestry, but now he read in Chuvan to his children. As he was one of just two thousand Chuvan people left on the planet, Petr's act of reading seemed futile in light of the metaphoric complexities that every language carried, beyond the literal meanings of the words.

The theme of the nuances embedded within language was one that I had heard at almost every stop along the way from Grímsey to Anadyr, and I was reminded of Mandar's explanation of the three types of language. The baffling part of all this common understanding was that it didn't register more forcefully. And the lessons about what was at stake when languages died were not limited, by any means, to the Arctic.

Petr explained that language was part of a much bigger picture, a more complex negotiation. He continued, adding the lawmaker's perspective to the discussion. "There are federal laws regarding the rights of Native peoples," he said. "Unfortunately, those laws are very formal. They talk about enabling municipalities to provide support to Native people through programs at that level. There is also a federal law on the books that has to do with local self-rule. But, at the municipal level, at the regional level, there is no mechanism to enact those laws. So nothing happens. We have raised this with committees looking at problems of the North. But I have to say we're not having much luck.

"I can say that this issue with the Native people is a difficult one," he said sadly. "When we visited Alaska and looked at land issues, mining interests, employment, and resource provisions, we were impressed with the amount of Native participation in those matters. If we had a system that worked like that, we could solve a lot of problems. My opinion is that our laws and our system for providing services for Native peoples in the North fall well behind international standards."

"It is almost as if you are invisible, as if you have been invisible all these years," I blurted out.

After murmurs of affirmation around the table, I heard about a new set of school textbooks that taught Russian not as an ethnic language but as a "government language." "They want children, regardless of background, to come to learn to be Russian. . . . Put another way, they say that to be Russian is to be a citizen of Russia without ethnicity," said Petr.

"How sad is that?" I asked under my breath.

"Of course," Larissa said, "we often struggle to be Russian, but what we strive to be is Chukchi, Eskimo, Chuvan, Even, Yukaghir—whatever we were born. We have to regain our self-respect. We have to develop our trades. We must strive to preserve and develop the cultures of our ancestors. We understand that you cannot run from civilization. We have to find a compromise between traditions and progress."

Knowing our time was over, I turned to Petr, struck by the resilience of these people and all that they have faced through the years, through the generations. I had to ask, "Where is the hope in all of this?"

Petr looked at me with his bright blue eyes and said, "For all its faults, the government of Chukotka has turned to face us. That gives me hope. We have agreements with the government to implement social programs. It shows us that cooperation is possible, even if progress is slow. The future of our children is what matters most to us. That is our goal, still."

The next day, at Elena's kitchen table in her two-room flat in Anadyr, Irina Tymnevye's composed expression didn't change but her beautiful Mongoloid eyes welled and tears dripped down her high cheekbones and onto her hand-crocheted top. At Elena's invitation, Irina, in her thirties, and her fiftysomething sister-in-law, Tamara, had come to show me the human side of the processes that the politicians and community leaders had sketched out. Both grew up in Chukchi reindeer-herding families on the north slope of Chukotka, in the tundra hills overlooking Chaunskaya Bay more than four hundred kilometres northwest of Anadyr. Both had been removed by Russian authorities to residential school at age seven. And although they fondly remembered summers with their families on the tundra, neither had been back or would be going back, and that memory stung like a lash on raw skin.

With a sheaf of well-thumbed snapshots, set out on a glass tabletop among bowls of sugared blueberries, chocolate biscuits, dried reindeer, and chunks of beluga *mattak* (frozen whale skin that Elena kept on hand for her young son, Dani, whose father was Eskimo), Tamara pointed out her father, mother, sister, and brother among a sea of reindeer swirling around the yaranga where she was born on a very cold day, March 11, 1959. "We lived in our own world. We had no idea that there were other countries out there. Or that there were people fighting wars. Our world was the reindeer. We had everything we needed."

In the fall of 1966, however, Tamara and the other boys and girls her age and older in the brigade were picked up by a Soviet Army helicopter and flown to Snezhnaya—a place called Snow Wind—to start school.

"It was a sorrow for the parents and a sorrow for the children," she said quietly, "but that's the way things worked back then. It was a shock to realize that the language we had been speaking since we were born was not the language that the teachers spoke. We didn't even know simple words like "table" or "wall." And the teachers made fun of us for that. We had grown up without electricity, without radio. We went from lamps that burned sea-mammal fat to light bulbs. It was very different. There were a lot of difficulties, a lot of stresses. But the happiest times were when our parents drove the reindeer close to Snezhnaya in the spring and we were able to spend the whole summer back in the yaranga, back with the family on the land, back speaking Chukchi."

"Do you miss the times with your family on the land?" I asked.

"Well," she replied, "life is easier here and it is nice to have money, but what I miss is family. For a long time, we had a band—tambourine, drum, *tumran* [jaw harp]. We sang and danced and performed around the place, which kept us together. I miss the reindeer, but I miss making music with the family as well."

Twenty years younger than her sister-in-law, Irina was born in a hospital but she too had been taken to residential school. As she grew up, she gravitated toward town. Her parents still spent time on the land as part of the thirteen brigades that tended the herds roaming on lands surrounding the Tavaivaam settlement and collective farm, not too far from Anadyr. She recalled the days when there were fifty thousand reindeer roaming the tundra. She visited her parents when she could, living in the yaranga. But she also remembered the 1990s, when the Soviet Union collapsed and those reindeer seemed to evaporate into thin air.

As she started to cry, lips quiverings, she recalled big celebrations, even as the herds were dwindling, in Anadyr. "Many people came from the tundra by dogsled and by reindeer sleds to take part in celebrations. We got together and exchanged skins and things that had been made. We dressed in our best fur clothing. Reindeer were tied up to blocks of flats, and it seemed completely normal. People didn't even notice when that was happening."

After pausing to collect herself, she carried on. "But there came a point when my parents had no reindeer and couldn't participate anymore. They decided to move off the land. They decided to move to town. But rather than let their yaranga and their sleds and harnesses and all their things gradually rot away on the tundra, they decided . . ."

She paused again and just stopped talking, as the intensity of the memory shook through her small frame. Head lowered, she said in barely a whisper, "They took their yaranga and all their everyday things and burned them. They didn't need that anymore."

"That is so sad," was all I could muster in response. "Were you there when that happened?"

"No," she replied, looking up at me, "I was studying here in Anadyr. I did not see it with my own eyes but many people told me of this. It was sad. Yes. But they had no choice. They said they were right to do that. I think I agree. It would have been a lot more difficult to see the yuranga spoiled during the years that no one was using it."

"How will your daughter Katya's children remember that history?" I asked, nodding to the five-year-old who was now roaring around the kitchen floor with her toddler friend, Elena's son Dani.

"I don't know. When my mother was alive, she taught my elder daughter the Chukchi language. She told her stories of being on the land and taught her Chukchi ways. But now that she is gone, there is no one to teach Katya those things. I remember, but my life has been more in town since I left the yaranga to attend school." She sobbed, choking up again. "I guess she will learn by our stories, spoken in Russian."

"What does the future hold for the Chukchi herders?" I ventured.

This time Tamara again joined the conversation. She too had been swept up in the quiet flood of emotion that surrounded us all. "What does the future hold?" she repeated. There was a long pause and a sigh. "It is difficult to say. It is difficult to answer. I suspect that if our dead ancestors were to arise from their graves, they would be shocked, because they could not have imagined the situation when we do not know our language, when we drink, when we die out. It would be a shock to them."

That evening, as I walked down the hill and back to the nicest hotel in town (the only one that accepted CP holders), I was glad to be out in the twilight of the midnight sun and back breathing clear Arctic air. Although the conversation with Tamara and Irina had not been totally devoid of hope, it had certainly sucked the air out of the room. On the way I passed huge murals painted on the windowless end walls of brightly striped Abramovich apartment blocks. One showed a huge raven standing on an outcropping of rock overlooking a wild tundra landscape. The other showed a larger-than-life polar bear swimming toward the corner of the building.

With Tamara's and Irina's faces and stories still very much front of mind, I attended my last event in Anadyr, which was an evening with the local indigenous cultural association. "Come in, come in," the organizers said, as if the nondescript classroom in which they were meeting was a grand ballroom. In chairs around the perimeter of the room were a couple of dozen people from eight to eighty, each one proudly decked out in traditional Eskimo, Chukchi, and other national outfits. Elena and I were offered seats at the front before a coffee table festooned with samplings of "this year's harvest," including *mattk*, dried reindeer meat, berries, and caviar on freshly baked bread.

In the manner of a ringmaster or impresario, the charming convener of the gathering, a Chukchi woman called Viktoria, stepped forward in her blue calico summer parka and redoubled the warm and expansive welcome that showed in people's faces. "Today we will show you," she said, sweeping her arm from one side of the room to the other, lighting up smiles as she pointed, "how we preserve the traditions of Chukchi people, culture, and language. We have representatives from our public organization. The chief of the Eskimo, or Yupik, group is here, as a representative of Chukchi and other ethnic peoples who have lived here for eons. We have young singers, dancers, and musicians from the Children's School of the Arts who will perform for you."

Viktoria continued, "Our honoured guests are also some of our finest writers and poets in the Chukchi language. We will show you some of our arts and crafts, like an exhibit of walrus tusk carving and Eskimo ball making, and also some models of skin houses and boats that we use in the schools to teach our young people about the traditions of our ancestors. You must understand that we all come from different villages across Chukotka, but we now live and work here in Anadyr. Later, everyone will speak briefly about themselves, and we will ask you to tell us about your project."

The room in which this remarkable cultural demonstration would be given was modest, to say the least. It was about the size of a normal elementary school classroom, with a suspended ceiling and fluorescent light fixtures. Light streamed in from a bank of windows covered with drawn white blinds to filter the energy of the Arctic evening sun. There was a desk in one corner. Smaller tables had been pushed to the walls and were covered with samples of sewing, artwork, and crafts. All the chairs had been moved to the end, by the teacher's desk, and set up in theatre-style rows to allow something of a stage area to be set out in the middle of the room.

The walls were papered with black-and-white images of elders and traditional activities on the land: reindeer herding, reindeer riding, berry picking, walrus hunting, yaranga life. The room was clean and tidy and clearly loved by these people, but what animated it was the energy of a group ready to put on their best face for a visitor. In months of travel eastward along the Arctic Circle from Iceland I had never been physically so close to home—after all, North America was only 90 kilometres away—and yet I had never felt so utterly distant either, having traversed eight time zones and 6,400 kilometres from Moscow—fifteen time zones and 14,000 kilometres from Toronto—to get here. But somehow, when I stepped over the threshold of this cross-cultural meeting place, any geographic, cultural, or language barrier had vanished.

Inside this remarkable bubble, a trio of girls in matching fox-trimmed summer parkas danced through a series of stylized domestic chores, while another small group of ladies sang of life on the land to the beat of a drum skinned with walrus stomach. That was followed by eleven-year-old Michael (Misha) Golbtsev, in a white cotton tunic trimmed with blue, expressively enacting a hunting story in a beguiling dance with a wooden spear as a partner.

If the girls' practised movements were elegant in a dance-class kind of way, Misha's movements, down to the tips of his fingers in beaded gloves and the tips of his toes in soft reindeer-hide moccasins, were positively balletic, as he searched, stalked, and speared his prey before dragging it home to camp with a leather rope slung over his shoulder. "In small settlements along the coast," Elena whispered, "these activities are still going on, but for the most part, these dances are how they are living in the minds and hearts of children in town."

An older Chukchi teen then stepped forward and talked of his journey to learn to play the *vargan*, or jaw harp. He had travelled to take master classes with players in the settlements and had learned a number of songs and techniques that, like the dances, connected him to his roots. With a combination of breathing and playing that emulated a screaming reindeer—a sound that every herder had to recognize instantly, no matter how faint, because in the safety and well-being of the reindeer was the safety and well-being of the people—he captivated the house. I thought of Mandar at his kitchen table and the woman in the Khanty winter house in Kyshik, turning their bodies into instruments by breathing through a piece of vibrating reindeer shin bone like the wind over snowswept tundra.

Next up was a filmmaker, who spoke of his efforts to capture and record the stories and faces and language of the elders. Master craftspeople then showed their work and talked about the process of keeping the traditions alive—I watched as a dog team on winter tundra emerged from the practised chisel scratches of beautiful, expressive aged hands on polished ivory. I was surprised to see these scrimshaw patterns enriched with stains from ordinary coloured pencils rubbed into the ivory with spittle from the old woman's tongue and oil from her fingers.

Another woman juggled two ornate Eskimo balls made of sealskin in her hands as she talked about how these "circles within circles allow us to capture and keep the image of the sun. After the long polar night, the sun rises and greets every person in the settlement. To children it is just a ball or a toy, but the ball's symbolic value is never lost. To pass on a ball is to give a gift of the sun."

There was an old lady who talked about how writing was used to capture some essence of local ethnography. "I have been playing with words since I was very young, but I only started writing poetry in 2001, for my children." She read a poem in Chukchi about her young son coming home dirty and how important that was because it showed that he was out learning from the land. "Most of my poems are about the tundra because the tundra charms me," she said. "I never grumbled when my son came home dirty because this was part of our tradition." This made people in the room laugh. Clearly, she was a much loved voice in the Chukchi literary community. She finished by saying she would like to read one of her favourites.

The room was instantly silent, except for Irina, my translator, who breathed English words in echo to those being spoken in Chukchi:

Look intently into the tender tundra
How it is quiet and calm
Inviting snow lies all around the quiet
The blizzard is sleeping
Don't wake it up

This brought clapping and laughter from throughout the room.

At this point, it was Viktoria's turn. She picked up some of the models—of a sled, snowshoes, a kayak, an umiak, and a yaranga—and began to tell her story. She had been an elementary school teacher on the coast in a little town called Uelen. Uelen, on the northwest corner of a lagoon protected by a sandspit on the point of Chukotka closest to Alaska, had always been a meeting place. At the time of my visit, it had a population of about eight hundred, she thought, but in the Soviet period this settlement had received people from communities like Nunak, Imaklik, Uyagak, and Mamrokhpak, which were officially closed. The residents were moved first to a settlement called Naukan and then to Uelen. There were local children in her school, but there were also many children who had been displaced from other communities and who, like Irina and Tamara, were removed from their families at seven years of age and whisked off to residential school by law. The same practice was continuing under the Russian Federation.

Holding up one of the models, she said, "These are to show our children the lives of our ancestors. This sled, these boats are made without a single nail. They are tied together with strips of leather, sometimes from seal or walrus, sometimes from reindeer. For the boats, the covering was always the hide of the female walrus because it is much smoother than the hide of the male walrus."

As she went on, I could see just how wilful and persistent and systematic the Chukchi people have been, working to preserve and maintain their traditions and livelihoods in the face of devastatingly overwhelming odds against living in this place: the coldest, most inhospitable place on earth outside of Antarctica, but also a place that has suffered the ravages of human conquest through wars, disease, and sheer brutality since the Cossacks first arrived in 1742. There was beauty alive in this room; there had been since the moment we'd arrived.

Through seventy years of total oppression, during which it was forbidden by law to practise Native religions—any religion at all, for that matter—or to carry forward any language or tradition if it was not Russian; through forced relocations and the killing of shamans or any contrarian; through generations and decades of interventions by administrations who have done everything they could possibly think of to Russify these nomads, the indigenous fire still burns.

Elena and I got into the van to head across town to my hotel. Just as the giant raven mural rolled into view, it dawned on me that when I'd first laid eyes on that raven image, presiding over an undeveloped landscape, it spoke to me of an absence of people. But that night I wondered if the raven *was* the people, hiding in plain sight. Maybe the bear was the same.

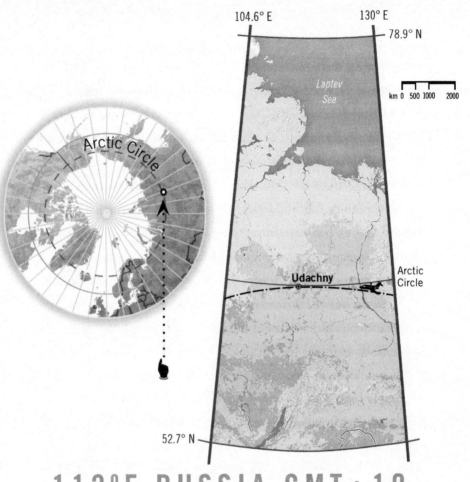

112°E RUSSIA GMT+10

15: FATE CONTROL

Although Chukotka actually hangs over the 180th meridian and the International Date Line and, on a good day, you might paddle a kayak east along the Arctic Circle to landfall in Alaska, because of Russian travel restrictions that were in place at the time, the only way home from Anadyr was to go west through Magadan, Moscow, Frankfurt, Washington, and Ottawa. Mercifully, the aged and comfort-challenged Russian plane on Flight 512 from Anadyr to Magadan had been replaced by a sparkling new Air Yakutia Boeing 757-200 leased from (and maintained by) Icelandair, in yet another creative collaboration between circumpolar nations. After half a world of Arctic experiences over nearly twenty-four months, there was something salutary in seeing my name in Cyrillic letters (my modest progress in learning to read simple Russian added its own measure of comfort) on a westbound boarding pass headed for home.

The day was crystal clear, even as we flew over great expanses of Siberian plains, wide winding Arctic rivers, and mountain ranges with their own little weather systems brewing at ground level. At one point, having arced north again on a great circle route, the shortest way to reach Moscow, we passed over mighty Eh-Beh and then over the scar of the mining town of Udachny on the Arctic Circle in western Yakutia. In their wisdom, the Soviets had approved a scheme to open a diamond mine there by exploding a 1.7-kilotonne nuclear bomb underground in 1974. It didn't go well, and they stopped doing that; but they weren't able to get close enough to cap the site at Udachny with twenty metres of concrete until 1992. Looking down from ten thousand metres, I wondered how the invisible reindeer people felt about that.

It's not that the indigenous people of the North have been totally invisible. Hundreds, even thousands of anthropologists, ethnologists, and social scientists have documented their travails in a myriad of ways since the beginning of their contact with outsiders. But as I thought about my snapshots taken at hearths and kitchen tables nearly halfway around the Arctic Circle, it was as if those fierce and gentle souls, those loud and quiet voices from the land, never had a chance. They welcomed the invaders into their chums, their yarangas, and their worlds, and yet social Darwinism had prevailed. The Western way would win, or try to win, all in the name of progress or national pride and security. The North was a place of discovery that became a repository of resources and, in Russia, a convenient backwater where dissidents would build the roads and miners would do the state's bidding as if the land were devoid of people or a culture of its own.

At best, when the people who lived there had entered the equation, they were a curiosity, a living museum, perhaps another source of cheap labour or proof of occupancy. In spite of the fact that peoples like the Sami, the Komi, the Nenets, the Yukaghirs, the Sakha, the Chuvans, the Evens, the Evenks, the Chukchi, and the Yupik had gotten along on their own for millennia, it was up to the conqueror to determine their fate and destiny from the moment of contact. The human traditions of these northern peoples were irrelevant. The bulldozing of these peoples, languages, and ways was of little consequence. It had happened in Africa. It had happened in Asia. It had happened to indigenous peoples in the Americas and the Middle East. And here in the North it was happening again, right in front of our eyes in real time. And yet the central element of the Chukotkan coat of arms, the poster child of informed compassionate progress, was the polar bear.

I opened my tray table, flipped open my computer, and pulled up the Arctic Council's latest statement on the well-being of northern peoples, the *Arctic Social Indicators* report, published by the Nordic Council of Ministers in Copenhagen in 2010. Following up on the first social-science-driven study commissioned by the eight-nation Arctic Council, called the *Arctic Human Development*

Report, the Arctic Social Indicators study was an attempt to put in place a systematic process for fathoming the human dimensions of the circumpolar North. The authors began with three indicators from the United Nations Human Development Index—health and population; material well-being; and education—and added to these "fate control," meaning the extent to which northern peoples are guiding their own destiny; "cultural integrity," meaning the extent to which individuals belong to a viable local culture; and "contact with nature," referring to the necessary connections between language, human enterprise, and the natural world.

Given the number of academics and researchers in eight countries who had contributed to this work, the report was surprisingly elegant in its design, execution, and presentation. From a host of possible indicators, the field of possible data sets was assessed and narrowed on the basis of what information was available, how hard that information was to collect if it was not currently available, how valid and reliable the information was, and whether the information was scalable from individuals to communities, regions, and beyond. Grigori Tynankergav, the member of the Chukotka Duma, had said the situation with Native people in Russia was complex; this report showed very clearly that he was an absolute master of understatement.

The only indicator that really resonated with me was "fate control." "Nobody ever asks us what we think," said person after person in one way or another on my travels. But Petr Klimov had said, "The government of Chukotka has turned to face us." And in that, he found hope. With that, and with an acknowledgement by all parties that self-determination matters, everything else could fall into place.

The ASI report read as follows:

Fate control, or the lack of it, can be experienced at the personal, household, community, and regional levels. Finnmark County in Norway, Greenland, Nunavut in Canada, or Sakha Republic in Russia may experience economic and political dependence on, respectively, Oslo, Copenhagen, Ottawa, or Moscow. Smaller communities in each of these regions may experience a lack of control in relation to the regional centre, Alta, Nuuk, Iqaluit, or Yakutsk, respectively. Individuals and households in an Arctic community may experience more or less control over their fate than do their neighbors, depending on their capacities and resources. Yet it is the collective control of fate that seems of critical concern to Arctic residents. Many communities and regions of the Arctic endure a residual dependence on outsiders, who play a major role in administering political, economic, and cultural institutions even at a local level, and notably on a higher scale. Boom-bust economic cycles characterize large parts of the Arctic, with concomitant high unemployment and underdevelopment in many regions, and dependence on transfer payments.

The breakdown of possible indicators of fate control was interesting. Under the heading of political power and activism, what was the level of participation and influence in local politics?

How strong was the political resistance? What was the proportion of local personnel in key decision-making positions? Who had control over place names? Who owned the rights to land and sea resources? In the economic realm, what was the level of self-generated income, and was it sufficient? Who had control of the local economy? In the broader sphere of knowledge construction, who had access to what information, who controlled the schools, and who controlled knowledge and information about politics? What was the language of power, and what was the retention rate of local indigenous languages?

On my journey so far I had seen that fate control for indigenous northerners, however measured, had often been so low that the hopelessness of the situation was reflected in levels of alcoholism, suicide, unemployment, and anomie many times the national and even international averages. The question was, how do you write "fate control" into even short-term development plans for the North when the pressing question of what was in the larder was singularly motivating everybody to focus on resource extraction? History seemed to indicate that it was impossible. Until we found the answer to that question, the future of the small peoples of the North would hang, still and always, somewhere between invisibility and active disregard, destined for almost certain cultural oblivion.

And still there were glimmers of hope, like a constellation of possibility across winter darkness of the back side of the circumpolar moon, not least the funnelling of funds from the Kupol gold mine into Aleksei Vakhrushev's film about reindeer herding in Chukotka. In this sense, my journey across Russia ended where it began.

Flashing back to the table in the RAIPON office in Moscow, I could see the humble Chukchi filmmaker explaining with smouldering passion his project to voice the old ways in the new world. Now that I had been to Chukotka, I had a much better sense of what was at stake and how he had raised the funds to make his film. I had found Aleksei's trail in Magadan and Kupol and again in Anadyr, when people spoke of his work and told me about his grant from the Kupol Social Development Foundation.

Not long after my return to Canada, in the spring of 2012, Aleksei brought his award-winning film—*The Tundra Book: A Tale of Vukvukai, the Little Rock*—to the Hot Docs film festival in Toronto, and I was able to see this remarkable work that had followed me, in a way, right across Siberia. It was a lyrical and arresting film that asked the viewer to take a breath and slow down. The story followed seventy-two-year-old Vukvukai—a Chukchi patriarch they called "the little rock"—through the seasons of the deer and the people with whom they intertwine. Except for occasional clues in clothing and equipment like knives and binoculars, it seemed almost impossible to believe that there were people living this self-sufficiently in the twenty-first century. Food, shelter, clothing, cordage, locomotion, transportation—all came from the reindeer.

In fact, Aleksei did not dwell on interactions with the world outside the cycles of the reindeer much at all, choosing to show Russian traders turning up with manufactured goods in tracked snow vehicles as if they were Martians from outer space. They communicated with the outside world with a wind-up two-way radio. The film was an engaging portrait of human enterprise that blurred the line, if there was one at all, between man and nature. It was as if Vukvukai and his family were one living breathing entity—right until the end of the film, when the spell was broken by the whack and whine of a government Sikorsky helicopter, coming in late summer to pick up the children in a whirl of Russian dust to take them off to residential school.

Goodbyes were said and the same fur-clad children who had played and learned so contentedly in the yaranga and on the windblown snow were drawn away from their parents in store-bought clothes and into the maw of a manmade machine. As the turbines spooled up, the steps were pulled up into the aging Mi-8 helicopter. Sad little sunny faces could be seen pressed against the convex windows.

Cut to a close-up on the face of Vukvukai, the old herder, who normally had all the answers but was clearly at a loss. In sub-titles, he said: "Why does the helicopter take them away? The boys and the girls. It's like it takes them to prison. And this is the end. They get used to living there. And they won't work in tundra. They don't want to. They will live over there. They'll become drunks. Or they'll end up in the grave. Just imagine—ten months of residential school and only two months in the tundra. It's like prison. Why are they doing this to our kids? The world has turned upside down. And then they'll leave their mother, leave their father. You see, in this tent, in that tent, their kids didn't come back. Why do they have this law? It is a stupid law."

Lest the film media not hear the call to action at the end of his 112-minute documentary, Aleksei took every opportunity, in far better English than he ever let on having when we spoke in Moscow through an interpreter, to hammer his point home again and again. When he won the prestigious NIKA award for best documentary from the Russian Academy of Motion Picture Arts and Sciences, in 2011, he reiterated his message on stage: "I am holding this award, the five-hundredth NIKA," he said, "and I see it not only as recognition of the merits of our film, but also as recognition of the rightness of the film's protagonist. I wish his point of view to be heard in some higher quarters. I wish that a more flexible law of the universal secondary education is adopted, so the residential schools can be closed and these reindeer-herders, Chukchi and other indigenous people that still retain their identity, stay alive. Let them live!"

In coverage of Aleksei's big win, I saw an indigenous man with a voice, speaking proudly about what concerned him. I saw a man controlling his own fate, or at least trying to with every bone in his body. But the significance of something else wasn't lost on me: in the credits, though buried among other acknowledgements and thank yous, was recognition of the Kupol foundation in helping to bring that voice, that creative energy, that compelling story to market.

Contemplating the second half of my journey, I sat at the kitchen table on a fine autumn day staring off into space. In front of me was the polar projection of the northern hemisphere, with little Post-it flags on all the stops I'd already made. Underneath the map was a sheaf of trail-worn journals that was growing by the minute. With 210 degrees of longitude behind me, I had about 150 yet to go, through Alaska, Canada, and Greenland, before I would cross over the Denmark Strait and back to Iceland.

Gail, having long since rolled with my yawning absences, was out for the day. My keys still fit the locks. The dog hadn't barked at me when I arrived home from the airport. And our two daughters, although they had more or less flown the coop since graduating from university, were present in the room, as was Gail, in a collage of family photos in frames hung on the kitchen wall. Suddenly I was awash in guilt. What had Gail and I ever done to deserve this privilege? And why was there not more generosity of spirit among the many who inhabit the middle latitudes, when we had so much?

Here we were, consuming with abandon, fretting about climate change, apparently oblivious to the fact that the attitudes and appetites driving global warming were no different from those that had powered policies of conquest and assimilation in the North. We talked of sovereignty and the resource potential of the North while northerners watched their land base and the sustenance it provided shrink with each passing season. They watched their babies die from disease and overcrowding. They worried about clean water and food security. They buried their elders, who took with them the last words of languages derived from a relationship with the land, knowing in their guts that it was possible to die of a broken heart. And they looked to the future, as they buried their teens, too many of whom have died at their own hands, suspended in a cultural muddle between cellphones and spears. And still, with unquenchable beauty and courage, they welcomed us.

168.8° W   160.8° W

70° N

Chukchi
Sea

km 0   100   200   300

ALASKA

Bering
Strait

Kotzebue

Arctic
Circle

Shishmaref

SEWARD PENINSULA

Nome

Norton Sound

From
Anchorage

62.1°N

Arctic Circle

166°W ALASKA GMT−8

16: NINETY-THREE-YEAR-OLD SOURDOUGH

The Arctic Circle comes ashore on Alaska's Seward Peninsula. The nearest town, Shishmaref, is an Inupiaq community of about six hundred souls that had been in the news almost enough to make it a household name in the early years of the twenty-first century. Because of the way that changing sea conditions—rising water levels, less sea ice, shorter winter season, fiercer storms—had been eroding the land on which this little village was located, Al Gore, among others, had taken to calling the residents of Shishmaref the "first victims of climate change," as they watched buildings on the edge of their community fall into the roiling waters of the Chukchi Sea.

As I planned the next leg of my journey, a web search revealed the site of the Shishmaref Erosion and Relocation Coalition, founded in 2001. Its newsletter of August 2005, the latest on the site, mentioned that media coverage over the previous year had brought to town representatives from *Time, National Geographic,* Alaska Public Radio, HBO, and a host of other outlets including the National Radio of Switzerland, ZDF German Television, the Swedish newpaper *Svenska Dagbladet,* and a French production company called Miroir Film.

A link led me to an elaborate website for a film called *The Last Days of Shishmaref: An Inupiaq Community Swallowed by the Sea.* A team including a Dutch large-format photographer, Dana Lixenberg, a web documentary maker, Jan Louter, and a filmmaker, Melle van Essen, were drawn by the worldwide attention surrounding the beleaguered community. They had found their way to Shishmaref in 2007 and captured an uncomfortably intimate portrait of faces, voices, and living conditions. Their work had been released the following year through multiple platforms—film, book, web—to great acclaim from almost every artistic and environmental organization.

The web documentary included Lixenberg's superb photographs, clips from van Essen's film coverage, and stories in the voices of the people of Shishmaref, interwoven with a theatrical-trailer-style narration and an orchestral score including Inupiaq drums. It had a kind of elegiac quality. That tone, combined with the definitive past tense "swallowed" in the film's title—it didn't say the community was "being swallowed" or was "soon to be swallowed"—did nothing to convey that there was a process under way here. No, Shishmaref appeared to be a community that had been *swallowed* by the sea: past tense, done deal.

Further searching revealed nothing more. The best I could determine from a distance was that Shishmaref indeed had become one of the first victims of a rising warming sea and the people who lived there had gone elsewhere. There was talk of picking out a new site on the mainland and of getting funds together to build a road to that site and one day, very soon, getting everybody moved there. But suddenly, around 2008, after the great wave of worldwide coverage had rolled up on the beach, the web had gone silent. It was as if Shishmaref and its six hundred residents had vanished into thin Arctic air. My challenge was to find them.

January 2012 found me in Nome, Alaska, where I had a good visit with Tom Gray, the head of the Alaskan Reindeer Herders Association. Aside from the fact that the head of the ARHA had no reindeer—in the last decade they had been scattered by incoming caribou herds and eaten by wolves, two-legged and four-legged, he said—I was surprised when he told me that Shishmaref was very much still on the map. If I wanted to go there, I should call either Fred Goodhope Jr. or Clifford Weyiouanna.

Without missing a beat, he picked up the phone and put a call in to the Weyiouanna household and found Clifford at home. "There's a guy here in Nome, a writer from Canada, who's interested in talking to you. Would you be interested in talking to him?" Apparently he was. Tom nodded and handed the phone to me. I needed to think fast.

"I've been talking to Tom about reindeer herding," I began. And before I could I say anything more, Clifford butted in and said, "You're talking to that guy, the old German. He's not Native. He just thinks he's Native. And anything he knows about reindeer he probably learned from me." Obviously these two guys knew each other quite well.

"I'm wondering if I might talk to you sometime about reindeer herding and climate change."

"Climate change!" He laughed. "There's no such thing as climate change. Sure," he replied. "Bering Air has a flight tomorrow morning and Era has a flight in the evening. Just let me know when you're arriving."

Suspecting that a small coastal community might not have a well-stocked local store, I asked, "Is there anything I can bring from Nome? Do you need any supplies or fresh groceries?"

"As a matter of fact I do," he said. I could hear the smile in his voice, and got some sense that this wouldn't be a request for fresh bread or lettuce. "I'm way low on Lea & Perrins Worcestershire Sauce."

The sun had just poked its nose over the horizon when the Bering Air flight to Shishmaref took off at 12:30 p.m. the following day. The outside temperature was a balmy minus forty-eight Celsius. It was about the same inside the plane for the first half hour of the journey; the windows were frosted over. Partway through the flight I went to chat with the pilots and looked out over their shoulders at the shining vista as we headed north over the frozen landscape.

The map in my hand, showing the borders of regional corporations owned by the indigenous peoples of America's forty-ninth state, made it clear that the relationship between the Native peoples of Alaska and the government of the United States was dramatically different than anything I'd encountered in Scandinavia or Russia. Signed in 1971, when the U.S. government was determined to bring oil from Prudhoe Bay to southern markets, the Alaska Native Claims Settlement Act was the first agreement of its kind in the circumpolar world to recognize First Peoples' claims to ownership of traditional territories.

In one fell swoop, ANCSA transferred title, including surface and subsurface rights, to forty million acres of land, established a royalty system for subsequent development on other Alaskan lands, and passed along US$960 million in cash, divided among twelve regional corporations and two hundred village corporations, including Shishmaref, which fell within the Bering Straits Native Corporation.

I survived the bitterly cold ten-minute "snogo" (Alaskan snowmobile) ride to Clifford Weyiouanna's house from the Shishmaref airstrip. One of the first things I learned from him was that the ANCSA had created at least as many problems as it had solved: "The problem is, back in '71 when we got the money and tried to set out a plan, we were not business people, never were. And all of a sudden we had some money to play with and a lot of big corporations played with it in the wrong way. And we had a lot of people come around to the village corporation trying to sell this and that, like from Anchorage and the lower forty-eight, and they never let us know that their business was failing. But they sweet-talked us. Those in Barrow are fortunate, because they have oil revenues and can pay dividends to the shareholders. Here, not so much. If the regional corporation doesn't make any money—and it doesn't—then there's no dividend. Before '71 people used to do things that needed doing: hunting, chopping wood. Now wood is seventy-five dollars a load. Everything is about money, especially since ANCSA was passed."

In his seventieth year, sitting like the laird of the manor in his fleece vest and checked flannel shirt, emphasizing points with an omnipresent cigarette clenched between the first two fingers of his left hand, Clifford took me through a life story that was almost as surprising as my discovery that Shishmaref had not actually been swallowed by the sea.

Born right there on this spit of shifting sand on June 26, 1942, Clifford learned to hunt and fish from his grandfather. When he had gone as far as he could in the local school, he and another promising student from town were awarded scholarships that took them to four years at a parochial school in Sioux Falls, South Dakota. After a short detour in the army he returned north and married into the Goodhopes, a reindeer-herding family. With his wife, Shirley, and their four children, he had built his own herd, which gave them a fine living, selling meat locally and antler velvet to the Koreans, until the same forces that had dissipated Tom Gray's herd took his as well in recent years.

"I knew things weren't going to last forever," he said, "so I took my last big cheque from the Koreans and invested it in the apartment complex here in town. I'm so glad I did that, because here we are with no reindeer and changing times. Really changing times."

"What about that?" I asked, hoping we might get onto the topic of climate change and the apparent evaporation of the whole community. "I'm glad you're here, but a little surprised, after hearing about the town that 'surrendered to the sea.'"

"Not yet," he said, lighting another Winston. "More hotcakes?"

Throughout our conversation, after he'd tucked away the four big bottles of Lea & Perrins I'd brought, Clifford moved back and forth between the dry sink and the kitchen table, keeping a steady flow of thick black coffee and homemade sourdough hotcakes. He told me the food was for his grandsons, who were working outside on this bitterly cold day to dig a grave for one of their friends, who had hanged himself the previous week. And then he told me the story of the sourdough, which was the same age as his dad, who lived next door. "Yup, that starter has been going as long as my dad has been alive. The hotcakes you're eating are the same culture that has been in this family for ninety-three years."

"What is it like for a young person, living in Shishmaref?" I ask. "Will your grandchildren be living here, keeping your starter going, when they're ninety-three years old?"

He laughed. "I doubt it. It's different now. It's all about computers. The school is the biggest employer in the community. Cooks, teacher's aides, custodians. We have two of our own local people who have come back as graduate teachers. We have one lawyer who had graduated from here. We have one pilot flying for Era Aviation. Having our own people teaching here is a big deal. Teachers from the lower forty-eight don't last very long. It's hard on the kids when teachers rotate too much. But other than that, kids have to leave town to get an education and a job. It's a dry town. We used to be 'damp,' which meant there were some controls on who could bring in liquor. Now we're dry. The richest guy in town is the bootlegger, selling booze at $250 a bottle. Go figure. I'm not sure there's a college in black market economics for that."

"What about the community relocation?" I tried again. "Five years ago, it sounded imminent."

Clifford leaned back in his chair and took a long draw on his cigarette, exhaling slowly and letting the smoke swirl around his head. "Yeah," he said, "it was. They said, 'Next year, next year.' But I've always wondered, how are you going to get the fuel and stuff up from barges on the ocean to a community up the hill on the mainland? Me and Shirley, before she passed, we liked the ocean. It provided us with food. But most of the village voted to move. We were two of the eighteen people who said no. Right now, I don't know what is going to happen. There are communities up and down the coast that are in the same situation. The government built up the seawall. And we could move, if there was money. But there isn't money. Or we could break the community apart and head to Nome or Kotzebue. I don't know. And in the meantime, with all this just hanging there, there's no money for fixing up what we have, keeping our water and sewer lines going, keeping the airport going. This is a very difficult place to live, and especially so for the young people. But it is our home. It's different now that the reindeer are gone, but I still have my cabin and the corrals and the grazing leases if they ever come back. And unless we have some kind of huge disaster, I think we're likely going to be here for quite a while yet."

True to his word, Clifford excused himself and packed up a picnic of hotcakes and Thermoses of hot coffee and headed to the edge of town on his snogo to resupply the gravediggers. During the hour or so he was gone, he suggested, I should put on my things and go for a wander through town, which I did. "People are friendly here. Just say hi and tell them what you're doing."

Later, Clifford's children and their spouses and his grandchildren came by. Respectfully, they checked out the stranger and asked a few questions of their own. Clifford took out some photo albums and walked me through nearly seventy years of life on the edge of North America. He showed me a guestbook with names of buyers from Korea and Japan and, of course, the names of some of the reporters and journalists who had come to document the end of days in Shishmaref.

"Are you the first victims of climate change?" I finally asked.

"I don't know. There's a lot going on here. And yes, things are changing. But things have always been changing. This is not an easy place to live. But we know how to make do. We know how to adapt."

"Are you worried about the rising sea levels?"

"Yes. But we have far more pressing problems that we need to deal with first. Like housing. And education. And giving our kids some options for the future."

"Do you think the move is going to happen one day?"

"I don't know. Maybe. I started a relocation committee but it kind of lost steam. I was acting chairman for quite a while. And I was sitting here at my kitchen table then and the phone rang. There was a lady on the phone. She said she had some money to help with our relocation. She said it was so-and-so from the Smithsonian. She told me that she could possibly fund about $200,000."

His black eyes burned into mine as the story continued: "I told her we were looking for money for a feasibility study to see about building a road to the new site. I asked her what the money was for. She said that it was to move the cemetery. I couldn't believe it. We'd already done a questionnaire, and 95 percent of people said leave their relations where they are. I told her that one of the last things Mom [his wife, Shirley] said before she died was 'Leave my body here.' She had money to move the cemetery, she said, from the Smithsonian. I said, 'Lady, we're more interested in the live ones than the dead ones.' And I hung up."

Before the evening Era Aviation flight back to Nome, Clifford offered me more hotcakes and a sample of the ninety-three-year-old starter to take home, along with a set of handwritten instructions on its care and feeding. We bundled up and headed out to the airstrip. There is no terminal building in Shishmaref, just a garage for the government snowplow, so we sat among a group of people on idling snogos and sleds waiting for the plane to arrive.

When it did land on the distant end of the runway and eventually taxied up, blasting ice crystals in everyone's faces, the pilot threw open the doors and called for people to help unload. Anxious to do something to keep the blood moving, I stepped forward and took my place handbalming cardboard boxes from the plane to waiting sleds.

There were a couple of mailbags and then cases of milk, bread, cereal, and fresh carrots. The last box was a corrugated container unlike any other, made of some kind of waxed cardboard and cinched tight with white plastic straps. Just as I read "Foot" on the top of the end that was emerging from the plane, I realized why Clifford's grandsons were digging a grave.

By chance, I had become part of a crew lining up on either side of a shipping crate cradling the body of nineteen-year-old Gilford Iyatunguk, back from autopsy in Anchorage. The last thing I saw, as I shook hands with Clifford and stepped into the dim yellow glow of the small plane's interior, was Gilford Iyatunguk's girlfriend in her parka, crumpled over his makeshift coffin as they got ready to take it to the newly prepared grave.

Back at the Nugget Inn in Nome, I couldn't get that box and Gilford Iyatunguk's unceremonious return to Shishmaref out of my mind. I paced my room. A fuzzy satellite connection fed to an ancient TV bolted to the wall brought images and commentary of the Australian Open tennis tournament, normally a functional diversion. A box. A cardboard box.

I got on the Web to see what I might learn about this young man. There he was on Facebook, large as life, one shot of Gilford in the kitchen and another selfie taken with his girlfriend. In his last status update, posted on December 31, he wished the world Happy New Year. His favourite quotation read: "Life moves pretty fast, if you don't stop and look around once in a while you could miss it. JUST DO IT!"

Life moves pretty fast. And then it doesn't. And then your body gets sent out to Anchorage for autopsy and you come home in a box. Nineteen years old. Poor Gilford.

While I was walking around Shishmaref during Clifford's supply run, word presumably had spread that there was a stray dog in town. A young lad who introduced himself as Dennis Davis pulled up on a snogo and asked if he could interview me on his video camera for a film he was making.

"Trying to capture the view from here," he said when I asked what it was he was trying to do. After all the media that had been through this town, it certainly made sense to me that people here would want to tell their side of the story. As we stood there in the bitter, bitter cold, as the wind whipped up off the frozen ocean, Dennis asked some very good questions about what I had found in my travels around the Arctic world so far. But the conversation didn't go much beyond that. Like me, he got cold and wanted to keep moving. As he was putting his helmet back on, he suggested we stay in touch and gave me his email address.

Looking at Gilford's smiling face on my computer screen, I emailed Dennis to ask what had happened. He replied almost immediately: "He was drinking and took his own life. It is sad that there is nothing to do in a small village hence this is one of the reasons for me doing this documentary video is to get people out in the world to see what it is like and to try and come up with things for people to do not just get stuck in a black hole."

So complex. So incredibly sad and simple. When every other aspect of your life and your being was shaped and controlled by outside forces, was the most definitive act of "fate control" taking your own life?

Alaska had the highest rate of suicide per capita in the United States in 2007; the U.S. average was 11.5 suicides per 100,000 population; Alaska's rate was nearly twice that, 21.8 per 100,000. The stats for young men in Gilford's age group (fifteen to twenty-four) were seven times higher than that: between 2000 and 2009, 141.6 per 100,000 each year, which is the overall suicide rate for *all* demographic groups in Chukotka.

Youth who are exposed to suicide or suicidal behaviour are at higher risk for attempting suicide than youths who are not. The Statewide Suicide Prevention Council said more than 90 percent of people who died by suicide had depression or another diagnosable, treatable mental or substance abuse disorder. As the feel of that box came back into my fingertips, I suspected this was not simply a suicide problem. It was a fate control problem. Either way, why weren't we who lit our lamps with northern coal and oil, we who were getting rich and fat from the bounty of the northern larder, we who were fussing about the fate of the polar bear—why were we choosing to do so little about it?

Next stop along the Circle was Kotzebue, population 3,200. In addition to being the centre and seat of the Northwest Arctic Borough, Kotzebue claimed to have been the home of the world's largest polar bear, a big male tipping in at over a thousand kilograms. It was also the main expediting and organizational centre for the massive Red Dog mine, the world's largest producer of zinc concentrate, located 150 kilometres northwest of town in the heart of the Brooks Mountain Range.

Kotzebue had been on my radar since I'd read *The Firecracker Boys*, a shocking account by Dan O'Neill of an American plan as crazy as the nuclear diamond-mining program at Udachny. Led by Edward Teller in 1958, Project Chariot, which was never realized, called for the opening of a massive harbour north of Kotzebue with "peaceful" nuclear explosions, to kick-start the economy of the state America had purchased from Russia a century earlier. In *The Genocide Machine in Canada*, Robert Davis said the real aim was to "measure the size of a bomb necessary to render a population dependent after local food sources have become too dangerous to eat due to extreme levels of radiation."

Disembarking from the Alaska Airlines Boeing 737 into the obscenely cold air in Kotzebue, I noticed the smiling, ruff-framed Inupiaq or Yupik man painted on the tail of the plane and made a mental note to see whose face had become a major company brand. Airline literature said simply, "Long known for its Alaskan roots, symbolized by the Eskimo on the tail of the aircraft, Alaska Airlines offers a friendly and relaxed style of service, one that we have come to appreciate as the 'Alaskan Spirit.'" In keeping with the trend of incomers in the North, Alaska Airlines had either created a logo figure from scratch or, more likely, appropriated someone's face without attribution or name.

A bit of digging led to a self-published book called *Know the Happy Face: Biography of Oliver Amouak*, by the man's granddaughter, Brenda Ritchey. Later I ordered the book from a used-book store. It categorically showed, with an original black-and-white photo with acetate overlay of the Alaskan Airlines logo, that the Mr. Mona Lisa of Eskimos was, in fact, her grandfather. They had tweaked his smile but that was Oliver, no doubt about it.

Interestingly, instead of being churlish about it, Ritchey had gone to some pains to retell some of her grandfather's stories and to teach her readers about where and how he had lived his life. With something of an ingenious design tweak of her own, the whole volume worked as a flip book, with little drawings of characters doing a dance that her granddad used to like very much. But there it was: Alaska Airlines had taken away the man's name, given him a smile, and continued to present him, anonymously, as some essence of Alaskan hospitality.

My first stop in Kotzebue was a morning with Zach Stevenson, the geographic information systems (GIS) professional working for the Subsistence Mapping Project in the Northwest Arctic Borough. As a fellow geographer, I had followed his trail electronically and was eager to see the work the group was doing with hunters, trappers, fishers, and gatherers along the coast of Alaska. The borough's goals, as set out in ANCSA, included maintaining Inupiaq culture, promoting traditional ways of life, and fostering local self-determination, and they seemed well served by the project being conducted by Stevenson and his team. Cultural and intellectual control of information about hunting and gathering of natural resources is surely at the core of local people taking local control over resources, even if the full measure of their knowledge of the place is often lost in translation. But the work was important and had helped not only to create all kinds of interviewing, clerical, administrative, recording, mapping, and analysis jobs in Kotzebue and beyond but also to provide a foundation of locally derived traditional knowledge that would be actively used alongside other types of science in determining the future of development projects in the region.

Between interviews, in cold like I had never felt, I tried something I had always wanted to do. Dark and early one morning, I took a cup of hot coffee into the minus-forty-eight air and fired the whole thing into the air. It was better than popular scientific legend had promised. The contents of the entire cup went *poooof!* with an audible pop and drifted as a puff of white vapour into the pool of light on the hotel porch. Very cool!

Martha Siikauraq Whiting, the Inupiaq mayor of the Northwest Arctic Borough, was up to her eyeballs in frozen water and sewer problems during this crazy cold snap but still found time to chat. With the unabashed smile of an optimist and expressive hands that could have sold diamond rings to royalty, she said, "Zach's project is a good opportunity to take the lead, to take the ownership. It's giving us more cards at the table, for policy-making and resource development. It's also a tool for us to learn these new skills, to learn about the language, the culture, the river. It's a chance for our community to perpetuate our culture. It is key that it is going to be written down. There's going to be a schoolbook. We need to take advantage of absolutely every opportunity we can to keep our culture and language strong. We need to have our voices heard."

"How is that going for you?" I asked.

"It's a struggle," she said quietly, as she straightened herself in her well-worn mayoral chair. She took a deep breath. "If I have a message for you to take away, it is that we—the indigenous peoples of Alaska—exist. We are here. I want people to know that we are unique and a national treasure. And we need to be part of the conversation when it comes to the Arctic. Even here in Alaska, we get a lot of people talking about the Arctic. It's climate change. It's offshore drilling. It's resource development. It's Arctic passage. As global warming is occurring, there's going to be a lot more marine traffic. So there is a lot of conversation about the Arctic."

She continued, "Too often we don't even *exist* in those conversations. We have to be the first and foremost people involved in what happens in the Arctic. So any time the word comes out about policy or next steps, they'd better make sure that we are involved because it's our backyard. It's our home. We have lived here for generations. We're going to stay here for generations to come. We're going to have the best interests for what happens in our environment, because we're going to be here forever."

Conscious of having a limited amount of time with the mayor, I drove on with queries about how climate change fitted into the picture. "It's like a phantom," Whiting said. "I won't say it's an organization, a presence maybe—that is right in our face. You see it. But it's kind of out there looming. So it's very difficult to address. There are changes we see with plants and insects and birds and berries, that we see with the weather patterns. It's so big but it's hard to grasp and certainly not as pressing as loss of culture or language or any of the thousand other things we're worrying about.

"And then there are other things we're looking at for policy, like the opening Arctic corridor and the increase in ocean traffic. I need to make sure that if there is money to be made from that—and there are expenses as well for search and rescue and environmental cleanup—I need to make sure that we get a share of revenues of that. I don't want to say that it's priority one, two, or three, but on a day like today, when I'm worried about getting water to our clinics, climate or climate change—whatever you call it—falls down our list of priorities. I'm hoping that this cold spell will not be too long."

But with grace and ease and by habit of mind, Whiting returned to where she began, cultural survival. She talked of her own daughter: as the offspring of a white father from Michigan and a mother who is three quarters Inupiaq, her Native blood quantum—the all-important measure of who receives govern-ment services for American aboriginal people—is only one quarter. If she, like her mother, had children with a non-Inupiaq father, her offspring would fall below the threshold. "We talk about that," she said.

She stiffened: "We will not, we cannot become a people of the museum. We will not become a people of the past. The last time I checked, we are a people. We exist. Even if my daughter doesn't know as much as I do or as my mother did, the important thing is that she knows who she is, that she knows her culture, she knows who she is as an Inupiaq person, and that she is proud as an Inupiaq person. She knows where she comes from. She knows who she is named after. She knows her internal spirituality as a people. And she is proud to carry that legacy for her own children. Cultural identity has changed in a generation. A lot of young people are asking, 'Who am I?'"

I told the mayor of my experience earlier in Shishmaref. "There is no doubt that this questioning can lead to suicide and to alcoholism," she responded. "We have to have a purpose. When we go to our fish camp, we have a purpose. We have to go hunt. We have to go fish. We have to prepare the camp for the winter. All kids have a role at the camp: bring the wood, take out garbage, dig a well to get water. Which is why kids like camp.

"We have the highest suicide rate in the state, and that's not something that we're proud of. A lot of it has to do with cultural identity. It gets tough. It gets really hard. At the same time you have to look at a lot of strength and resilience that we do have. We have a strong language. We have a strong culture. It's my job as mayor to make sure that we provide people with hope."

On the way back to the hotel, I picked up a newspaper that highlighted the importance of Whiting's optimism, something of the essential power of her leadership in the face of dark realities that shade, it seems, all post-colonial northern life. A front-page story detailed the case of a fifty-three-year-old Kotzebue man who slashed his sister multiple times with an ulu, shot her, then shot himself but not fatally, leaving him able to present himself to the Norton Sound Hospital ER. His lawyer was requesting a change of venue because of fear that the man wouldn't get a fair trial in his hometown.

As an effective counterpoint to the raw violence in the paper, and presenting an excellent sense of the substance underpinning Mayor Whiting's optimism, I spent a morning at Nikaitchuat Ilisagviat, the tribal immersion school in Kotzebue. It was another dark mid-winter day with temperatures that turned diesel fuel to wax, but the welcome I received and the colour and the chortling of happy children in this one-room school warmed me from the inside out. The school operated outside of the formal Alaskan system, run as a private non-governmental institution, but the Northwest Arctic Borough and NANA Regional Corporation (one of thirteen for-profit Alaska Native Corporations set up as part of ANCSA) were supporting the place because of its role in strengthening Inupiaq pride and confidence in the community.

Children of various Native backgrounds, not just Inupiaq youngsters, were in a circle with the teachers on a bright blue carpet. Their parents had to pay $500 a month tuition for them to be there. It was clear that they were thoroughly enjoying games and exercises and stories in the Inupiaq language. The director, Mickey Nanouk, explained, "Nikaitchuat is based on the understanding that culture resides in language, and from that all else flows. If they can get a good start here, this gives the children an early childhood foundation in Inupiaq before attending regular school, where they might get twenty minutes a week in their native language."

Clearly, whatever was happening here was generating pride both in the students, whom I watched going through their paces so willingly, and in the community, where a visit had been highly recommended to me. The tribal immersion school was also garnering interest from other northern jurisdictions. "Representatives from Statoil in Norway are coming here next week to see what we're up to," Nanouk said. "Our mission is simple to say, harder to enact. What we are trying to do here is instill the knowledge of Inupiaq identity, dignity, and respect, and to cultivate a love of lifelong learning." I couldn't help but wonder how life might have been different for Gilford had he experienced tribal immersion like this in his formative years.

Walking back across town in the forenoon, the sun just poking up over the horizon, I heard a clatter of sound from above. I stopped and turned to see what looked like forty or fifty ravens, all gathered in the pool of sunlight that was hitting the top of the insulated water tower, or perhaps the fuel tank. Like a romp of river otters on a frozen bank, the ravens were crowding together at the cusp of the curve where the gently sloping top of the tower arced down. In ones and twos, birds were sliding on their bellies until gravity cast them off into space, where they caught the air, did a barrel roll or two, and circled back to the pack on the top of the tank.

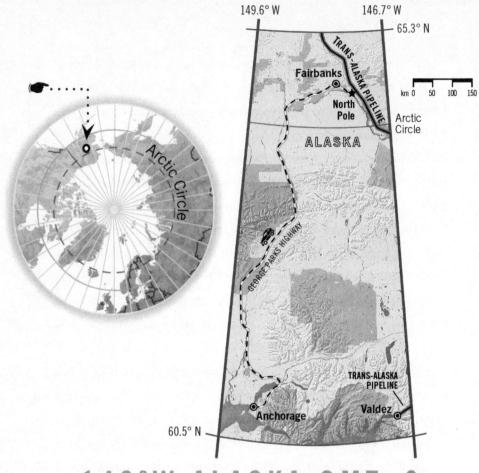

Fairbanks

TRANS-ALASKA PIPELINE

North
Pole

ALASKA

GEORGE PARKS HIGHWAY

TRANS-ALASKA
PIPELINE

Valdez

Anchorage

60.5° N

Arctic Circle

148°W ALASKA GMT–8

17: HO, HO, HO

The only figure of northern myth older and more persistent than the "Happy Eskimo" has got to be good old Santa Claus. After Rovaniemi, Finland, which may hold the title of the HQ of Santa Inc.—being right *on* the Arctic Circle—the next most enduring point in the Coke constellation is south of Fairbanks in a little place called—what else?—North Pole, Alaska.

On the off-ramp from Alaska Highway 2, in the shadow of a set of McDonald's golden arches, was a large sign made of ice: "Welcome to North Pole where the spirit of Christmas lives year round." It didn't take long to find Santa Claus House at 101 St. Nicholas Drive in the village of North Pole, but I was a little surprised at how much it seemed like a roadside attraction set between two oil refineries on one axis and two military installations on another.

Sadly, although it is "Christmas every day of the year" in North Pole, it was mid-week in January when I arrived, and Santa was only at home on Saturdays and Sundays. So I had to settle for a walk around the exterior. It looks far more European and less Coke-like than Santa's main office in Rovaniemi, but the fat man is still wearing red. The day was, as my musical idol Tom Waits liked to say, "colder than a well digger's ass," so I headed back to the car, noticing that the water vapour in the exhaust had created a sail-shaped icicle that was nearly dragging on the ground.

Over coffee and free Wi-Fi at the North Pole McDonald's (which, ironically, is south of the Arctic Circle McDonald's in Rovaniemi), I learned the cute story of how the Alaskan zip code 99705 has become the same as postal code H0H 0H0 in Canada, the address to which letters to Santa are sent and from which good boys and girls will receive a letter back, no charge. If you want the letter personalized or with customized text, or if you'd like an authentic deed for one square inch of North Pole property, or if you'd like to purchase any number of other cool things—a "Santa dollar," a jumbo sticker proclaiming the bearer to be on "Santa's Good List"—then that costs a bit extra. And in true northern gold-rush style, the backstory of Santa Claus House has a frontier family thread woven right in.

"When Con and Nellie Miller arrived in Fairbanks, Alaska, in 1949," the story goes, "they had $1.40 in cash and two hungry kids. Determined to carve out a living in the new territory of Alaska, Con soon became a merchant and fur buyer in the surrounding villages. Donning an old red Santa suit each Christmas, Con earned celebrity status as Santa Claus in the eyes of the village children—the first St. Nick many had ever seen."

One thing led to another, and the store became "Santa Claus House." Nellie got the contract to run North Pole's first post office, Con became the mayor, and Nellie became a state marriage commissioner and could officially marry the giddy couples who flocked to Santa's lap to say their vows. They added a new wing and commissioned a three-dimensional thirteen-metre-tall plastic Santa (gone in January 2012, having been replaced by a much taller two-dimensional plywood one). Sixty years later Santa Claus House is one of the top attractions in Interior Alaska, having welcomed millions of visitors from all over the world in person and online.

From North Pole, I got back on Highway 2 and continued to Fairbanks. My original plan was to take a few days and drive down through the Kuskokwim Mountains, past Denali National Park and Mount McKinley to Wasilla, north of Anchorage—

where, if Sarah Palin wasn't available for lunch or tea, I was going to search for a lake named after a friend's father who'd been seconded to the U.S. Army Corps of Engineers during the Second World War. On my earlier flight to Nome from Anchorage, those majestic peaks and snow-filled valleys had been bathed in starlight, leaving an image that stirred the wilderness wanderer in me. To come here without taking at least a few steps on snowshoes would have been a travesty.

The first indicator that it was not to be came at the rental agency. The clerk asked what I was planning to do with her bottom-of-the-line super-sub-compact, and I told her about the planned expedition down to Anchorage. She blurted, "Are you nuts?" After composing herself, she flatly refused to rent me that car.

"Do you have any idea how cold it has been, how snowy it will be in the mountains, how lonely that road is in the winter, how long you would last if you broke down, and how stupid you would be to go down that way this week by yourself? I can't rent you that little car. At the very least, you must take an all-wheel-drive and promise me that you will put a survival kit together and tell somebody when you're leaving and where you expect to be at what time along the way. Is this your first time in the Arctic?"

"Well, no. But I get your point. I'll take the all-wheel drive, and the chains."

I ventured out onto the four-lane George Parks Highway, heading south from Fairbanks, at ten the next morning, in darkness. The first thing I noticed was that there were no trucks on the road—I thought there would be freight running up and down the highway, but I'd neglected to consider that in this part of the world, everything goes by train between Anchorage and Fairbanks. After half an hour of driving at speed, the heater still hadn't heated the cab sufficiently for me to remove my mitts and balaclava.

The shivering was all the worse because somewhere along the way, I'd contracted some kind of flu, just as I had in Siberia. I couldn't hold anything down. I had a temperature of 39.7 degrees and had awoken in my Fairbanks hotel room wrapped in wet sheets. So much for the glamour of round-the-world travel. I was beginning to think it might be better to rest my jet-lagged, travel-ravaged carcass for a day or so in a Hotwire hotel than it would be to die of flu-induced carbon monoxide poisoning, in a flapjack of my own frozen sweat, in a candlelit Ford sarcophagus in a Denali ditch at seventy below.

The final and by far most compelling reason to turn around was that after an hour plugged into the cigarette lighter in the car, my mobile came back to life with news that the Gwich'in holy man Evon Peter had returned my call, placed a few days before after I'd heard about his remarkable work in Kotzebue. He was indeed interested in sitting down with me to talk about his work with the youth camps and other projects he directed through his work with the Northern Alaska Wellness Initiative.

I had learned about Peter's work with youth in both Shishmaref and Kotzebue, where he had convened some of those all-important cultural summer camps, helping young people find themselves in the land-based subsistence harvesting activities of their ancestors. He was married to a Navajo woman and spent at least part of his year in the American Southwest. But everyone who recommended that I talk to him said that if he wasn't speaking somewhere, or running a community wellness workshop, he would be at home in Fairbanks. And suddenly there was a message on my phone saying that a meeting was possible. Sarah Palin and Bruce Lake would have to wait.

While I rested up, trying to shake the plague, I got an introduction to Evon Peter online. In a speech he gave to the Tanana Chiefs Conference in 2009, he talked about being the son of a Neets'aii Gwich'in mother and a Jewish father. He became chief of the community of Arctic Village—Vashraii K'oo—in 2000 at age twenty-four. Since that time, he had travelled all over the world. Although he was likely still the youngest of the forty-three chiefs in the room, he stood and spoke before his peers with the poise and confidence of a man twice or three times his age.

"I have been seeing the challenges the world is facing, not just our own people. And I have learned a lot and I have shared a lot. And one thing that I learned is that the traditions, the culture, the traditional wisdom and knowledge that our people carry, the way and form of our leadership is direly needed all around the world, not only here. We are in a unique role as Alaskan Natives or as indigenous people, where people want to understand what it is that we understand, about what it takes to live in community for long periods of time with one another, what it is to live closely to the land in a sustainable way. That sort of knowledge is becoming more and more important.

"I would go as far to say that, without us all doing the work of becoming healthier and stronger, wiser, more aware and conscious of becoming trained to garner skills for ourselves, the other political, economic, and social changes we make won't succeed, because our people need to be able to fill those positions that

Chief Jerry Isaac [president of the Tanana Chiefs Conference] is talking about, at the CEO levels, to be able to run the shows. To do that we have to have a lot of self-discipline, and carry ourselves and be responsible.

"We define ourselves by respecting ourselves. When we respect our own spirit, our own actions, then it is hard for anyone to break us down because we become so strong and so grounded. We grow roots into the earth. We build that connection to our elders and our ancestors and then it is hard to shake us."

The audience stood in an ovation that went on and on, and I wondered if this deeply charismatic young man I was to meet the following day was the next Nelson Mandela. He was so grounded, so self-assured, so solid in his convictions, so magnetic, all without a trace of arrogance. Further digging turned up more information about how he had consciously turned away from political leadership and toward projects and activities that would make his people better and more whole, particularly the summer camps for youth throughout Alaska that many credit as turning points in their young lives.

When I found him in his unassuming windowless office in the basement of a strip mall in Fairbanks, I asked him about that ovation. He said that this was an important speech because it was given after he'd been living for five years with the Navajo in the South, just after he had decided that he would take a much more traditional leadership role among his people.

Big and strong, with clear eyes and a memorable handshake, he presented himself as a very serious guy, not inclined in the least to accept any kind of credit for what I had seen in his address to the Tanana chiefs. But he did explain why he had chosen not to re-enter conventional band politics as a chief or councillor: "On my return, I had decided that I didn't want to move back into this Western structured leadership system, but I would fulfill that more traditional leadership role put on me by an older man, Chief Peter John. He was an elder who lived to be 102 years old. He was from the Minto tribe. And when he was 99, he invited me—this was before I was chief of Arctic Village—to this gathering called Inakanaga, a gathering of elders and youth and most of the chiefs.

"He showed up about ten a.m. He was getting kind of old, not moving too fast. It was in a gym. He came in late, all bent over . . . and called for me. There were the chiefs sitting on the gym floor; the rest of us and other guests were in the bleachers. He asked if I was there and then he called for me to come down. There was a circle of chairs. So I stood up and went down, and he and I sat in the circle with the elders. He spoke in his language, which is different from mine. So an elder sat next to me to interpret," Peter explained.

"I had sat with him several times in my life so he was one of the traditional mentors for me, of understanding what it means to live life based on a set of values and understandings, which manifests as wisdom over time, as you experience life, when you're going along that path and that trajectory of what it really means to be a traditional leader or chief.

"He explained several things to me. He was even able to foretell the future. He said, 'Only if you continue to live the path you have been leading so far in your life will your destiny be fulfilled.'

At that point he placed a chief's necklace on my neck. That was when I began that path of taking on a role of a traditional leader among Athabascan people."

While in Nome, after my experience in Shishmaref, I'd clipped an article and editorial about suicide in the *Arctic Sounder*. Before I knew anything of Evon Peter, I'd read about the key leadership role that he was taking across Alaska and beyond, not on what might be considered the conventional paths through the state social and mental health systems, as laid out in a government document called the *Alaska Suicide Prevention Plan*, but from a much more synoptic and potent viewpoint.

In the editorial, Carey Restino summed up her response to Peter this way: "This week . . . I met someone who made me embarrassed to have ever whined, even internally, about my work. I met someone whose job is so overwhelming that he ought to be hiding under his desk. Instead, this person is full of energy and enthusiasm for what he does. . . . Imagine that your job is trying to stop an epidemic that is killing young people throughout your region. It brings you nose-to-nose with every piece of community and culture that is broken—every heartbreak and sad story you can imagine. And your job, simply put, is to fix it all."

Sitting across from the man himself in the basement of a Fairbanks strip mall, I had to ask: "Is that what you're trying to do, fix it all? Where do you begin? And how do these summer camps fit into the plan?"

Over the next six or seven minutes, I sat listening, amazed at the clarity of his calm words and the evident fire in his belly. Chief Peter John was right about this remarkable young man's potential.

"These camps are focused on young people," Peter began. "We aim at youth thirteen to eighteen years old. We try to give them a chance to meet other young people from around the region and to learn ways to be able to live life well and to have a healthy life, rooted in the cultural values of the people of the area. We talk about the rapid cultural change that our peoples are going through. Then you look at the grandparents, the great-grandparents of these people, pretty much living a traditional life on the land, all speaking their language, living off the land. No electricity. No running water. Living a real culturally, traditionally based lifestyle. You go from that to bringing in a lot of outside influences—my mother is an example of a person who was taken out to a boarding school at five years old, to California or some place, and told that her language is wrong, that our culture is wrong, that who we are as a people is wrong, or evil or backwards."

The dark eyes had an intensity that drew me in. He continued: "At the same time, they were facing a lot of physical, emotional, spiritual abuse through the process of being told those things. Some of the elders who spoke before me today talked about being hit because they were speaking their language in the schools. So you have that coupled with alcohol being introduced, sexual abuse that started coming into communities. . . . There's a lot of hardships that have been passed down over a couple of generations now in some of the communities. The cultural values that were intact, that sustained our people for thousands of years were kind of fragmented and broken apart.

"So a lot of our work with healing is mending or re-mending

those bonds, those relationships, so that they can be healthy and strong and provide for our people again," Peter went on. "But that has to begin with each individual deciding to live the values that our people embraced for so long. And to be able to walk a path that way. To build that strength with each other. And that's what our work is about, not only with young people but in the communities and with the elders as well, encouraging people to take the steps and to break the cycles of violence or harm and to begin to have a solid foundation underneath their feet again."

He even looked balanced in his chair, with both forearms at rest on the desk in front of him. There was no tension in his body. He just talked: "So we do that. In supporting young people, I know that maybe some of the hardships they may have seen in their communities or their families or that people are facing isn't the way that it has to be. And that if we choose to shift our own life path, then we can change that within our families and our communities. That's basically the work that we do."

Since that day, I have followed the Gwich'in apostle Evon Peter online and in the press when I can, watching how peoples of the circumpolar North tried to bottle what he had to say and franchise his methods—creating a team that always worked with local elders and leaders wherever he went, unfailingly returning the credit and the thanks to them for making things happen— for finding a way to ignite the possibilities of pride and place in the hearts and minds of young northerners. Undaunted by the statistics and the often seeming hopelessness of it all, Evon Peter made putting fate control in the hands and hearts of northerners job one, his mission in life.

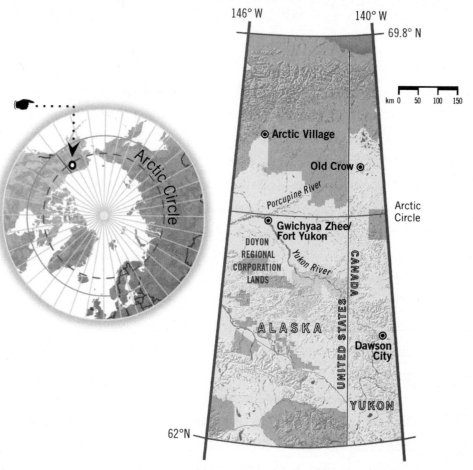

145°W ALASKA GMT-8

18: BREAKFAST WITH CLARENCE

Like a character out of a Robert Service poem, Clarence Alexander, seventy-two-year-old former grand chief of the Alaska Gwich'in, stepped out of the darkness and into the Snowdrift B&B in Gwichyaa Zhee. He stomped the loose snow off his moosehide moccasins and removed his glasses, which had fogged instantly in the warmth of a very familiar kitchen. He removed his muskrat hat, patched nylon parka, and slim-hipped snow pants, hung them on pegs behind the door, and then padded across the kitchen floor and dropped into a chair at the head of the table, set with a placemat and a new place setting.

His ex-wife, Ginny, proprietress, cook, and philosopher-in-residence at the Snowdrift, whisked a full breakfast of sausages and pancakes out of the oven and plunked it down in front of him. She poured a steaming cup of coffee and only then said, "Clarence, this is James. He's a writer from Canada travelling around the world at the Arctic Circle."

His oversized seventies-style specs had steamed again a little, but with his hands on his lap he turned and looked at me with clear, dark eyes that looked far younger than his slow and deliberate movements would suggest. After a pause, just long enough for me to feel uncomfortable, he reached out a weathered hand and took mine with a grip that, like his gaze, belied his years. "From Canada, eh? Is that why you're so quiet?"

As the son of a Yorkshireman who had a similarly arid sense of humour, I could spot an almost imperceptible smirk on that handsome Gwich'in face. By the look and by his tone, I knew I was going to like this guy.

"Hmm, Canada," he continued. "Maybe you can tell those people in Dawson City to stop dumping raw sewage in the river."

"Yes, sir. I'll be over that way at the end of the month."

"Good. Tell Mayor Jenkins I say hi. And then tell him to clean up his act."

Another pause, which I came to learn was just the natural cadence of his speech. Eventually, he said, "I don't know if my husband ran off with another woman that I'd invite him back for breakfast when the other woman buggers off."

Ginny, who'd just poured herself another cup, sat back down at the table. "Who said you're invited?" she said to Clarence. And then, turning back to me, she added, "I just couldn't kick him out of the family home that he built."

This was going to be a different sort of breakfast.

As I made my way from Anchorage to Nome, Shishmaref, Kotzebue, Fairbanks, and North Pole, people asked about my plans for travelling along the Arctic Circle in Alaska. My story would end with mention of going to Gwichyaa Zhee, or Fort Yukon. "You're going to FYU? Why the hell would you want to do that? Nobody wants to go to Fort Yukon. They're all busy going the other way to get patched up in hospital or to get liquored up in Fairbanks."

It was crystal clear to me, given the mandate of my project, why I might want to spend some time in Fort Yukon, a Gwich'in community of 589: it was just thirteen kilometres above the Arctic Circle. But it wasn't exactly a tourist destination. Fortunately, an online notice about a 2010 gathering hosted by the Gwichyaa Zhee Gwich'in Tribal Government opened a small window to goings-on in the village, which allowed me to connect with the band and the school, which, in turn, connected me with Ginny Alexander and the Snowdrift B&B.

I did wonder if I'd made the right choice when I was the only person on the Wright Air flight to FYU from Fairbanks. The only passenger instruction on that flight was, "We gotta lot of mail and fresh groceries in the back, so sit in the front row. Take your pick." And standing alone in the dark on the ramp outside a locked terminal (at least, unlike Shishmaref, FYU had one), turning my back to the blast of prop wash as the plane departed, didn't make me any more sure. Mercifully a guy in a pickup came for the last of the boxes on the ramp and offered me a lift to Ginny's.

By then it was late. Ginny was still up and expecting me. We had tea and agreed to talk more in the morning, but she said I might want to check out her friend Hanne Bergman's book *The North Star: My Sign of Peace*, which was all about her life in Fort Yukon. "It's on the night table," she said, as she shut off the lights and headed for bed.

Hanne's first line amplified my uncertainty, but things improved after that. She wrote:

> All the bad things have been said already, and it seems we have a pretty bad reputation. But when all is said and done I don't believe Fort Yukon is so different from the rest of the world. We have a lot of very smart people and we have some incredibly stupid people. We have child molesters, murderers, drunks and druggies just like the rest of the world, and just like the rest of the world we have all those good people who do the best they can. They go to

work, they raise their kids, and sometimes even their grandkids and they don't make waves so we don't notice them much. The difference is that because we live in such a small community we see and hear everything, so we know who is who and that is a good thing. . . . I would not want to be anywhere else.

In truth, what had intrigued me from what little I could find out about the local politics of the spectacular Yukon Flats area of the Alaskan interior was the fact that the people of Fort Yukon—half of whom were children—were counted among the 18,600 shareholders of ANCSA-created Doyon, Limited, the regional Alaska Native Corporation for Interior Alaska and the largest private landowner in Alaska. The locals had said no to a proposal to swap some of their land, with strong oil and gas potential, for an equivalent piece of public land, so that Doyon might get the test drilling under way. I'd been moved by published testimony by the Gwichyaa Zhee first chief, Dacho Alexander, Clarence and Ginny's son.

Speaking to a tribunal about the land exchange deal, the younger Alexander said he'd realized his dad had been telling him they lived in paradise. As a young man he couldn't see that, so he left town, as so many youth did, and roamed for ten years. But he came home and saw the place with fresh eyes. And what he saw was a Native corporation that was betraying the very people it had been created to serve.

"The transformation of Doyon is complete," Dacho Alexander said. "They are no longer a Native corporation. And now they are willing to sell you out. They are selling you out. They put a price tag on everyone in here. This is how much you are worth to Doyon. Doyon has put a price on our land. Who here can do that? I think you have to be thirty-seven years removed from the village to be able to do that. And now that's exactly what it is. We have been marginalized. A price tag has been put on everything that is in Doyon land, on Doyon land. That tree over there, it's got a price tag. That blade of grass, that has a price tag now. That muskrat that's swimming down the creek, that's got a price tag. Every single thing within our area, our traditional area here that Doyon owns has a price tag now. All you have to do is come up with the money to offer them."

Led by the Alexanders, FYU had turned down its Native corporation's plan. Six days in FYU gave me a chance to explore that issue from a variety of perspectives but none richer or more entertaining than subsequent go-rounds at Ginny's kitchen table, which included a couple of chats with Hanne and, of course, breakfasts with Clarence.

Ginny warned me, "Beware. He hates when people repeat what he says. And, whatever you do, don't say, 'Really?' because he didn't take well to a journalist who was here who said that all the time. Clarence got mad and blasted him. He yelled, 'Do you think that I am lying to you all the time? I'm not a goddamn liar.' And that's the last thing he said to that guy."

Ginny had told me that they were both concerned about possible untoward health outcomes that happen in association with oil and gas development. They were also aware of impact studies on the North Slope and elsewhere that showed the sociological outcomes of major petroleum development on local land and people. "But ask him yourself," she said, knowing that her ex could just as easily dismiss the question with a wave of his hand or a diatribe on another subject.

What I did learn from Ginny was that in his lifetime, Clarence had spent a lot of time on the land. He was sent to residential school in Wrangell after grade six and then to Mount Edgecumbe, a state-run boarding high school in Sitka, for one or two years. He had also done a whole variety of jobs—training for tool and die making in Chicago, odd jobs in California, a long stint in the National Guard.

But at some point he ended up back in Chicago, binge drinking, running with the wrong crowd, and eventually being beaten senseless and ending up in the Cook County Hospital with no idea how he'd got there. That turned him back toward the North, toward home, and into twenty years of service with the Alaska Department of Fish and Game. And after that, at almost every turn in his life, he had stepped into leadership roles.

He had been first chief of the band from 1980 to 1994; for part of that time, he had also been grand chief of the Alaska Gwich'in. In 1988, he'd co-founded the Council of Athabascan Tribal Governments, arguing—always—on behalf of his people, traditional values, making an honest living, *and* keeping connected to the land. But he had also been one of four co-founders of the Yukon River Inter-Tribal Watershed Council, an international organization uniting more than seventy First Nations up and down the length of the Yukon River in the protection and preservation of the watershed.

For his efforts he had won a US$20,000 Ecotrust Indigenous

Leadership Award. And in 2011, the whole family—Ginny and their four children, with spouses and grandchildren—had gone to Washington to see Clarence receive the Presidential Citizens Medal, pinned on his suit by Barack Obama. Just because he lived in a five-by-five-metre cabin in the woods at the edge of town, walking the couple of kilometres into the village now and again only to have breakfast, that was no reason to think he wasn't a man with a mission.

Next time he blew in from the cold into Ginny's kitchen— Super Bowl Sunday, I believe—he showed me how he had lined the knees and shins of his snow pants with kangaroo fur that somebody had given him. "Great when you're kneeling in the snow," he said. After dismissing the manufacturer of the pants (Columbia), he showed me how he had replaced all the nylon zippers with heavy metal ones from the Alaska Commercial Company ("Serving Rural Alaska Since 1867") and created moosehide tabs and buttons to reinforce the Velcro that was supposed to hold the leg flaps together. He had also created denim cuffs to go inside the bottom of the snow pants, to keep the snow from riding up his legs when he was snowshoeing in the bush. "Sewed all this myself," he said in a deadpan voice. Far be it from Clarence to allow some snow pant designer in Zhejiang Province in China to decide what winter is like in FYU!

After he'd settled at the table, I plucked up courage and asked him about the land swap and why he felt it was a bad idea. He turned and paused, and those mischievous bespectacled eyes started to dance. I started to think about the journalist he'd yelled at. But then he began, and what he said—not that by this time I was surprised—came at the question from an unexpected starting point.

"I wish the hell we could do better with getting to a common language," he said. By now, I knew that there was no better strategy for keeping the conversation going than to stay quiet.

"Subsistence," he spat. "That's a term folk in the lower forty-eight give to what we do. 'Subsistence' comes from 'subsidy.' Subsidy is what they pay farmers in the lower forty-eight not to farm. We piss those politicians and farmers off because we're so rich. So they call what we do 'subsistence.' Subsistence hunting. It's not subsistence. It's not a goddamn subsidy. It's more like self-reliance. It's more like living off the land, with the land, on the land. Those guys from down south come up with all kinds of stupid terms for what we do."

He launched into a diatribe about water rights and the creation of the Inter-Tribal Watershed Council. Mines need water, doesn't matter if it's placer mining or underground. Miners need water. Oil drillers need water. And the communities along the mighty Yukon need water, and they use the river to catch what they throw away. That was what Clarence had been doing, trying to get people to the table to talk about water.

But then he flipped to salmon. New topic. No: same topic. Different angle of approach. He told me that he'd noticed—others had too—that there were white specks in the meat of some salmon, particularly in the meat of female salmon. Down by the mouth of the Yukon, he said, where it flows out into the Bering Sea, they had some specks in their meat; the farther upriver you go, the more specks there were in the meat.

"And those clowns in Dawson are still dumping raw sewage into the river," he scoffed. "Fairbanks allows raw sewage to be dumped in the Chena [a tributary of the Tanana River, which in turn flows into the Yukon River], and that's why their salmon are disappearing. So I've been thinking about water. I've been thinking about salmon. I've been thinking about us, the people in the seventy communities up and down the river."

He took a breath and continued, "I went down to Portland one time to talk about the Salmon Nation, about bringing together *all* of the people and communities up and down the west coast of North America and maybe into Russia and down into Japan and Korea too. I thought everybody who is in one way or another dependent on salmon should get together. Other people had that idea too. But somebody thought I should get that Ecotrust thing. It was twenty grand. Good money, but I gave it away.

"Nobody who knows what they're doing eats salmon around here anymore, because the Yukon River water is not the same. Nowadays, you eat salmon, your hair goes white. You eat whitefish, your hair stays dark."

Nodding at his ponytail and full head of mostly jet-black hair, I said, "I take it you eat only whitefish." Again he paused, giving me reason to think I'd crossed the line. But then he continued.

"Only whitefish. That's how you stay healthy. But to stay healthy, you have to have healthy food. And to have healthy food, you have to look after the river.

"I went to a Gwich'in Gathering in Old Crow a while back"—given that the 2010 biannual gathering was in FYU, I gathered this had to be 2008 or earlier. "I was sick in my tent for three days with some kind of weird chest infection, some kind of respiratory condition. There was a Chinese doctor there. He pinned me [acupuncture], told me to eat pears, and I've been breathing fine ever since. That's four-thousand-year-old knowledge. There's a lot that our modern medical people don't know."

I was beginning to wonder if he would ever get around to telling me why he opposed the land swap deal, as he launched into a related story about natural healing. He had an infection, "dysenteric disease," he called it, ulcers in his stomach and intestines that he felt were caused by stress and too many people asking him to do things (or too many people asking him stupid questions). Food would turn to liquid in his guts, he said.

To try to get better, he went out to a camp near Shoo Taii (Happy Hill), also known as Alexander Village, about thirty kilometres north of FYU, where his family had lived for generations. He went for a month or six weeks and lived off the land, trying to cleanse his body and soul. He stayed until the snow came but still he wasn't better, or as much better as he had hoped to be with clean water and nourishment from the land.

Around then—it might have been an accident, or it might have been providential in some way—Clarence happened to meet a 104-year-old Inupiaq man from Noatak, north of Kotzebue. He remembered him as a big man, like a walrus. Like the Chinese healer, the old Inupiaq man gave Clarence some advice, and he listened. What he needed to heal his insides, the old man said, was porcupine droppings!

"Ginny calls it porcupine shit," he said with a smirk. "What she cooks is shit. What I'm talking about here is porcupine droppings."

So he found a pile of porcupine pellets. He took four, broke them up into a bowl, and added some broth from a rabbit he was stewing on the stove. He ate that and immediately got really dizzy. "I knew right away," he said, "I took too much. But in three hours, it completely cleaned me out. The infection was gone! And about an hour after that, I got really, really hungry. So I ate and ate, as much rabbit stew as I could, and—I couldn't believe it—it stayed with me. It didn't go to liquid. And that treatment lasted more than a year. I didn't try it again until a year later, but this time I only took a couple of drops." He laughed. "And I got better again.

"So there it is, the most perfect machine made by nature. A medicine-making machine, a porcupine. What it needs from its food, it takes, and then it puts the rest, the toxins, in its droppings. But what a porcupine doesn't need is medicine for a man."

As casually as he would arrive at Ginny's, Clarence would suit up and drift back out into the community. Through the kindness of Ginny and the band council, I was able to meet a number of elders in town as well as a number of key officers in the band office who were only too happy to talk or to take me to places around the village where things were happening. People were cutting wood north of town, some of them accessing the sites by dog team. Friday, the elders were treated to a hot lunch at the band office. There was work to do on the town's new water and sewer system. And there were a few people running in and out of town with traps and rifles, obviously involved in bringing country food back into the little community.

One day, when Clarence was nowhere to be found for break-fast, Ginny's friend Hanne, the author, came for morning coffee. Both she and Ginny had raised kids in town, and they talked about the pros and cons of living in such a small community.

"When my kids were small," Ginny said, with Hanne in full agreement, "we might have to entertain the kids at home for as much as two months in January and February and March, off and on, because when it was below minus fifty-five [minus forty-eight Celsius], there was no school. But last year, school was closed only one day. There's an indication of global warming for you. And so far this year, we haven't even come close, despite the fervent prayers of our grandchildren. And I just bought the first snow shovel since I left Idaho back in the dark ages! That means in my book Fort Yukon wins the Fickle Finger of Frigidity Award."

I had connected, before arriving, with the principal at Fort Yukon School. Unlike her counterparts on the coast, who were not interested in my presentation—"Too many visitors get the kids off track and it's hard to bring them back," a couple of them said—she accepted my offer to come in and speak to some classes about my journey so far. I reported to the office on the appointed day, but she was running out as I went in. The secretary said simply that there'd been "an incident" and that I should come another day.

I went back the following day, and the principal was all smiles. She led me into the senior half of the school and to the end of the hall, where a large and unkempt white teacher named Bob was sitting at his desk, reading, while the kids in his grade nine physical education class were sitting on the desks and talking among themselves. They were quite interested when someone new walked into the room. Their teacher was not. He said a perfunctory hello when his boss introduced us. She left. He said, "Knock yourself out. The projector's over there." And he left the room. He was missing in action as well when I began a presentation with his grades seven and eight social studies class, who were studying Canada.

When my presentation was finished, the class—fifteen in all—insisted on signing my journal as a way of wishing me well, letting me know in no uncertain terms that they expected me to be showing their pictures to kids in other classrooms I might get into as my journey continued. Their teacher was in the hall when the period ended, looking bored. Packing up, I kept looking to see if he might catch my eye. Nothing. I slipped out without saying goodbye. An impromptu encounter with a grade five class in the elementary wing of the school, hastily arranged with another teacher by the principal, was marginally more welcoming, but I left the school feeling as if I needed a good gulp of fresh air.

"No Child Left Behind," Ginny scoffed, as I decanted this underwhelming experience as a guest presenter. She was referring to the federal law on educational standards brought in under President George W. Bush, whose main premise was that high standards and explicitly stated measurable goals can improve individual outcomes in education, particularly for disadvantaged students. "All students across the U.S. are tested at certain grades, and all schools are rated on how well their students do on these standardized tests," she explained. "In the last results that were published, Alaska came forty-eighth out of fifty, and Fort Yukon was the last of all the schools in Alaska. Things are so uninspired here we actually had no senior class last year. *No senior class!* Of the ten or twelve kids who started in kindergarten together, how is it that not one of them is in school in their final year?

"Now, they probably all didn't drop out," she said. "Some probably went to Fairbanks and went to school there, or wherever. A lot of people here have family in Fairbanks. But isn't that a travesty to have no senior class? The school provides nearly half the employment in this town. What's up with that? I lay part of the blame on the teachers: they rotate in and out of here like they do across the North. But I also blame the school board, which is nominally responsible for hiring and firing the teachers and for the overall quality of education. I ran for the school board when I had five children in the school but lost to a guy who had no kids in the system. He sent his kids out to school. And *that's* who they voted in. *What were they thinking?*"

The next morning, Clarence's take on the educational system was characteristically acerbic. "All my life in *school* I got Ds. All my life in *life*, I got As. What's up with that? These evaluations for No Child Left Behind—No Child Left Behind, *pfffft*—these evaluations are being done with outside values and outside standards. How can our kids do so badly when they are so smart?"

This, and comments from others in the community, echoed

Evon Peter's observations about the systemic effects of colonization and ongoing government policies of assimilation. Being a child growing up caught between worlds, with traditional northern values at home and traditional southern values in school, was difficult at many levels.

As it happened, Evon's cousin Mike Peter (their grandmothers were sisters), past chief of Gwichyaa Zhee (2008 to 2011), had just returned to Fort Yukon with his wife and family from Fairbanks to assume the position of environmental coordinator in the community. Having been on the job just a couple of months, he was still getting used to the position. He was working on planning the annual spring cleanup, including the removal of derelict vehicles and old household appliances from the community by barge, and generally figuring out what to do about garbage and how to keep community members safe from fuel spills and environmental toxins. He invited me into his space in the band office. He was forty-seven, but, like so many northerners to whom I'd now spoken throughout the circumpolar world, he seemed old beyond his years, with the wisdom of a survivor.

For Mike Peter, the Fort Yukon School was not a good experience, but that was the least of his problems growing up. He had his first drink of alcohol as a young teen, and by sixteen, he told me, "I was right into drinking and right out of control." Somehow Peter realized through the haze of that existence that something had to happen. Something told him that he had to break the cycle.

So, like many young people from FYU, he headed south to Fairbanks and signed up for the Job Corps, which took him to the Yakima First Nation in Washington State, where he was eventually adopted (in the manner of many First Peoples) by a woman called Florence Haggerty. She counselled him, loved him, and helped him get himself organized and back in control of his own affairs.

"What would have happened if you had stayed in town?" I asked.

"If I'd stayed here, I probably wouldn't be alive. It's as simple as that," he replied.

He went back and forth between Alaska and Washington for some years. In 1982, in his late teens, his work with Florence Haggerty gave him the inclination to get more connected to the land, which led him back to his family and a couple of influential summers in a fish camp on the river with his grandfather. "That was a huge part of figuring out who I was, who I am, and what is important," he said.

Even when he was chief, the constant travel between Fort Yukon and Fairbanks and the South continued, which seemed to work. "A lot of travel. Money for meetings but no salary. And it's kind of a thankless job, really, but fulfilling in its own way." For the last while, Peter had been working in Fairbanks, living with his university-educated wife and three children, two boys and a girl. I asked him what went into the decision to move back to FYU with the family.

"Things are better now. Environmental coordinator is a paid position. And I know what at least some of the problems are, and that I can be part of the solution. And we didn't want to raise our kids in car seats."

"What will life be like for them here?"

That, it turned out, was a much tougher question to answer,

for once they got much beyond elementary school and immediate parental control and influence, there was no telling what could happen. The trade-off, of course, was that proximity to family and to opportunities to hunt and fish came with the challenges of isolation and the ongoing pathologies of conquest and assimilation.

The official FYU unemployment rate was 21 percent, which included people who were looking for work as well as those who were not, and finding meaningful work was difficult. The hard truth was that the number of jobs inside the community was much smaller than the number of employable people. Because of ANCSA, if you had Native status (the blood quantum had to be greater than 25 percent), said Mike Peter, and if you could get four walls of some kind raised out of logs or dimensional lumber, there would likely be some kind of program that would help with the doors, windows, roof, plumbing (if applicable), electrical work, and interior finishing. And there were other sources of money as well.

For any band member who chose to stay in town without work, there was general assistance to the tune of about a thousand dollars a month. Recipients of this benefit could be asked to work. People who refused to work could be refused the money, but that money was available. It certainly didn't go very far for hunting on the land with gas at eight dollars a gallon, said Peter. Shells cost more than a dollar a shot, and the already high Alaska prices for food were amplified by the cost of barging or air freight.

There was the Quest Card, Peter told me, which provided a

form of income supplement to offset the high cost of living for Native people. A single person might get $250 to $350, and a family of five might get something like $1,400 a month, he said. There was also a WIC (Women in Crisis) card, which was meant to ensure that children one to five years old received at least some eggs, dairy, fresh vegetables, brown rice, and non-sugared cereal. But food security was an issue. People here weren't rich. But that was the trade-off for living here.

One of the provisions of ANCSA that went along with the transfer of land and cash and the establishment of regional and local corporations was the designation of an expanse of land for the purposes of wildlife conservation and for the conservation of traditional lifestyles—or to at least make that possible. Fort Yukon is more or less in the middle of the massive Yukon Flats National Wildlife Refuge. Upstream on the Yukon River is the Yukon-Charley Rivers National Preserve. To the north is the Arctic National Wildlife Refuge, summer home of the Porcupine Caribou Herd. And all around, of course, is oil, gas, coal, and untold mineral potential.

And yet the people of Gwichyaa Zhee, knowing there would be revenue from a land swap that might see the oil and gas potential south of them being realized, had voted not to get more involved. As I listened to many takes on this decision, I thought of the people in Jokkmokk who wrote with such passion and elegance about slow food and the importance of food sovereignty, meaning the care and keeping of the habitats in which their food species thrive.

For FYU, the land in question was their piece of the revered

Han Gwachoh, the mighty Yukon River. For a southerner or anyone with a more instrumental view of land as a commodity, the deep rootedness of these connections, and why these might take precedence over what seemed to some like a reasonable land swap, could be hard to fathom. The two perspectives were as different as a realtor's rulebook might be from an award-winning novel called *Two Old Women*, by Velma Wallis of Gwichyaa Zhee. Wallis's story was based on an Athabascan legend that took readers into the Yukon Flats at the confluence of the Porcupine and Yukon Rivers, where for generations, for millennia, her people had hunted moose and caribou and wolf and trapped everything from fox to marten and beaver. But in order to fully appreciate the significance of the story, both the storyteller and the reader had to enter Ch'idzigyaak's world unfettered by conventional notions of linear time and physical distance. These understandings of how space became place had something essential to do with a real fear on the part of the Gwich'in of Fort Yukon that quick cash from development might compromise their very essence.

I finally asked Clarence about that during our last time together at the breakfast table in the Snowdrift B&B. As ever, he answered from an unexpected place. First, he said, "I see you were walking on the ice out by the barge landing. I think those were your footprints in the snow."

"How did you know they were mine?"

"Two reasons: I like those mukluks you're wearing with the rubberized soles. And secondly, no one around here would be stupid enough to walk on such unsafe ice at the corner in the river."

On he went with a story about Venezuelan president Hugo

Chávez, who, "just to piss off George Bush," had conspired to donate a hundred gallons (about 375 litres) of stove oil each to "poor" Americans living in the North.

"Yeah," he said with his trademark smirk, "he chartered a 737 to take a bunch of us from Anchorage to New York City. Why me? Because I am considered 'more honest'—you can put that in quotation marks—than most. Apparently I can turn the heads of the federal government with them sitting right in front of me. Anyway, Chávez put forty of us up in the finest hotels, and we eventually met with the man. He was all riled up, saying that America is the richest country in the world, with billions and billions of dollars in coal and oil flowing out of Alaska, and yet the indigenous people of this state are among the poorest in the country because of how the system is treating us. I think that lasted about four years. Who were we to refuse?" I didn't have the nerve to ask whether the relationship between the indigenous people in Venezuela and the Chávez administration was something that the Alaskans took into consideration before accepting the dictator's kind offer.

Eventually, the topic of the expansion of the Arctic National Wildlife Refuge came around. In the months leading up to my visit to Alaska, this had been a hot topic of discussion in Washington, with much backtalk from the environmental lobby and Native communities as well, including voices from Fort Yukon. It turned out that, with many other accomplishments, the man with the kangaroo fur in his snow pants, the man President Obama called "the grandfather of tribal government in Alaska," had been on the Alaskan Steering Committee advising the government on this decision. Not that, by now, that surprised me; at this point, I would have believed that Clarence had advised the pope on matters of northern decorum and Native spirituality.

"What was your perspective on this?" I asked. Without the characteristic pause, he growled, "I said they'd have to shoot me to make that swap happen." And then came the blast.

"They ask what happened to all the passive Indians. The nice ones. I didn't say yes, yes, yes, yes, like a passive Indian should. I say FUCK YOU! I don't know what passive means. And they say, Clarence, you shouldn't talk to our leaders like that. I say again, FUCK YOU! Why are you robbing me of more land?"

Clarence was nowhere to be found on my last morning at the Snowdrift B&B. I packed my things, said my goodbyes and thank yous, and readied my gear for an afternoon departure. I hadn't actually visited—or been invited to—Clarence's cabin in the woods at the edge of town, but on the basis of things he'd said and places I'd seen him walking in town, I reckoned he was in the woods back behind the barge landing dock where he'd seen my footprints in the snow.

Standing at the counter in the Alaska Commercial Company store, I debated whether to get him some tobacco to say thank you, or something else. Tobacco might make him think that I was trying to be an Indian. And then, if I gave him something else—but what?—he might think I was patronizing. In the end, I bought two large chocolate bars and put them in my pocket for the half-hour walk to the end of the road.

It was a dandy Arctic morning. The temperature had moderated a bit, but my mukluks still squeaked on a skiff of new-fallen snow. For the first time in a while, although I was all trussed up in snow pants and parka with multiple layers underneath, I didn't feel the need to have a scarf or neoprene mask blocking the raw cold from my face. And the sun—even though it was only February and sunrise was at about ten thirty—felt strong, as if spring might be crawling north. Buntings and crossbills were out and about and busy picking at the last of the freeze-dried alder catkins along the side of the road.

I walked past Nyharn 17, Hanne and Grafton Bergman's place (named after their boat, which was named after a street in the red-light district of Copenhagen), past the south end of the runway and the old jail, and on down the frozen tracks of wood sleds and snogos that had made their way in and out of town for firewood.

At the Indian Graveyard, which was separate from the graveyard outside the first trading post, I stopped and just soaked up the sun filtering through the rime-laden branches of poplars and conifers that poked through the snow among the mostly wooden grave markers. A guttural croak to my immediate left, almost a greeting, came from a raven sitting on one of the gravestones. Another big black bird in a tree swooped down, as if to join the conversation.

From there to Clarence's place, which I found at the end of a fresh trail of his footprints leading into the woods from the barge landing, these two birds appeared to follow along, perching in the trees on the side of the road and then flying ahead, feathers glistening with every colour of the rainbow in the brilliance of the morning sun. They headed down to the pile of backhaul vehicles down by the frozen wharf when I turned onto what I thought had to be the trail to Clarence's.

"I came to say thanks and goodbye," I said, standing in the warmth of his tiny cabin.

"Thanks for what?"

"Thanks for the chats. I enjoyed them."

Then, as he just looked at me with an awkward silence, I listened as my mouth said, "Nice stove" to fill the dead air.

"Made it myself out of parts I scavenged from cabins all around here."

"Cool. Brought you some chocolate."

"What time's your flight?"

"Two thirty."

"Good luck with your book."

"And to you, with Doyon, or whatever."

"Don't forget to tell those fuckers in Dawson to stop putting their shit in our river."

"Right."

"Till next time."

"Yeah."

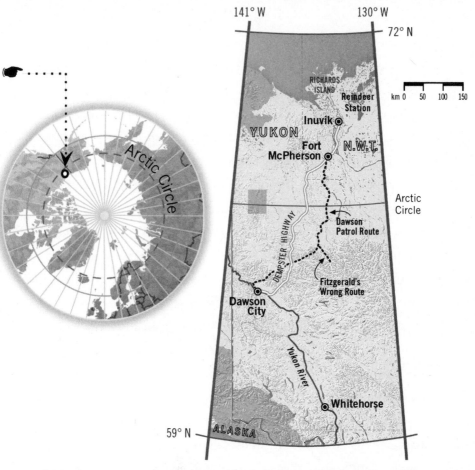

137°W CANADA PST (GMT−7)

19: LANDSCAPE AND MEMORY

As I made my way over the border from Alaska to Yukon and the Northwest Territories in the winter of 2012, the details of some memories of earlier trips to this corner of the Arctic seemed a bit faded with time, but the impact of the conversation I'd had in 1978 with an octogenarian Gwich'in elder, Andrew Kunezi, on the worn wooden steps of the Northern Store in Fort McPherson, N.W.T., was probably stronger than it was back then.

I met Andrew when I had just crossed the Peel River on a one-vehicle barge tied to a wooden skiff built and owned by Eight-Mile Joe Vittrekwa, having driven north on the nearly completed Dempster Highway, the only all-weather road in Canada that crossed the Arctic Circle. The summer before, sick and tired of petri dishes, the mathematics of ecology, and other biological minutiae, I'd tucked away my new science degree and flown to Inuvik, N.W.T., where I secured a job building metal buildings for Esso. It was grunt work but I loved it, putting in sixteen-hour days by the light of the midnight sun. It had been so wonderful that I'd gone back for another summer, this time by road, pulled by the inexorable draw of the North and by wages sufficient to cover exotic Arctic canoe trips before heading back to graduate school.

Looking back, those two hours on the steps with Andrew Kunezi—while people in wellies clumped up and down past us, going in and out of the one store in town—were a turning point in my life and maybe even *the* moment in which a dawning fascination with the human stories of the North eclipsed my early inclination toward natural science as a career choice.

His new-moon eyes were wolf grey and shaded with the brim of a cap much faded by the sun. His face was burnished like hand-rubbed harness leather and surprisingly unlined for a man of his advanced years. Crinkles in his brow and crow's feet, in white circles around his eyes where sunglasses protected his skin, appeared only when he smiled. He wore a hunter's padded vest, stained green on the outside and patched red on the inside, and a blue plaid shirt that had clearly spent a lot of time on the old man's back, judging from the way the colours inside his cuffs were so much darker than the fabric on the outside.

He talked about Corporal Dempster, after whom the new highway had been named. Whatever Dempster had done as a police operative, he had truly made a name for himself by discovering the fate of the infamous Lost Patrol led by Inspector F.J. Fitzgerald. En route from Fort McPherson to Dawson City, Yukon, over Christmas and the New Year in 1910–11, Fitzgerald and three others had perished like characters in an instructive Jack London tale. Three had succumbed to starvation and cold, and the fourth, seeing no way out, had died at his own frozen hand, which delivered a final single carbine shot to the face.

What followed was a glimpse into Andrew's remarkable mental map, as he recounted the trail taken by the Lost Patrol. "From McPherson, you go south on the Peel," he said, "about seventy miles [110 kilometres] to the Trail River. And then, to cut off the big bend in the Peel, you head upriver and across open ground at the foot of the Richardson Mountains, which roll away to the north, until you pick up Mountain Creek and follow that back down to the Peel." It was a route that he had travelled with his father and grandfather many times.

Then up the Peel for maybe fifteen kilometres. The water was fast underneath but the ice was good there, Andrew said. Then left, heading southwest up the Wind River, maybe eighty kilometres, taking the fork at the Little Wind to head more west than south. It was as if he were giving directions in a city and these river confluences were the Times Square of the Yukon wilderness. "Follow your dogs," he said. "They'll remember the trail if they have been on it before."

Depending on conditions, you'd go for one day, maybe two, up the Little Wind. You had to watch for Forrest Creek, which took you up and over the divide into Waugh Creek and down north to the Hart River. This was where Fitzgerald went wrong, said Andrew.

That corner on the Little Wind could change when the river froze when the water was high. There were certain rocks and certain crooks in tree branches that you had to learn, to make sure that you didn't miss this right-hand turn. Fitzgerald had passed by the turnoff and ended up following the Little Wind until it petered out into a little brook in a tundra meadow in the Blackstone Range, and they knew they were in trouble.

"If they had watched their lead dog, they would have known when to turn, even if they didn't know exactly what it looked like. It was their mistake to have Carter"—Special Constable Sam Carter—"and not a local guide with them. That's why they died," he explained.

As Andrew talked, I had my Yukon road map on my lap. He pointed at it from time to time to help me get my bearings, but it was pretty clear that the map he was following was in his head. His map, I was sure, painted in multiple dimensions and in many layers, was what my map tried to convey on a piece of paper.

The heat of the northern sun was beating down on us that July day. As I returned to the Mackenzie more than thirty years later, I thought again of how this man, who was born around the time of the Yukon gold rush, had shared personal experiences that encompassed every single change—good, bad, and indifferent—

that had occurred in the lives of northerners in his lifetime. The richness of his memories and how they tied the man to the land amazed me still.

Since 1978, the changes that had occurred in this northwest corner of the Canadian North had been dramatic. But the promise of the Dempster Highway as the key to unlocking the resource riches of the Mackenzie Delta had not, as yet, been realized. The pipeline it was to support was never built. Justice Thomas Berger had led an inquiry into the feasibility of creating an energy corridor and, after listening to indigenous voices up and down the Mackenzie River valley, had written a pivotal report called *Northern Frontier, Northern Homeland*, released in 1977. It recommended a ten-year moratorium on any pipeline development.

That, in the short term, was probably a good thing for the people of Fort McPherson and the Mackenzie Delta. The Tetlit Gwich'in of Fort McPherson had signed Treaty 11 back in 1921, but all that had really done was connect Andrew and his people to the Canadian government's policies of assimilation. Berger and the members of the Mackenzie Valley Pipeline Inquiry knew that more needed to happen in order for the indigenous people of the Mackenzie River valley to participate as equals in development. Only then could a more equitable arrangement be struck with the Crown.

Indeed, in January 1987, almost ten years after the Berger

Report was published, the Inuvialut of the Mackenzie Delta signed a first Comprehensive Land Claim Agreement. That was followed by the Yukon Umbrella Final Agreement in 1990 and the Gwich'in Comprehensive Land Claim Agreement in 1992. Each of the fourteen Yukon First Nations settled with the Crown one by one after that.

These agreements accomplished exactly what the Sami and the indigenous peoples of Russia hungered for as they continued to suffer the lingering consequences of conquest and assimilation. The deals all included provision for cash and land transfer, resource royalty sharing, and a host of other benefits that allowed these indigenous communities to move back toward independence and self-government. Like ANCSA, each of these agreements in its own way acknowledged and honoured wrongs that had been committed along the way.

Interestingly, these documents also built on the Alaskan example of how beneficiaries were established. "Who counts" in the agreements was generally based on a blood quantum of 25 percent. But, as if responding to the concerns of Mayor Martha Whiting in Kotzebue, the Canadian settlements added a variety of measures that allowed tribal affiliation, community acceptance, living an Aboriginal lifestyle, and personal family lineage to be added to the mix. Who was in and who was out of the Canadian land claim agreements was broader, more flexible, and more in the hands of the First Nations themselves, but the quantum was still a matter of contention in many quarters.

What it had taken to build or rebuild these relationships between First Nations and government after a century or more of discord had been courageous acts on both sides of the northern culture divide. Perhaps the most inspirational document for Aboriginal negotiators was a letter from Chief Jim Boss, of the Ta'an Kwäch'än (living in the area of Whitehorse and Lake Laberge). He wrote to the Canadian government in 1902 to express his displeasure with the land grabs and damage wrought on his homeland by the gold rush of 1898.

Not surprisingly, perhaps, Chief Boss's letter was more or less ignored by the government for decades. But with the signing of ANCSA in 1971, which precipitated the building of the Dalton Highway and the Trans-Alaska Pipeline to bring oil south from Prudhoe Bay on the Alaskan North Slope, Chief Elijah Smith, first president of the Yukon Native Brotherhood, dug out Jim Boss's letter. Inspired by Boss's courage and clarity, Chief Smith collaborated with other Yukon First Nations to write *Together Today for Our Children Tomorrow: A Statement of Grievances and an Approach to Settlement by the Yukon Indian People.* This remarkable document, published in January 1973, became the basis and inspiration for the Yukon Umbrella Final Agreement, signed in 1990.

Like Clarence Alexander, Chief Smith spoke the truth—but in slightly more diplomatic language.

Many people say all we want to do is go back to the bush. This is NOT true for all of us, but it IS true for some. We are talking about going back to a set of Indian Values which will help our young people understand who they are. At the same time, many of our older people would rather move back to the bush where they would be free, independent and comfortable with a way of life that they know and understand.

The culture, values and traditions of the native people amount to a great deal more than crafts and carvings. Their respect for the wisdom of the elders, their concept of family responsibilities, their willingness to share, their special relationship with the land—all of these values persist today, although native people have been under almost unremitting pressure to abandon them.

Native society is not static. The things the native people have said . . . should not be regarded as a lament for a lost way of life, but as a plea for an opportunity to shape their own future, out of their own past. They are not seeking to entrench the past, but to build on it.

In early April 2012, I headed to Inuvik. I padded in my mukluks from the main street toward the blue oil tanks by the river on Veteran's Way, headed for the McInnes Branch 220 of the Royal Canadian Legion. A raven ahead of me on the road was kicking something along like a soccer ball. On closer inspection, it looked like a puppy that had succumbed to the cold.

It was two in the afternoon and the proprietor of Kunnek Resource Development Corp, a.k.a. Canadian Reindeer, Lloyd

Binder—nickname Kunnek, meaning "reindeer"—was fed up. He had taken the rest of the day off to relax a bit before he returned to the endless battle of trying to keep Canada's only reindeer-herding operation afloat. "They're just north of town but they're all spread out, some of them anyway. I have no idea where the rest of them are. And right now, I couldn't give a shit. Come and have a beer," he had said on a crackly cellphone.

Dressed in an old hoodie and sporting whiskers of varying lengths, Lloyd had something of a lived-in look. But his blue Sami eyes flashing through owlish specs on a round wind-polished face were fresh and credible. He took a long tug on his beer. "Yeah," he said, lighting a cigarette (cupping his hands around the lighter as if it were windy in the Legion) and tipping back on a stacking chair, "I'm not entirely sure why I keep doing this, but I know it's sure as hell not for the money or peace of mind."

The lingering smell of smoke, two-stroke exhaust, and old beer amid the murmur of contented voices and canned country music took me back to my first nights in Inuvik back in May 1977, working a summer job above the Arctic Circle for the first time. That aroma brought to mind the Mad Trapper Lounge, where I heard Charlie Patagoniak for the first time, whining his way through the entire Hank Williams songbook, in Inuvialuktun. And, to add to that memory of Arctic romance was the image of bar fights spilling out onto the street at closing time. I'd sit on the boardwalk watching the drunks duke it out by the light of the midnight sun.

Inuvik in those days was aswarm with southerners animating Dome Petroleum's drive to get the gas out from under the Beaufort Sea. The Committee for Original People's Entitlement, founded in 1970 after the discovery of oil in the Mackenzie Delta, had made the government listen. And everyone's interests in northern development had been sharply focused by the just-released Berger Report, which said there should be no pipeline until the indigenous peoples of the valley were equal beneficiaries of the proceeds.

Thirty-plus years later, I was back in Inuvik, still puckered up for a cold beer. It was winter outside Branch 220; still lots of snow around. The river was covered with ice and snow and more or less continuous with the land, leaving the shore marked by parked boats and barges dressed in the lopsided millinery of aging snowdrifts. But I could feel the strengthening sun on my face. And it was the lengthening day that had stirred the reindeer cows in Kunnek's herd to move, as they did every summer.

But before they moved too far north toward their summer range on Richards Island, it was time to harvest a few animals. Kunnek had rounded up a portable abattoir somewhere down around Fort Smith and flown it up at great expense. He'd hired a couple of "rough butchers" (slaughterhouse workers) from Edmonton. There was a vet on standby from the Canadian Food Inspection Agency. And he'd corralled a few locals to help with the cull. But the herd was so scattered, he wasn't sure if they'd be able to get any animals to the processing facility on the north edge of town, let alone to markets in Alberta and beyond.

Having known Kunnek for at least a decade, I knew that he was only ever half serious when he threw up his hands in disgust. As the grandson of Mikkel Pulk, one of the Sami reindeer herders engaged by the Canadian government in the 1930s to drive 3,500 animals from the coast of Alaska to the Mackenzie Delta, he was made of tough stock. The Canadian government had learned that the people of the Mackenzie Delta had not been doing well since the signing of Treaty 11, and and even as far back as the First World War. To stave off hunger in the local indigenous populations when traditional game species went elsewhere, Ottawa decided to bring reindeer to Canada.

The drive was supposed to take eighteen months. It actually took five years. In the preface to *Arctic Exodus*, Dick North wrote, "Called by many persons familiar with the livestock industry the most spectacular trail drive in the history of North America, the five-year hegira of three thousand reindeer under the guidance of Laplander Andrew Bahr (known later as 'The Arctic Moses') was to win a permanent niche in the lore of the North as one of the great feats of modern times."

Through North's book and several others published over the years, as well as through films like Marc Winkler's *Tundra Cowboy*, the story of the great Alaskan drive and the creation of the Mackenzie Delta reindeer herd was well publicized, even if it was not well known. What was not present in the public consciousness was the details, the shifting fortunes and cruel ironies of the politics behind the incentive to move the animals in the first place. Nor was it well known what happened when the reindeer finally got to the forty-seven-thousand-square-kilometre Mackenzie Delta Reindeer Grazing Reserve in the east of the sprawling delta. Kunnek had lived this history. He was a player in it. And, in spite of the setbacks, he continued to push to see that reindeer would have a future in the continuing evolution of the people and processes in the Mackenzie Delta.

In previous years, Kunnek had taken me with him as he and his crew moved the herd from its winter range near Jimmy Lake on the mainland, up and across the ice road from Inuvik toward Tuktoyaktuk and onto the summer range on Richards Island. One hard cold day, I had done my level best to keep up with him as we bumped over windswept winter tundra at high speed on snowmobiles. In the end, we had run out of gas. But Kunnek just said, "I'll be back. Do some sightseeing." And without more said than that, he was off. He came back in a couple of hours with two jerry cans of gas he'd known were stashed somewhere not too far away. Back in business, we caught up again to the herd and watched an amazing fog of seething, moving life rise over the herd as the animals mosied and jostled ahead of our sleds, exhaling hot moist breath en masse into minus-forty air.

Another time I watched from a distance on the Arctic prairie as Lloyd rode the range, doing his best to cut infiltrating caribou from the herd. We had hot meals at a Petro-Canada exploration camp at Swimming Point. Lloyd talked, I listened, and some of what I heard ended up in radio documentaries and magazine articles about his most unusual occupation.

In the late nineteenth century in Alaska, after the introduction of the rifle and in concert with intensifying whaling activity in the Bering Strait, the coastal peoples along the strait and the Chukchi Sea were starving. That was when the Presbyterian Church, in a venture initiated by Rev. Sheldon Jackson and supported by the U.S. Congress, raised $2,000 and brought reindeer across the Bering Strait from Chukotka. Reindeer herding was readily taken up by the Inupiat on the coast of Alaska, but also by non-Native Alaskans like the Lomen brothers of Nome (from whom the Canadian government would eventually purchase the animals that were herded to the Mackenzie Delta).

By the mid-1920s there were more than half a million reindeer in Alaska. Because the American government was concerned that the Inupiat might get squeezed out of the reindeer business by non-Native businessmen, it passed the Reindeer Act in 1937, which restricted reindeer ownership to Native Alaskans.

It struck me that in Alaska and in the Mackenzie Delta, reindeer herding was a government-initiated activity; in the U.S., it was even a government-sponsored economic activity. Russia and Scandinavia had a much more organic evolution of the domestication of ungulates, going back thousands of years, but reindeer herding in Alaska was only a century old and in Canada it was four decades younger than that. Both industries were reactive, intended to alter the ecology and economy of the North in an effort to undo changes wrought by the incursion of southern appetites.

It was the growing southern appetite for petroleum that etched the Mackenzie District in national, indeed international consciousness. The discovery of oil at Norman Wells in 1920 prompted the Canadian government to send representatives up the Mackenzie River to see if it might settle with the Dene, who lived along its banks, about getting unfettered access to this valuable resource. Treaty 11, the last of the numbered treaties in Canada, was signed by all parties in 1921.

Although the Inuit of the Mackenzie Delta were not part of the Treaty 11 process, they were affected by government intervention and the beginnings of exploration and development in the Mackenzie Valley. By the mid-1920s, government agents realized that there was little game in the area, and it looked much like the coast of Alaska twenty years earlier. The government became concerned that the people of the Mackenzie Delta were slowly starving to death. And so, following the apparent success of the American model, the Canadian government set aside a grazing reserve, built Reindeer Station (where Kunnek was born in 1952) on the edge of these lands, purchased a herd from the Americans, and drove it into place.

But the problems that extended the drive from eighteen months to five years were doubled and redoubled when the herd finally got to Canada in March 1935. The original idea was to set up a main government-owned herd, portions of which—perhaps a thousand animals at a time—could be turned over to interested Inuvialuit families, each of whom would be assigned winter and summer ranges within the main reindeer reserve. Between 1938 and 1954, six such locally owned herds were established, but all of these, after early success, eventually declined.

By 1964, all of the Mackenzie Delta reindeer were back in government control, and the Canadian government had just

d dog in Nome, Alaska, howling to greet a minus-sixty-degree February sunrise—at
30 am.

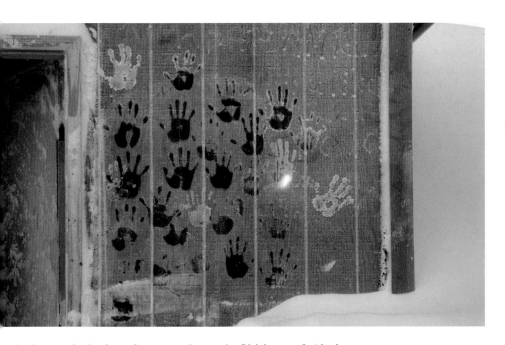

ndprints melt the hoarfrost on a home in Shishmaref, Alaska.

Clifford Weyiouanna, in his home in Shishmaref, mixes a sourdough starter that has been living and in continuous use for more than ninety years.

Gilford Iyatunguk's body, back from autopsy in Anchorage, is ushered back into town from the Shishmaref airstrip on a sled in a snogo cortège.

Martha Siikauraq Whiting, Inupiaq mayor of the Northwest Arctic Borough in Alaska, says, "We will not, we cannot become a people of the museum. We will not become a people of the past."

Bobbi Rose Koe, Tetlit Gwich'in and Students on Ice ambassador for Tetlit Zheh (Fort McPherson, Northwest Territories), with an image she painted to explain fishing and ratting at her family's camp in the delta region of the Peel and Mackenzie River confluence.

Lloyd Binder, a.k.a Kunnek, drives his reindeer north toward Richards Island, not far from Tuktoyaktuk, on the edge of the Beaufort Sea. The hot breath of the reindeer condenses in the cold air and forms a fog over the herd.

y McWilliam (*far left*) beside the author and the rest of the Atanigi Coppermine River xpedition, organized by Angulalik Pedersen (*far right, back row*).

Atanigi Expedition members Philip von Hahn (*left*) and Charlie Walker laugh afte[r] round of Inuit muskox push, while Billy McWilliam referees and Kenny Taptuna (*cen.*) looks on.

Summer twilight around the circumpolar world brings out the Arctic Air Force—mosquit[o]

On a crisp cold winter night at Campbell Lake, near the Nunavut–Northwest Territories border, a wood-heated, gas lamp–lit canvas tent stands against a conjunction of celestial bodies on the southwestern horizon.

...est of strength and agility, the one-foot high kick is considered to be among the most ...cult Inuit traditional games. One must land on the same foot that touched the sealskin ...et. The 2012 world record for women was 7'8", for men, 9'9".

Ihalmiut elder and teacher David Serkoak (Hiquaq) relaxes beneath a bowhead-wh
skull on Kekerten Island, near Pangnirtung, Nunavut.

The Canadian Coast Guard icebreaker *Louis S. St-Laurent* makes its way through broken
in Peel Sound, en route from Resolute Bay to Kugluktuk through the Northwest Passa

...mpressive places like the Prince Christian Sound fjord on the southern tip of Green-...l, summer visitors can watch the glaciers recede almost in real time.

...festive houses of Nanortalik ("Place of the Polar Bear"). The southernmost town ...reenland is home to about one thousand people, as well as world-renowned soft ice ...m cones, and is the expediting point for Nalunaq, Greenland's only gold mine.

Two Students on Ice ambassadors entertain a large crowd with a traditional Inuit thr singing duet, playing off each other with sounds, rhythms, and breathing to see who last longer.

Massive iceberg in Disko Bay, near the outflow of the Ilulissat (Jakobshavn) Icefjor western Greenland. When this glacier recedes, as glaciers worldwide are doing, cal ice will eventually fall and melt on land instead of into the water, ending the flov icebergs.

completed building the model northern town of Inuvik, with modern buildings on stilts in the permafrost and water and sewer lines running in heated aboveground "utilidors." Inuvik was sited on the east bank of the river because there were worries about the ground underneath the town of Aklavik, on the other side of the river, being washed away by flooding and erosion.

By the early 1970s, as the oil and gas exploration boom was in full swing and hope was reviving for the future of the Mackenzie Delta, the Canadian government had other things on its mind. Any lingering affection it might have had for the reindeer business was long gone. Finally, in 1974, the government sold the whole operation—the animals and the rights to the Mackenzie Delta Reindeer Grazing Reserve—to Silas Kanagegama, a man who had for a time been chief herder. Kanagegama gave it a good shot but ultimately fell short of making the business viable as a private enterprise.

Four years later, in 1978, Kanagegama flipped the operation to William Nasogaluak, a hunter and trapper from Tuktoyaktuk who, after some early problems with cash flow and finding markets, found success selling meat and, like the Alaskans, connecting with antler buyers in the Pacific Rim. Kunnek still found it in his heart to laugh when he told me about Nasogaluak ordering a navy-blue Cadillac Coupe de Ville with air conditioning and plush powder-blue upholstery that he had barged to Inuvik from Hay River. "He did very well. Between 1974 and somewhere around 1980, the herd grew from five thousand to nearly thirteen thousand animals. But that's when the story gets really complicated."

Representatives of the Canadian and territorial governments, knowing by now that existing treaties and the long-standing policies of assimilation—the horrors of which had crystallized around the whole history of residential schools—needed to be replaced by fresh foundational documents, sat down with the leadership of the Committee for Original People's Entitlement in Inuvik and began hammering out what became the Inuvialuit Final Agreement. Fortunately for the Inuvialuit of the Delta Region, this agreement transferred ownership of the lands of the Mackenzie Delta Reindeer Grazing Reserve from the Crown to them. Unfortunately for William Nasogaluak, who was Inuvialuit but essentially a private businessman, the new land claim agreement meant that he was now expected to pay fees for the privilege of grazing his animals on their established summer and winter ranges. Compounding the complexity of the situation, the ownership change also removed any worries, on the part of locals, about federal consequences for poaching the Crown's reindeer. More "two-legged wolves" were born. Nasogaluak's business began to falter.

Just as he was starting to think about getting a dairy operation going and wondering what the tourism potential of the herd might be, the federal government began issuing oil and gas exploration permits throughout the grazing lands. With the signing of the Inuvialuit Final Agreement in 1984, they handed off the ownership of the land, leaving him more or less alone to fend for himself.

In time, the Inuvialuit Regional Corporation, which oversaw the management of the land claim monies and resources, sued Nasogaluak, who in turn sued the federal government for failing to protect his grazing rights through the process and finalization of the Inuvialuit land claim settlement. "It was a mess," said Kunnek. "But, being a glutton for punishment, that's when I thought it might be an excellent time to quit my job and get into the family business."

Working with the Inuvialuit Regional Corporation, encouraged by his mother, Ellen (Mikkel Pulk's daughter), and father, Otto Binder, and using his own family funds supplemented by an additional business development loan from the government of the Northwest Territories, Kunnek became the owner and manager of the herd in 2002, knowing that his parents were there for advice and moral support. But by this time, to his surprise and disappointment, there was a palpable sense of resentment toward the whole idea of reindeer herding, which many of his neighbours viewed as just another spoke in the wheel of colonialism. "Accidental hunting" became a serious threat to the herd, he explained, "especially when the herd is close to town or winter road."

Ten years later, Kunnek had persevered. He had faced just about every problem a reindeer herder in any other place in the circumpolar world might have encountered: truck strikes on the winter road, market problems (chronic wasting disease found in elk in Alberta effectively ended any Asian interest in reindeer antler products from Canada), continued predation by two- and four-legged hunters, the death of his cousin Hiram, who was working by himself trying to contain the herd during a particularly wicked winter storm, problems with finding helpers at roundup time, overlap with oil and gas exploration activity, cash flow, and so on. And over the years he connected and reconnected with his relatives and fellow herders in Sápmi, both in northern Norway and Sweden and in his Jimmy Lake cabin, near the winter range of his herd northeast of Inuvik.

When I talked to Kunnek, whether in person or on the phone or via email, he was often chuntering on about something. But it was his absolutely irrepressible optimism that somehow always poked through. The image in my mind's eye during these conversations was of the man himself, during my 2012 visit, kneeling on an idling snow machine on a snow-covered hill on the high ground east of the delta, north of Reindeer Station. The crust of the snow all around us had been broken where, through the night and the previous day, his animals had used their sharp hooves to get access to the still green and lush lichen beds below.

We had picked up this trail and had been following it for some time. Ahead in the distance, on the ice of Parson Lake, a shifting peppered pattern on the snow emerged. That was the herd, making its way north and east to the summer range on Richards Island. Beyond that was the orange glow of a gas flare burning from a thin stack that stuck up above the horizon into an uncertain sky. It was chilly, even by northern standards, and the two-hour journey from Reindeer Station had dusted his face and collar and the ruff of his parka with hoarfrost. His was not an easy path, but it was the one Kunnek had chosen, for better or worse. During a break from the driving, we stopped. He pulled a mangled cigarette package out of his parka pocket, lit one, and said with a smile, "Beats the shit out of an office any day."

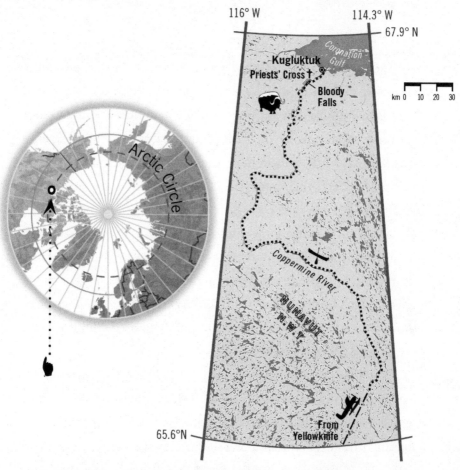

116° W   114.3° W
67.9° N

Kugluktuk
Priests' Cross †
Bloody
Falls

km 0   10   20   30

Coronation Gulf

Coppermine River

NUNAVUT
N.W.T.

Arctic Circle

65.6°N
From
Yellowknife

115°W CANADA MDT (GMT−6)

20: THE ATANIGI EXPEDITION

By the next time I ventured north of the Arctic Circle, later that year, the solstice had passed. It was late June and I was on the shore of the Coppermine River. Thirty-four-year-old Kenny Taptuna was washing the dishes in a collapsible green sink. We were on a cross-cultural canoe trip with teens from Toronto and from the Nunavut hamlet of Kugluktuk, which sits at the mouth of the Coppermine on the Arctic Ocean. The adults were expected to take a turn now and again with camp chores; on this chilly evening, the wash water felt warm on our hands. After the flurry of a typical canoe-tripping day, it was a chance to chat quietly by the lingering light of the Arctic summer sun.

Kenny lifted a dripping plastic plate from the grey dishwater and passed it over. "This trip is significant to me, personally," he said, "but it's also important to our community. What we're doing is historic. We are the first from our community, the first Inuit from Kugluktuk to have actually paddled the Coppermine River, which has been our back yard as long as people have been around the area." The town was originally named after the river; it was called Coppermine until 1996.

The Coppermine River valley breathed all around us. Evoking memories of Lovozero or Bayaga, sapphire-blue lupins swayed contentedly among the pastel boulders along the bank, soaking up the sun and making seeds, as Kenny and I talked and watched. Our eyes wandered from the dishes to the river and to the green hills beyond. A flight of tundra swans lifted on an easterly breeze and circled up and over our heads, the squeak of their wings hanging on the thrum of mosquitoes and the quiet clatter of our own making. That day, I saw majestic birds in a remote wilderness setting. Kenny saw beauty too but he was also eyeballing lunch: perhaps roast swan sandwiches with a chaser of hot sugared tea.

It had taken the ingenuity and imagination of Angulalik— Angut for short—Pedersen, a young man from Kugluktuk, to inspire this unlikely connection between North and South. Back in 2004, a teacher from his school in Kugluktuk had crossed paths with a staff member from Upper Canada College in Toronto on a beach in Mexico one holiday season. Surprising as it may sound, they found a possible match between a new Aboriginal scholarship and a promising middle school Inuk from Kugluktuk. The next thing Angut knew, he was flying to Toronto to do his high school education at UCC on a full scholarship. From the moment he arrived in Toronto, he dreamt of one day taking some of his southern classmates to his northern home.

We were sixteen in total in eight canoes. My participation with these youth came about after Angut's geography teacher at UCC, Craig Parkinson, suggested he contact me about helping to find some sponsors for the journey. I'd written a letter of support, saying what a fine idea I thought this cross-cultural expedition to be. Angut got the funding. I had offered, but in jest, to come along, so I was surprised but delighted to receive an invitation to join the trip.

In the group were three guides from a company of outfitters; Craig with four students and a parent from the South; Kenny, with five students from the North, including Angut; and me. The problem of challenging the rapids with a crew that had a potentially disastrous range of canoeing expertise (from extensive to none) was adeptly handled by the guides; they paired novices with experienced paddlers in six canoes and then, in an ingenious bit of problem solving, plopped the most fearful expeditioners in an almost unsinkable catamaran—lovingly called the party barge—made of two 5.5-metre blue canoes lashed together, with the senior guide at the helm.

One of the first issues to be worked out was trail hygiene. Colin Smith, the chief guide, gathered everyone around and tackled the delicate topic of elimination. "These," he said, holding up two blue waterproof sacks, "are the poo bags. Each one contains a trowel and toilet paper, some paper bags and one plastic bag. The trowel you use to make a small hole in the active layer of the tundra. If you use paper, and we might recommend that you don't, but if you do, we'd request that you place your used toilet paper into one of these paper bags. Then put the paper bag into the plastic bag. And, at the end of the day, after the dinner is cooked, one of the chores we'll all have to attend to is to empty the plastic bag and burn all the paper bags." No one said anything, although by the look on Kenny's face—he had spent a good portion of his thirty-four years on the land doing what bears do in the woods without the benefit of bags of any kind—I could see that he was trying hard to comprehend why all of this might be necessary.

Colin continued. "Now, about washing. You can use sand in the river to wash your hands, which works quite well. But if you're doing any washing with soap, we ask you to do that well away from the river. We have a bladder that can be hung with the poo bags that contains water that can be used to wash your hands after going to the bathroom. And, if you're wanting to wash more than your hands, I'm going to ask that you get one of the collapsible basins—you can use hot water if you want from the fire—and go back well away from the river to have a sponge bath."

After Colin was finished, Kenny put up his hand, as if in

school. "Why would you want to do that?" he asked. Colin looked at him and, without missing a beat, said, "Because we're trying to have as little impact as possible on *your* river."

It was clear from the outset that this trip was not really about canoeing or learning to camp, although that was surely a necessary part of the agenda. It was about connecting students from North and South. In fact, Kenny suggested that we call ourselves the Atanigi Expedition, from the Inuinnaqtun word that means "coming together."

It was that. One of the southern students was surprised that the iPods and cellphones belonging to the Inuit youth (the organizers had decreed that iPods were off limits and we were well out of cellphone range, but it seemed everyone had one or the other in their pack somewhere) were the same as his, or in some cases fancier. "I was expecting that there would be an old guy in a parka on this trip who could sniff the wind and tell the weather, stuff like that."

From the moment we'd landed and put our canoes into the Coppermine River just over the Nunavut-N.W.T. border, my canoeing partner, fifteen-year-old Billy McWilliam, had been fishing, in his dreams and in every waking moment on the river and off. Others tried their luck but no one except Billy had been catching anything much. Billy had been hauling them in—lake trout, grayling, and char, some for fun, some for the pot. This young northern man, who in everything but name looked and sounded Inuit, and even spoke a little Inuinnaqtun, appeared to be able to sniff the water and divine where the fish were. I took to calling him Billy McWilly, Fish Whisperer, and it made him smile, crinkling his almond eyes and revealing the dimples in his tanned and handsome face.

Billy was new to canoeing but, based on his exquisite balance as he fiddled with his rod and turned this way and that to cast, he was more comfortable in a boat than anybody I knew. We paddled and chatted. His father was born in southern Ontario and grew up on the French River. That taste for Canada's hinterland on the Voyageur Highway had led him to apply for a job in one of the Northern Stores scattered in out-of-the-way places across Canada. (This is the chain of stores created by the venerable Hudson's Bay Company and sold in 1987, in a transaction awash in irony, to a group of investors and employees who took the name of the HBC's corporate nemesis, the Northwest Company.) Billy's father started in Black Lake, Saskatchewan. A move to the store in Cambridge Bay on Victoria Island gave him a taste of the Arctic and introduced him to a Kugluktuk girl who was working there. Together, they moved on to other postings across the North, eventually ending up living in Kugluktuk with three beautiful girls and a handsome boy.

Billy's mom worked for a cultural group in Kugluktuk called CLEY, standing for Culture, Language, Elders and Youth. As part of her work in the community, she had been piecing together the way that today's Inuit in Kugluktuk connected to their history, finding ways to get elders and their wisdom into the school curriculum. Along the way, she had told Billy about a murder.

One day, Billy asked me if I knew the story of Uluksuk and Sinnisiak, two Inuit from the Kugluktuk area who were charged a long time back with the murder of two priests. At first the names were not familiar. But then, with astonishment, I realized that although I had never heard the two names spoken, a book that I had brought along with me on the trip, about two murders on the Coppermine River back in 1913, was about the same story. Just before I'd left home, a friend had brought the book around, thinking I might like to read it while on the expedition.

In *Bloody Falls of the Coppermine*, a *New York Times* feature writer, McKay Jenkins, had related how in 1911 or 1912, word filtered up the Mackenzie River valley from the Arctic that there was a group of Eskimos living at the mouth of the Coppermine River who were yet to be saved. This news made its way to Bishop Gabriel Breynat, who, at a scant thirty-two years of age, was in charge of all operations of the Catholic Church in Canada's Northwest and was eager to beat the Anglicans to these souls. He dispatched two young Oblates, Jean-Baptiste Rouvière and Guillaume LeRoux. The two met up at Great Bear Lake and travelled north together by canoe. They arrived in October 1913, dressed in their cassocks, rosaries around their necks, Bibles in hand, communion kits in their backpacks. But they had no store of food and no winter shelter.

The half dozen families who were indeed living at the mouth of the Coppermine took one look at the strangers and realized that the last thing they needed was two more mouths to feed and two more bodies to keep warm, when survival for their own numbers was not assured through the dark months to come. They might have tried to accommodate the intrusion if one of the visitors hadn't had an altercation over a rifle with one of the senior men in the encampment. This fight prompted another man to insist that, for their safety, the priests should pack up and head back south. They were given a sled and a couple of dogs to assist with an expeditious departure.

Though what happened next is far from clear in anyone's mind, two men from the settlement, Uluksuk and Sinnisiak, caught up with the priests on the banks of the river. Somehow the priests convinced the two men to help them move more quickly and, before they knew it, the two Inuit were in harness with the dogs, helping to pull the sled. But at some point very soon after that, hardly surprisingly, the whole situation spiralled totally out of control.

The Inuit rebelled. The priests tried to bring them back into line. A gun was taken from the sled and brought into the mix. And then, according to Uluksuk (from trial transcripts in the book): "Sinnisiak dropped the rifle and took an axe and a knife. I had a knife and we ran after him. When we got up to Kuleavik [Father LeRoux], Sinnisiak told me to stab him again, I did not want to stab him first, then Sinnisiak told me to stab him and I stabbed him again in the side and the blood came out and he was not yet dead. I did not stab him again and Sinnisiak took the axe and chopped his neck and killed him."

When all was said and done, both priests were dead on the snow. Then, as they had learned to do with other large mammals in the hunt, Uluksuk and Sinnisiak removed a portion of the priests' livers and ate them to prevent the ghosts of the departed from following those who had taken their lives. It was a grisly scene, to be sure, at least according to Jenkins.

I told Billy I was familiar with the story, and I asked him how he'd learned it.

"Uluksuk is my mom's great-uncle." Little did I know the coincidences wouldn't stop there.

Several days after this conversation, we pitched into a back eddy to bail our canoes after a particularly harrowing close call on a series of sandstone ledges in the river. Somehow we'd ended up on the outside of a turn instead of the inside, and all eight canoes, including the party barge, took on water, even over and through the spray decks that were supposed to keep us dry. By then, Billy was very much into the canoeing thing. When the whitewater got intense, it appeared that he even stopped thinking about fish momentarily as we pulled, pried, backpaddled, and manoeuvred our way to safety.

He turned to me as we powered into the eddy after bumping down the ledges and crashing through the waves below, his smooth brown face absolutely radiant and covered with sparkling drops of icy river water. "That was totally fun," he said breathlessly. "But James, we should have scouted that one."

"How right you are, my friend. You're getting the hang of this."

From the eddy, as we waited for everyone to get bailed out and prepared for more whitewater action, someone noticed a small wooden cross high on a bluff on the opposite bank of the river. Although the guides and, by now, all of us were eager to continue the roller coaster ride down the river, the group decided that it might help get the blood flowing again in our legs if we ferried across and hiked up to check out the cross. So across and up we went, in our multi-hued helmets, life vests, and squeaky rubber wetsuits.

The cross was made of wooden two-by-fours that had long since lost their paint and sharp edges over years of incessant tundra winds and driving snow. Two carriage bolts, their heads still painted white, affixed the spars. Dual triangular cuts in the three finials of the cross gave a cared-for, almost Celtic look to what might have been, in other hands, two rough boards and a prayer. By the look of it, the memorial had been here, stuck in its cairn of stones, for some time. The only fresh blond wood we could see was a splinter from a shot from a small-bore rifle from somewhere to the west. A .22, Billy thought; somebody hunting ptarmigan.

The mosquitoes were horrendous, and everybody was fussing and fidgeting to wipe greasy bugs from their hair and faces. But the silent mystery of the site became more and more captivating. It was likely not a grave, given the conical form of the cairn. We poked a bit through the rocks at the base of the cross and came up with what appeared to be the threaded top of a broken Mason jar. Energized by the idea that it might contain a note placed by the cross maker, we dug a little deeper and the bug flailing ceased. To everyone's astonishment, out came the pro-verbial treasure map.

We pulled out a piece of paper that had been folded four or five times. The paper, now a bit crispy with time, was stained with water and other organics that gave it an almost golden tone at the folds. At this point, I was imagining the rising swell of a movie score.

Gingerly, we opened it. In faded pencil were printed the following words:

THIS CROSS ERECTED
AT THE SPOT WHERE
FATHERS ROUVIERE AND
LEROUX WERE MURDERED
IN SEPTEMBER 1913.
[*unclear*] OF COPPERMINE
JULY 30, 1990

Until now, I had said nothing to anyone except Billy about the strange connection between this story, Billy, and the book that was in my pack. However, as I was absorbing this next bit of serendipity, I noticed Billy backing away from the cross and starting to slouch down the hill. It dawned on me that instead of feeling a geographical connection to an interesting historical event, he might be feeling diminished by being related, however tangentially, to a murderer. Hard enough being a fifteen-year-old in a strange new social and cultural situation, doing your best to fit in, without being connected to the nasty turn of events that had transpired at the exact spot where we had all just been standing.

After dinner, still a little dumbfounded by the sequence of coincidences through which the story of Uluksuk, Sinnisiak, Rouvière, LeRoux, and Billy had found its way into the Atanigi Expedition, I invited everyone who wanted to hear McKay Jenkins's account of what had happened at the cross we had just visited to gather round the campfire.

Jenkins related how the weather that fall, as the priests headed south with the two hunters pulling their sleds, had turned from bad to worse. Uluksuk and Sinnisiak knew the white men were desperate, but they too were anxious to return home. They were leading the priests back to the river so that they might follow it south, the way they had come, when they came across a cache of goods beside the river (perhaps made with some of the same stones used to erect the cross at this place), including a rifle and ammunition, apparently left by the priests on their way north.

At some point Father LeRoux picked up the gun as if to coerce the two Inuit to get back to the task at hand. Simultaneously, Father Rouvière, the more peaceable of the two, started throwing cartridges into the river. This confused everyone, especially the hunters, who knew that the only thing between these priests and certain death from starvation on the way home was shells for their rifle. As far as they knew, the priests were going insane. They began to fear for their lives. The two priests, as we all knew by now, came to a bloody end in the snow, and the two hunters headed back north to tell the head man in the encampment what had happened.

There was silence around the fire as everyone realized that what they had heard was not just a story but something that had actually happened, high on the bank of the river where we had stopped earlier in the day. Before anyone said anything more, I gently put the book down beside me on the riverbank and said, "Right. That's one account of this story, researched and written by a southern reporter. Because of who we are, the members of the Atanigi Expedition, I'm going to ask if there are other versions of the story to be told. I suspect there are a few people at this campfire who know this story and who have never read this book."

Kenny spoke up and told us that, like Billy, he was related to one of the characters in the story: one Patsy Klengenberg, a man of Danish-Inuit origin who accompanied the two hunters as a translator when they were shipped south to Edmonton for trial by the Mounties, after being apprehended a year or so after the killing. Kenny's account did not depart too dramatically in the details of the story, except to emphasize how presumptuous it was for southerners to turn up in October with no real resources of their own, expecting to be looked after by the people whose souls they were sent to save. Where Kenny's account did differ was in what happened at the trial in Edmonton.

The story he had learned around the kitchen table was that Uluksuk and Sinnisiak were sentenced to death for killing the priests and hanged. That brought nods from other Kugluktukmiut around the fire. They had heard the same thing.

By that point, I had not read on in the book far enough to know the eventual fate of the two hunters. So I flipped through to see if Jenkins's account jibed with Kenny's. It became apparent that the two men had first been acquitted (on an argument that they had not been tried by a jury of their peers, that a group of Edmonton businessmen did not constitute "peers" for Inuit hunters from the Arctic coast). But on appeal the same judge who had presided over the first trial found them guilty and indeed sentenced them to death by hanging.

However, because of the circumstances surrounding the

self-defence claim of the defendants and the nature of the evidence as presented, that mandatory death sentence for murder had been commuted to two years in a jail at Fort Resolution, on the south shore of Great Slave Lake. According to Jenkins, Uluksuk eventually returned home; never the same, he was later murdered by one of his own following a dispute over a dog. Sinnisiak was released as well and died in 1930 of tuberculosis contracted while in prison.

All eyes at the fire turned to Kenny, who was shifting his position on the ground. "Not much different than hanging," he said, after a moment of reflection. "A rope or a disease—he's still dead as a result of his trip to Edmonton to stand trial."

Back on the water the next day, I asked Billy what he thought about the whole cross episode. He didn't say much at all, choosing instead to dig his paddle a little harder and scan the eddies for fish. Slowly, though, as we paddled on through the magnificent valley that his ancestors on his mother's side had walked for generations, hunting caribou, muskox, wolf, hare, fox, and bear, we talked about how most Kugluktukmiut now have ancestry that intersects with white people—whalers, trappers, or traders, like his dad—in one way or another.

In many places throughout Canada, I explained, the idea of blood quantum—how indigenous a person is on a genetic basis—was often a precondition to who could and who could not be included as signatories to land claim agreements. Was this something that got talked about in school or in town at all? "Not really," he replied quietly. Then I asked him whether he identified more with his mother's or his father's side of the family.

"I'm white," he said. And that was the end of the conversation. With the obvious affection he had for his mother and her cultural work on the Inuit side of the family, I could only think that this response was a way to distance himself from the nasty story we had stumbled upon on this journey.

The rhythm of paddling lets the mind wander to other journeys. A previous visit to see Frank Ipakohak in the winter of 2004 to do some ice fishing had brought similar tensions to the surface. On the way from the airport to his house on the back of his snow machine, Frank had stopped en route to show me the charred ruin of Our Lady of the Light Catholic Church, which had mysteriously burned down.

He knew this had been a favourite place of mine since my first visit in the 1970s, when I had been captivated by the sealskin tapestries around the walls of the sanctuary depicting the Last Supper and the Crucifixion. Although the figures in the wall hangings were Semitic-looking, the way they had been rendered in different shades and textures of animal hides was distinctly northern and uniquely Inuit, as if the church had come some way in bridging the gap between the disastrous first contact of Fathers Rouvière and LeRoux and the present. But in the place of the church in my memory was a black hole that smelled vaguely of varnish and wet ash, inside a white picket fence and snow-covered yard.

"Was anyone hurt in the fire?" I asked.

"Not in the original fire," Frank replied. "But a week or so after the building burned, a local man committed suicide in the ruin. He stabbed himself and then lit himself and the rest of the building on fire with gasoline." That news hit with a thump on my chest, to think that for one poor soul, life had come to a place as dark as that.

During the Coppermine River trip, chatting around the campfire, I learned that the man who had died in the second church fire was Angut Pedersen's cousin.

The Atanigi Expedition arrived in Kugluktuk triumphant, in the middle of a storm front. As dreary as the day was, the gravel beach by the town's freshwater intake was illuminated by the glowing faces of family who had come out with no regard for the weather. Long before the canoes made it to shore, we could hear shouts of greeting and congratulation drifting over the whitecaps with the wind. Billy's mother and father and grandmother were there. Kenny's partner, Darlene, was there with their three children, who ran to their dad and wouldn't let go. Red Pedersen, Angut's Danish grandfather, who had arrived as a Hudson's Bay Company fur trader in 1952, was there. And many others too from the community of 1,300, rain dripping off multicoloured coats, hoodies, and ball caps, who knew that this really was a historic moment.

Within seconds, or so it seemed, the expedition was swallowed by hugs and we disappeared in a flotilla of all-terrain vehicles and dirty pickup trucks. Kenny and Darlene invited Craig Parkinson and me to billet at their place. "The baby sleeps in our room anyway," he said. The other two young ones would sleep on the couch while we inhabited their room. Amid the welcoming clutter of family photos, toys, coverlets, baby shoes, and baby blankets, Kenny turned back to the topic of the expedition, with his middle daughter on his knee and his son on the floor at his feet.

"This is an amazing thing for these kids to have done," he explained. "So many of the young people in this town are caught because they have to live simultaneously in two worlds. And for many of them—you've heard some of the stories and statistics—that's often almost impossible to do with the land, Inuit culture, and their language on one side and iPods, English, and all the other stuff they see on TV and on the Net on the other. It's hard just being, for many of them, when they don't know what to be, if they don't know how to connect to either world."

I asked him, "Why now? Why has it taken until 2010 for the first people ever to arrive in town via the river that was its namesake?"

"Why not now?" He was standing at the sink in his kitchen, scraping remains of ketchup and caribou stew off plates that had just fed the whole crew in his crowded living room. Half the window in front of him was covered with duct tape, cardboard, and plywood, waiting for a new one to arrive via sealift. The wraparound sunglasses he had worn every day of the trip had left him looking like a raccoon, with a light band around the eyes over sun-darkened nose and cheeks. But his eyes danced and his face shone with the joy of travel and homecoming.

"If these kids are going to survive and thrive, they need to learn to live in both worlds. But to do that they need confidence in who they are, and then they will realize what they can do. I think this trip helped them do that. Climate change is focusing attention on the North, and that's certainly something that northerners will have to deal with. But, in the meantime, there are other things that need to get done, and done soon, like making more trips and exchanges like this one happen."

With a whoosh of dust from pickup trucks loaded with canoes, packs, and kids of all ages, we rumbled through town the next day to the airport. Amid a flood of tears and goodbyes at the tiny terminal, Billy was doing wheelies on his souped-up ATV in the parking lot. As I watched, it occurred to me that he wanted to be there, at the airport—to be a part of that—but didn't really know how to say goodbye.

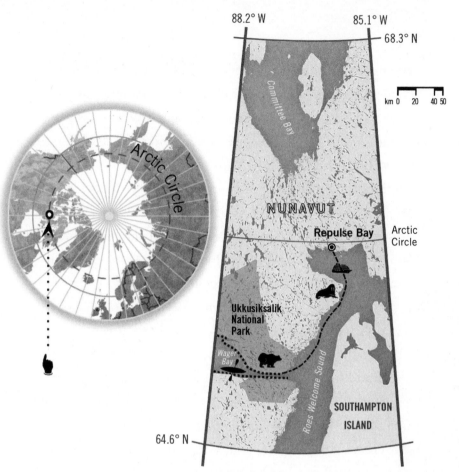

88.2° W 85.1° W

68.3° N

km 0 20 40 50

Committee Bay

Arctic Circle

NUNAVUT

Repulse Bay Arctic Circle

Ukkusiksalik National Park

Wager Bay

Roes Welcome Sound

SOUTHAMPTON ISLAND

64.6° N

86°W CANADA CDT (GMT-5)

21: BEARNESS

The Arctic summer rolled on. Having flown east across the barrens into the Kivalliq Region of Nunavut, over routes of past canoe journeys, I was in a bright red folding sea kayak on Wager Bay in Ukkusiksalik National Park, north of Hudson Bay. With three other paddlers, I was headed for Repulse Bay, "the only North American community on the Arctic Circle." (Clarence

Alexander and the good people of FYU, who are closer to the actual line, might dispute that claim.) On that gloriously sunny day, with a brisk following wind, the others had been flying parafoil kites, which had pulled their boats almost out of view on the eastern horizon.

Idling along on my own a couple of hundred metres offshore and just south of the Arctic Circle, there was time to daydream and soak up the day. I'd come here to get a fix on the natural and cultural features of the park, but it was also a chance to have a bit of an adventure. And all was idyllic until I spied a white lump on the shore, moving in the same direction and at about the same speed as I was paddling.

Part of the promise for this part of the world was that in summer, a traveller could expect to encounter about eighty polar bears per thousand kilometres of coastline. Next to Churchill, Manitoba, in the fall, Polar Bear Pass on Ellesmere Island, and Coke coolers around the world, Wager Bay has one of the highest concentrations of polar bears anywhere. In my week or so of staying with an Inuit family (engaged by the founders of Sila Lodge, an ecotourism facility on the north shore of Wager Bay that struggled after its creation in the 1980s), we had seen plenty of bears in the water and on the land from big aluminum motorboats. But now we were on our own. This moving white lump presented a whole different scenario.

During my undergraduate years in biology, my summer job at the University of Guelph had put me among researchers in an active marine biology research facility where a polar bear named Huxley was a resident. As I worked with the team investigating bear and seal vision, my friend and colleague Robin Best was working on energetics. In fact, one of the reasons why Huxley was in Guelph was that after he had been run on a treadmill in the energetics lab at the old American air force base in Churchill, he had become habituated to humans—they didn't scare him one bit, in spite of all the crazy stuff that had been done to him as part of the research project. He was too dangerous to be returned to the Churchill area, where he was born.

Having had coffee with Robin many mornings and attended seminars he'd given as patterns were forming in his data, I knew that bears' core temperature limited their ability to run and swim. But I also knew that one of the many beautiful things about bears was their incredible ability to regulate heat, especially when running hard or swimming. And somewhere in the back of my mind, I recalled that bears could swim at eight knots almost indefinitely and that it was not unusual to see them eighty kilometres from land or fast ice.

Eight knots: that was faster than a kayak. Eighty kilometres: that was farther than our group would paddle in a day, even with a tailwind. At that point, however, with the bear ambling along the shore, it was more of a wildlife viewing opportunity than anything else. Just to be safe, though, I turned the kayak slightly to starboard and paddled just a little bit harder to see about putting a little more distance between the two of us. But what a sight it was, ambling along in the sunshine, its feet padding along the rocks on the shore and its musculature rippling through and under its splendid white coat.

It was difficult to tell how big the bear was—at least as big as

Huxley, who weighed in at four hundred kilos. And it was alone, so, given its size and the absence of cubs, I had to conclude that it was very likely a male. The good news was that, male or female, polar bears didn't eat much in the summer. Their percentage of body fat was lowest at that season because without ice cover their open water hunting success rate was very low.

Since those days in the mid-1970s, the summer season had lengthened because of climate change, and polar bear fat had become something of an indicator of change. The thinning of polar bear fat had been the cause of considerable worry because of its direct correlation with the shortening of the winter hunting season for ringed seal, their favourite prey. But what if this bear was tired of being hungry? And what if this thing flailing away with a double-bladed paddle out on the water looked even remotely sealish?

With visions of Huxley's massive black claws and gleaming canines and razor-sharp carnassials, I looked down at the flimsy red neoprene hull of my trusty kayak and thought that it wouldn't take much for Br'er Bear to bite right through into the chewy flesh on the inside. That thought caused an involuntary flexion of my right leg, which pushed the rudder pedal and turned the boat on a steeper angle out to open water. And the image of white teeth poking through red neoprene had a similar effect on the vigour of my paddling. It was about that time, as I looked over my left shoulder, that I noticed the bear drop into the water with a visible splash, definitely heading my way.

The churning in my guts at that point felt a little like the time in the Lab Animals Building at the University of Guelph when, after anaesthetizing Huxley to take blood and do some routine measurements, I thought I'd do some work on the electrical relays and switches on the roof of his cage while he was asleep. While I was up there, alone, he woke up and started pounding on the plate-steel door of the cage. I'd assumed he had no idea where the door actually was, because we opened it only when he was tranquilized. Apparently not!

Looking over the top of the five-by-three-metre steel-barred cage, I saw the seventy-five-millimetre plate-steel door bending a little farther outward with each bang, as Huxley sat on his haunches, punching it repeatedly with his front paws. I'd had no idea, no idea at all how powerful he really was. I jumped from the roof of the cage, slipped on the wet cement floor, slammed my head into the corner of the food-prep table, and hotfooted it out the door in my rubber boots to get as many barriers as possible, as quickly as possible, between me and a loose bear in a U of G research suite.

Of course Huxley didn't break out that day. But he made his point. And that was about the time when my budding career as a marine biologist took an abrupt turn away from bears in cages and toward bears in the wild, and the people who knew them best, native northerners.

Out on the bay, I had the ultimate chance to get up close and personal—just prior to being eaten. It was another of those moments when, as any shaman can tell you, time "becomes a substance of infinite elasticity." Let's just say that in those few heartbeats, when the bear hit the water and started swimming out toward my kayak, the world stood still.

The only sensible conclusion to draw was that I had just become the object of a polar bear hunt. I had become prey. My understanding and appreciation of the whole idea of food chains, food webs, and the flow of energy through the Arctic aquatic ecosystems suddenly crystallized into one overriding and overwhelming powerful instinct: to flee. To release the freeze-frame pause button and paddle for dear life.

After digging in mightily for a few dozen strokes, I began to wonder how much longer I had to live. Strangely, the bear was no closer. Flailing on, I turned again. To my great surprise and relief, it was actually farther away and paddling back toward the shore again. As the angels of deliverance began to take their places on the park benches of my overwrought imagination, I saw clearly what had happened and why the bear had plopped into the water in the first place.

There was a sheer cliff, perhaps ten metres tall, dropping straight into the water at that exact point on the shore. Rather than heft that large beautiful carnivorous frame up and around the cliff, a route that would have required a bit of mountain climbing, he had just dropped into the water and swum around, to continue scavenging on the low ground at the water's edge. He might not have even noticed I was there. Polar bears are, after all, *marine* mammals.

By prior arrangement, the Wager Bay kayaking group connected with Joani Kringayark, an outfitter from Repulse Bay, in big wooden motor canoes at the mouth of Wager Bay to take us up Roes Welcome Sound and back to town. If we'd had more time, and more on-the-land intelligence about tides and fresh water, we might have paddled this ourselves, but it always enriches a trip such as this to connect with the local guides and outfitters to glean their knowledge. In the bay, wind had not been a huge problem, but as we tied our kayaks under tarps on the canvas-covered canoes, a wind came right out of the north and stayed with us for the 150-kilometre journey up the coast. As we huddled in the boats pounding north through the heavy seas, I was mighty glad that this support was available. There was no way we could have paddled against this wind—even with a bear in hot pursuit.

As we crested the north end of Southampton Island, which had been a sliver of green on the eastern horizon for much of our journey, the wind mercifully dropped. Joani at the wheel didn't have to hang on quite as tightly to keep the boat on course. With his .303 at the ready beside him at the helm, the quiet Inuk moved closer to shore, scanning for anything he could see with binoculars.

Patience rewards. Two walruses were resting on a big rock on the shore. Two fast shots. And suddenly our kayaking back-haul to Repulse Bay had become a community hunting trip. In no time at all, with many hands pitching in, the animals were expertly butchered, the meat and blubber plopped onto blue Fabrene tarps in the boats, and we were back on our way, surrounded by happy hunters and the pungent smell of fresh blood and walrus. No sooner had we pulled up on the beach, unlashed our kayaks, and retrieved our gear than the proceeds of the hunt were leaving the beach in cardboard boxes on the back racks of a small herd of ATVs headed for houses all over town.

Like all but one of the twenty-five communities in three

time zones across Nunavut, Repulse Bay is a coastal community. Ongoing connection and activity on the sea in summer and on the sea ice in winter were indicated by a scattering of boats, komatiks, snow machines, sheds, and other hunting paraphernalia along shore. As in the rest of Nunavut, half the population of about a thousand was under twenty. This fact was most evident when visitors arrived by land or sea because it was the children, on their bikes and running along in ones and twos, who were the welcoming committee. After weeks of solitude and a few hours of travel on the open sea, where conversation was not possible because of the roar of the outboards and the wind, we were surrounded by pint-sized ball caps, T-shirts, and questions flying everywhere.

You would never know by their toothy smiles and innocence that these children lived in the most difficult circumstances of young people anywhere in the world—seven out of ten of them lived in houses without adequate food, fewer than one in ten would graduate from high school, and if they did finish high school and stay in town, they'd have to deal with the fact that only four in ten adults actually had jobs.

Ten out of ten residents had already coped with the effects of alcohol and drug abuse and rates of family violence and violent crime that had affected each one of them directly—although Repulse stands out among Nunavut communities as one of the few places with a crime rate low enough to approach the national average. And they had to know and be affected by the fact that when they became teenagers, especially the boys, they would be forty times more likely to take their own lives than their counterparts in southern Canada.

Nunavut is Canada's newest territory and the circumpolar world's grandest social experiment yet in self-government initiatives. It began with the splitting of the Northwest Territories in two and the signing of the Nunavut Land Claims Agreement on July 9, 1993, which made the twenty-seven thousand Inuit of the central and eastern Arctic the largest private landowners in Canada. It was the largest Aboriginal land claim settlement in Canadian history, involving transfer of title to Inuit ownership of 350,000 square kilometres, of which 35,000 square kilometres included mineral rights (the total land area of Nunavut is 1.9 million square kilometres). The settlement also included a wide variety of provisions for transferring and devolving a host of responsibilities from the federal and territorial governments to the Inuit themselves. Parallel legislation that came into force on April 1, 1999, provided for the creation of a new territory with a public government, called Nunavut, that would serve all residents, 80 percent of whom were Inuit.

The Nunavut land claim settlement also involved the transfer of $1.15 billion over fourteen years, which sounded like a lot— but the annual budget of Nunavut for 2013–14 was $1.7 billion, and 82 percent of that ($39,373 per capita) came in federal transfer payments. On just about every measure of success and social satisfaction—education, general health, life expectancy, substance abuse, employment, income, and housing—Nunavut was still at the bottom of the heap in Canada.

In the heady years between the signing of the land claim and the creation of Nunavut, there was hope in Repulse that the creation of a new national park around Wager Bay—Ukkusiksalik was one of four parks written into the land claim agreement—

would be an economic driver for the community. Indeed, when I first went to Wager Bay, it was with the two Inuit businessmen from Rankin Inlet who were in the process of establishing Sila Lodge. The lodge did reasonably well for a decade or so but eventually collapsed due to "high operational costs."

The park is rich in wildlife and spectacular scenery. But because of the still high incidence of polar bears (park literature recommended "hard-sided accommodations" for visitors, if one could imagine a kayaker pulling such a thing out of a waterproof hatch), the remoteness of the location, and the lack of infrastructural support, the park had not lived up to expectations, not so much in its mandate to protect important natural and cultural resources but as a source of tourism dollars on which to build the local economy. There was a park office in town that got the odd project going, providing various types of short- and long-term employment, but the dream that the park would one day be an economic boon for Repulse Bay had yet to be realized.

There was potential for new mines in the area to become part of the Repulse economy, but there too problems arose. Gold and diamonds have both been found in commercially viable deposits. Meadowbank, the first of several potential gold mines nearby, opened in June 2010. But in April 2012, Denis Gourde, general manager of Meadowbank, told the Nunavut Mining Symposium in Iqaluit that his most persistent problems in making it profitable were absenteeism and high turnover within the Inuit workforce. "We have an average of twenty-two missing, not for the first half hour, but for the full day, twenty-two missing people. You can imagine the financial burden on the operation when you have that much absenteeism." Apparently, it is an almost impossibly long way from walrus hunting to wage work following the tick-tock of a southern clock.

A renewable-resource-based industry that also brought people to town from time to time was big game hunting—walrus, caribou (when they are around), muskox, wolf, and polar bear—which, though contentious, did at least inject some cash into the local economy. But it too was fraught with issues, usually including collisions between southern expectations (instant electronic and telephone communication, weatherproof dates, and flexible airline scheduling) and northern realities.

For the last of the elders in Repulse and the other Nunavut communities—who in seventy or eighty years have gone from chatting among family in the star-spattered silence of the barrens to having satellite TV and Internet bombard their "hard-sided accommodations" with news and weather from around the world—the relocation from the land, residential schools, and the forced rethinking of the whole idea of economy and employment were things that, for better or worse, had been taken in stride. But life was accelerating. As elders took with them to icy graves Inuktitut words that would never again be spoken and as young people, in disturbingly unacceptable numbers, took with them to their early graves the promise of the future, life in the rest of the world went merrily on.

As my friend Ipak in Kugluktuk had often reminded me, "The thing that runs through it all is the land, and our connection to the land, and to the water, and to the animals, through who we are and how we live. Country food is what keeps us whole." That night, some of those elders in Repulse Bay would be remembering all that with big pots of walrus stew.

Walking around the hamlet, getting our kayaks sorted out and arranging for our flight out, I passed a shed on which a full polar bear hide was nailed, drying in the sun and the wind. I thought of Terry Audla, president of Inuit Tapiriit Kanatami, the pan-Canadian Inuit organization, and his dogged work, on behalf of the Inuit of Nunavut, Nunavik (northern Quebec), and Nunatsiavut (Labrador) as well as the Inuvialuit, to have the views and data of northerners valued and included in conversations about the world status of polar bear populations.

Polar bear hunting, especially as it came up against the Convention on International Trade in Endangered Species, was another hot political topic. As I looked at the inside of the hide, which covered almost a full wall of the shed, it occurred to me that one of the great differences between northerners and southerners was in how we see and interpret this iconic animal. With the memory of paddling for my life in Wager Bay still fresh, images from Felix Lajeunesse and Paul Raphael's remarkable film *Tungijuq* (What We Eat) came to mind. The short film opens with a Cambridge Bay singer and actress, Tanya Tagaq, covered with the pelt of a wolf on an ethereal white background. Through the magic of animation and special affects, Tagaq morphed into a wolf that then hunted, chased, and killed a caribou, which was the woman herself once again. She then stepped in bare feet across a frozen ocean and dove into an open lead, where she underwent a third transformation, this time into a seal that was harpooned and eaten by a hunter and his wife, actor Zach Kunuk and Tagaq herself. With these cinematic images clicking by in memory against the stretched hide on the wall, I recalled the voice from Kyshik that said, "We were all bears once."

On a fine day, regardless of where visitors were in the town or what they might be doing, it never took long for some of the beach kids, or maybe their older siblings, or even their parents, to present themselves to us with crafts, sewn items or carvings, to sell. Often the best parka makers, hat crocheters, and carvers had their work spoken for by outside dealers or through prior arrangements with the local co-op, so the kind of work for sale on the street was what was left over. The makers knew it could go to less knowledgeable, less discriminating buyers, but cash was cash.

Naming the national park Ukkusiksalik, meaning "where there is pot stone," honoured a quarry in the area where soapstone for kudliks (seal-oil lamps) and other vessels was mined from talc-rich rock. I was hoping I might find a stone carving as a memento of my time at Wager Bay. The piece that ended up in my hands from a little girl on the dusty summer streets of Repulse Bay was a figure on all fours, with head low down, front legs walking and back legs, under ample rump, following along.

A bear. Perfect. But as I took it in my hands, I realized that there was a line like the curving hem of a traditional sealskin parka where the tail of a bear might be. Turning it over, I realized the front paws were actually hands, curled in mittens on the ground. Further, the bear had the face of a person.

A dealer would look at the imperfect lines and the rasp marks that hadn't yet been sanded out and would pass on this work, for sure. But I was captivated by the idea of transformation, connection, and a world and a way long gone, or so I thought. The language was fading. The deep connection to the land was less strong. The shaman was buried (or hidden in plain sight) but maybe not that deeply, because here, in a piece of art, was an essential element of a way of thinking about the world that very much blurred the line between species, between organisms, between bears and people. Perhaps that was the essence of the power and the beauty that I was holding in my hands.

"Did you make it?"

"No, my uncle did. Twenty bucks."

"Sold."

And it sat on my desk as I wrote these words, still challenging me, still speaking to me about the "bearness" we'd do well to better appreciate and comprehend.

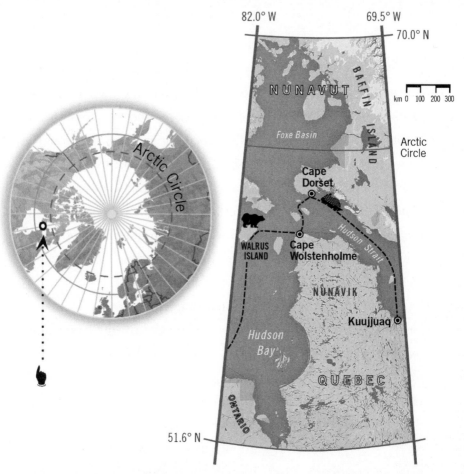

76°W CANADA EDT (GMT−4)

22: WALKING BACKWARDS INTO THE FUTURE

Later that summer I switched from a kayak to an ice-hardened ship called the *Clipper Adventurer*, working as an educator for Students on Ice (SOI), an Ottawa-based organization whose mission was to bring together youth from around the world on expeditions to the Arctic, to build international connections and to explore change, climate change in particular, through experience. On this journey, we started in Kuujjuaq on Ungava Bay in Nunavik and sailed west into Hudson Bay, then along the south shore of Southampton Island, just around the corner from Wager Bay. Standing off the shore of Walrus Island in inflatable boats, we were treated to the sight of a polar bear sow and yearling cub feasting on the carcass of a massive male walrus. It was almost comical to see their white faces reddened by gorging on fresh meat, and even funnier to watch the mother pad down the beach and into the sea, apparently to wash off the blood and to encourage her young one to do the same.

It was only on closer inspection through high-powered binoculars that we saw the walrus had died not from four-legged predation but from a gunshot. Speculation among the SOI staff was that this was the remains of a sport hunting expedition, likely from Coral Harbour, which had taken the tusked and bewhiskered head of the magnificent animal and left the rest on the pebble beach. With eighty young people from around the world on board, including twenty-three Native youth from across the North, it was a surreal moment. The southern youth looked on, soaking up images of charismatic megafauna in the wild. The northern youth, on the other hand, were seeing a picnic of country food, be that bear or walrus. As with the Atanigi Expedition, it was this cross-cultural mix that gave Students on Ice its essential power and purpose as an organization, especially when we debriefed each day and explored these different perspectives aboard ship.

Joining the education staff for this expedition was CBC News anchor and chief correspondent Peter Mansbridge, who came with his teenage son, Will. Given the huge role that he played in keeping Canadians from coast to coast to coast connected to each other and to the world, going ashore with Mansbridge the following morning at Cape Dorset, on an island off the south coast of Baffin Island, was like being in the vanguard of a rock star. People had lined up on shore to meet him and have their hands shaken. Eager faces wanted T-shirts signed, babies kissed . . . babies signed. Mostly, they wanted to speak to the man and have their stories affirmed of how CBC radio and television stitched North to South.

As we milled about, a hunter appeared with a small ringed seal in a cardboard box on the back of an ATV. In no time, the seal was cut up, and our northern kids were chowing down on raw seal meat and encouraging the others to do the same. Local boys then set up an adjustable wooden stand for some games. Like the seal butchering, the games began as a demonstration but very quickly turned into fully participatory activities, with teenage boys from SOI competing to match the physical prowess and dexterity displayed by their local counterparts.

By and by, there was first feedback and then the crackling of voices on the public address system. Cary Merritt, mayor of Cape Dorset, said a few words of formal welcome to our group. Next came a couple of local young women throat singing and laughing. The other ships that occasionally drop anchor here don't often have onboard throat singers, so the local women took the unusual opportunity to join with Inuit members of our crew in a joyous meeting of voices.

Peter Mansbridge was invited to say a few words. He told a rapt audience that were it not for the manager of the CBC station in Churchill, way back when, who'd heard his mellifluous voice announcing a flight when he was working as a ramp rat for a small northern airline, he might still be loading bags and trying to figure out what to do with his life. The biggest ovation, however, was reserved for another member of our education crew, Mary Simon, former broadcaster, former Canadian Arctic ambassador, and much loved former head of Inuit Tapiriit Kanatami.

But then the whole northern community welcome ceremony went in an unexpected direction. After this delightful cultural program, suddenly climate change was centre stage, in the strangest way. Mayor Merritt announced that another group of visitors were in town that week, and he'd asked them to join the celebration and say a few words. Instead of speaking, they had asked to sing their message.

Three strapping lads in their late twenties or early thirties—a Fijian, a New Zealander, and a Solomon Islander—in surf shorts and singlets stepped into the centre of the circle and started strumming ukuleles and singing a song of the South Pacific. When their first number was done, they explained that through their church, NGOs like the Norwegian environmental organization GRID-Arendal, and the magic of digital communication, they had learned that many small island states around the planet were increasingly at risk of storms and rising sea levels, and they knew that many northern peoples had exactly the same concerns.

Their leader, a generously tattooed Maori, spoke: "We have come here to see what the people in Cape Dorset are doing. And it is our great pleasure to have come here and to learn and to share some of our stories and traditions as well. Our elders tell us that we should walk backwards into the future with humility, gentleness, and courage. We are learning that the traditions of the Inuit of Cape Dorset are similar to ours, but that we need all the help we can get in these changing times." My mind flipped back to Maxime Duran and his cryptic observation about me walking backwards up a blue mountain on my way around the Arctic Circle. It was another strange and thought-provoking coincidence.

The clapping of the Cape Dorset audience brought me back to hear the visitors perform another song of the South Pacific that would have made Richard Rodgers proud. Then down went the ukuleles, off came the shirts, and out came acres of new body ink. Each man struck a stance that you might see the New Zealand All Blacks take at a championship rugby match. Then the three of them chanted a haka, screaming, beating their chests, and making menacing moves in unison, to squeals of delight from the crowd.

When welcome activities wound down, the youth and staff from the expedition drifted off into the village with various community members. I ended up joining a tour of the famous printmaking facilities here. Cape Dorset is probably the most well known of all Nunavut communities, having made its way onto southern radar through its printmakers and artists like Ningeokuluk Teevee and Kenojuak Ashevak.

Inside the facility, the prints that caught my eye were ones with unconventional imagery, the ones that had replaced or added to the traditional images—animals and fish, igloos and life on the land. I noticed a sampling of TV and Internet iconography, like stiletto heels and images of the space shuttle. "Our dealers in the South aren't much interested in those," said our guide. "They'd still much rather have the classic Eskimo stuff. That's what sells."

That night we said our goodbyes at Cape Dorset and sailed on. Mary Simon spoke in the main conference room of the ship that evening and helped put our Cape Dorset experience in a larger and more comprehensive frame than our one-day shore visit had allowed.

"I was born in the small village of Kangiqsualujjuaq on the eastern shore of Ungava Bay in Arctic Quebec," she began. "My mother was Inuit and my father, originally from southern Canada, was a fur trader and started in Arctic Bay and moved on to different Hudson's Bay posts. He ended up in Kangiqsualujjuaq as the post manager, and this is where he met my mother." To an attentive audience, in her grandmotherly way, Simon talked about her experience in federal day school, about being punished for speaking Inuktitut, and how when she thought back on those times, two Inuktitut words came to mind: *iliranaqtuq* and *kappianaqtuq*, which described the combination of fear, respect, and nervous apprehension that Inuit felt at that time about southerners and southern institutions.

In the ensuing days, the group heard much from working researchers aboard the ship about the science of climate change, of the flora and fauna of the North and the ways in which rising temperatures and shifting ecological parameters are affecting their yearly cycles. What set SOI apart from so many other climate change education programs was that participants were able to join these same scientists in the field, on the land, and on the water, where we were able to touch and count, examine and behold the organisms at first hand, with our own hands, our own eyes. These raw encounters with the passion of scientists were something to behold as well—who knew passion for herbaceous plants, mosses, lichen, and even phytoplankton from tow samples of the sea could be so incredibly captivating?

The elegance of science and its compelling nature seem all-consuming to those of us who look up from the middle latitudes. After exploration, which often places scientific interests in the forefront and encounters with Native peoples as a sidebar, science has been and remains the principal lens through which incomers view the North. Scientific expeditions and subsequent analysis of the data, especially when presented in four-colour maps and graphs showing trends and patterns, are in their own way both captivating and reassuring. Ethnographic inquiry, the gathering of cultural data and what is now referred to as traditional ecological knowledge, or TEK, is, when done properly, equally rigorous and replicable but often far more complicated, context bound, and conflicted than the findings of physical science.

It is far easier, more certain—and maybe safer as well—to measure ice and its decay than it is to measure decay of language or culture. The ice—the alluring and eminently measurable ice—is melting, and at the same time, as I learned at kitchen tables and hearths around the Arctic Circle, cultures—whole peoples—are melting away too, right in front of our eyes. What is interesting and perhaps sad about that is that both these phenomena are happening in real time and both are being affected and accelerated, in one way or another, by climate change.

Scientific exploration has made a huge contribution to humanity's understanding of the past. When the legendary glaciologist Dr. Fritz Koerner and his team started drilling into the Penny Ice Cap on Baffin Island in the 1950s, the assumption was that these ice cores would allow the past to be reconstructed with year-by-year, season-by-season certainty. It was fascinating to discover that climate had fluctuated quite dramatically over millennia. But as we became aware (thanks to St. Albert of Gore) that the fluctuations of our time were well beyond the expected deviations, it became apparent that careful analysis of ice caps and glaciers around the world could tell us not only about the past but about the present as well.

New analytical techniques came along, including a variety of remote-sensing instruments mounted in aircraft and on satellites, which improved the acuity and precision of data collection and analysis. For example, laser airborne altimetry surveys, which precisely measure the height above sea level of any point on the earth's surface, showed that mass loss (melting) on the Penny Ice Cap had tripled since 1995. Combined with other types of data and other clever and sophisticated analytical techniques employed by scientists around the world, these measurements showed that ice caps, on average, had shrunk by half in the past fifty years.

For several decades following the Second World War, the majority of this research was happening in the relative isolation of particular disciplines or subdisciplines, and there was almost no crossover between the so-called natural sciences and the social sciences. So compartmentalized was science that when the idea of anthropogenic climate change first surfaced in public consciousness in the early 1990s, the naysayers got industry-financed traction and a substantial head start before science pulled itself together. Science eventually compiled its findings and presented what turned out to be incontrovertible proof that climate change was indeed happening, at a rate much faster than anything that had happened in the past, and that these wide-reaching changes were probably—and in very significant measure—caused by humans. It became common to hear scientists talking about the Anthropocene, the new geological epoch we live in, in which humanity is the biggest agent of change.

The first comprehensively researched, exhaustively documented, and independently reviewed evaluation of the effects of climate change on the part of the world where the metrics of flux were most obvious was the Arctic Climate Impact Assessment (ACIA), organized by the Arctic Council and the International Arctic Science Committee and chaired by Robert Corell from the University of Alaska, Fairbanks. Three hundred scientists from every available discipline and throughout the circumpolar world took three years to create this document. A plain-language overview was released in 2004–5, followed by a more comprehensive and technical scientific report. Finally, after much chatter about whether global warming was real or a hoax brought about by government and business-unfriendly cranks, the ACIA presented ten key and incontrovertible findings:

1. Arctic climate is now warming rapidly and much larger changes are projected.
2. Arctic warming and its consequences have worldwide implications.
3. Arctic vegetation zones are very likely to shift, causing wide-ranging impacts.
4. Animal species' diversity, ranges, and distribution will change.
5. Many coastal communities and facilities face increasing exposure to storms.
6. Reduced sea ice is very likely to increase marine transport and access to resources.
7. Thawing ground will disrupt transportation, buildings, and other infrastructure.
8. Indigenous communities are facing major economic and cultural impacts.
9. Elevated ultraviolet radiation levels will affect people, plants, and animals.
10. Multiple influences interact to cause impacts to people and ecosystems.

Feeding into this comprehensive research process were indigenous people around the circumpolar world, who were only too happy to be asked and to use the funds that were made available to put their heads together about their sense of what was happening with climate change. Concurrent with the ACIA research process, Inuit Tapiriit Kanatami collaborated with the Nasivvik Centre for Inuit Health and Changing Environments at Laval University and the Ajunnginiq Centre at the National Aboriginal Health Organization, along with regional land claim organizations across northern Canada, to produce in 2005 an important study called *Unikkaaqatigiit: Putting the Human Face on Climate Change.*

As with the broadly based roundup of scientific findings in ACIA, *Unikkaaqatigiit* brought community voices to the wider world, talking about a wide range of concerns: changing ice and weather patterns, effects on drinking water sources, changes in access to and availability of country food sources, worries about the safety of hunters, and increased costs to get out on the land to fish and hunt. Sadly, what this important and elegant report did not say, at least in its main narrative, was that of all the priorities in their communities, climate change was not anywhere near the top of the list.

A concluding paragraph in the executive summary does broach this topic:

It is clear that Inuit have been adapting to the effects of climate change for some time. This puts Inuit in the rare position to teach the rest of the world about what may be to come. Inuit ingenuity and knowledge in adapting to local-scale environmental change can set an example for communities that may face these issues in the near and distant future. Regrettably, this ability to adapt has never been more important for Inuit than it is today. Environmental changes—of all kinds—are coming at a rate and to an extent that may exceed the threshold of Arctic peoples' capacity to respond.

And that painful honesty and achingly sad understatement was presaged, also somewhat parenthetically, in a foreword to the work by Jose Kusugak, president of Inuit Tapiriit Kanatami at the time. He wrote, "Inuit across the Arctic and Canada have made tackling climate change a priority. But [we] don't have the monetary, infrastructure, or human resource capacity to go it alone. . . . Our millennia-old traditions are already being altered because of the warming Arctic, and we face the possibility of having to completely reinvent what it means to be Inuit. This is a prospect that we fear."

In the following paragraph, in plain words, Kusugak told the world what he saw, in a refrain that I have seen and heard over and over and over again throughout the circumpolar world, but one that never seems to register with middle-latitudes dwellers: "We have already undergone immense changes as a result of colonization and modernization. We are still struggling to deal with these changes, and having to adapt our ways completely to a different world is not only far from ideal, it is unacceptable. I hope processes like the one that led to *Unikkaaqatigiit*, where

Inuit and non-Inuit [worked] together to face the challenges of climate change, will continue on a larger scale with our full participation, because our very way of life is at stake."

Somewhere there was a fundamental disconnect that had to do with acknowledging the possible existence of other ways of knowing, other ways of viewing, interacting with, and interpreting the world, and trying to catalogue that knowledge with tools designed for the products of the Western intellectual tradition. When I was doing my doctoral research in the Barren Lands in the early 1990s, gathering stories to help the arbitrator John Parker draw the line that would divide the Northwest Territories from Nunavut, there was much talk about TEK and the importance of bringing indigenous voices to the table—although not, interestingly, about bringing science onto the land and into the camps and cabins of the people who live there. In addition to sorting out land claims, health, housing, justice, and wildlife management, the government of the Northwest Territories was working flat out at the time to get a handle on where indigenous knowledge overlapped or intersected with science. The territorial government struck a committee to wrangle a common definition of that term "traditional knowledge." The committee considered this problem for two years and, at the conclusion of those deliberations, wrote:

The lack of common understanding about the meaning of traditional knowledge is frustrating for those who advocate or attempt in practical ways to recognize and use traditional knowledge. For some, traditional knowledge is simply information which aboriginal peoples have about the land and animals with which they have a special relationship. But for aboriginal people, traditional knowledge is much more. One elder calls it "a common understanding of what life is about."

Knowledge is the condition of knowing something with familiarity gained through experience or association. The traditional knowledge of northern aboriginal peoples has roots based firmly in the northern landscape and a land-based life experience of thousands of years. Traditional knowledge offers a view of the world, aspirations, and an avenue to 'truth,' different from those held by non-aboriginal people whose knowledge is based largely on European philosophies.

More recently, the great Inuit leader and organizer Rosemarie Kuptana clarified that traditional knowledge was a product, like science, but it was also a process. "Indigenous Knowledge is rarely communicated in a direct manner," she wrote. "Instead, it is communicated in stories, events, dances, songs and dreams. . . . The very premise underpinning Inuit Indigenous Knowledge is that it must be shared; otherwise it is no longer knowledge. . . . There is a place for Indigenous Knowledge. It needs to be respected for what it is, a science, in its own right, that can work in concert with western science to solve the complex problems of the world. However, it must be respected and must be used to benefit the holders of this knowledge." And we all nod in agreement and go to the subsistence harvesting and the cultural land use maps and then to Amazon.com to find the TEK encyclopedia so that we might write indigenous perspectives into our development plans.

As I engaged with the scientists on the *Clipper Adventurer* through experiments and data gathering projects on the land and in the floating labs, I heard Jose Kusugak's voice, from those times when we'd crossed paths in airports or at meetings in Iqaluit or Ottawa. He always seemed a little bit angry and always out of breath, but he always made his point: that the Inuit perspective mattered and must be heard, that the creation of Nunavut was an essential first step in the journey back to self-determination. I also heard the clipped voices of crouched women, tending children in tents and laughing, as they fed the family from pots over a sealskin lamp. I heard dogs barking as they bedded down on a line staked out in the snow, and sounds of men mudding sled runners and scraping them smooth for tomorrow's journey. I heard throat singing. I heard drumming and stories. I heard the sounds of impending silence.

What had we done? What were we doing? How was it that a way of life, or a cascade of ways of life around the circumpolar world, could disappear in front of our eyes, while we petted polar bears, venerated Western science, and turned a blind eye to the obvious?

It should come as no surprise that no one seemed to notice that the northern indigenous youth in the SOI group—each of whom had overcome heavy odds just to be there—tended to get restless. Often they tuned out completely during the science lectures, choosing to nap on the cushions or on the floor at the back of the salon rather than hanging on each lecturer's every word.

Nevertheless, impromptu workshops on throat singing and drumming, led by the same northern youth who seemed intellectually adrift when faced with the science, became increasingly popular. Sometimes staff had to almost physically break up these sessions to bring the whole group to attention to introduce another presentation in the "polar fundamentals" curriculum.

As I reflected on Mary Simon's words about federal school, it became apparent that the exact same divide, in spite of our best educational intentions, was alive and well in this twenty-first-century floating school. The message seemed to be that there were many ways to learn, and many cultures, each with its own way of doing things, but that when it came to the serious business of school, it was all about science—physical science, natural science, empirical observation, measurement, analysis.

The rest was, well, social context at best. The science of story, of relationship, of cultural upheaval, of residential schooling, of the struggle to maintain subsistence hunting on the land—all of this and more was deemed second-class, if it was science at all. The southern, Western educational agenda prevailed, in spite of dialogue and moving presentations to the contrary.

One evening, after a full day wandering through the old settlement of Cape Wolstenholme, at the extreme northwest tip of Nunavik, where Mary's grandmother had lived and was buried, the group was treated to a different type of presentation by David Serkoak, an Inuit elder teaching at a unique eight-month all-Inuit college program called Nunavut Sivuniksavut, based in Ottawa. David would be teaching us about drumming. Indeed, that's what he did. But first, he said, he wanted to tell us a story.

"My name is Hiquaq," he began quietly. "Hiquaq is my only name. I was born in a tent at Hicks Lake. Hiquaq is a name given to me by my parents after an elder in our group. The government couldn't keep track of us, so they gave me, like everyone else, a number, just like you give a dog. I was E1-602. I went from being a boy with a proud name, Hiquaq, to a person with a number, maybe just a number in the government's eyes."

By now, the room was quiet as a cave. "Then, when the church came, we went to church and I was given another name, a so-called Christian name, by the Anglican minister. He said, 'Father, you will be Silas. Mother, you will be Mary. Sister, you will be Winnie. Brother, you will be David. These are your new names. Don't forget them.' But Hiquaq is my only name."

Standing there in his fringed white summer parka with green seam binding and a coloured sash, he opted not to say anything more about the distant past. Instead, he turned to positive lessons, taught with his drum. On a flip chart page stuck to the lounge wall, he had posted a message in syllabics, and he spoke the words in Inuktitut for everyone to hear. It was important to Hiquaq to speak these words—and to have us hear them—in his own language.

And then, with beguiling, engaging candour, he uncovered a

second flip chart page where he had written an English translation of what he had just said and read it aloud: "The late Donald Suluk, a respected elder from Arviat, once said, 'When I was a child I didn't know the meaning of the songs. I thought they were just for fun and that they belonged to the shamans. Now I know they are not only for the shamans, they are for the world to enjoy.'"

And with that, slowly, rhythmically, he began to strike his large flat drum, first on one side, then the other, his whole thick and aging body undulating with fluid movements punctuated by the resonant beating heart of all that had gone before, all that was yet to come.

With the other drums he had brought, as he continued to sing and to move, he invited the audience, six at a time, to pick up a drum and join him, if only for a turn or two. When as many of the assembly with a yen to try had done so, Hiquaq scanned the room. Everyone, northern and southern students alike, was connected. Then he set down the drum and picked up his button accordion, and in no time the whole room was swirling in rhythm with the music.

Early the following morning, the northern light streaming through my cabin window was too much to ignore, so I headed out on the aft deck to greet the day. Far off was the distant coastline of Baffin Island. From about forty kilometres offshore, high

cliffs were reduced to a jagged thin white-on-black line that separated water from sky. Daydreaming about the drumming and
the dancing that had taken place in the ship's main lounge the
night before, I looked back at gulls and fulmars wheeling in air
currents created by the ship and marvelled as they dropped,
scooping up the fish turned up in the churning wake. The thrum
of the engine evoked Hiquaq's drum, and the reedy bird cries
were not unlike the notes of his magic accordion.

Inside, drawn to the smell of fresh-brewed coffee in the ship's
library, I was delighted to see Hiquaq sitting in the five o'clock
sun, enjoying a cup.

"Good morning, Hiquaq. That was quite an evening last
night. Thank you for your stories and your songs."

"You're welcome," he said, with a broad smile.

"You mentioned last night you were born at Hicks Lake," I
said. "Would this be the Hicks Lake inland from Arviat?"

"That's the one," he replied. "I grew up in a place called
Hudson Bay Padlei."

"Are you one of the Ihalmiut?" I blurted out. "And did I read
about you in Farley Mowat's *The Desperate People?*"

"I am. And yes, you did."

Shocked to be sitting down for a morning coffee with a character out of a book that I had read a number of times over the
years, all I could muster by way of response was, "No shit!"

"Yes," he said, with a twinkle in his eye. "I guess it was important for Farley Mowat to tell our story. But there were things he
didn't get right."

"Like what?"

"I started making a list of things that I wanted to correct, things I wanted to say to him, starting with the fact that he got my name, age, and gender wrong. One day—I think I was teaching then—I saw an article in *Maclean's* magazine that Farley Mowat had written, and it said that he was living in Port Hope, Ontario. So I called up directory assistance, got his number, and called him."

"Did he answer the phone?" I asked, still not really believing what I was hearing.

"I had my list and I was very angry," he replied. "Farley actually answered the phone. I explained who I was. And I started in with the items on my list, but before long we were just talking. The anger faded away and we just talked. We talked and talked."

Hiquaq was a babe in arms in the late 1940s when Mowat came through. And although my coffee companion's version and the author's version differ in many details, the broad strokes are the same. Diseases—influenza and diphtheria and tuberculosis—were brought into the Barren Lands by traders in the early years of the twentieth century. These germs, against which the Inuit had no natural immunity, combined with seasonal fluctuations in the movements of the caribou, their main food source, to result in a huge number of deaths from disease and from starvation. Hiquaq told me of vague memories of sucking on a bone for days because there was just nothing else to assuage his hunger.

When the Canadian federal government responded to Mowat's call and intervened with well-meaning but badly conceived programs to assist Hiquaq and his people, the community was being forcibly moved from one place to another, so that government programs might be more easily and universally applied. Hiquaq, in spite of the odds, ended up in Rankin Inlet and managed to survive. He became a teacher and had a family of his own.

"How do you feel about all that now?" I asked.

"There is still a lot of anger," he said quietly, staring into the middle distance.

How that anger was expressed as part of his teaching on this expedition and in his life was perhaps the most poignant lesson of all. Instead of lashing out at the injustices that had been visited upon the Inuit by circumstance, by the government, by the mechanics and legacies of conquest that had usurped the Inuit's power over their own lives, Hiquaq chose to teach through kindness, through inclusion, using music and storytelling as the vehicle. In this choice there was quiet pride and satisfaction.

His story, as I learned over coffee in the tranquility of the early morning, was there for the telling, for the listening, for anyone willing to ask. But Hiquaq's goal in life, it seemed, was not to foist it upon anyone. Like the rest of us on board, he sat through trenchant treatises on climate change and issues of sovereignty in the circumpolar Arctic, topic after topic that all somehow missed the point.

The point was that in the sixty-plus years since the Ihalmiut were weakened by disease and nearly wiped out through starvation, the situation for the Inuit had changed substantively in many ways, but all was far from well. Nearly three quarters of Nunavutmiut, preschoolers, youth, and adults alike, still did not have secure access to food. Despite all the government programs designed to make things better, despite all the attempts to mix and blend Inuit culture with the dominant culture of the South, eight in ten Inuit throughout northern Canada were going hungry in 2010, which was just one of many indicators of cultural malaise.

I had been watching the young Inuit on this journey tune out during presentations. I had been conscious that when on the land, they had often just clustered among themselves instead of joining workshop stations on plant identification, pond sampling, rock analysis, or whatever else was being offered on the more scientific end of the educational spectrum. But I had also watched as Mary Simon and some of the other Inuit leaders aboard had taken these same youth, one by one, and started what looked to be heart-to-heart chats during free time in the program.

Toward the end of the expedition, word rippled through the staff that some of the Nunavik youth had received devastating news: one of their classmates back home had taken his own life. These young participants withdrew even more. It brought some measure of solace to me to see Mary Simon sitting in the back of the main lounge, long after curfew, with her arm around one or another of these young women, consoling them, talking to them, giving them strength by her example.

But nothing was said about any of this in the public opportunities for comment aboard ship. Throughout time, incomers had arrived on Arctic shores, bringing with them—bringing with us—economic possibilities, a hunger for northern resources, a hunger for trade and social intercourse. But we also brought disease and a Darwinian sense of privilege. Slowly, almost imperceptibly, northerners' control of their own destiny has slipped from their hands.

Being Inuit, living in the harshest and most difficult climates and geographies on the planet, was never easy. It involved privation and starvation. But in this harsh and unforgiving place emerged a way, a beautiful, simple way that saw northern nomads build their culture and thrive in their own way of relating to each other, to the land, to the sea, to the cosmos. And all those skills and ways of adapting were ready to be brought to bear on today's issues. But southerners entered the picture, controlling schools and northern policies with the best of intentions, and initiated a long slow slide into oblivion for the indigenous inhabitants of the Arctic—a long slow slide that was so much more difficult to quantify than the physical, chemical, and barometric changes so well suited to scientific measurement.

Where did all that energy of doubt, that history of conquest, go, after it was internalized by those who were living it day by day?

Mary Simon had touched on the answer to this question in her talk after our Cape Dorset day when she spoke of challenges that must be overcome by Inuit if they were to make their way back to self-determination. She talked of food security, how young people were six times more likely to go hungry in the North than they were in the South. She talked about the high school dropout rate of 75 percent, and of social passing (students who did not meet academic standards being put into the next grade for the sole benefit of staying with their peers).

She talked of the few students who did graduate from northern high schools but who couldn't really be competitive for places in post-secondary institutions with their counterparts from southern schools because their literacy and numeracy skills, as well as their general knowledge, were below par. And, ever so gently, she mentioned suicide and how "historical trauma" was a key social determinant across indigenous populations around the world, particularly the Inuit.

But even in the enlightened confines of the SOI expedition, these remarks were somehow peripheral, folded into a socio-cultural agenda that by habit, if not by design, was considered less important than the main scientific learning objectives of the expedition. And so it went, as we continued with visits to communities and remote scientific research camps, with encounters with bears, seals, walruses, and whales in open water.

The community visits were all focused on traditional Inuit life. We would be treated to demonstrations of Inuit games, often with chances for members of the expedition to get involved. There would be feasts of local foods. Elders would speak about changes they'd noticed—insects, like biting flies and spiders, had come north with the warming weather; animal behaviour and patterns were different; ice was thinner, or non-existent, in places where they used to be able to go without worry. But no one, it seemed, would speak about the elephant in the room, the decay of culture and its heart-rending effects. This was a very difficult topic to broach, but not impossible. And the cross-cultural conversation was long overdue.

The Students on Ice Expedition ended happily: action plans were created and commitments were made to stay in touch on social media on various projects, including organizing a student delegation to the next meeting of the Arctic Council. Many of the northern youth left the expedition in Iqaluit, where the shipboard portion of the expedition terminated, but those from the western Arctic and farther afield in Nunavut, Nunavik, and Nunatsiavut came south with the rest of the staff and participants on a chartered flight to Ottawa, from where they would find their way home.

A group of perhaps thirty youth, including six or eight northerners, convened in a residence common room at Carleton University in Ottawa to see what everyone might like to do in the time together that was left. After three weeks of shared and intense experience aboard the ship and on stops in Arctic Quebec, Baffin Island, and smaller islands in northern Hudson Bay, this group had an intimacy, a familiarity with one another, and a level of trust that went well beyond anything we'd felt on the ship.

Bound by a common desire to decant, to process, to make sense of what had happened, without any prompting from the remaining staff, these young people started to talk about highlights of the expeditions, points of stress and challenge, and how different people had responded differently. Clear-eyed, sometimes with tears, some spoke about the life-changing intensity of friendship, of the remarkable intermixing of lives and dreams that had taken place aboard ship. Others spoke about their resolve to keep the feelings going, taking them into their schools, environment clubs, or home communities to raise awareness about climate change and expedite strategies to reduce dependence on fossil fuels, to become part of the solution rather than part of the problem.

Permission to speak was being passed, by silent agreement, in a clockwise direction around the circle. Some people were on stacking chairs, others on the carpet, still others on couches. But with the greatest respect for space and the intensely personal nature of what was being shared, the group managed to hear from everybody who wanted to speak, one by one.

When it came time for the first of the northerners to speak, there was a pause, indicating that she was going to exercise her right to be silent. And in that pause, which drew itself out as tension increased, I thought that if there was ever a time for this group to experience the power of learning in this cross-cultural expeditionary setting, then this was it.

Finally, she spoke. "I have been hurting through this whole expedition," she said. "I didn't want to leave home. It was hard to leave home, even for a short time. I was homesick. I have never been this far away from home. Never been away for this long. And then, when we were in Kimmirut, I heard from my aunt that one of my friends had died. He had taken his own life." With that, her head went down and her dark hair covered her face, as tears fell and the young woman beside her consoled her. But instead of continuing to collapse into her pain, she looked up through her hair and her tears at the circle of faces who were holding her, helping her to persist, with their eyes and their supportive body language.

"We have to start talking about this," she stammered. "In my community alone, there have been more than one hundred suicides in the last few years, and most of the people who have died are young, mostly boys but all young. And why did they die? There is drinking. There are drugs. People break up. There are lots of reasons, but we have to stop being quiet about this. We have to talk about this. Many of us can't say anything about climate change, we can't do anything else, until we get other things in our lives figured out."

And that started a flow of support and stories from the other northerners. I wished the whole expedition could have sat in and heard what they had to say. That was not to be, because in a bigger group, without this one's intrinsically, organically organized go-round, conditions would likely not have been right for these brave young women to speak.

But what a truly remarkable moment it was, what an awe-inspiring scene, to see the bright, motivated southern students on the expedition realize for the first time that the perspective they had brought to the expedition was just one way of looking at the world. It was an indelible lesson about parallel lives, worlds as separate as two ships on the open sea that for a moment came toward one another, giving up truths that, if nothing more, illustrate the importance of creating spaces to listen and learn.

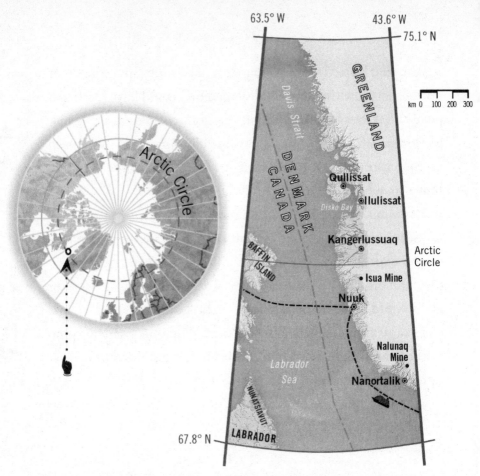

63.5° W   43.6° W

75.1° N

km 0   100   200   300

GREENLAND

Davis Strait

DENMARK

CANADA

Qullissat

Ilulissat

Disko Bay

Kangerlussuaq

Arctic Circle

BAFFIN ISLAND

• Isua Mine

Nuuk

Nalunaq Mine

Labrador Sea

Nanortalik

NUNATSIAVUT

67.8° N   LABRADOR

45°W GREENLAND GMT–2

23: GREENLAND LEADING THE WAY

Anytime I have been in or even over the waters of the Davis Strait between Canada and Greenland, a traditional sailor's ritual has come flooding back to mind. I experienced it aboard the Canadian Coast Guard icebreaker *Louis S. St-Laurent*, heading north in July 2006. About twenty-four hours before we were to cross the Arctic Circle, Captain Anthony Potts handed personnel who had never previously crossed the line on a Coast Guard ship a raw white egg, signed and stamped with the ship's postmark. "You're to carry these on your person at all times," intoned Captain Potts, "and when you're called to report to various places on the ship over the next twenty-four to thirty-six hours, you're to bring your egg. Look after them." The game was on.

Coached by a gaggle of off-duty officers and crew, we were all encouraged to make some kind of protective carrying case for our egg. Thinking I'd found the perfect waterproof, shockproof container for my egg in a small camera case, I popped in the egg and snapped the clasp shut. The shell cracked. "King Neptune will not be amused," said the chief engineer, when I confided in him.

The egg was damaged but it wasn't leaking. Over the next twenty-four hours, there were announcements at all hours that we had to report with our eggs to Monkey's Island, Jack's Mast, and a host of other obscure places on a five-engined 120-metre ship of 13,899 tonnes displacement. The first mate always had his pen and clipboard at the ready when we would eventually turn up, noting how long it had taken us to find the place and the condition of our egg. These tasks were set for the newbies to determine if we were fit to cross the Arctic Circle, as judged, apparently, by Neptune, king of the sea.

On the day of reckoning, we were all given a full physical by the ship's doctor. Then we were dressed in old Coast Guard coveralls and locked in a paint locker off the flight deck. The door opened and one of the sailors was collared by a couple of large ordinary seamen and escorted out. Those of us inside the locker heard a mixture of cheering, screaming, and shouting.

After a few minutes, the door opened again and the sailor was tossed back in the cell, soaking wet, with half of his hair missing. He also reeked of food compost and vinegar.

One by one, the others were escorted out but none came back. When it was my turn, the glorious details of the extended practical joke were revealed. I was blindfolded, hands tied behind my back, and walked along the flight deck and down a companionway to the boat deck below, where the commotion was louder and even more raucous than it had sounded from above.

First I was ushered onto a chair. Something touched my ear and I heard the unmistakable buzz of industrial hair clippers. I felt the vibration on my scalp as the clippers set into my hairline and over the curve of my head. My brain finally sorted out the sensation and I realized there was some kind of plastic guard on the actual blades of the clippers that allowed them to pass over my hair without cutting it. Very realistic. The demi-shaven sailor had been a plant! Phew.

Off came the blindfold and I found myself seated before King and Queen Neptune, who turned out to be Bob the bosun and Natalie the second engineer decked out in mop wigs and splendid costumes as rulers of the sea, complete with broom handles and tin foil to make a pair of royal tridents.

The king and queen had been fully apprised of my performance in the egg charade, including the fact that I'd come into the actual initiation bereft of my egg. "You have lost your egg," the bosun boomed. "That will never do. You must pay in the belly of the whale."

And with that I was blindfolded again, led around a corner rail on the boat deck, and told to make my way to the other end of the boat deck on my belly, as if swimming. Easy enough, or so I thought, except that for the week or so we had been at sea, every bit of old spaghetti, soup, mashed potatoes, sour milk, vegetable peelings, and other miscellaneous compostable liquids and food solids had been saved by the cooks, all to be dumped out now on the deck.

The belly of the whale, sure enough. "Swim through the belly of the whale," the voices said. "Swim. Swim!" More mushy solids than liquid, at first it just seemed disgusting, but after a few minutes of flailing, the smell was evoking a gag reflex.

"You must be thirsty," a voice said, as hands grabbed my arms and rescued me from the whale's belly. "Drink this. It's an iceworm cocktail." Set up by the feel and smell of swimming through old food, I found this mixture of every condiment in the ship's fridge—ketchup, mustard, vinegar, soy sauce, horseradish, wasabi, the lot—acidic, salty, and putrid. It came up almost as quickly as it had gone down.

Fully blindfolded, we continued through a series of physical and psychological trials until each of us in turn was locked into a set of old-fashioned head and hand stocks, blasted with an onboard firehose, and doused with buckets of sea water from the deck above.

Finally we were released to rewarm in the shower and put on new clothes. This grotty Arctic Circle initiation ended with a celebration in the officers' mess, with drinks and a feed of finger food. Captain Potts presented each of us with a very official-looking Arctic Circle Certificate: "Be it known to all Narwhal, Walrus and Seal that Our Loyal Subject, James Raffan, hath this day crossed the Arctic Circle. Captain Anthony Potts, Master, Canadian Coast Guard Ship Louis S. St-Laurent."

In days of yore, these lands at the northern end of the earth turned up on maps with that middle-latitudes perspective built right in. The Arctic was *terra incognita, mare incognitum*—unknown ground, unknown seas. And in mythical King Neptune's Greco-Roman tradition, the Arctic was *terra nullius,* "land belonging to no one." Little wonder, then, that explorers considered these northern lands unpeopled spaces that could be claimed by simple declaration or occupation with the planting of a national flag.

Years later, crossing the Arctic Circle in more or less the same spot in the Davis Strait where my initiation occurred, thinking of Frobisher, Parry, Ross, Franklin, and the rest, I couldn't help but laugh. It was suddenly crystal clear to me that the whole idea of the earth's grid—lines of latitude and longitude, parallels and meridians—was so ingrained in my own thinking that I had been oblivious to a big disconnect. I had told indigenous people around the circumpolar world that I was following the Arctic Circle, but the concept of the Circle was totally irrelevant in their own knowledge and traditions. The joke was on me.

Back aboard the *Clipper Adventurer* on another educational journey, sailing through the waters of the eastern Labrador Sea off

Nuuk, Greenland, I found the sea alive with the scattering rays of a strengthening spring sun. Across the water, past lingering icebergs in the bay, there was a freshness and confidence to the rusts, reds, blues, perky yellows, and spectral greens of these classic Greenlandic houses, piled in good order on the frozen rock along the shore. Beyond these, adding to the decidedly Scandinavian feel of the world's largest island, was Sermitsiaq, the 1,210-metre mountain beyond the town that looked a bit like snow-covered Stetind from the ocean.

In a couple of days, senior ministers from the eight member countries of the Arctic Council and representatives from the permanent indigenous member organizations of the council would gather in Nuuk at the ultra-modern Katuaq Cultural Centre and do something pivotal. This Ministerial Meeting of the Arctic Council hoped to ratify the first legally binding agreement in the history of the intergovernmental body. Nuuk would become the venue for the coming-of-age party for the Arctic Council.

Boats buzzed in the harbour. Snow still lay everywhere, but the streets were open and water was starting to run in the gutters and ditches. There was fresh dolphin for sale at the Nuuk fish market; the heads of three of Flipper's northern cousins were smiling up from a stainless steel table. Across from the arched main entrance of the Pisiffik Nuussuaq supermarket, people on the plaza were selling crafts from folding tables, as mothers with strollers, business people, children on bicycles, and elders opened the zippers of their parkas and enjoyed the relative warmth, ignoring the chill that was definitely still in the air.

Across Aqqusinersuaq Street and down closer to the water, the heads of the various national delegations were meeting at Katuaq, working to put everything in order. They would ensure that when the politicians arrived, the report of the Seventh Ministerial Meeting of the Arctic Council would include the much heralded first Agreement on Cooperation on Aeronautical and Maritime Search and Rescue in the Arctic.

Although the Arctic Council was created officially in Canada in 1998, the idea to bring representatives from the eight circumpolar nations together came from the Finns, who convened a conference in the late 1980s to talk about monitoring, assessment, emergency preparedness and response, and conservation of the Arctic environment. Scientific, academic, and governmental representatives from Iceland, Finland, Sweden, Norway, Canada, Denmark (Greenland), the United States, and the Soviet Union met in Rovaniemi in January 1989.

What made that gathering different from other such conferences was that, in addition to representatives of the eight circumpolar nations, there were also representatives of Arctic indigenous organizations at the table, in the spirit of the Berger Report. This was the first time that the Saami Council, the Inuit Circumpolar Council, and RAIPON had participated as equals in the preparation of an international declaration.

The formation of the Arctic Council was a seismic event in the history and evolution of the Arctic for many reasons. Inclusion of indigenous representatives was a major one, but perhaps most dramatic was one of the provisions set out in the founding declaration, item 7: "Decisions of the Arctic Council are to be by consensus of the Members." Although consensus decision making honoured the governance process used widely and for millennia by the indigenous peoples of the circumpolar world, the essential power of the Arctic Council that would emerge would be derived from *who* was at the table.

So perhaps the most complex problem in founding the Arctic Council was membership: who was in and who was out. Partly this question had to do with how the Arctic was defined; partly it was about political authority and, significantly, which states actually border the Arctic Ocean and which do not. Greenland, Norway, Russia, the U.S., and Canada all have Arctic coastlines. Sweden, Finland, and Iceland (somewhat strangely, because there is ocean between Grímsey and the pole), though within the Arctic Circle, do not border on Arctic waters. But these became the eight members of the Arctic Council.

After a day of speeches and deliberations inside the Katuaq Cultural Centre, Chair Lene Espersen, surrounded by smiles and pats of congratulation, emerged to say how pleased she was that this meeting had witnessed the transformation of the Arctic Council from "a decision-shaping organization to a decision-making council." Indeed, as the draft declaration regarding search and rescue was circulated, it was headed "Strengthening the Arctic Council." Among other provisions, it included a call for establishment of a permanent Arctic Council Secretariat in Tromsø, Norway, by 2013.

The creation of the Arctic Council and its growing power and stature have shaped the Arctic's future in three significant ways: first, the council strongly affirms that northern people, particularly indigenous northerners, will be involved in decisions and will benefit from any developments that proceed; second, it makes clear that any environmental consequences of Arctic development are a circumpolar matter, involving everyone who lives there; and third, with the creation of a permanent Arctic Council Secretariat, it establishes a continuum of process, concern, and decision making that will allow for better prosecution of long-term plans even as democratically elected politicians cycle in and out of office.

Near the southern tip of Greenland, with Nuuk behind us to the north, we stopped at the town of Nanortalik, meaning "place of the polar bear," although bears hadn't been seen for almost a generation. We disembarked and learned about Nalunaq, Greenland's only gold mine, just up the fjord. Owned by Crew Gold Corporation, a U.K.-based junior mining and exploration company, and operated by Procon, a Canadian mine services company, this mine produced more than 8,500 kilograms of gold (small compared with Kupol's 56,700 kilograms since 2000, but a boon to the local economy nonetheless) between 2004 and 2008. Nalunaq gold was used for Danish royal wedding rings and a series of commemorative coins to mark International Polar Year (2007–8), and it was an indicator of what natural resource extraction meant to Greenland (and Denmark) in the past and what it could mean in the future.

As early as 1260, Greenland was considered a colony of the Danish-Norwegian territory because its Norse communities at the time agreed to pay taxes to the Norwegian king. By 1721, a Danish expedition had established a *niuertogarfik* or trade station near the modern-day location of Nuuk. A century later, in 1854, cryolite (a valuable mineral often called "white gold") was discovered, and a mine that operated for the next 130 years was established at Ivittuut on the west coast. With that mine going strong, Denmark established a committee in the 1950s to regularize procedures for resource extraction: a committee to create a mining act for Greenland that was devoid of Greenlanders.

The effort to regulate mining at that time was part of the Grønlandskommissionen of 1950, known as G50: a much more comprehensive plan for public investment in infrastructure that was designed to help nurture private investment in Greenlandic industry. Although G50 did not work nearly as well as the government of Denmark had hoped, it did set the stage for Greenland to move from being a colony of Denmark to a semi-autonomous state in 1953. The move led to a series of initiatives to improve health conditions (tuberculosis was the main cause of death at that time), to educate the Inuit with a Danish-style school system, and to industrialize fishing, particularly along the west and southwest coasts. Although Greenland ceased to be a colony, legislation continued to come from Copenhagen, and in many respects, the Danization or modernization process made Greenlanders more dependent than ever on social and financial assistance from Denmark.

A second pan-Greenland development initiative, called the

G60 plan, did what most colonizing governments have tried to do at one time or another: it enacted policies to concentrate the family groups scattered between the ice cap and the sea all the way around this massive island. This was done partly through positive incentives like the promise of new housing and access to schools, shops, and health care in the bigger settlements; and partly through negative incentives, like the closing of public facilities in the smaller settlements.

Of course, resettlement, as it was throughout the circumpolar world, was a huge perturbation to families and communities who had lived for centuries quite happily on their own paths and by their own devices. Lines were drawn to create arbitrary administrative jurisdictions; the process reminded me of a story I'd heard about when Sápmi was divided into four different nations. The Sami chastised each other in jest for being too Norwegian, Swedish, Finnish, or Russian (pick one) in their dealings with others after the new map had been drawn.

The "Second Copernican Revolution" in the late 1960s, when images of Spaceship Earth came back from the Apollo missions to the moon, increased awareness of humanity's effect on the environment and on its indigenous people. Greenland saw the same increase in awareness and activism that occurred elsewhere. But what was emerging was a deeply seated sense of pride and nascent national identity that allowed the people of Greenland to create, preserve, and protect who they were. For many years, I learned, Coca-Cola was not allowed on the product import list, for fear of the American cultural baggage that might arrive with it.

The Greenlanders themselves created a National Council. It

had no legislative power, but the power of the people and positive communication began to take hold, and in 1975 the idea of Greenlanders owning Greenland was adopted by the National Council. This idea, and the critically important corollary of ownership of subsurface mineral rights, did not sit well with the Danes, but by this time the thought of Greenlanders taking some responsibility for their own affairs was out there. From 1975 to 1978 these ideas were hotly debated between Danish and Greenlandic representatives on the Home Rule Commission.

On January 17, 1979, Greenlanders overwhelmingly adopted Home Rule in a referendum. In May of that year, the Danish constitution was amended to create the Greenlandic parliament. As an autonomous country within the Kingdom of Denmark, Greenland assumed control of health, education, and social services but not—and this was key—mineral rights and resources. But this move was pivotal in giving Greenlanders a palpable sense of control over their own destiny as a northern people. A quick scan of current cultural institutions, like the museums in Nanortalik and other communities and the University of Greenland, shows that these were created after the establishment of Home Rule, a significant outcome of this devolution of power and the beginnings of intellectual and political autonomy.

The international financial community wasn't sure what to make of Home Rule, but through the 1980s and '90s Greenland went about its business, winning on some fronts and losing on others. The Ivittuut cryolite mine and the Maamorilik lead and zinc mine closed. But commercial fishing, particularly for shrimp, continued.

Although social problems still plagued those who remained in the settlements—caught betwixt and between cultures, environments, and worlds—there was a pride evident throughout the land, particularly in the larger settlements. Fortunes in and on the water turned to economic opportunities on the land. In 2004, Crew Gold announced that the Nalunaq mine would begin commercial production. Gold, as ever, was highly emblematic of the possible promise of a new prosperity.

That prosperity did arrive, not via an offshore refinery but because of a decision taken in the Folketinget, the Danish national parliament. Following a second mega-referendum, Queen Margrethe II stood on June 12, 2009, and announced the passage of Act 743, the Act on Greenland Self-Government. This legislation honoured Greenland's democratically elected assembly, called the Inatsisartut, and its government, and it devolved responsibility for the administration of justice, border controls, financial regulation and supervision, and a host of other new powers, including total control of mineral resource activities both on land and offshore.

The self-government law fixed the Danish government's subsidy to Greenland at its 2009 level, 3.4 billion kroner (US$600 million). Unlike the Nunavut Land Claim Agreement, which devolved power to Canada's newest northern territory with everything it needed to succeed except resource-revenue-generating potential, the Danish law gave Greenland the first 75 million kroner (US$12 million) in rates and royalties; after that, half the revenue over the 75 million kroner would be subtracted from the annual subsidy. Greenlanders were in a unique position in the circumpolar world: they got the necessary legislation to eventually take charge of their own affairs as well as the wherewithal to pay for them, through the royalty sharing agreement with Denmark.

What self-government would mean for Greenland remained to be seen, but one metric that stood out was that exploration for oil and minerals in Greenlandic lands and waters more than doubled in one year—from thirty-four permits issued and US$402 million spent in 2009 to forty-nine active permits and US$1.1 billion spent on exploration in 2010. Although these were not the actual revenues going into Greenland's coffers, the numbers did indicate the scope of activity and the emergence of the very real possibility that Greenlanders might one day achieve total independence as a result of Denmark's move.

After rounding the southern end of Greenland, we cut through Prince Christian Sound and turned up a smaller fjord to approach the tip of one of the many fingers of glacial ice that snake down to the sea from the Greenland ice cap. It was almost impossible to get any sense of scale or distance there, with sheer rock cliffs towering overhead on both shores. I went up to the bridge and looked to see where we were on the chart. Although the chart was only five years old, it showed ice where we were sailing. For more than four kilometres beyond where the map said the ice would start, we sailed through open water, as if chasing the glacier as it retreated back toward the mainland.

The effects of climate change are most evident in the North, and nowhere on my journey more than in Greenland. Change, at least politically and environmentally, seemed more a part of life in Greenland than almost anywhere else. And nowhere was that fact reflected more engagingly than in the politics of this harsh northern place.

On the same day that Queen Margrethe proclaimed Greenland's self-government in 2009, there was a federal election that saw Jakob Edvard Kuupik Kleist sworn in as Greenland's fourth prime minister. As a member of the Danish parliament and a vocal member of the leftist Inuit Atagatigiit (Unified Inuit) party, Kleist had been a great proponent of self-rule. His people-centric focus led him to concentrate on addressing the post-colonial social issues that plagued Greenland and so many other northern jurisdictions—alcoholism, domestic violence, and high suicide rates.

But he also wanted to make it known that Greenland was open for business, particularly in the resource extraction sector. Born in a small mining town called Qullissat on Disko Island, a place now abandoned by progress but surrounded by Cairn Energy's offshore wells, Kleist knew both the economic benefits and the social costs of boom-and-bust development. Forward progress had to take into account the fate of people who lived in the place where the development was happening.

While the self-government campaign was building steam in the mid-2000s, a massive inland high-grade iron ore deposit called Isua was sold to a U.K.-based producer of iron ore for the global steel industry called London Mining. On the very edge of the ice sheet in the wilderness between Nuuk and Kangurlussuaq, Isua had been discovered in 1960, explored by one company, and further investigated by another in the 1990s.

London Mining, which had done very well in Sierra Leone at the Marampa iron ore mine, saw dramatic potential for its shareholders in the Isua project. Scoping studies in the summer of 2009 showed that, with the right permits to build infrastructure including an airstrip, a deepwater port, and a 105-kilometre pipeline to move the concentrated ore to the coast as a slurry, the company might build the Arctic business on the export of five million tonnes of concentrated ore per annum. Further investigations in 2010 doubled that number. The following summer, a team of contract hard-rock geologists and hydro geologists, along with experts in geomorphology, did more geotechnical and geomechanical drilling and completed a glacier-melting-rate study that allowed the projected annual output from the mine to jump to a seriously bankable fifteen million tonnes.

London Mining had engaged since 2009, it said, in two-way dialogue with local communities, civic organizations, and government agencies and was ready to go as soon as the exploitation licence and construction permits could be issued by the Greenland Bureau of Minerals and Petroleum. It sounded almost too good to be true, until it became clear who was going to be buying all that iron ore: China.

The People's Republic of China had been cozying up to Iceland next door, and ramping up its icebreaker program with the hope of sending 250,000-tonne ore-carrying ships over the pole as soon as the mine started to produce. In addition to bulk transit of commodities like iron ore, China was planning on running 5 to 15 percent of its shipping to the West through Arctic waters by 2020. Word got out that one of the consequences of China's involvement in the Isua project was that London Mining was planning to operate the mine with as many as two thousand labourers flown over in shifts from Shanghai and Beijing.

Suddenly, Isua became a major issue in the 2013 Greenlandic federal election, with Prime Minister Kleist fighting for his political career. Given the strength of this possible new relationship with China, the electorate worried that he was giving away jobs and potential revenue in the continuing rush toward independence.

The other contender for the top political job in Greenland who was making herself known to the voters, 89 percent of whom were Inuit, was the clever and vivacious Aleqa Hammond, leader of the Siumut (Forward) social democratic party. She had found her political feet as a commissioner of the Inuit Circumpolar Council in the early 2000s and was first elected to the Inatsisartut in 2005. She was appointed to the Department of Families and Justice in 2007, and then to Finance and Foreign Affairs, from which she resigned in 2008 to protest the government's budget deficit.

But with Kleist looking ready to sell the farm to the Chinese, she was convinced to run again, this time campaigning on greater government control of resources, heavier taxation of foreign mining, and stiffer controls on foreign workers. On April 5, 2013, having won 43 percent of the vote in the general election, she forged a coalition and became Greenland's fifth prime minister.

In her first interview after assuming office, Hammond said, "We are welcoming companies and countries that are interested in investing in Greenland. At the same time we have to be aware of the consequences as a people. Greenland should work with countries that have the same values as we have, on how human rights should be respected. We are not giving up our values for investors' sake."

Greenlanders, like all their neighbours around the pole, still struggled with the legacies of colonialism. Greenland was not without its continuing social ills. Alcoholism, family violence, drug abuse, and suicide remained issues that demanded the attention of decision makers, from the heads of families to the heads of municipalities and regions, right up to the prime minister herself.

But with the control of fate came pride that was definitely starting to show itself. This pride and its consequences were continuing to set Greenland apart from its immediate neighbour Nunavut, across the Davis Strait, where infant mortality, for example—a measure of maternal, prenatal, and postnatal health but also of housing and other challenging circumstances—was twice Greenland's and nearly four times the Canadian national average.

Greenlanders cut their average annual alcohol consumption by 50 percent. They instituted a national suicide prevention strategy. But most of all, they were talking to one another about what they needed to do to take back control of their lives. Without the help of the Danish government's enlightened push toward self-determination, which in large measure was shaped by voters who actively wanted to make Greenland work, this would have not been possible at all.

What happened in Greenland is so far from what was happening in the fate control arena for any other indigenous group in the circumpolar world that the rest of the world must pay attention. Greenland had political parties of indigenous people competing for the ears and the votes of the nation. Nina Afanasyeva and her Sami colleagues in the Kola Peninsula would have found this almost impossible to fathom.

Greenlanders were governing themselves. Greenlandic was the language of their self-government. They had decision-making power, and they were working toward economic independence and intellectual control of education and public policy. There were lessons in Greenland for every other country around the circumpolar world, just as there were lessons in every country on the Arctic Circle for every other country in the world.

With the swirling summer mists of Greenland's eastern shore astern, I thought of Sweden's massive iron ore trove and its powerlessness to do anything other than capitulate when Hitler came looking for resources to fuel his expanding geopolitical aspirations. Although the wars of the future will very likely play out in the major stock markets of the world, the ability of northerners to secure and maintain control over their destiny remained tenuous. There were 57,000 Greenlanders. Greenland's gross domestic product was US$1.3 billion. There were 1.3 billion Chinese, and China's GDP was US$7.3 trillion, making its economy five thousand times bigger than Greenland's. Anybody who has played the game of Risk knows who wins when the odds are stacked like that.

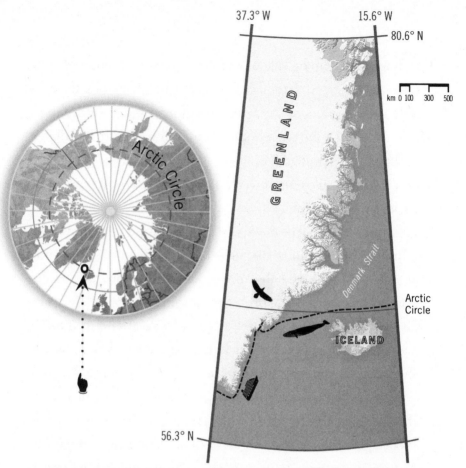

20°W INTERNATIONAL WATERS GMT–1

24: HOME STRETCH

On the home stretch in the Denmark Strait, as the *Clipper Adventurer* steamed just below the Arctic Circle toward Iceland, the close fog and thick scatterings of southbound ice gave way to open water, and we got a sense of being on something of a two-lane ocean highway. Along the Greenland shore, the East Greenland Current brings icy water south into the North Atlantic Ocean.

And on the Icelandic side of the three-hundred-kilometre strait is the ice-free North Irminger Current, which is moving the relatively warm waters of the Gulf Stream and the North Atlantic Drift up toward the pole. Somewhere in the middle, in brilliant sunshine, I was sitting aft on the ship, looking back at the line I'd been following for thousands of kilometres, imagining the Arctic Circle curling back on itself on the Isle of Grímsey—that strange geographic monument made of drill pipe—and remembering.

In this monochromatic scene of Arctic water and sky, the odd raft of ice drifted by. I thought of the Coke bears, or the animated polar bear in Al Gore's film, swimming into oblivion in a warming sea. And I thought of Huxley the bear and my time in the sciences, when personifying a research subject was absolutely taboo. My supervisor back in those days would chastise anyone in the lab who referred to Huxley as anything other than Bear 007 or Double Oh Seven. (Just like Hiquaq, the bears were numbered so that their activities were easier to administer.) But it was a natural thing to do, to honour a glorious beast like a full-grown male polar bear with a name.

As I was scanning the sea for drowning bears, Richard Sears, the ship's resident whale expert, came breathlessly over the ship's public address system to say that he was pretty sure he had sighted two blue whales off the port bow. Everyone scuttled to a rail to have a look.

Knowing that Richard would be where he had always been on this expedition, standing all bundled up on the flying bridge with his binoculars affixed to his face, I headed there instead. "That is the largest living organism on earth," he said, as he pointed to a spout in the distance.

"How do you know they are blue whales?" I had to ask.

"I don't know," he replied. "They look like blues. You can tell by the size of the animals. By the small size of their dorsal fins. By the height and frequency of their blows. They could be bowheads, but I'm pretty sure they're blues. If they get closer, we may see mottled colouring. Up close, we'll get a better idea of size and I'll know for sure."

The ship slowed and steered to a place where it looked like these magnificent animals might come up if they continued their gently arcing course. On the flying bridge my conversation with Richard bounced all over the whale map: Of the estimates of perhaps a quarter million originally in two main populations, one in the northern hemisphere, one in the southern hemisphere. Of nineteenth-century humanity's quest for baleen and meat and oil, mostly oil, and the wholesale slaughter of these and other species of whales to near extinction. And of the moratorium on hunting, with the slow recovery of the population. "You don't get to see the greatest of the great whales very often," said Richard. "Pay attention."

For a time, it looked as though these two whales were playing with the ship or vamping for a very appreciative audience. With the ship more or less stopped in the water, they cruised around, often breathing in unison—one big, the size of a couple of school buses, and one smaller, so perhaps a male and a female or a cow and a calf. The sheer size and ease of movement in the cold ocean, the streamlined beauty of the twin nostrils of the blowhole, releasing air and drawing breath in one smooth movement, riding up out of the water and back down. After a while their backs arched more than before. I watched as they dived deep and disappeared, turning up the next time about ten minutes later far off the starboard bow.

Facts and figures were flying in the excitement that attended this remarkable sighting. "What effect does climate change have on these animals?" one of the students asked. Someone explained their diet and how the krill were affected by water quality and water temperature; this might be altering the whales' distribution and fortunes.

Someone else reminded anyone who was listening about the increasing amount of fresh water that was entering the ocean from melting glaciers and sea ice, and how this was affecting the thermohaline conveyor, the deep ocean currents that move heat around the planet; these were thought to have some relationship to the whales' migration patterns. Others talked of carbon dioxide being absorbed by the ocean and what we had learned about ocean acidification and its effect on the micro-life of the oceans, through the trophic exchanges that move energy up through the food chain. This too was a way in which humanity was affecting the whales.

A student said, "Their breath stinks!" I looked at her and laughed. "You're one of a very select group of people on the planet who know that from personal experience. Count yourself lucky." Out of the corner of my eye I saw an SOI expedition leader, Geoff Green, standing at the railing with his three-year-old son, Fletcher, in his arms so that he might see over the rail. He was pointing at the whales, by then far away, drawing attention to the spouting that was still visible out on the calm sea. "Fletcher, those are the biggest animals in the world," said Green.

"I know, Dad, you said that already."

I was now perhaps a hundred kilometres shy of the end of the 17,662-kilometre line and a full circumnavigation of the world at the Arctic Circle. I'd heard Semjon's stories in the Kola Peninsula that blurred the line between people and reindeer, and Slava's story in Yakutsk about the man who became a wolf who became a man. I recalled several people who'd assured me that "we were bears once." These perspectives were leading me to question the whole idea of the certainty of science and the front-brain ways we relate to the natural world as separate from human existence. What about Captain Ahab? What about Jonah? And what about the day Raven was out in his kayak and saw a great blue whale loafing on the ocean? It was an old Inuit story I'd heard along the way.

Raven saw the whale, said hello, and asked if he might have a peek inside to see what was going on in that massive body that was rolling through the sea. The whale was still thinking about an answer when Raven faked a big yawn. As so often happens, the whale yawned too, and Raven paddled into his mouth, hitched his kayak to one of the big baleen plates, and started to wander back toward the whale's stomach.

Raven hadn't gone more than a few steps into the whale's esophagus when he heard drumming. He followed the sound and saw a circle of drummers playing and singing while a beautiful girl danced like no one he had ever seen dance before. Raven was totally captivated. In the centre of the circle was a kudlik, a seal-oil lamp, which cast shadows of the drums and the drummers and the girl onto the shiny white ribs.

When the beautiful girl danced slowly, the whale moved slowly. But when the drumbeats increased, she would dance more wildly and the whale would speed up, sometimes zooming right out of the water, sometimes turning in the air and crashing back into the blue ocean in time to the music.

As these massive blue whales moved slowly, smoothly, rhythmically through the Denmark Strait, I imagined the girl to be dancing unhurriedly, with precision and intention and almost hypnotically slow. Breathing in. Breathing out. Sliding through the sea.

But that day, as Raven watched the beautiful girl and her movements within the circle of light, he noticed that there were strings attaching her arms and legs to the whale's heart, like a marionette. Raven told the girl that he was absolutely smitten with her beauty and wanted to take her home to be his wife. Of course, she politely declined, saying that she needed to be with the whale. He was welcome to stay, she explained, but she could not leave.

Raven being Raven—after all, he was the creator of the world and could do more or less whatever he pleased, or so he thought—he waited until the beautiful girl took a rest and the whale dozed. With the stealth of thousands of years of trickery, and with the quickness of a twitch of a caribou's ear, he wrapped his wings around the girl, snapped her strings, and ran back the way he'd come in. He untied his kayak and quickly made it disappear. Stepping out of the sleeping whale's mouth, he lifted into the air and flew to the beach with the girl in his talons.

Suddenly Raven had two problems on his hands. The whale

started thrashing in the water, twisting and turning in agony until it ended up on the beach. And as the whale was taking its last breath, the beautiful girl got smaller and smaller in his hands until she disappeared altogether.

Raven was devastated. He sat down beside the dead whale and started to cry. He cried and cried. For weeks he cried. Then he began to sing. For weeks he sang. And then he danced. For weeks he danced, and finally he started to feel more like his old self. But he had learned a lesson.

And it was a lesson that Raven felt he had to share with everyone else on earth. He promised all the fish and the birds, all the insects and the animals, including the people, that he would continue to return to their world from his world as long as they would remember to look after each other and to honour the truth that everything must live and eventually everything must die, but all life is sacred.

And they say that the tears that Raven shed were the first tears, and that those songs and those dances were the first healing songs and the first dances of forgiveness.

When this journey began, the story of Raven and the whale, and countless others like it that are told and retold on radio, stage, and television and in ordinary family dwellings throughout the circumpolar world, registered as folk tales, as myths, as stories of indigenous origins—fictions. After 17,562 kilometres, I wasn't so sure that they were any less true, any less profound, than the pronouncements of other arts or sciences.

Raven, my friend Raven, was the only living creature that was with me at every step of the way. It didn't seem to matter where I went; Raven was there, literally, metaphorically, mythic-ally—shape shifting, playing, calling, signalling, speaking of life and death, guiding some in healing, others in understanding. For others, like Clifford Weyiouanna in Shishmaref, ravens were the bane of his existence as a reindeer herder.

On the open sea between Greenland and Iceland, I looked east to see if the *Nunni* and her crew might be far out in western waters, and I thought of those two ravens—only two—who lived on Grímsey, who have always lived on Grímsey. Huginn and Muninn: the god Odin's eyes and ears. Huginn and Muninn: thought and memory. The image of Odin's two black birds with minds of their own stuck like a burr on my parka.

The idea came from the Old Norse Poetic Edda, written down in the thirteenth century but probably older than that. One stanza, verse 20, from "The Speech of the Masked One (Odin)," transcribed at the Culture House in Reykjavik, stands out. I've written and rewritten it into various journals along the way, to keep it close at hand:

> *Hugin ok Munin*
> *fljúga hverjan dag*
> *Jörmungrund yfir;*
> *óumk ek of Hugin,*
> *at hann aftr né komi-t,*
> *þó sjámk meir of Munin.*

Hugin and Munin
Fly every day
Over all the world;
I worry for Hugin
That he might not return
But I worry more for Munin.

These lines from the Poetic Edda had gone around and around in my mind, as I watched ravens do all the crazy things they did along my way. They were an enduring presence through-out the seasons and through nearly 360 degrees of longitude. And the more I researched and read and wrote, the more I was convinced of the deep relevance today of the wisdom of our ancestral elders.

One of the indigenous philosophers, Windhawk, said this: "Raven speaks of the process of death and birth. It guides us to healing, to an initiation that signals the end of one part of life and the beginning of something new. Out of the darkness, out of the Void of Creation we are guided by Raven to become that which we are destined to become. This, like all such pronounce-ments, is based on a host of teachings and an ocean of belief from a variety of cultures that science would be quick to point out are very difficult, if not impossible, to verify."

In her book *The Masks of Odin*, Elsa-Brita Titchenell explored the lure of the material world and how humanity's "cosmic purpose" was to choose to connect the here and now to "the divine source of their existence." She wrote, "The critical choice is not made all at once; it is the cumulative effect of numberless small choices made through progressive stages of life. In the natural course of growth the soul unites each increment of experience with its divine source and so little by little merges with it."

Thought can get diverted away from "cosmic purpose," which, in many respects, describes exactly where we are today with the decisions we persist in making that are fundamentally changing the environment we occupy. And one of these diversions must surely be this: perhaps because we are so enamoured of our own ways and our own beings, we have chosen to ignore or disregard other ways and other beings, such as the residents of the circumpolar world, particularly the indigenous residents of the Arctic. We have become slaves to corporations, choosing to measure wealth in economic terms rather than by any of the host of other indicators of social well-being.

We have set up an elegant framework for assessing the wellness of northern peoples and communities: health and population; material well-being; education; cultural well-being and cultural vitality; contact with nature; and, of course, fate control. But perhaps the way we gather information to assess these indices says as much about ourselves as about northerners. The Poetic Edda warned of this in the thirteenth century, and to my mind, the admonition reads as profoundly now as it might have done then. Thought—volition and the ability to choose—has disconnected us from balance and some key fundamental truths of our lives.

When we lose touch with the contradictions of our own existence, Huginn fails to return, as Odin worried many years ago.

Odin worries about Huginn, but he worries more about Muninn, memory, failing to return. To lose memory would be far worse than to lose thought, if such a grand distinction can be made. We must walk backwards up the mountain.

Titchenell, a scholar of the Poetic Edda, interprets the end of the poem like this: "Hugin returns to Odin, bringing tidings of the manifest world. It is on the report of Munin that is built all attainment, as memory remains eternally as the foundation of future awareness." Throughout my journey, everyone talked about remembering and why that might be important, even if the memory was from a past life or from a life that was yet to come.

Why does difference matter? In difference is memory. In the same way the pharmacologists went to the tropical rainforest to find drugs to treat the emerging diseases of the developed world, I went to the North hoping to find wisdom that could come to bear on the problems the earth is facing, particularly climate change. Again and again, I found at hearths and kitchen tables, in tents, yurangas, and chums from Siberia to Shishmaref and Reykjavik to Repulse Bay, northerners who understood change—particularly cultural change—and whose voices, views, and visions were not being heard.

What northerners know, where they have been, what they have endured, what they have loved, how they have lived and died, how they *are* living and how they *are* dying, is part of the great treasure trove of human knowledge, of thought and memory, of understanding.

"Memory remains eternally as the foundation of future awareness." But much of that wisdom, those memories, is found in languages and ways of knowing that don't easily translate into categories of the Library of Congress or conventional Western epistemological frameworks.

Contained in the hearts and minds of people of many different dying language groups, many different cultures in crisis, may be solutions to the essential problems of humankind, the keys to "future awareness." Climate change is just the tip of that melting iceberg.

In that great open changing sea, the bear swims, and swims, and swims, its future more uncertain with every heartbeat. As most northerners would tell us, solutions can begin with a simple shift of perspective, a switch in point of view that could lead to profound changes in approach, in lifestyle, in inclusion, in wealth, in happiness, in fate control and all the rest.

We are the bear.

EPILOGUE

AFTER THE COLD RUSH

It seemed fitting at the end of my journey to return to Iceland for a conference called Arctic Circle, convened in October 2013 by the irrepressible Ólafur Ragnar Grímsson. Big money and big business had come together to talk about climate change as opportunity. Although Arctic NGOs, women, youth, and indigenous people were in noticeably short supply, particularly on the speakers' list, there was a warmth and collegiality among the thousand delegates from forty countries that could have led an observer to the conclusion that the world was indeed warming—but that, all things considered, science was doing what it needed to do, meetings were being convened, and things were generally where they should be at the top of the world.

Standing under a giant screen bearing the logo of a major international shipping company, President Grímsson welcomed everyone to an evening reception at the Icelandic National Art Gallery, housed in a repurposed warehouse on the Reykjavik waterfront: "It is fitting that we gather in this old warehouse where Iceland first did business with its neighbours around the circumpolar world."

On the way north, as a guest of the ever-hospitable Icelandair (suddenly wistful that I wasn't on one of the planes it had leased to Air Yakutia in deepest darkest Siberia), I ticked over in my mind some of the things that had happened in the three and a half years that it had taken me to make my way around the Circle.

In 2013, the Intergovernmental Panel on Climate Change issued another report that stated that it was "extremely likely" that climate change was of anthropogenic origin. Also in 2013, as summer minimums of northern ice cover continued to decline, two voyages of note took place in the mild months. In August, the first ever commercial container vessel to take the Northern Sea Route, the *Yong Sheng*, knocked a full two weeks off the conventional journey from Dalian, a port in northeastern China, to Rotterdam by sailing east across the top of Russia. And in September, the ice-strengthened seventy-five-thousand-tonne *Nordic Orion*, with a load of coal (how ironic was that in an age of global warming?), became the first bulk carrier to transit the Northwest Passage over the top of Canada, en route to the furnaces of a steel producer called Ruukki Metals in Pori, Finland. Although the journey from Vancouver was only four days shorter than passage through the Panama Canal, analysts estimate that Nordic Bulk Carriers, the Danish owner of the ship, saved something in the order of US$200,000.

In anticipation of this increase in ship traffic around the pole, and following its first legally binding resolution in Nuuk regarding search and rescue, the Arctic Council unanimously passed an agreement on marine oil pollution preparedness and response. Critics were quick to dismiss the agreement as inadequate, given that it failed to impose any practical minimum standard on governments regarding preparedness or on-the-ground response capability, nor did it do anything to increase the level of liability for companies operating in the North in the event of an actual spill. Supporters, however, said that cooperation of this sort was a significant step in the right direction.

Still in the political arena, a federal election in Norway in September 2013 saw the ouster of the incumbent prime minister in favour of a four-party coalition that, as part of a common platform, had agreed to halt drilling and further oil exploration in Lofoten, Vesterålen, and the areas close to the ice edge in the High Arctic. And political decisions made as if the natural environment mattered had been matched occasionally by similarly enlightened public processes conducted as if the Arctic were a peopled place. An example of that happened at a meeting in Bangkok on March 7, 2013, when delegates voted *not* to ban commercial exports of polar bear parts in the Convention on International Trade in Endangered Species—a move that particularly delighted the Canadian Inuit leader Terry Audla. Score one for Arctic indigenous peoples.

But in late 2012, the Russian government had moved unilaterally to suspend the operations of RAIPON, the only organization representing *all* three hundred thousand indigenous people in forty-one different groups across Russia's 172 degrees of longitude. Happily, the international community rallied to protest this action, reminding Moscow that the well-being of indigenous peoples was a stated priority in a host of official Russian policies; after a moment of studied indifference, the Kremlin caved and allowed the organization to be reinstated, but not before meddling in the election of its next president. My friend from Salekhard, Sergey Kharyuchi, whose signature on a letter of introduction had been instrumental in my journey, was out; after the people's favourite candidate, Pavel Sulyandziga, withdrew, Moscow-friendly Grigory Ledkov was in.

In a move that was quietly celebrated by almost all concerned, Canada returned to the chair of the Arctic Council, and in the leading role was Leona Aglukkaq, an Inuk from Nunavut. The move was trumpeted by the Canadian federal government as one that "underlines the priority that the Government of Canada places on the Arctic as well as its commitment to ensure that the region's future is in the hands of Northerners." With all due respect to Minister Aglukkaq, having a northerner in this position was a promising start, but when it came to the lives of everyday northerners in 2013, nothing could be farther from the truth. The region's future was *not* in the hands of northerners.

Every day, stories on the inside pages of newspapers around the world—if they even got that far—told of continued heartache in communities around the circumpolar world: suicide, substance abuse, kids dropping out of school, family violence, incest, crime, and unemployment, all at levels that spiked well beyond the national and international averages. If I had learned anything from visiting with northerners around the circumpolar world, it was that in spite of the enormous challenges they faced, most had found ways to cope, even to thrive; without a strong sense of well-being, however, nothing more was possible, including participation in anything beyond their immediate sphere of living—traditional, modern, conventional, or otherwise.

And so it was with a sense of hope and optimism that I disembarked at Keflavík Airport and headed toward the Arctic Circle conference. Outside the impressively glazed Harpa conference centre venue—"If people have been wondering what Icelanders have been doing since the economic collapse of 2008," quipped Ólafur Grímsson in his opening remarks, "we have been building an amazing meeting venue"—were four Greenpeace volunteers in polar bear suits, protesting Russia's incarceration of thirty of their peers, who had been arrested trying to draw attention to an offshore drilling platform in the Barents Sea. The first thing I learned about the Arctic Circle conference was that bears were not welcome—indeed, any mention of Greenpeace brought audible scoffs from the audience, strange as that seemed, given Grímsson's call for open dialogue as "House Rule Number One" for a successful conference.

House Rule Number Two was that fact-based science should guide all decision making, and Rule Number Three was that indigenous peoples of the North should be a "significant part of the process." The problem was that although, presumably, indigenous peoples had been invited to attend, only one of the six permanent participants in the Arctic Council was represented. For the Inuit Circumpolar Council, with 155,000 members in Canada, Alaska, Greenland, and Russia, Aqqaluk Lynge was present, but there was no one officially representing the Saami Council, RAIPON, the Aleut International Association, the Arctic Athabascan Council, or the Gwich'in Council International. That, for me, was a problem.

Of course, many northerners might have wanted to come but couldn't afford the ticket to Iceland. But I knew of others who felt that President Grímsson's initiative ran contrary to the intentions of the Arctic Council and its multitude of working groups and adherent forums. Although it was not clearly specified in the pre-conference literature, the lingua franca of the conference was English, so participants needed personal translators; there was no simultaneous translation of any kind. And yet, as Alice Rogoff, an Alaskan publisher and co-founder of the conference, said in her opening remarks, the gathering was open to all comers (excluding bears). In contrast to more formal gatherings, she said—referring however obliquely to the protocols and communiqués of the Arctic Council—delegates might think of the Arctic Circle conference as a "cross between Davos and Woodstock" or as conversations around the "Arctic water cooler."

There were quite a number of heavy hitters around that water cooler. United Nations secretary general Ban Ki-Moon opened the conference by video. He was followed by an impressive parade of current and former heads of state, ambassadors, government ministers, Arctic officials, legal specialists, scientists, explorers, financiers, and delegates of every conceivable industry, shipping company, tourism operation, university, or financial institution with Arctic interests. Significantly (and controversially), President Grímsson had made a point of inviting and making especially welcome some of the new countries that had been awarded observer status at the recent Arctic Council Ministerial Meeting. Presenters from Singapore, Korea, and

China were on the program, alongside representatives from a number of the eight countries of the so-called Himalayan/ Third Pole Region of mid-Asia, all gathered to talk about the challenges and opportunities—mostly opportunities—of climate change. The "cold rush" was on.

While the bears did sun salutations on the concrete plaza outside the conference, delegates were offered twenty plenary sessions and at least twice that many breakout sessions over three days with names like "Arctic Energy Cooperation," "Arctic Security," "Selling the Climate Crisis Message," "Arctic Resource Development and Indigenous Religious Rights," "Industry Leadership and Collaboration for Responsible Economic Development of the Arctic," "Northern Sea Routes," "Singapore and the Arctic," "The Alaskan State of the Arctic," "The Future of Arctic Cooperation," "Polar Law: The Rights of Indigenous Peoples," and "The Emerging Risks of the Arctic Bioeconomy."

It was a veritable feast of Arctic information and know-how. To be sure—wide swings in subject matter, speaking style, and quality of visuals notwithstanding—it was a stimulating talkfest, with as much going on in the corridors and around the refreshment stations as there ever was around the metaphoric water cooler. Good people. Good ideas.

Things intensified during the Q & A session after a talk about Russia and the Arctic led by my Moscow friend, the explorer, Hero of the Russian Federation, and special envoy of President Vladimir Putin to the Arctic, Arthur Chilingarov. With the Sami parliamentarian Josefina Skerk at his side, Greenpeace International executive director Kumi Naidoo stepped up to the aisle microphone in the audience to ask if, given the speaker's previous support of conservation causes, there was some way that he might intervene with his government to have the charges of piracy dropped or reduced for the thirty protesters involved in the Barents Sea rig incident. As he spoke, there was an audible groan in the room, as if this question were somehow offside. Chilingarov was, of course, on stage and took this as an opportunity to belittle Naidoo by saying that it was here, in forums like this, that they should make their points, not by breaking laws on the open sea. Until that point, Chilingarov had used a translator, who had delivered his formal remarks in English. But now he answered questions directly, clearly understanding and speaking English perfectly well. It was good theatre.

Naidoo persisted, saying, "Some months ago, my colleague Josefina and others dropped a flag through the ice at the North Pole, where you famously dropped your flag from a submersible, only our flag was signed by 2.7 million supporters who wish to save the Arctic on behalf of all nations, not to claim it for just one nation." By then, delegates were shifting in their seats and clearing their throats.

Josefina Skerk stood poised, blond and beautiful in her traditional *gákti*, throughout this exchange. I'd met the twenty-six-year-old at the opening reception and learned that in addition to being part of the Greenpeace team that had taken the flag and signature capsule to the North Pole, she was a member of the Swedish Sami parliament, chair of the Sami Youth Council, and, in her spare time, studying law at Umeå University. "Is the Sami parliament a place to practise law when you graduate?" I had asked her. She sighed and said, "No. I think not. Perhaps I will work in the international sphere. It might have more effect there."

That's when it struck me: this gathering was mostly about energy, Arctic energy, hydrocarbons in the ocean floor. In fact, depending on whom you listened to and where they were getting their numbers, the received wisdom from science was that 10 to 15 percent of the planet's undiscovered oil and gas is in sediment-ary rock under the Arctic Ocean. It's a huge number. Something like ninety billion barrels of oil is part of the Eldorado that is the melting Arctic. But at current consumption rates, the prize that industry is scrambling for would fuel the entire world for only three years. Moreover, there are new and growing fears that methane hydrates would be released from sediments into warm-ing ocean waters by drilling, and many enlightened scientists are insisting that the only workable future for humankind involves leaving much of this petroleum in the ground.

Thanks to the work of the Arctic Council with the United Nations Convention on the Law of the Sea, which almost every-one (except the Americans) agrees is a workable mechanism for determining who owns what in the Arctic, sovereignty was not an issue. The Arctic pie had been divvied up, with some small areas still being negotiated. Big business and big money were there to talk about what might be done collectively, collabora-tively, capitalistically, to make Arctic ventures work for all con-cerned—well, almost all concerned. There stood Josefina Skerk. For her, and four hundred thousand indigenous people around the circumpolar world, sovereignty *is* an issue.

It seems to me that this juncture in history is our last chance to put things right with indigenous peoples and with the environment, while there are still indigenous peoples and still parts of the natural environment that remain more or less pristine. And for all intents and purposes, both of these interests were absent or systematically excluded from the conversation in Reykjavik.

Johan van de Gronden, chief executive officer of the World Wildlife Fund Netherlands, had the courage to stand up and say, "The Arctic should be a zone of peace. I ask you humbly to bring [the issue of the jailed environmentalists to] a peaceful resolution so that these people might go free." But then he went on to say what had not been said—and he was the only one to do so: "The proclaimed oil and gas bonanza is a chimera. You cannot safely mine for oil and gas in the Arctic. Full stop."

The final plenary voice at the Arctic Circle was that of a university student from Greenland, a young, female, indigenous voice that filtered through the suits like a cool breeze. Her name was Naja Carina Steenholdt, and she was as aware as anyone that Greenland was really at the vanguard, among northern indigenous peoples, of emerging power through devolution. She acknowledged those who would say that taking power back from Denmark, only to have that hierarchical relationship replaced by massive inflows of cash from China or other major market players, was tantamount to cultural suicide.

But unlike so many who had spoken before her during the three-day "Arctic marathon" (so described by President Grímsson as the conference entered its final day), and like the Nenets elder in Salekhard who said he was looking forward to the day that the oil runs out, Naja Steenholdt had her young eyes up, looking over the horizon. She had been thinking about Greenland's long game, in particular what would happen after the cold rush, how Greenlanders might navigate through those newly ice-free waters and what kind of priorities should guide them on the way. Before they could fully embrace self-rule, she said, "we need to educate ourselves." In a voice that belied her young age and slight stature, tucked behind Harpa's ponderous podium, she continued, "In order to carry out future responsibilities in our pursuit for independence, we need to empower our people with knowledge and competence."

As her brief speech wound to a close, she asked questions that brought winter tundra silence to the room. "Do we want independence? Do we want to export uranium? Do we want to drill for oil? Can we comprehend the risks? Do we know the consequences? And if the answer is yes, will we then be ready to pay the price?"

Naja was listed on the program as "Student from the University of Greenland." The panel, entitled "Greenland's Perspective on the Arctic," included a professor from the University of Greenland, the deputy manager of the Greenlandic Association of Fishermen, and an executive from the Royal Arctic Line. And it had been business as usual until Naja stepped forward and said her piece. Now far from anonymous, she concluded by saying, "These questions cannot be answered in the present; however, the future of Greenland is created by initially addressing the challenges we face today. We as a people have to acknowledge that each and every one of us shares a responsibility to carry out this difficult task."

Although by this last session in the conference, many seats in the auditorium were vacant, I was among many who stood to applaud this remarkable young Greenlander who dared to ask questions that went beyond expedient resource extraction and corporate politics, and who acknowledged that none of her peers would join the conversation until they were empowered through education to shape their own destiny. In thanking her for this remarkable speech, former Greenlandic prime minister Kuupik Kleist—obviously delighted with what she had said—turned to the audience and said, in his distinctive gravelly voice, "If I had to put the future of Greenland in one word, it would be 'education.'"

If this is our last chance to get things right with indigenous peoples and with the environment, and if Naja and Josefina, Angut and Billy, Ingrid and so many other youth I met in my travels around the Arctic Circle are living testament to the wisdom of Kleist's words, then the challenge for the rest of us is to educate ourselves to empower and support northerners to fly their own arcs toward sustainable self-determination and to confront issues like climate change and the cold rush head on.

But to do that we must shine a light into the shadows of conquest. We must spend as much time and money on relationship building as we spend on science and industry, and invest with every available resource to ensure that this illumination and these investments persist until, as our minister for the Arctic Council dreams, the Arctic's future is truly in the hands of northerners.

Lined up in Keflavík, ready to head home, I recalled a moment during a presentation about Alaska, when the presenter looked out on the sea of delegates and asked for a show of hands to indicate how many Alaskans were in the audience. There were three score or more. Later that day, during a presentation about indigenous rights, a presenter asked how many indigenous people were present in the audience. Eight hands went up. Visibly embarrassed by this, conference co-founder Alice Rogoff picked up the stage mike and said, "We'll do better next time." Amen, Sister Alice.

Our future depends on it. In a world where climate change affects every living soul, we are all northerners.

ACKNOWLEDGEMENTS

This odyssey would just *not* have happened but for the love and care of my spouse and partner of thirty-five years, Gail Cole Simmons—911 operator, home fire stoker, in-house editor, and confidante through more than a few scrapes, long absences, and missed connections.

I must also acknowledge the pivotal contributions of former Canadian diplomat and Queen's University policy studies professor Bob Wolfe, and Canadian Ambassador to Russia John Sloan, who were instrumental in helping to make the first official connections in Moscow for this project. Special thanks and appreciation as well to Evgenia Titovskaya and my hero, Venera Niyazova, from the Yamal Department of Culture, who vouched for my character and the soundness of this project with almost no information to go on, and helped to secure a long-term, multiple-entry visa to conduct the Russian legs of the research.

Official access to communities across the Russian Arctic was also crucially aided by Russian Ministry of Foreign Affairs Ambassador-at-Large Anton Vasiliev, who provided strategic advice, as well as Executive Director Elena U and Board Chair Sergey Nikolayevich Kharyuchi of RAIPON—the Russian Association of Indigenous Peoples of the North, Siberia, and the Far East—whose written support for this project opened many doors. Finally, without the dogged determination of Elena Bologova in Anadyr and Elena Gaisina at the Canadian Embassy in Moscow, this project's Chukotka permit would never have been issued.

Others whose counsel came at multiple points throughout the research and writing process include my friend and long-time editor and publisher, Phyllis Bruce; Arctic ambassador Mary Simon; International Polar Year conference chair Peter Harrison; Students on Ice founder Geoff Green, who seems to know just about everybody in the boreal and austral circumpolar worlds; reindeer herder and indefatigable northern entrepreneur Lloyd Binder; my ebullient literary agent, Hilary McMahon at Westwood Creative Artists; historian David Finch in Calgary; vice president and general director of the Moscow Representative Office of Kinross Gold Corporation, Lou Naumovski; Arctic Institute of North America co-conspirator Mike Robinson; and mentors Brian Osborne and Bert Horwood, who always manage to slip alternative perspectives into a conversation just when things are settling.

Top list kudos, too, to the hardest working e-agent in the Russian travel biz, Nina Abrosimova in Moscow, who coached me through reading as much Russian as necessary to understand complicated itineraries and who extinguished flash fires at the most crucial times.

And then, at each stop along the way, there were contributors, informants, guides, translators, hosts, fixers, and friends old and new who, without exception, sometimes with my knowledge and often without, or without mentioning in any detail just how far out of their way they had gone to make things happen, bent over backwards to welcome and assist a northern neighbour.

In **Iceland**: Svafar Gylfasson, his wife, Unnur, and their delightful children, Gyda, Sigrun Edda, Bra, and Ingólfur Bjarni, who introduced me to the secret life of birds on Grímsey. On the fishing vessel *Nunni*, Svafar's twin brother Bjarni Gylfasson and crew, Arni Mar Olafsson and Adam Petur Petursson, who humoured me as I asked incessant questions between dashes to the rail. Invaluable insight and advice in Reyjkavik came from Ari Trausti Guðmundsson, who, among other things, taught me about ravens. My thanks as well to Icelandic President Olafur Ragnar Grímsson, whose iconoclastic and courageous thinking about circumpolar affairs was always thought-provoking. And to the hardest-working polar bears in Iceland, who protested the Arctic Circle Conference on behalf of the imprisoned Arctic 30, Caterina Torresani and Leena Lahti—you too added signifi-cantly to the round-the-world experience.

In **Scandinavia**: Ingrid Skjoldvaer and her mother, Torhild Morsund, welcomed Canadian visitors into their lives in Sigerfjord, **Norway**. Gyrid Celius, counsellor at the Royal Norwegian Embassy in Moscow, also provided crucial advice about Norwegian travel. In **Sweden**, Elisabeth Ohlsson helped me connect to Terra Madre delegates, and her son Daniel Ohlsson welcomed us into his farm kitchen right on the Arctic Circle in Kuouka. Then in **Finland** there were guides and interpreters at cultural sites along the way, and delighting us in a wonderfully weird Finnish interpretation of *Peter Pan* was the theatre troupe on the MS *Silja Serenade*, on the night cruise between Helsinki and Stockholm. And the guy at the Koskenniemi Gasthaus, ninety kilometres south of Jyväskylä, who lent us the canoe for a day without anything other than the warmest and most trusting welcome—thank you.

In **Russia** (working west to east through 172 degrees of longitude): In **Sápmi**, on the Kola Peninsula, were the incomparable Anna Prakhova, Nina Afanasieva, Anna Afanasieva, Olga Egorova, Valentina Sovkina, Semjon Bolshunov, Olga Sergeiova, and their families and friends, and whose special anniversary candle we burn still on June 30th each year. In **Murmansk**, Nathan Hunt, Ludmila Kondratenko, Maria Ilicheva, Grigory Stratiy, and Evgeniy V. Nikora, speaker of the Murmansk Regional Duma. In **Moscow**, Maria Ilicheva, Gilles Breton, Eugene Berg, Mikhail Slavin, Evgeny Pimenov, Prof. Tatiana Vladsova, Arthur N. Chilingarov, Ivan V. Rozhin, Prof. Vera Smorchkova, Prof. Tatiana Dmitrievna Pivovarova, Nikolay Dmitrievich Smirnov, Natalia Muradova, Aleksey Vakhrushev, Alexander Mikhailovich Konstantinov, Dr. Natalia Rybczymski, and my old friend from elementary and secondary school, Mark Gilbert, and his wife, Lois, who made me so welcome when passing through Moscow. In **Yamal**, Alina and Yana Lyaskovik, Ljudmila Lipatova, Roman Yando, Lidiya Patievna Vello, Keonid Ivanovich Khudi, Vanentina Ivanova Shakhova, Nadezhda Larivna Serpivo, Oleg Prokop'evich Siugney. In **Aksarka**, Viktor and Olga Laptender and not too far away in their chum on the frozen tundra, Nikolai and Oustinia

Laptender, and their families. In **Khanty-Mansiysk**, Vladislav Ivanovich Rishkolaevich Shestalov, Oleg Gustavovich Shatin, Prof. Romanov Konstantin, Dina Gherasimova Vasilievna, and Nikolai V. Chepurnyh. In **Kyshik**, Yefim Mikolaevich and his wife, Natalya Paulovna Bachman. In **Yakutsk**, Sardana Boyakova, Prof. Aitalina A. Borisova, Ekaterina Evseyeva, Alexandr P. Isaev, Valentina Dmitrievna, Afanasiy V. Migalkin, Ruslan Skrybykin, Vaycheslav Shadrin, Igor and Marina Makarov, Sardana Boyakova, Maxime Duran, Natalia Harlumphia, Nikolai Louguinov, and Aiza P. Reshetnikova. In **Oktyomtsy**, Marta Alexandra and Olga Uvarov. In **Bayaga**, Boris Fedorovich Neustroev and his wife, Fedora. In **Magadan**, Brad Margeson and Roman Karabets, the Kinross driver. At **Kupol**, Lyudmila Ukhtomskaya, Alexander Petrovich Romanov, Evgeniya Saevich, Pavel Ermakov, Nikolay Rol'tykvy, Vladimir Korange, Vladislav Itegin, and Jason Lever. In **Chukotka**, Grigori Tynankergav, Elena Bologova, Anna Otke, Petr Klimov, André Alexandravich Klimko, Irina Tymnevye, and Michael Golbtsev. And finally, kudos to the lady at the Russian Consulate in Ottawa, who brought me to tears with her tough love.

In **Alaska**: With an introduction from Geoff Green, Lieutenant Governor Mead Treadwell personally opened a number of doors leading to wonderful encounters in **Nome** with Tom Gray; in **Shishmaref** with Clifford Weyiouanna and Dennis Davis; and in **Kotzabue** with Zach Stevenson, Martha Siikauraq Whiting, Dolly K. Holley, Mickey Nanouk, and the incomparable whale hunter/culturalist-cum-actor, John Chase. In **Fairbanks**, Evon Peter made me think of Nelson Mandela and his work; and in **Fort Yukon,** Ginny Alexander made me welcome in her house, the Snowdrift B&B, where she introduced me to her ex-husband, Clarence, as well as to Hanne Bergman and Mike Peter.

In **Greenland**: Again, assistance, information, guidance and advice came from a wealth of likely and unlikely sources: David Fletcher, Rassy Alataq, Ludvig Hammeken, Kristine Klemensen, Esther Olsen, Kim Rasmussen, Ania Drechsel, Liv Lynge, Naja Carina Steenholdt, and Mikkel Lund, who piqued my interest in the Arctic Circle trail east from Kangerlussuaq with offer of accommodations in his coastal home in Sisimiut. A strong vote of support for the project from a pivotal conversation with Prime Minister Aleqa Hammond after singing for her on stage with the Students on Ice Chorus at the 250th Anniversary Celebration in Uummanaq in the summer of 2013.

In **Canada**: Advisors, travelling companions, teachers, and confidants across the country helped in variety of contexts: Patrick Borbey, Andrew Kunezi, Frank and Margaret Ipakohak, Pascal Baillargeon, Elaine Alexie, *Up Here* magazine publisher Marion Lavigne, Elizabeth Basil, Martin Bergmann, Grant Linney, Michael Greco, Larry Biemann, Mike Robinson, Peter Harrison, Whit Fraser, Tony Penikett, Bruce Rigby, John Crump, Faruk Ekich, Steve Mitchell, Ed Opitz, Mat Wilcox, Farley Mowat, Commander Jeffrey McRae and Col. Pierre St-Cyr, Jeff Anderson, Johnny "Awesome" Issaluk, Jesse Mike, Jason Annahatak, Whitney Lackenbauer, and in Repulse Bay, hunter, boat driver and guide, the late Joani Kringayark. You have all been instrumental in one way or another in circling the midnight sun. And on the **Coppermine River**, members of the Atanigi Expedition described in Chapter 20 were Craig Parkinson, Angulalik Pedersen, Katrina Hotogina, Billy McWilliam, Carla Algona, Colin Smith, Ken MacDiarmid, Andrew Aziz, John Aziz, Charlie Walker, Rob Willoughby, Philip von Hahn, Kevin Ongahak, Molly Prendergast and Kenny Taptuna, who gave me the Inuinnaqtun name "Aiuituk" (meaning "teacher" or "bearded guitar player from the south"), which I cherish.

My travelling mates on ships in the Arctic—Captain Anthony Potts, Jolly Atagoyak, Captain Norm Baker, Mike Beedell, Michael Byers, JR Carey, Borden Chapman, Sira Chayer, Gary Donaldson, Kathleen Edwards, Jane Eert, David Fletcher, Whit Fraser, David Freese, Eric Galbraith, Diz Glithero, Geoff Green, David Gray, Peter Harrison, Bobby Rose Koe, Shirley Manh, Peter Mansbridge, Eric Mattson, Jeannete Menzies, Daniel Meyok, Alanna Mitchell, Lee Narraway, Joanne Palituq, Bianca Perrin, Annie Petalaussie, Scobie Pye, Richard Sears, David Serkoak, Tim Straka, Ian Tamblyn, Donavin Taplin, Alex Taylor, Trevor Taylor, Lucy van Oldenbarneveld, and the members of South Pacific ukulele ensemble Island Breeze, who rocked the ball diamond in Cape Dorset one sunny Arctic summer afternoon.

Besides various and more anonymous snogos, ATVs, canoes, kayaks, dog sleds, cars, 4 x 4s, eighteen-wheelers, motor canoes, Peterheads, reindeer sleds, bicycles and dirt bikes that got me from A to B along the way, the internationally registered oceangoing ships and their unseen crew members that deserve a vote of thanks as well for safe passage: *Nunni* EA-87 around Iceland; CCGS *Des Groseilliers* on scientific assignment with the Bedford Oceanographic Institute in Lancaster Sound and Wellington Channel; CCGS *Louis S. St-Laurent*, sailing through the Northwest Passage from Halifax to Kugluktuk; MV *Clipper Adventurer* (MV *Sea Adventurer* since she was renamed in October 2012) on various Arctic expeditions with Students on Ice and Adventure Canada. And, of course, there was the *Sea Adventurer*'s Yugoslavian-built sister ship, the inimitable MV *Lyubov Orlova*, now a ghost ship drifting, so they say, somewhere in the north Atlantic, which carried my dreams along with those of many others through Arctic waters.

And finally, heartfelt appreciation to the whole team at HarperCollins Canada: my new editor, Jane Warren; production editor Maria Golikova; illustrator Dawn Huck; publicists Rob Firing and Lauren Morocco; and my long-time friend at reception, Norma Cody.

Pakka þér, takk, takk, kiitos, giitu, спасибо, mutna, ᕐᖀᕙᐅᒃᓂ, whakawhetai ki a koutou, quyanainni, mahsi' choo, quana, ma'na, qujannamiik, nakurmiik, qujan—*thank you* all.

James Raffan
Pugwash, Nova Scotia
June 30, 2014